THE COMPONENTS OF THE RABBINIC DOCUMENTS

From the Whole to the Parts

SOUTH FLORIDA ACADEMIC COMMENTARY SERIES

Edited by
Jacob Neusner,
William Scott Green, James Strange
Darrell J. Fasching, Sara Mandell, Bruce D. Chilton

Number 82

THE COMPONENTS OF THE RABBINIC DOCUMENTS
From the Whole to the Parts
V.
SONG OF SONGS RABBAH
PART ONE

by
Jacob Neusner

THE COMPONENTS OF THE RABBINIC DOCUMENTS
From the Whole to the Parts

V.
SONG OF SONGS RABBAH

Part One

by

Jacob Neusner

Scholars Press
Atlanta, Georgia

THE COMPONENTS OF THE RABBINIC DOCUMENTS
From the Whole to the Parts

V.
SONG OF SONGS RABBAH
Part One

Publication of this book was made possible by a grant from the Tisch Family Foundation, New York City. The University of South Florida acknowledges with thanks this important support for its scholarly projects.

Library of Congress Cataloging in Publication Data

Neusner, Jacob, 1932–
    The components of the rabbinic documents : from the whole to the parts / by Jacob Neusner.
      p.   cm. — (South Florida academic commentary series : no. 81)
    Includes bibliographical references.
      Contents: 1. Sifra. pt.1 — V. Song of Songs Rabbah
    ISBN 0-7885-0358-8 (cloth : alk. paper)
    ISBN 0-7885-0372-3 (cloth : alk. paper)
    1. Halakhic Midrashim—History and criticism. 2. Midrash rabbah—Criticism, interpretation, etc. I. Title. II. Series.
BM514.N464   1997
296.1'406—dc21   97-9249
                                      CIP

Printed in the United States of America
on acid-free paper

TABLE OF CONTENTS

PART ONE

PARASHAH ONE

PARASHAH TWO

PART TWO

PARASHAH FIVE

PARASHAH SIX

Parashah Seven

Parashah Eight

Preface

     This work forms the logical second stage in my systematic and comprehensive inquiry into the character of the Rabbinic literature and its formation, viewed phenomenologically. It commences at the point at which I have completed my academic commentaries to both Talmuds, my outlines of both Talmuds, and my comparison of the outlines of both Talmuds. We now have a complete account, mainly in graphics and in outline form, of the components of the two Talmuds: the composites and compositions that comprise the Talmuds. These large-scale results now await comparison with a complete account of the components of the Midrash-compilations, that is, the composites and compositions of which they are made up. When that work is complete, two further, and quite distinct projects will demand attention. First, we shall have to identify the free-standing, whole and complete units of thought that do not take part in the formation of a composition (all the more so, of a composite), that is, the smallest whole units of cognition in the Rabbinic literature. These will require examination in their own terms. Second, we shall find necessary the comparison of the characteristics of the components of the Rabbinic literature, Talmud and Midrash together, just as we have now described, analyzed, and compared the entire documents of the Rabbinic literature, Mishnah, Tosefta, Talmud and Midrash all together.

     To do this work for all but the Mishnah and the Tosefta, I have had systematically to review nearly the whole of my complete translation of the Rabbinic literature beginning to end, and, in this second complete go-around, to identify what I deemed primary to a document's construction, and what I held secondary. This is now done for both Talmuds and all the Midrash-compilations of late antiquity, and I have furthermore outlined both Talmuds and compared the outlines, side-by-side. The work of documentary analysis can therefore turn to the question of what components of each document belong to the work of framing that document, and what parts of each document stand separate from that document (and perhaps all documents now in our possession). With the completion of my translation of Sifré to Numbers, I have brought to a conclusion the entire project, there being no further definitively-Rabbinic documents of late antiquity that I have left untranslated. In due course, I shall have occasion to work through the entire canon yet a third and a fourth time, for two purposes, which, at this time, I am thinking through but had best leave unspecified; but I cannot imagine a life without words of our sages framing my work for the day, every day.

     This entire project of form-analysis of the Rabbinic documents rests on a simple theory of formal, phenomenological classification of the Rabbinic writings, viewed whole. It may be stated in a few words. All the Rabbinic documents are made up of three distinct types of writing,

[1] writing that conforms to the documentary program of the framers of the document, realizing that program in formal and logical ways;

[2] writing that does not conform to that program but that appears, nonetheless, only in said document;

[3] and writing that not only does not conform to the formal and logical program of the document in which it occurs but also appears in two or more documents.

In this study and its eleven companions, we analyze the properties of the three constituent parts of the Rabbinic Midrash-compilations, respectively, systematically asking a uniform set of questions about them. These constituent parts are documentary and non-documentary. The first type carries out the principal tasks of a given documentary and characterize that document in particular. In my outline, these are flush with the left-hand margin. The second proves extrinsic to the paramount, governing formal traits of the document and occupy a subordinate position, both ordinally and otherwise. In my outline these are indented, as the case requires. As with my *Academic Commentaries* to the Talmuds, the results are set forth in graphics, rather than in words. By signaling the components and identifying the normative forms, I mark out the aberrational ones as well. In Part VIII of the Introduction I amplify this matter and explain the procedures of the project of which this monograph forms a part.

Since, it is quite obvious, this project forms part of a much larger inquiry and refers for context to a considerable vision of the whole, readers may wonder, what comes next? When, as I hinted in the opening remarks, this work on aberrational forms is complete for all dozen Midrash-compilations of late antiquity, I shall address yet another, also-obvious problem,[1] the free-standing saying. I refer to the saying that does not form part of a composition, all the more so of a composite. Free-standing sayings do not relate to the context in which they stand, fore or aft, and they (ordinarily) expose their sense without requiring attention to that context. In every Rabbinic document but one the smallest whole unit of discourse ordinarily puts together two or more such sayings, neither of which makes

---

[1] In my own defense, I hasten to note, it is not a problem of any proportion or consequence in the Rabbinic documents, comprised as they are of whole compositions and large composites.

sense on its own. Most of those collected in tractate Abot[2] by contrast stand on their own. Extra-contextual autonomous sentences — not absorbed within the contiguous composition (all the more so composite) — occasionally make their appearance but rarely make a difference in the presentation of a comprehensive and fully-articulated Rabbinic construction.[3] When we have a clear picture of the parts, as we now have of the whole and the principal parts of the documents, we will proceed to take that third step in the form-analysis of the Rabbinic literature of late antiquity.

I refer, in formal terms, to the sentence essentially independent of its context in the composition in which it occurs. Anyone who has conducted systematic form-analyses of Rabbinic documents knows that such wholly-free-standing, utterly-autonomous sentences occur very rarely in the situation of the Rabbinic writing, nearly all of which takes the form of compositions, themselves cast into still-larger composites. For example, we look in vain in the present document for sentences fully and exhaustively comprehensible without reference to their context. Virtually every line of the document is tightly woven into a broader setting of a coherent composition, and the compositions and even large-scale composites, we shall see, are modeled on a few, quite rigid patterns.

But even if we had a large corpus of free-standing sayings, whole documents made up in considerable proportion of them, a second problem presently awaits attention. While we may develop hypotheses on the formation of documents and even on the conglomeration of their composites and on the formulation of their compositions, I cannot conceive of a hypothesis on how such free-standing sayings were given final form and so formulated for transmission and utilization here and there. Those who conduct exegetical work within the anti-documentary hermeneutics that identifies the free-standing saying as the building block of Rabbinic discourse offer no theory of literary history: formulation and transmission.

---

[2] Rabbinic literature as a whole contains a negligible proportion of free-standing sayings, Abot being unique among the complete documents of the canon in both its definitive form — X says, or he used to say, + a wise saying — and also in its genre, wisdom. There is no other wisdom-document in the Rabbinic canon, and even the talmud to Abot, The Fathers According to Rabbi Nathan, likewise takes a form other than that paramount in Abot itself. I discussed the relationship of The Fathers According to Rabbi Nathan to tractate Abot in my *Judaism and Story: The Evidence of The Fathers According to Rabbi Nathan.* Chicago, 1992: University of Chicago Press.

[3] As to the portion of these free-standing sayings that are itinerant, these I treated briefly in my initial exercise on the present problem, *The Peripatetic Saying: The Problem of the Thrice-Told Tale in Talmudic Literature.* Chico, 1985: Scholars Press for Brown Judaic Studies. But that is only a preliminary study, and in the projected documentary form-history of Rabbinic literature, I shall have to address non-documentary forms as well, thus free-standing sayings.

Since the normal situation of a sentence in the Rabbinic documents is contextual, precisely what we are to make of the aberration of the extra-contextual sentence presently eludes me. But, predictably, while I conduct the present large-scale exercise, I reflect on what is to come.

And that is, as I now project matters, *The Documentary Form-History of Rabbinic Literature* — including, it goes without saying, non-documentary forms. In this work I take as established facts the results of my documentary descriptions, now complete. It suffices to refer readers to the research that is in print on the strength of which I characterize the indicative formal, material traits of the Midrash-compilation under study here and of its companions. For the convenience of librarians and scholars who follow the unfolding of my *oeuvre*, I include in Volume XII Part iii of this work a complete and up-to-date bibliography, as of June 1, 1996. This allows ready reference to my presentation of the documents as autonomous and my comparison thereof as well as to my commentaries that identify what is primary and what is secondary in the two Talmuds, and my outlines of the two Talmuds and systematic comparison of the same. The plan of this part of the entire project is as follows::

The Components of the Rabbinic Documents: From the Whole to the Parts. Volume
    I. *Sifra.* Atlanta, 1996: Scholars Press for South Florida Studies in the
    History of Judaism.

    Part i.   *Introduction. And Parts One through Three, Chapters One
                through Ninety-Eight*
    Part ii.   *Parts Four through Nine. Chapters Ninety-Nine through One
                Hundred Ninety-Four*
    Part iii.   *Parts Ten through Thirteen. One Hundred Ninety-Five through
                Two Hundred Seventy-Seven*
    Part iv.   *A Topical and Methodological Outline of Sifra*

The Components of the Rabbinic Documents: From the Whole to the Parts. Volume
    II. *Esther Rabbah I.* Atlanta, 1996: Scholars Press for South Florida Studies
    in the History of Judaism.

The Components of the Rabbinic Documents: From the Whole to the Parts. Volume
    III. *Ruth Rabbah.* Atlanta, 1996: Scholars Press for South Florida Studies
    in the History of Judaism.

The Components of the Rabbinic Documents: From the Whole to the Parts. Volume
    IV. *Lamentations Rabbati.* Atlanta, 1996: Scholars Press for South Florida
    Studies in the History of Judaism.

The Components of the Rabbinic Documents: From the Whole to the Parts. Volume
V. *Song of Songs Rabbah.* Atlanta, 1996: Scholars Press for South Florida
Studies in the History of Judaism.

Part i.   *Introduction. And Parashiyyot One through Four*
Part ii. *Parashiyyot Five through Eight. And a Topical and
         Methodological Outline of Song of Songs Rabbah*

The Components of the Rabbinic Documents: From the Whole to the Parts. VI.
The Fathers Attributed to Rabbi Nathan. Atlanta, 1996: Scholars Press
for South Florida Studies in the History of Judaism.

The Components of the Rabbinic Documents: From the Whole to the Parts. VII.
Sifré to Deuteronomy. Atlanta, 1996: Scholars Press for South Florida
Studies in the History of Judaism.

Part i.   *Introduction. And Parts One through Four*
Part ii. *Parts Five through Ten*
Part iii. *A Topical and Methodological Outline of Sifré to Deuteronomy*

The Components of the Rabbinic Documents: From the Whole to the Parts. VIII.
Mekhilta Attributed to R. Ishmael.   Atlanta, 1996: Scholars Press for
South Florida Studies in the History of Judaism.

Part i.   *Introduction. Pisha, Beshallah and Shirata*
Part ii   *Vayassa, Amalek, Bahodesh, Neziqin, Kaspa and Shabbata*
Part iii. *A Topical and Methodological Outline of Mekhilta Attributed to
         R. Ishmael.*

The Components of the Rabbinic Documents: From the Whole to the Parts. IX.
Genesis Rabbah. Atlanta, 1996: Scholars Press for South Florida Studies
in the History of Judaism.

Part i.   *Introduction. Genesis Rabbah Chapters One through
         Twenty-One*
Part ii. *Genesis Rabbah Chapters Twenty-Two through Forty-Eight*
Part iii. *Genesis Rabbah Chapters Forty-Nine through Seventy-Three*
Part iv. *Genesis Rabbah Chapters Seventy-Four through One Hundred*
Part v.   *Topical and Methodological Outline of Genesis Rabbah. Bereshit
         through Vaere, Chapters One through Fifty-Seven*
Part vi. *Topical and Methodological Outline of Genesis Rabbah. Hayye
         Sarah through Miqqes. Chapters Fifty-Eight through One
         Hundred*

The Components of the Rabbinic Documents: From the Whole to the Parts. X. *Leviticus Rabbah.* Atlanta, 1996: Scholars Press for South Florida Studies in the History of Judaism.

Part i.   *Introduction. Leviticus Rabbah Parashiyyot One through Seventeen*
Part ii.   *Leviticus Rabbah Parashiyyot Eighteen through Thirty-Seven*
Part iii. *Leviticus Rabbah. A Topical and Methodical Outline*

The Components of the Rabbinic Documents: From the Whole to the Parts. XI. *Pesiqta deRab Kahana.* Atlanta, 1997: Scholars Press for South Florida Studies in the History of Judaism.

Part i.   *Introduction. Pesiqta deRab Kahana Parashiyyot One through Twelve*
Part ii.   *Pesiqta deRab Kahana Parashiyyot Thirteen through Twenty-Eight*
Part iii. *Pesiqta deRab Kahana. A Topical and Methodical Outline*

The Components of the Rabbinic Documents: From the Whole to the Parts. XII. *Sifré to Numbers.* Atlanta, 1997: Scholars Press for South Florida Studies in the History of Judaism.

Part i.   *Introduction. Pisqaot One through Eighty-Four*
Part ii   *Pisqaot Eighty-Five through One Hundred Twenty-Two*
Part iii   *Pisqaot One Hundred Twenty-Three through One Hundred Sixty-One*
Part iv   *Sifré to Numbers. A Topical and Methodical Outline*

As Professor of Religious Studies at Bard College (through 2003), I receive a research grant, which has materially assisted in preparing the camera-ready copy of the present book. I express my thanks to the President and the Dean of the Faculty of Bard College, Dr. Leon Botstein and Dr. Stuart Levine, respectively, for their cordial interest in my research. During the period of work on this project, from the status of Visiting Professor, the terms of my appointment were revised, and I was appointed Professor of Religious Studies at Bard College, in terms compatible with my tenured professorship at the University of South Florida. I am delighted with the challenges and opportunities offered by both settings, a small, elite liberal arts college in the countryside of the Hudson valley, and a huge, mass-enrollment, full-service university on the urban frontier. No one in American higher education enjoys a more favorable situation than I do, certainly none who values both scholarship and teaching at one and the same moment. That is why combining Bard and USF has presented so splendid a situation to me.

No work of mine can omit reference to the exceptionally favorable circumstances in which I conduct my research. I wrote this book mainly at the University of South Florida, which has afforded me an ideal situation in which to conduct a scholarly life. I express my thanks for not only the advantage of a Distinguished Research Professorship, which must be the best job in the world for a scholar, but also of a substantial research expense fund, ample research time, and some stimulating and cordial colleagues. In the prior chapters of my career, I never knew a university that prized professors' scholarship and publication and treated with respect those professors who actively and methodically pursue research. The University of South Florida, and all ten universities that comprise the Florida State University System as a whole, exemplify the high standards of professionalism that prevail in publicly-sponsored higher education in the USA and provide the model that privately-sponsored universities would do well to emulate. Here there are rules, achievement counts, and presidents, provosts, and deans honor and respect the University's principal mission: scholarship, scholarship alone — both in the classroom and in publication. Here at last I find integrity, governing in the lives of people true to their vocation and their mission.

JACOB NEUSNER
DISTINGUISHED RESEARCH PROFESSOR OF RELIGIOUS STUDIES
UNIVERSITY OF SOUTH FLORIDA, TAMPA
AND
PROFESSOR OF RELIGIOUS STUDIES
BARD COLLEGE
ANNANDALE-ON-HUDSON, NEW YORK

Introduction
Identifying the Parts

I.   EXPLAINING THE PROJECT

Here I carry forward a new phase in my inquiry into the properties of the Rabbinic literature of late antiquity. Let me begin the account by placing the present project into the context of my on-going work. The presentation of the entirety of documents, seen one by one, each in its own terms, has allowed me to define the indicative traits of each canonical writing or document.[1] We now know in detail the formal conventions and protocols that characterize each of the several documents of the Rabbinic canon, respectively. Having completed the characterization of the whole documents, I move from the whole to the parts.

Since we have learned to regard rabbinic compilations[2] as purposive, not a mere scrap book but a deliberate and well-crafted compilation of materials to cohere in some way(s), a new set of questions comes to the fore. What elements of a document carry out the purposes of the compilers? These we may regard as primary to the document. What compositions and even whole composites do not conform to the definitive protocol, the indicative traits of the document? These we may regard as secondary to the document. Seeing the whole and defining its particular qualities, therefore, we are able to discern, also, those parts, distinct from the whole, over which the framers of the document, those who defined its characteristic traits, cannot necessarily claim authorship. Here and in the companion-studies of the other eleven principal Midrash-compilations I proceed to the re-presentation of those same documents, now as composites, and to the analysis of the composite of which the documents are comprised severally and jointly.

---

[1] The project of documentary description to date has received only episodic, and, on the whole, trivial and uncomprehending criticism, most of those who undertake to criticize the documentary reading of the Rabbinic canon exhibiting imperfect understanding of the work, its scope and purposes, and even its methods. I deal with most of the critics in *The Documentary Foundation of Rabbinic Culture. Mopping Up after Debates with Gerald L. Bruns, S. J. D. Cohen, Arnold Maria Goldberg, Susan Handelman, Christine Hayes, James Kugel, Peter Schaefer, Eliezer Segal, E. P. Sanders, and Lawrence H. Schiffman.* Atlanta, 1995: Scholars Press for South Florida Studies in the History of Judaism.

[2] Except for Mekhilta attributed to R. Ishmael, and I plan to return to that document in the present project and to attempt a different mode of description.

Nearly a quarter-century ago, frustrated by an important and insoluble problem of critical historical research using Rabbinic literature as the principal source,[3] I decided to turn from historical to religions-historical and therefore also literary work, to investigate the character and history of the documents that purport to supply the facts out of which conventional[4] history is to be constructed, and to utilize the results in the study of the history of the formation of Rabbinic Judaism as the documentary evidence yields that history.[5] Now, to do that work of documentary analysis I considered two starting points: the whole or the smallest part. That is to say, do I start from the document as a whole and examine its indicative traits? Or do I begin with the smallest whole unit of thought, the free-standing sentence, or, at least, with the completed composition, entire in its realization of the intent of its writer(s) but treated out of relationship to its documentary context in particular? The highly formalized character of the writing compiled in the Rabbinic documents, which had struck me from the very beginning of my studies,[6] dictated the answer: work from the whole to the parts. That is

---

[3] I could not devise a method for testing the validity of attributions of sayings to named authorities, let alone the veracity of stories as accounts of things really said and done. The methods I did work out served limited purposes and rested on undemonstrated premises. Several critical exercises showed possibility, but also underscored the limitation of taking stories or sayings out of their documentary context. Hence the documents as a whole had to be investigated, before attempting to evaluate details here and there. In that recognition was born the documentary hypothesis. The beginnings of the new and ending of the old are spelled out in these works: *Development of a Legend. Studies on the Traditions Concerning Yohanan ben Zakkai.* Leiden, 1970: Brill; *The Rabbinic Traditions about the Pharisees before 70.* Leiden, 1971: Brill. I-III; *Eliezer ben Hyrcanus. The Tradition and the Man.* Leiden, 1973: Brill. I-II.

[4] The historical work that I have done with the results of the documentary reading of the canonical books constitutes history too, but it is not the sort that "Talmudic historians" wished to write and thought that the sources as they read them could sustain. The documentary work began with *A History of the Mishnaic Law of Purities* and led to *Judaism: The Evidence of the Mishnah* (Chicago, University of Chicago Press, 1981). That too contributes a study of a historical problem, but one of a different kind from the history I had had in mind from 1960 through 1970. It is one of the history of religions: the ideas of a religion in relationship to the social order that realizes those ideas. The successive studies of documents are listed in the bibliography given in the Preface. The further studies of the documentary history of Judaism, culminating in *The Transformation of Judaism* (Urbana, 1991: University of Illinois Press), do not require summary here.

[5] The most important monographs in the religions-historical work were *Judaism. The Evidence of the Mishnah.* and *The Transformation of Judaism. From Philosophy to Religion* The complete results are summarized in *Rabbinic Judaism. The Documentary History of the Formative Age.* Bethesda, 1994: CDL Press, and *Rabbinic Judaism. Structure and System.* Minneapolis, 1995: Fortress Press.

[6] *A History of the Mishnaic Law of Purities.* Leiden, 1977: Brill. XXI. *The Redaction and Formulation of the Order of Purities in the Mishnah and Tosefta* spells out the initial results and places them in the context of linguistic theory as I grasped matters at that time.

because the writing that is collected is not random but patterned, and the patterns work in large-scale aggregates, not in small and random units of thought.

Accordingly, the former choice defined the norm on the base-line of the whole and asked where, how, and why the parts diverge from the norm. That is the mode of comparison and contrast that would then generate hypotheses of literary history and purpose — and also, therefore hermeneutics.[7] The manner of analysis dictated by the entry from the outermost layer is simple. We commence our analytical inquiry from a completed document and peal back its layers, from the ultimate one of closure and redaction, to the penultimate, and onward into the innermost formation of the smallest whole units of thought of which a document is comprised. In so doing, we treat the writing as a document that has come to closure at some fixed point and through the intellection of purposeful framers or redactor. We start the analytical process by asking what those framers — that authorship — have wanted their document to accomplish and by pointing to the means by which that authorship achieved its purposes. Issues of prevailing rhetoric and logic, as well as the topical program of the whole, guide us in our definition of the document as a whole. The parts then come under study under the aspect of the whole. Knowing the intent of the framers, we ask whether, and how, materials they have used have been shaped in response to the program of the document's authorship.

The alternative point of entry — from the smallest of the parts outward — requires beginning with the smallest building block of any and all documents. That is the "lemma" or irreducible minimum of completed thought. From that

---

[7] A theory of the character of the document is required to shape the hermeneutics that guide the reading of the document, and the hermeneutics is prior to the exegesis of the same document. Exegetical work without an articulated hermeneutics produces incoherent results and obscures the field of inquiry. The assumption that exegesis means, philological exegesis, on the one side, and the collection and arrangement of textual variants, on the other, leaves without articulation the basis for the assumption that the only, or the main, point of interest of a text is its material character: its wording, the meaning (out of specific, textual context!) of words used therein. Most historical work on the same documents rests on the premise that with a well-criticized text, all the words being understood, all the wordings being secured by surveys of manuscript variants, we have solid historical facts, on the basis of which we may build our historical reconstructions. Called critical and positive, that historical reconstruction rests on credulity and gullibility readily characterized: if the source says it, it must be so.

point, text-study works upward and outward from the innermost layer of the writing.[8] That point of entry ignores the boundaries of discrete documents and asks what we find common within and among all documents. There is the starting point, and the norm is defined by the traits of the saying or lemma as it moves from here to there. Within this theory of the history of the literature, the boundary-lines of documents do not demarcate important classifications of data; all data are uniform, wherever they occur. The stress then lies not on the differentiating traits of documents, but the points shared in common among them; these points are sayings that occur in two or more places. Literary history consists in the inquiry into the fate of sayings as they move from one place to another. The hermeneutics of course will focus upon the saying and its history, rather than on the program and plan of documents that encompass, also, the discrete saying. The advantage of this approach, of course, is that it takes account of what is shared among documents, on the one side, and also of what exhibits none of the characteristic traits definitive of given documents, on the other.

---

[8] This contrary approach is taken by David Weiss Halivni. He is in a well-established tradition, for the received method of study of the holy books of Judaism focuses upon discrete sentences, rarely reaching the level of whole paragraphs. "Commentaries" in the primary encounter with texts ordinarily take shape around words, phrases, and sentences, and the commentary-form matches the program. Halivni maintains that the indicative and definitive building block of a document is its smallest whole unit of thought or saying ("lemma"). That is where matters start, and that is, therefore, the point at which we should commence our analysis. But the document defines the traits of a sizable proportion of its contents, and that means the authorship bears responsibility for the composition of much, though not all, that that authorship has compiled. Some materials, to be sure, exhibit traits of composition that in no way respond to the program of any authorship known to us . But even here, the differentiating criteria *to begin with* derive from the traits of the document as a whole, and not from the character of the sayings or lemmas of which a document is — also, as a matter of fact, in a sizable proportion of the contents — comprised. Now to the matter of the null-hypothesis, what it is, how it may be tested. If Halivni were right that documents begin from "the beginning," that is, the individual sentences of which they are composed, then principles of [1] composition and [2] conglomeration would prove contradictory, so that a discourse or sustained discussion of a problem would appear jerry-built, episodic, rough-hewn, and *ad hoc*. But any analysis of whole units of discourse, as distinct from the sentences that define the arena for Halivni's analysis, shows the opposite. Analysis of any passage of the Yerushalmi, for example, or of the Bavli, beginning to end demonstrates that the whole is the work of the one who decided to make up the discussion on the atemporal logic of the

As I said, in determining to conduct a set of form-analytical studies of the Mishnah and the Tosefta, which I thought would yield history, I chose the first of the two approaches. That struck me as the right way to go, because no one had ever before explored the proposition that Rabbinic compilations constituted coherent statements. It struck me as an idea awaiting investigation, at least worth a systematic and thorough test. I have now completed that work for the Mishnah, Talmuds, and Midrash-compilations. Every important document in the canon of formative Rabbinic Judaism has yielded its data. Each has been given an introduction, that is to say, a description of the whole.[9]

II. FROM THE WHOLE TO THE PARTS

That is why I move from the whole to the parts. Specifically, from the whole — examining within a uniform category-formation the traits of cogency and coherence of each of the authoritative Rabbinic documents seen in its entirety — we now move to the analysis of the parts, the elements that all together comprise a given document. We may do so because we may now say with some certainty what distinctively characterizes and sets apart from all others each of the compilations of the Rabbinic canon of late antiquity. I have set forth in detail, precisely what traits of rhetoric, logic of coherent discourse, and topical and even propositional program (where relevant) characterize each one individually and, moreover, distinguish one from all others, or one group from the other groups of the documents. So much for the whole, the document seen in one piece.

---

point at issue. Otherwise — again the null-hypothesis, that would favor Halivni's position — the discussion would be not the way it is: continuous. Rather, discourse would prove disjointed, full of seams and margins, marks of the existence of prior conglomerations of materials that have now been sewn together. What we have are not patchwork quilts, but woven fabric. Along these same lines, we may find discussions in which opinions of Palestinians, such as Yohanan and Simon b. Laqish, will be joined together side by side with opinions of Babylonians, such as Rab and Samuel. The whole, once again, will unfold in a smooth way, so that the issues at hand define the sole focus of discourse. The logic of those issues will be fully exposed. Considerations of the origin of a saying in one country or the other will play no role whatsoever in the rhetoric or literary forms of argument. There will be no possibility of differentiation among opinions on the basis of where, when, by whom, or how they are formulated, only on the basis of what, in fact, is said. I have elaborated on these matters in a variety of books, several of them explicitly devoted to Halivni's position. To date, there has been no published response to criticism of Halivni's view, and he has not communicated in any other way with the criticism I have set forth.

[9] , That uniform pattern of introduction is set forth in rhetoric, logic of coherent discourse, and topical program, terms defined later in this Introduction.

Now, everyone familiar with the documentary reading of the canonical writings understands, that is only part of the task. For the work of documentary description leaves open questions concerning what (if anything) the framers of the documents utilized but did not themselves invent for the purposes they realized in said documents, severally, all the more so, jointly. The building blocks are to be identified and analyzed too.[10] That is what I mean when I say that we have now to move from the whole to the parts. A simple definition of what is, in context-ready made and not tailored for the document is required at the outset. Once we know what defines a document's rhetorical traits, its logic of cogent discourse, and its topical program, we may single out those components of the document that serve to realize the document's compilers' definition of their work. And that makes possible the identification of those components that do not serve the document's established purpose.[11]

These are to be divided into two parts, components that do not conform to the document's protocol but occur only there, and those that do not conform but also occur in more than a single document.[12] All of this is to be indicated in visual signals. When the document as a whole has been so analyzed, we shall know the proportions of the document contributed by three parts that make up the whole. We also shall have criteria for the analysis of the three types of writing and may address further questions to each type. Whether from identifying the parts we may propose to uncover a history behind the documents — the pre-history of the ideas

---

[10] The theoretical statement of what we can mean by "building blocks," short of simple sentences treated out of all intelligible context, is *The Rules of Composition of the Talmud of Babylonia. The Cogency of the Bavli's Composite.* Atlanta, 1991: Scholars Press for South Florida Studies in the History of Judaism. The distinction between the composite and the composition, worked out there, has proven critical in all documents, not only the Bavli.

[11] I originally spelled out the criteria of documentary differentiation among the components of a document in *Making the Classics in Judaism: The Three Stages of Literary Formation.* Atlanta, 1990: Scholars Press for Brown Judaic Studies. Readers will note that a large part of the theoretical work for my movement from documents to their components was completed in the earliest 1990s. Once I finished *Transformation of Judaism,* I was able to give sustained thought to this next phase of the work, and the several theoretical exercises followed. Most of this work was done at the Institute for Advanced Study, and the rest was completed in my earliest years at the University of South Florida. But nothing could have been done without first working through the documents, one by one, in the manner ultimately summarized in *Introduction to Rabbinic Literature.* N.Y., 1994: Doubleday. The Doubleday Anchor Reference Library. Most of that work was completed before I went to the Institute with *Transformation* as the ultimate statement of the intellectual history of Rabbinic Judaism in mind.

[12] This distinction is explained below.

finally set forth in the documents[13] — remains to be seen. What we do here is to identify the differentiating phenomena, not recount the temporal sequence ("history") in which they took shape, either severally or jointly. All of this remains to be spelled out presently. For at this point, I have gotten ahead of my story. Let us start back with the fundamental questions of classification: comparison, contrast, and differentiation.

III. DIFFERENTIATING THE RABBINIC CANON FROM THE CANONICAL WRITINGS OF ALL OTHER JUDAISMS IN ANCIENT TIMES: THE NECESSARY TRAITS

First we describe jointly, as a whole, the entire corpus of writings not only deemed authoritative by the Judaism of the dual Torah,[14] but also unique to that Judaism. We shall then consider what is required to define the entirety of the respective documents. At that point, what I mean by "the parts" will become fully exposed. The reason is simple. If I claim to speak of "the whole," then I must begin with all of the Rabbinic documents viewed all together. To move from the whole to the parts, I characterize the whole Rabbinic canon, viewed in the aggregate..

In any labor of classification and differentiation, we identify traits that are necessary but not sufficient, and and those that are necessary and sufficient. Each set of traits serves its purpose, the one exclusionary, the other, inclusionary. We commence with traits that are necessary to assign to a document a place in the canon of the Judaism of the dual Torah, or, if absent, to deny a document a place in that canon. We then proceed to the traits that are both necessary and sufficient. Documents exhibiting those traits can find a place only within the Rabbinic canon and in no other canonical context of a Judaism (all the more so, any other set of religious systems or religion).

---

[13] No one can imagine that a given idea is to be assigned the date of the document in which it first surfaces. That is something we cannot show and therefore do not know. In many instances we know the opposite. That is, we can find in much earlier documents reference to a rule or a conception that, in the Rabbinic canon, first occurs in the Mishnah. It follows that, for some group or other, that same rule or conception bore consequence. But what we are to make of that fact is not clear. Do we then have a history of an idea as it wended its way from here to there, from one circle of Judaic faithful to another? But out of all context, ideas standing alone bear slight weight. Knowing, for example, that Jesus held vowing was disreputable, and knowing that third century rabbis held that vowing was a mark of poor character, tells us something about what different people had to say about the same thing. But what more we know, if we know that obvious fact, is unclear. The basic organizing unit for religious ideas is the system that utilizes them for its larger purpose and forms of them a coherent statement — whether the system put forth in the name of Jesus in one or another of the Gospels, whether the system set out in a given document such as the Mishnah. In response to that set of problems, I formulated the much more modest notion of not the history of Judaism and its ideas, but the documentary history of Rabbinic Judaism.

[14] I clarify this claim presently.

The canon of Rabbinic Judaism encompasses[15] the following: the Mishnah; the Tosefta; the Talmud of the Land of Israel; the Talmud of Babylonia; tractate Abot (the Fathers); the Fathers According to Rabbi Nathan; the Hebrew Scriptures; Mekhilta attributed to R. Ishmael (for Exodus); Sifra (Leviticus); Sifré to Numbers; Sifré to Deuteronomy; Genesis Rabbah; Leviticus Rabbah; Pesiqta deRab Kahana; Song of Songs Rabbah; Ruth Rabbah; Esther Rabbah I; and Lamentations Rabbati.[16] Viewed as a whole, the canon of Rabbinic Judaism allows us readily to distinguish any typical document of the Judaism of the dual Torah from any and all documents put forth by other Judaisms of the time from Ezra to the closure of the Talmud of Babylonia, roughly a millennium.[17]

---

[15] But is not limited to the named items. These are principal and definitive. The items I omit are not particular in sponsorship to the Rabbinic sages; or do not clearly derive from the period under discussion, the first through seventh centuries; or are derivative and subordinate. I leave out only one Rabbinic document that meets the criteria just now indicated — particular to sages, from the period at hand, original and important — and that is Targum Onqelos, which awaits the kind of systematic study I have given to the main documents that permits further work of classification and analysis.

[16] My purpose, clearly, is to characterize the principal, influential writings particular to "our sages of blessed memory." Their canon is not limited to the writings distinctive to the sages, but canonical description requires that we limit ourselves to those particular documents. We should take note of others, though these will not require attention, each for its own reason. Certain other documents, such as Ben Sira and Megillat Taanit, are cited as authoritative within the canonical books; but while "our sages of blessed memory" deemed them to be normative, they do not find a place in the presentation of the canonical documents, whether Scripture or post-Scripture. Alone these same lines, some others, such as the Siddur (order of prayer for weekdays, Sabbaths, and festivals), Mahzor (order of prayer for the Days of Awe), and the like, clearly found approval within the canonical books. But while, it is clear, sages made rules about the recitation of one prayer or another, it is equally obvious that sages deemed normative liturgical practices that they do not claim to have originated, such as the recitation of the Shema, the formulation of The Prayer (attributed, after all, in part to Abraham, Isaac, and Jacob). So an account of Rabbinic theology would have to encompass the liturgical writings, but an account of Rabbinic literature does not. The standing of still other compilations, e.g., certain mystical texts, liturgical poetry, and the like, has no bearing upon our problem, since these writings all come to closure after the period under discussion here. I also do not make reference to the minor tractates of the Talmud, since these seem derivative, compiled out of available materials rather than formulated in the processes that came to fruition in the tractates of the Talmud of Babylonia. But I readily concede that further work is required on these unimportant compilations, whether mystical or halakhic. As to the Targumim, Onqelos certainly is Rabbinic, others surely belong within other Judaisms; but no work on the systematic description of the Targumim one by one, in the manner of my *Judaism: The Evidence of the Mishnah,* permits us to classify the Targumim among, or as, Judaisms. As to Onqelos, it must be deemed an exception to the rules set forth in the following paragraph.

[17] Let alone all other religious traditions, systems, or groups of the same, e.g., Christianity, Gnosticism, Manichaeism, Mithraism, and so on and so forth.

How so? It is the simple fact that, given any 250 words of the writings collected as a random sample out of writing in the Apocrypha and Pseudepigrapha, the Elephantine papyri, the Dead Sea library, the magical bowls and papyri, the so-called mystical writings, and any and all other writings attributed to the authorship of any Judaism of antiquity (including authorships that deemed themselves "Israel" and their writings "Torah," within Christianity) — given any 250 consecutive words chosen at random, we could without the possibility of any error whatsoever assign those words to either Rabbinic Judaism or some other Judaism. So marked and distinctive are the definitive traits of the documents of the Rabbinic canon.

What are these traits? The necessary, but not sufficient, traits are easily set forth. A canonical document of Rabbinic Judaism produced in that thousand-year span will exhibit, among others, at least these three necessary traits:

[1] it will cite a corps of authorities that occur in no other Judaism's writings;

[2] it will constantly cite verses of Scripture, particularly of the Pentateuch for legal matters, as proof for its propositions, and disputes about the exegesis of those verses of Scripture will prove ubiquitous;

[3] all normative statements will be made in the Hebrew language.[18]

All of these traits are necessary to the characterization of a document of the Rabbinic canon,[19] and any document that lacks them will find no place in that

---

[18] The privileging of Mishnaic or Middle Hebrew goes along with the privileging of the Mishnah, since it is the Mishnah's Hebrew that governs in the Rabbinic canon. On the Mishnah's language as the language of an occasion, see my *A History of the Mishnaic Law of Purities.* Leiden, 1977: Brill. XXI. *The Redaction and Formulation of the Order of Purities in the Mishnah and Tosefta.* All normative statements — those of law in particular — in that canon occur in Mishnaic Hebrew or a simile thereof. The Talmuds use Hebrew or Aramaic for give and take, analytical argument, and a fair part of the narrative corpus of precedents as well as tales; but Hebrew alone is used in the presentation of norms of law, rules of conduct, and the like. See my *Language as Taxonomy. The Rules for Using Hebrew and Aramaic in the Babylonian Talmud.* Atlanta, 1990: Scholars Press for South Florida Studies in the History of Judaism; and also *Are the Talmuds Interchangeable? Christine Hayes's Blunder.* Atlanta, 1996: Scholars Press for South Florida Studies on the History of Judaism. Hebrew also is the paramount language of the Midrash-compilations, where Aramaic makes only a very rare occurrence, and then in the context of narratives. The requirement of Hebrew for normative statements is violated by Megillat Ta'anit, which sages cite as authoritative, and very rarely in the Mishnah, e.g., in a few lines of Eduyyot. Interestingly, whenever the Bavli's composites' framers wish to set forth a general proposition for dialectical analysis, it will be stated in Hebrew, though the discussion will proceed in Aramaic. But the language-protocol is not violated by Onqelos, which is the Rabbinic Targum, and that is by reason of the task undertaken by that writing, translation into Aramaic.

[19] Necessary for the description of the documents jointly, but not sufficient for the characterization of the documents severally, as I shall explain in the next section.

canon.[20] Any other document, whether in Hebrew or in Aramaic or in Greek, valued by a Judaism, will exhibit these (negative) traits:

[1] it will cite no figures prominent in the Rabbinic canon;

[2] it will not systematically accord a privileged position to the Pentateuch and to the synagogal lections of the Five Scrolls, to the near exclusion of all other books of Scripture, in discussions of problems of law and theology;

[3] it may or may not make its normative statements in the Hebrew language.

Any document that originates among Jews and purports to set forth law, theology, or exegesis, for a Judaism that bears these negative traits will find no place in the Rabbinic canon and most such documents will make statements in one way or another conflicting with the dogmas or norms of the Rabbinic canon.

Of the necessary traits, the third requires comment. The other-than-Rabbinic writings refer to Pentateuchal books; Philo discusses Genesis at great length, for example. The Damascus Covenant obviously knows a great deal about the Sabbath law of Exodus, for another. But the systematic, orderly, and, we may say, relentless pursuit of Pentateuchal law, cited and amplified, that is characteristic of the Mishnah and Tosefta and two Talmuds and various Midrash-compilations has no counterpart in the canon of any other Judaism. These, for instance, may deem equally urgent the systematic exegesis of prophetic books, which takes no prominent place within any Rabbinic document and defines the purpose of no free-standing document. Fragments of this and that scarcely compare to the unique privileging of the Pentateuch that is achieved in the books of the Oral Torah.

IV.   DIFFERENTIATING THE RABBINIC CANON FROM THE CANONICAL WRITINGS OF ALL OTHER JUDAISMS IN ANCIENT TIMES. THE SUFFICIENT TRAIT

One trait is both necessary and sufficient uniquely to assign to the canon of Rabbinic Judaism any coherent piece of writing out of antiquity, and that is, the constant presence of disputes (with or without articulated debates).[21] The dispute-form is ubiquitous in Rabbinic literature, and it is unique to that literature within the larger set of writings of various Judaisms. The dispute consists of the articulation of conflicting positions on a common issue, each position being assigned to a

---

[20] Defining what characterizes the canonical writings of all Judaisms but of no other religious writings of any sort need not detain us.

[21] There is a second trait that is characteristic of Rabbinic rhetoric but that is not unique to Rabbinic literature, and that is the exegetical form — citation of a verse of Scripture followed by a few words, whether or not bearing an attributive, Rabbi X says, in which the meaning or application of the cited verse is spelled out. I cannot regard the simple exegetical form as either necessary to, or sufficient for, the designation of a piece of writing as part of the Rabbinic canon. But adding the attributive changes everything.

named authority, or one position being given anonymously and the other in a name.[22] It goes without saying that that name signals the presence of one of "our sages of blessed memory" who collectively set forth the Judaic religious system of the dual Torah.

The dispute constitutes a rhetorical form.[23] It also stands for a principle of logic, and one bearing the deepest implications for the social culture of our sages' textual community. If I had to choose a single trait that is unique to the Rabbinic canon and absent from the canonical writings of all other Judaisms, it would be the matter of articulated disputes about important principles. That trait is not only necessary, but also sufficient for differentiating the Rabbinic canonical documents from all other writings of Judaisms from Scripture to the closure of the Talmud in opening years of the seventh century. Not only so, but it is a form that bears the deepest meanings of Rabbinic Judaism, the one that is ubiquitous because it everywhere imparts the basic intellectual quality to whatever is said. Let me expand this point, since the dispute-form is as definitive of Rabbinic Judaism as the myth of the dual Torah. And any attention to the parts of the documents will always encompass the disputes that at many points constitute free-standing parts of discourse, not only documentary building blocks.

In its persistent attention to the conflict of opinion and in the critical importance of articulated dispute and debate, the Rabbinic literature recapitulates that the remarkable discovery of Classical philosophy, the critical importance of debate. So native to the Mishnah, Talmuds, and Midrash alike,[24] so essential in

---

[22] When a position is given anonymously, the articulated intent is to indicate that that is the normative rule on a disputed point. It is rarely claimed that what is anonymous also is "older" than what is assigned to an authority, but it is commonly made explicit that anonymity marks authority, specification of a name marks the schismatic view. Since both views are treated as equally plausible and since each one is allowed to claim authority, it is not possible to entertain the notion that anonymity is synonymous with antiquity. That theory of matters as presently articulated rests on unproven premises, which beg the question.

[23] The dispute-form tends to vary somewhat from document to document, and I plan a monograph on that problem, paying attention to the places and circumstances at which a debate is appended to a dispute. This is tentatively titled, *Forms of Rabbinic Discourse: A Documentary History of the Dispute and Debate*. Atlanta, Date to be determined: Scholars Press for South Florida Studies in the History of Judaism.

[24] The only Rabbinic document that does not conduct its exposition through exposing difference of opinion in dispute-form is tractate Abot, where "X says" introduces not a point of conflict but a free-standing wisdom-saying. Even the talmud to tractate Abot, the Fathers according to Rabbi Nathan, includes some dispute-materials (though nowhere near in the proportion characteristic of the conventional talmuds to the Mishnah-tractates set forth in the Talmud of the Land of Israel and the Talmud of Babylonia). Tractate Abot is also exceptional in providing wisdom-sayings, not law nor exegesis nor theology in the exegetical mode, such as fill the Mishnah, Talmuds, and Midrash-compilations. Everything that follows, therefore, must bear the qualification, except for tractate Abot.

Classical science and philosophy, debate marks the Rabbinic canon as unique in the Israelite context, but natural in the Classical philosophical one. Articulated debate on a single program, one side insisting that it is right and the other wrong, further identifies the Greek philosophers as singular in the context of world civilization.[25] G. E. R. Lloyd describes this matter in language that serves equally well for the various Judaic systems except the Rabbinic one:

> The Egyptians...had various beliefs about the way the sky is held up. One idea was that it is supported on posts, another that it is held up by a god, a third that it rests on walls, a fourth that it is a cow or a goddess...but a story-teller recounting anyone such myth need pay no attention to other beliefs about the sky, and he would hardly have been troubled by any inconsistency between them. Nor, one may assume, did he feel that his own account was in competition with any other in the sense that it might be more or less correct or have better or worse grounds for its support than some other belief.[26]

If we examine the two creation-myths of Genesis, or the two stories of the Flood, we see how readily conflicting stories might be joined together, and how little credence was placed on the possibility that one theory of matters, embodied in one version, might be correct, the other wrong. In search of dispute and debate, articulated and pursued, we simply look in vain through the entire heritage of Israelite Scriptures and through all extra-scriptural writings of various Judaic systems.

We look in vain in the writings of other Judaic systems, such as those collected in the Old Testament Apocrypha and Pseudepigrapha, in the library found at Qumran, in the papyri discovered at Elephantine, for instance, for anything

---

[25] The comparison of religions in antiquity has now to turn to the comparison of the logics of coherent discourse. The dispute-form (with or without the debate), for example, has no counterpart in Christian theological writing, just as the systematic demonstration along philosophical lines of theological propositions, such as is so brilliantly executed by Aphrahat, has no counterpart in Judaic-rabbinic theological writing. Professor Bruce D. Chilton and I plan a preliminary sounding of these data in *Confronting Conflict, Seeking Truth: Judaic and Christian Modes of Conducting Arguments in the Formative Age*. London, 1998: Routledge. [With Bruce D. Chilton.]

[26] G. E. R. Lloyd, *Early Greek Science. Thales to Aristotle*. New York, 1970: W. W. Norton & Co., pp. 11-12. Note in addition his *Greek Science after Aristotle*. N.Y., 1973: W. W. Norton Co., and, especially, *Polarity and Analogy. Two Types of Argumentation in Early Greek Thought*. Cambridge, 1966: Cambridge University Press.

comparable to the notes for a public argument that the dispute represents.[27] Greek philosophy and Rabbinic writing, by contrast, articulately faced the possibility that differing opinion competed and that the thinker must advocate the claim that his theory was right, the other's wrong. Conflicting principles both cannot be right, and merely announcing an opinion without considering alternatives and proposing to falsify them does not suffice for intellectual endeavor. And with the recognition of that possibility of not only opinion but argument, Greek philosophy engaged in debate:

> When we turn to the early Greek philosophers, there is a fundamental difference. Many of them tackle the same problems and investigate the same natural phenomena [as Egyptian and other science], but it is tacitly assumed that the various theories and explanations they propose are directly competing with one another. The urge is towards finding the best explanation, the most adequate theory, and they are then forced to consider the grounds for their ideas, the evidence and arguments in their favor, as well as the weak points in their opponents' theories.[28]

---

[27] For a comparison with the Zoroastrian Rivayat-writing of the period just beyond the closure of the Talmud, see my *Judaism and Zoroastrianism at the Dusk of Late Antiquity. How Two Ancient Faiths Wrote Down Their Great Traditions.* Atlanta, 1993: Scholars Press for South Florida Studies in the History of Judaism. There the oral setting is presupposed, but the exchange is one involving only information, not dispute. My result may be simply stated. Some authors find it sufficient to give [1] a rule alone, some want [2] a myth to accompany the rule, but one authorship — the Talmud's alone — insists that [3] the rule be subordinated to a process of critical analytical reason. Specifically: [1] in the first category fall Aturfarnbag's Rivayat, on the one side, and the Mishnah, on the other. In the second we find [2] the other rivayat, the one that accompanies the Datestan i Denig, — not to mention on the Israelite side all of the Pentateuchal law codes. In the third is only [3] the Bavli, which so reformulates discourse as to redefine what can be meant by "tradition." Of the documents I survey in the cited work, two suffice with [1] the statement of rules alone, Aturfarnbag's Rivayat, which sets forth rules in the form of questions and answers, and the Mishnah, which uses simple declarative sentences, statements of fact, with the same effect. A third document, the Yerushalmi, wants a rule with secondary clarification, and forms a secondary development within this same category. Further, the Pursishniha — called by its editors "a Zoroastrian catechism" — exhibits the same general characteristics: convey information through unadorned statements of fact in the form of questions and answers. Its governing form does not greatly vary from Aturfarnbag's

[28] Lloyd, *op. cit.,* p. 12.

And what was true of science pertained to civilization in all aspects:

> In their very different spheres of activity, the philosopher Thales and the
> law-giver Solon may be said to have had at least two things in common. First,
> both disclaimed any supernatural authority for their own ideas, and, secondly,
> both accepted the principles of free debate and of public access to the information
> on which a person or an idea should be judged. The essence of the Milesians'
> contribution was to introduce a new critical spirit into man's attitude to the world
> of nature, but this should be seen as a counterpart to, and offshoot of, the
> contemporary development of the practice of free debate and open discussion in
> the context of politics and law throughout the Greek world.[29]

And for its part the Rabbinic canon may lay claim to fundamental intellectual
novelty. In no prior writing deriving from Israelite sources, e.g., a writing of some
other, earlier Judaism, is a debate conducted, or the premise of a debate allowed to
govern in the formulation of conflicting views. In those other, prior Judaic systems
opinions conflict throughout, but never do they compete in articulate fashion as
they do in the dialogic writing of the Mishnah and analytical dialectics of the
Gemara. And, essential as well, never do they derive from a specific, named
authority in conflict with another named authority of equal standing.[30] The
presentation of two sides to the same exegetical debate finds no counterpart in
Israelite writing outside of the Rabbinic canon.

　　Disputes form not details let alone mere formalities, but the essence of
the whole. For the received Israelite writing in Hebrew and Aramaic prior to the
Mishnah (all the more so, contemporary and posterior writing outside of documents
produced by our sages) contains no counterpart to a document largely made up of
disputes, with conflicting opinions given in accord with named authorities on a
common agendum of difference. The dispute-form, indicative of the Mishnah and
Tosefta, amplified in the Gemaras and commonplace in the Midrash-compilations

---

[29] Lloyd, *op. cit.* p. 15.

[30] The teacher of righteousness of the Qumran texts does not enter an opinion in a dispute
with some other authority of the same community. Jesus and the Pharisees do not conduct
disputes set forth in the way in which the House of Shammai and the House of Hillel conduct
disputes. "Woe unto you, scribes, Pharisees, hypocrites" hardly constitutes a compelling
argument against the position of the other side. And at no point in the Gospels are Jesus's
opponents allowed to argue their case as equals.

as well,[31] finds no counterpart in a single earlier writing in Israel. In all of the Hebrew Scriptures, for example, with their rich record of conflicting viewpoint we have nothing like a public dispute, a debate comprising balanced, reasonable arguments (prophets, for instance, do not debate with kings or priests, and only Abraham and Moses debate with God, and then not on equal terms but only in a very careful negotiation indeed). Not only so, but while more than a single opinion may register in a given context, one opinion is never juxtaposed with some other and set out with arguments in behalf of the superiority of one position over another, or one explanation over another, for the purposes of a reasoned exchange of opinion and argument. That is to say, Elijah and the priests of Baal do not enjoy equal time to explain why fire consumed Elijah's but not the priests' offerings. But Meir and Judah in the Mishnah, or Yohanan and Simeon b. Laqish in the Yerushalmi, or Abbayye and Raba in the Bavli, always do.

The singularity of the dispute-form proves still more striking when we examine the genre of Israelite literature to which the Mishnah most obviously may be alleged to correspond, law codes.[32] The manner in which laws are set forth in Exodus (JE), the Holiness Code (P), Deuteronomy, let alone the library at Qumran and in the Elephantine papyri, for example, in no way proves congruent with the manner in which the Mishnah sets forth laws. To take two striking differences already adumbrated, the former attribute nothing to named authorities, the latter names authorities in nearly every composition; further, the former never contain articulated debates on laws but only apodictic laws; the latter is made up of explicit disputes of rulings on a shared agendum of issues. A third difference, from Scripture's codes in particular, is to be noted: the absence of a myth of authority, corresponding to "The Lord spoke to Moses saying, speak to the children of Israel and say to them." To take an obvious point of comparison, set side by side, the Mishnah's presentation of Sabbath law and that in the Dead Sea library bear few points of formal comparability at all.

---

[31] But that statement will be qualified in each documentary context. Sifra, as we shall see, is rich in disputes, but the basic formulary pattern of the document is executed without reliance on disputes between named authorities. Indeed, I find it quite striking that the proposal of a basis in the natural traits of things, not in Scripture's categories, for reliable generalizations, and the definitive rejection of that proposal, seldom bear attributions. It is not, "Said R. Simeon, 'Is it not a matter of reason?'" but only, "Is it not a matter of reason?" And the opposite position also is given anonymously. So the dispute overall plays a subordinated formal role in Sifra, even while the dispute as a mode of inquiry, in all of its dialectical glory, defines Sifra! So the generalizations offered here are to be refined as we proceed from one document to the next.

[32] I do not concur in that allegation as to the "genre" of the Mishnah, but once more introduce it for the sake of argument. In fact a single document cannot define, or constitute, a genre at all. And the Mishnah's singularity is its indicative trait in Israelite context.

True, the Mishnah's law refers constantly to the substance of Scripture, even though citations of scriptural proof-texts prove rare and at best episodic. That makes all the more remarkable the persistence of disputes as the norm, unattributed, normative law as the mere background for the setting of vivid discourse. It is equally true that the Mishnah's law intersects with the law portrayed in prior collections, which is hardly surprising given the reference-point of all collections in Scripture. That again underscores the significant point: while in some details, the snippets of laws preserved at Qumran intersect in contents with bits of the laws of the Mishnah and related writings, in form we find only differences.[33] While the Mishnah frames much of its materials in the form of public exchanges, the other Judaisms' law codes give no hint as to their framers' expectations on how their writings were to be received and read. The Mishnah is a document to be memorized and performed — a kind of mimetic version of the law — and the formal traits that so indicate in the case of the Mishnah simply do not characterize those other law codes at all.[34] It is the striking fact, therefore, that the first piece of writing in the history of Judaic religious systems to set forth a program of debate is the Mishnah.[35] And the only subsequent documents that carried forward the disputes and debates of the Mishnah are the two Talmuds' Gemaras, and, in different ways, the Midrash-compilations as well.[36] Elsewhere, differing opinions prove abundant. But occasions in which differing opinions are set forth in the form, and for the purpose, of debate prove few indeed.[37]

The Mishnah, Talmuds, and Midrash-compilations, start to finish, form a vast arena for debate. And, as Lloyd points out, beyond the recognition that "natural phenomena are not the products of random or arbitrary influences but regular and governed by determinable sequences of cause and effect,"[38] it is debate that forms the distinguishing mark of Greek science and philosophy, and it is with the Mishnah that debate entered the public discourse of the Judaism put forth by our sages of blessed memory. In the Mishnah's representation of matters, the sages always

---

[33] On the relationship of Qumran and Rabbinic Sabbath law, see Lawrence H. Schiffman, *The Halakhah at Qumran* (Leiden, 1975). Schiffman does not undertake form-analytical comparisons.

[34] If we further consider the literary ambition exhibited in the massive size of the Mishnah as compared with the paltry volume of laws preserved among other Judaisms, that point is reenforced.

[35] We make provision for a possible exception in the case of Job, but supernatural debate and debate between men surely are to be classified differently.

[36] Sifra is a prominent example but not the only one by any means.

[37] The dispute in the Midrash-compilations must be addressed in its own terms. But when it comes to debates and extended dialogues, the Gemaras of the two Talmuds stand by themselves even when compared with the later Midrash-compilations, beyond Sifra.

[38] Lloyd, *Early Greek Science,* p. 8.

"knew and criticized one another's ideas," just as did the early Greek philosophers. And, in the context of prior Israelite writing, they find no antecedents or models or precedents for their insistence upon debate, (implicit) face-to-face exchange of contradictory views, with provision for sorting out difference through reasoned exchange.

If we cannot find an Israelite "tradition" realized, also, in the Mishnah and Midrash-compilations, then when we come to the Talmud's Gemara, we find ourselves still further away from the received and typical rhetoric of Israelite writing. It is there, and only there, that we find the sustained, dialectical argument that transforms law into jurisprudence and the arena for philosophical speculation and argument.[39] Except for the Gemara of the Talmud of the Land of Israel,[40] no other writing out of the Judaisms of antiquity, whether of the Rabbinic or any other Judaism, is comprised of fully-exposed disputes and debates and protracted analytical arguments as is the Bavli. It follows that had the authors of compositions of dialectical analysis for use in the Bavli wished to find models for their work in the prior literature of Israel — whether of their own Judaism or of some other — they would have looked in vain for guidance. The very conception of the written-down argument, or rather, the provision of notes for the reconstituting of an oral argument, in the Israelite setting is unique to the Mishnah's two Gemaras, the Yerushalmi, the Bavli, and, in context, the Midrash-compilations, from Sifra through Song of Songs Rabbah.

V. DIFFERENTIATING CANONICAL DOCUMENTS FROM ONE ANOTHER

Now that we see how we may characterize the Rabbinic canon as a whole and complete entity, to be differentiated from all other entities of its class, we have to analyze the canon's components and briefly indicate how these are to be differentiated, whole and complete, from one another. Since, in a variety of books listed in the Preface, I have demonstrated beyond any doubt that rabbinic texts are purposive documents, well-crafted texts and not merely compilations of this and that, and since I have further specified in acute detail precisely the aesthetic, formal, and logical program followed by each of those texts, we need not be detained at this point with a systematic reprise of well-known facts.[41]

---

[39] What I said about the points of commonality and difference with the Zoroastrian Rivayat-writing of a somewhat later period pertains here as well.

[40] There, as I have already noted, the dispute gives way to considerable analytical arguments. These are different from the kind we find in the Bavli, as I said, since they prefer the form of the axiom-theorem, rather than the open-ended dialectics of the Bavli. But in the Yerushalmi we do find disputes and debates as we do in the Bavli.

[41] For a complete survey, see *Introduction to Rabbinic Literature.* N.Y., 1994: Doubleday. The Doubleday Anchor Reference Library.

It suffices here to state the basic principles of differentiation. Three definitive traits permit differentiating one document from another in Rabbinic literature, and correct translation of a Rabbinic document makes possible the identification of these traits:

[1] the rhetoric or formal preferences of a piece of writing, which dictate , without respect to meaning, how sentences will be composed;[42]

[2] the logic of coherent discourse, which determines how one sentence will be joined to others in context; and how groups of sentences will cohere and form completed units of thought, and, finally, how said units of thought agglutinate or are otherwise held together in large-scale components of complete documents;

[3] the topical program of the writing, which indicates the subject and may also indicate the problematic — what we wish to know about the subject — of that same writing.

By invoking these three criteria, which are entirely familiar in the analysis of literature in antiquity, we may distinguish each document from all others and establish a clear definition for every piece of writing in the literature. The reason is simple. A received discipline of thought and expression governed all writing that has survived in Rabbinic literature.

[1] RHETORIC: Writers in this literature followed formal conventions, making choices never particular to a given "author" (that is, the authorship of a composition, the compilers of a composite) let alone a particular, individual sage who is named and quoted but always set forth, to begin with, by a repertoire of commonly-understood fixed arrangements of words.[43] These fixed arrangements, transcending particular meanings, signaled the purpose and even the context of a given set of sentences; following one form, rather than another, therefore dictated to the reader of a passage the character and intent of that passage: its classification. Correct translation will underscore the regularities of form and formulation.

[2] LOGIC OF COHERENT DISCOURSE: Since the Rabbinic writings ordinarily set forth not discrete sentences — aphorisms that stand, each in lapidary splendor — but cogent sets of sentences forming whole units of coherent thought

---

[42] One of the many problems to be solved in the study of the free-standing sentence is the relationship between the formalization of such a sentence in its context and the alleged autonomy of what is said. I should have thought that the proponents of the atomistic exegesis of sentences out of context would have found it necessary to demonstrate the formal autonomy of those sentences, or at least to explain the formal conventionality of many of them.

[43] That is not to claim we never find idiosyncrasies of formulation, for the opposite is the case. We do find them — occasionally. But a theory of how individual formulations are preserved and transmitted and ultimately utilized in otherwise highly-formalized compositions has not yet been put forth; people simple assume that if a saying is attributed to an authority, he really said it, and that is without differentiation of the formal and contextual traits of what is said.

("paragraphs") in our language, we also have to identify the principles of logic that connect one sentence to another. That logic of coherent discourse has the power to make of a group of sentences a whole that is greater than the sum of the parts. Proper translation will point up the distinct small whole units of thought ("sentences") and further show how these units of thought coalesce in completed units of thought (paragraphs), and how sets of paragraphs hold together to make coherent statements ("chapters" or major parts thereof).

[3] TOPIC, PROPOSITION: Every document treats a specific topic. Moreover, many documents set forth sustained exercises in the analysis of a concrete problem pertinent to a given topic. Some entire documents, early and late in the formation of the literature, are so set forth as to demonstrate propositions we are able to identify and define. Few books in Rabbinic literature aim merely at collecting and arranging information. Nearly all documents, to the contrary, work on not a topic in general but a specific problem concerning that topic, that is, a problematic; most of the documents set forth propositions that emerge out of masses of detail and may come to concrete expression through diverse details.

The governing protocols served because no document in Rabbinic literature ever accommodated idiosyncratic preference. Not a single one comes to us from an individual writer or author (e.g., Paul, Josephus, Philo); none systematically collects the sayings or composites formulated in a single, clearly identifiable school (e.g., Matthew). All documents — by definition, that is, by their acceptance into the authoritative canon, indicated by their cross-referencing — enjoy the sponsorship of sages as a group, whether we call the group an authorship, or redactors or compilers or editors. Not only so, but the compositions of which the composites are comprised themselves follow rigid rules of formulation and expression. When, therefore, we identify those rules, we can classify documents by differentiating among a limited repertoire of available choices.

Each document requires close analysis within its own limits, then comparison with other documents, first, those of its species, then, those not of its species. When compared as to rhetoric, topic, and logic of coherent discourse, nearly all of the documents will yield ample evidence that a restricted formal repertoire dictated to writers how they were to formulate their ideas if those ideas were to find a place in this particular document.

Some forms appear in more than one document, others are unique to the documents (or to the genre of documents) in which they appear. Two examples of the former are the exegetical form and the dispute.

[1] EXEGETICAL FORM: The exegetical form requires two elements only: citation of a phrase of Scripture or a clause of the Mishnah, followed by a few words of paraphrase or other explanation.

[2] THE DISPUTE: Already discussed earlier, the dispute form requires the presentation in a single syntactic pattern of two or more conflicting opinions on a given problem. The form will commonly have a topic sentences that implicitly

conveys a problem and two or more elliptical solutions to the problem, each bearing attribution to a named authority. An alternative will have a problem and solution assigned to one authority, or given anonymously, followed by, And Rabbi X says..., with a contrary opinion. Dominant in the Midrash-compilations but paramount also in the two Talmuds' treatment of the Mishnah, the exegetical form commonly defines the smallest whole unit of thought ("sentence") in a larger composition or composite ("paragraph," "chapter," respectively). No Midrash-compilation relies solely on the exegetical form for the formulation of its materials; every one of them uses that form as a building block. The dispute-form serves both legal and exegetical writers, the Mishnah and Talmuds and Midrash-compilations as well. It proves definitive in some documents, the Mishnah and Tosefta in particular, subordinate in others, Midrash-compilations, the two Talmuds.

VI.   THE CONSTRUCTION OF DOCUMENTS: "THE PARTS" DEFINED

This sizable account of the whole brings us to the point: the parts. What exactly do I mean by "the parts" of the whole constituted by a given document? By moving from the whole to the parts, I intend to identify each one of the constituent components of the Midrash-compilations. These I take to fall into three classes by reason of their formal traits, that is, to be subject to differentiation in solely phenomenological classes:

[1] what is primary to the document and conforms to its indicative forms and program,

[2] what does not exhibit the definitive traits of the document but occurs only in that document, and

[3] what is shared by two or more of the documents of the canon.

The distinctions upon which these analytical taxonomies rest are objective and in no way subjective, since they depend upon the fixed and factual relationship between a piece of writing and a larger redactional context. We now know the requirements of redactors of the several documents of the rabbinic canon, because I have already shown what they are in the case of a large variety of documents. When, therefore, we judge a piece of writing to serve the program of the document in which that writing occurs, it is not because of a personal impulse or a private and incommunicable insight, but because the traits of that writing self-evidently respond to the documentary program of the book in which the writing is located. Writing that does not conform to the documentary protocol is readily identified for the same reason. And it is a matter of fact that a given composition or composite appears in more than a single document.

To do this work we begin with the whole and work inward, as we peel an onion. As to the parts, we classify them by their indicative traits of relationship with the plan and program of the whole. That is to say, are writings responsive to the program of the compilation in which they occur? Are they responsive to the program of some other compilation, not the one where they now are? Or are they utterly autonomous of the requirements of any redactional setting we have or can envisage? In the present context, these categories may be defined with greater precision:

[1] Some writings in a given Midrash-compilation clearly realize the redactional program of the framers of the document in which those writings occur.

[2] Some writings in a given Midrash-compilation do realize the redactional program of the document in which they occur, but do not occur anywhere else. These are anomalous.

[3] Some writings now found in a given Midrash-compilation stand autonomous of any redactional program we have because they take a comfortable position in two or more compilations.

These are the three types of parts of the whole that we may discern by an objective examination of the formal traits of a piece of writing. Once we know the governing protocol of a document, we recognize that in the background of the documents that we have is writing that is not shaped by documentary requirements, writing that is not shaped by the documentary requirements of the compilations we now have, and also writing that is entirely formed within the rules of the documents that now present that writing. These are the three formally-distinctive kinds of writing. My purpose is to portray each Midrash-compilation as a composite of writing of these three kinds, and when I have done so, I shall have set forth the parts that all together form the whole of the document.

My analytical taxonomy of the writings now collected in various Midrash-compilations points to not only three types of writing in our documents. It also suggests that writing went on both outside of the framework of the editing of documents, and also within the limits of the formation and framing of documents. Writing of the former kind then constituted a kind of literary work on which redactional planning made no impact.

We have now to ask what is at stake in this study. Specifically, what do we know when we have identified the parts that comprise a document, and what do we not know? Or, to put matters slightly differently, if we know how a document breaks down into its components parts — its composites, its compositions, their components — what else do we know?

At stake is further perspective on the character of each document, whole and in its constitutive components. With the work in hand we are able to assess the coherence of the document and the role assigned therein to materials composed for some other purpose than that defined by the compilers. But we may move a step further, behind the surface of the document, into its situation in the process of construction. For we may further examine the traits of these atypical, or a-documentary parts of the document, comparing the character of the peripatetic from the stationary ones. Once we differentiate the documentary from the non-documentary components of a document and further identify, among the latter, the non-documentary from the a-documentary, peripatetic ones, we open a variety of new problems for inquiry into the canon's other-than-documentary writing. Does the result promise insight into something we may call "the 'tradition'[44] prior to the documentary (re-)formulation of the 'tradition'"? I see no historical questions that we may answer, e.g., is one kind of writing prior in time to another, for diverse traits of compositions and composites in relationship to the character of the document have no bearing upon such temporal questions as priority or posteriority.[45] People in the same period, even in the same place, write in more than one way and for more than a single purpose. But one thing seems to me clear: what conforms to the paramount documentary protocol in literary terms surely belongs to the period in which the document was put together — the compositions written according to a single rule, the composites formed with a uniform purpose in mind, the whole assembled in response to a coherent plan. An agglutinative process yields clues of the stratification of a document that a process operative for a determinate period does not. A comparison of the Mishnah and the Mekhilta attributed to R. Ishmael, at opposite extremes of the formal spectrum, makes that fact clear.

---

[44] "Tradition" bears within itself a variety of senses and claims, and it is a word that cannot serve any valid exercise of description. For if we know to begin with that we deal with a "tradition," then we have answered the question that we ask simply by making use of the right word. We want to know whether we can gain access to a "Judaism" that is behind the texts, and to one that is prior to the texts. Once we label non- and extra-documentary writings as "traditional," we have answered our question.

[45] All the more so, I see no questions of broad historical interest about the general character of "Judaism," or the social realities of Rabbinic Judaism, that this literary inquiry can answer. The documents tell us about the Judaism that is within or behind the texts, but not — on the face of matters — about the Judaism that is beyond them, in the world at large. I have dealt at some length, and in some detail, with that question, in the monograph set: *The Judaism Behind the Texts. The Generative Premises of Rabbinic Literature*. I. *The Mishnah*. A. *The Division of Agriculture*. Atlanta, 1993: Scholars Press for South Florida Studies in the History of Judaism; *The Judaism Behind the Texts. The Generative Premises of Rabbinic Literature*. I. *The Mishnah*. B. *The Divisions of Appointed Times, Women, and Damages (through Sanhedrin)*. Atlanta, 1993: Scholars Press for South Florida Studies in the History of Judaism; *The Judaism Behind the Texts. The Generative Premises of Rabbinic Literature*. I. *The Mishnah*. C. *The Divisions of Damages (from Makkot), Holy Things and Purities*. Atlanta, 1993: Scholars Press for South Florida Studies in the History of Judaism; *The Judaism Behind the Texts. The Generative Premises of Rabbinic Literature*. II. *The Tosefta, Tractate Abot, and the Earlier Midrash-Compilations: Sifra, Sifré to Numbers, and Sifré to*

What about the history of ideas? In terms of the ideas that are put forth, differentiating between what is said and the way in which it is said proves an uncertain art, often practiced but seldom carefully defined and defended. Subjectivity and impressionism govern. A document that time and again makes a single point in a single way, covering diverse materials, surely speaks out of the age at which that single point was selected for repetition. Then we know that a given idea, of indeterminate antiquity, was deemed urgent at a specific moment. The situation of a document that does not make some few points over and over again yields less clear results. Each document with its components is to be considered in its own terms.

As to what does not conform to the documentary protocol, matters seem to me still less clear. Such compositions need not find a temporal position alongside the documentary compositions, but they also cannot arbitrarily be assigned to some earlier stage in the formation of the writings. I am inclined to think that what is shared among two or more documents was written to circulate on its own, outside of all documentary frameworks. But whether that means that writing was done before people began to assemble Midrash-compilations of the kind we now have, or simply outside of the framework of documentary composition, I do not know. More than a single type of writing takes place at any period, and people are quite able to write for publication in more than a single medium. That is to say, they may write brief, coherent compositions for circulation as stories, independent of further acts of agglutination and conglomeration, and they may also write brief, coherent compositions that are meant to help build a large-scale document or a major composite thereof. So I do not see how we may draw any historical conclusions about either kind of extra-documentary writing that we find in a given compilation.

Deuteronomy. Atlanta, 1993.: Scholars Press for South Florida Studies in the History of Judaism; *The Judaism Behind the Texts. The Generative Premises of Rabbinic Literature.* III. *The Later Midrash-Compilations: Genesis Rabbah, Leviticus Rabbah and Pesiqta deRab Kahana.* Atlanta, 1994: Scholars Press for South Florida Studies in the History of Judaism; *The Judaism Behind the Texts. The Generative Premises of Rabbinic Literature.* IV. *The Latest Midrash-Compilations: Song of Songs Rabbah, Ruth Rabbah, Esther Rabbah I, and Lamentations Rabbati. And The Fathers According to Rabbi Nathan.* Atlanta, 1994: Scholars Press for South Florida Studies in the History of Judaism; *The Judaism Behind the Texts. The Generative Premises of Rabbinic Literature.* V. *The Talmuds of the Land of Israel and Babylonia.* Atlanta, 1994: Scholars Press for South Florida Studies in the History of Judaism; *The Judaism the Rabbis Take for Granted.* Atlanta, 1995: Scholars Press for South Florida Studies in the History of Judaism.

VII.   SIGNALING THE PARTS AND THEIR PLACE IN THE WHOLE

It remains to explain how I propose to indicate what I conceive to be the constitutive parts of the document. As in my academic commentaries to the two Talmuds, I utilize visual signals to indicate my judgment on what is primary to a document and what is secondary and further to differentiate secondary compositions and composites between those particular to a document and those shared with other documents. To make matters immediately clear, I print from one margin to the other the passages that conform to the documentary protocol. Within these compositions and composites, I identify interpolations and appendices and other sorts of extraneous intruded material by centering the passage within the larger frame in which it finds its place.

I then indent, toward the middle of the page, ending once more at the right hand margin, passages that do not conform to the document's plan, but that also do not occur elsewhere.

In this way we identify the parts out of which the whole is put together. We also form an accurate assessment of the proportions of the document made up of the several types of parts. So we are able immediately to see how much of a given document conforms to its overall plan, how much of it is shared with other documents, and how much is anomalous (in the framework spelled out in the previous section). So far as formal traits permit identifying the sources of a document, this systematic work of identifying the parts provides information for source-research.

VIII.   DOCUMENTARY DESCRIPTION AND FORM-ANALYSIS: THE INTERPLAY. THE SPECIFIC RESULTS PRESENTED IN THIS MONOGRAPH

The definition of documentary as against aberrational forms requires some refinement. The principle of form-analysis that governs is simple: a document defines its purposes, therefore identifies for us the forms that the framers require to carry out that purpose. Hence the specification of the forms that fulfil the documentary program depends upon the character of the document at hand, not on the traits of the principal forms thereof. A given form may serve in one document as integral, in another as peripheral. At the end of the outline-chapter, I specify what the outline identifies for us as documentary preferences as to form, and the remainder falls outside of the range of discussion. That remainder constitutes the document's corpus of aberrational forms.

It follows that, integral to the project are my systematic outlines of the several compilations. There I portray the compilation in such a way that the primary and secondary and derivative components are shown in relationship with one another. At this stage of the work we may proceed no further. When all twelve Midrash-compilations have been systematically described through form-analysis of the type defined here, we shall address the question of form-analysis of the Rabbinic literature as a whole, that is, in canonical, not narrowly documentary, terms. Enough has been said so that readers can work out for themselves precisely of what those terms will consist. At the intersection of documentary description and systematic form-analysis we shall finally reach the facts that permit us to turn outward, toward the history of documents and the history of the components that comprise those documents, viewed whole through the traits of the parts and still smaller components. But we remain some distance from that encounter.

With the outlines of the two Talmuds fully exposed and systematically compared with one another, we are able to attempt the same procedure for the Midrash-compilations. But the purpose of the outline is now analytical, not merely descriptive of the topical and propositional program of the document as was the case with the two Talmuds. A profound difference between the Talmuds and the Midrash-compilations defines our problem. The Talmuds follow the formal and topical outline of the Mishnah and are exceedingly well organized in accord with that program. But the Midrash-compilations follow a different principle of organization altogether, a far more complex set of principles, in fact.

To explain briefly: in the case of my now-complete, *The Talmud of Babylonia. A Complete Outline,* and *The Talmud of The Land of Israel.. An Outline of the Second, Third, and Fourth Division,*[46] an outline of a document serves both as a descriptive mechanism and also as a medium of analysis. That is, an outline allows us both to follow the unfolding of the propositional program of a document (if it has such a program), and also to identify the main elements of argument and evidence in support of the propositions. If following the protocols of outlining — first the primary assertions, and, now indented and so subordinated, the secondary, derivative, or illustrative ones, and then the further-indented and subordinated evidence and argument in behalf of the initial allegations — we can derive from a document a conventional outline, the character of the document itself emerges in a clear way. That is, the document that conforms to the protocol finds its place within the logical system of propositional, topical, and argumentative documents that, in general, conform. But the character of the Midrash-compilations imposes its own logic, therefore the possibilities and tasks of an outline must define themselves in their own terms.

Specifically, in the case of the Midrash-compilations, the procedures of outlining produce something other than a conventional result, so the document itself will attest to its own classification. The outline that the document produces will tell us about the character of the document and permit the comparison and contrast of that document with others, both like and unlike, subjected to the same procedure. That, in a very few words, is what the third element of the present

---

[46] Atlanta, 1995: Scholars Press for *USF Academic Commentary Series.*

exercise is meant to make possible. Because of the rigidly phenomenological character of my proposition, evidence, and argument, I do not present the documents in their generally-accepted chronological order; in form-analysis, considerations of temporality do not apply.

Now we know how to see the compilations whole and complete, so that we are able to distinguish one document from another by appeal to objective facts concerning their respective characteristics in rhetoric, logic of coherent discourse, and topical program (*topoi* in the philosophical framework). We therefore are able to define the definitive, indicative traits of documents and we know those characteristic types of composites and compositions that the compilers of the several documents chose for their work. These, further, allow us to identify, in a given document, what is aberrant, what clearly does not conform to the indicative traits of the document as a whole: how much, in what proportion, with what effect, and comprised by what kinds of formations? So once we know how documents define themselves, the logical next step is to identify the principal parts of those same wholes that do not conform to the documentary definition.

How are we to do so? Since we can define the indicative traits of a document, we now identify and examine components of said document that do not conform to those governing traits. Now with the comprehensive form-analysis complete, we can reliably identify compositions and composites within a document that do not exhibit those traits and therefore do not conform to the documentary program of that particular compilation. In this project and its eleven companions bearing the same subtitle, "from the whole to the parts," I turn from description of the several Midrash-compilations seen whole, respectively, to the analysis of the principal parts thereof.

What I wish to find out in detail is simple, though finding the answer requires much detailed work. Beyond the formal norms of a document, of what large-scale types of writing of an aberrational character are the Midrash-compilations comprised? Since I have defined the governing formal conventions of the various documents, I am able to ask, what of the components that do not conform to those conventions? My special interest lies in identifying the anomalous, non-documentary writing in the several compilations, namely, the components of Midrash-compilations that do not replicate to the protocol that governs the formation of those compilations overall. I wish to find out what traits we discern in the compositions and composites that stand separately from documents' principal parts. Each of the twelve principal Midrash-compilations is examined in this protracted project. In due course we shall identify the aberrational (in context: extra-documentary or non-documentary) forms of a given document and compare them with those of another, and of the whole lot.[47]

---

[47] The first study that I presently plan will be *The Aberrational Forms of Rabbinic Discourse. I. A Documentary History of the Dispute and Debate.* Atlanta, Date to be determined: Scholars Press for South Florida Studies in the History of Judaism.

IX.   THE TRAITS OF SONG OF SONGS RABBAH IN PARTICULAR

The Song of Songs (in the Christian Bible, "the Song of Solomon") —
both referring to the opening line, "The Song of Songs, which is Solomon's" —
finds a place in the Torah because the collection of love-songs in fact speaks about
the relationship between God and Israel. The intent of the compilers of Song of
Songs Rabbah is to justify that reading.[48] What this means is that Midrash-exegesis
turns to everyday experience — the love of husband and wife — for a metaphor of
God's love for Israel and Israel's love for God. Then, when Solomon's song says,
"O that you would kiss me with the kisses of your mouth! For your love is better
than wine," (Song 1:2), sages of blessed memory think of how God kissed Israel.
Reading the Song of Songs as a metaphor, the Judaic sages state in a systematic
and orderly way their entire structure and system.

If, as noted in Chapter Four, the Talmud of Babylonia joined the Mishnah
to Scripture in its formation of the structure of the dual Torah as one, so too, Song
of Songs Rabbah joined metaphor to theology, symbol to structure, in setting forth
that same whole. Standing in the same period, at the end of the canonical process,
in the sixth century, its authorship accomplished in its way that same summa that
the authorship of the Bavli set forth. But the writers and compilers worked with
far more delicacy, those deal with not intellect but sentiment, not proposition but
attitude and emotion. For the Bavli rules over the mind and tells what to think and
do, while Song of Songs Rabbah tells how to think and feel, especially how to
make the heart at one with God.

Mishnah-tractate Yadayim 3:5 defines the setting in which sages took up
the Song of Songs. The issue was, which documents are regarded as holy, among
the received canon of ancient Israel. The specific problem focuses upon Qohelet
("Ecclesiastes") and the Song of Songs. The terms of the issue derive from the
matter of uncleanness. For our purpose, it suffices to know that if a document is
holy, then it is held to be unclean, meaning, if one touches the document, he has to
undergo a process of purification before he can eat food in a certain status of
sanctification (the details are unimportant here) or, when the Temple stood, go to
the Temple. What that meant in practice is, people will be quite cautious about

---

[48] For further reading and bibliography on the topic of this chapter, see the following:
Bowker, p. 83.
Moses D. Herr, "Song of Songs Rabbah," *Encyclopaedia Judaica* 15:152-4: the name of the
    compilation, definition, language, sources, date: Land of Israel, middle of the
    sixth century.
Maccoby omits this document from his introduction.
Stemberger-Strack, pp. pp. 342-4: text, translation.
    This writer's introduction is *The Midrash Compilations of the Sixth and Seventh
    Centuries: An Introduction to the Rhetorical Logical, and Topical Program.* IV.
    Song of Songs Rabbah. Atlanta, 1990: Scholars Press for Brown Judaic Studies.

handling such documents, which then will be regarded as subject to special protection. So when sages declare that a parchment or hide on which certain words are written imparts uncleanness to hands, they mean to say, those words, and the object on which they are written, must be handled reverently and thoughtfully.

> All sacred scriptures impart uncleanness to hands. The Song of Songs and Qohelet impart uncleanness to hands.
>
> R. Judah says, "The Song of Songs imparts uncleanness to hands, but as to Qohelet there is dispute."
>
> R. Yosé says, "Qohelet does not impart uncleanness to hands, but as to Song of Songs there is dispute."
>
> Rabbi Simeon says, "Qohelet is among the lenient rulings of the House of Shammai and strict rulings of the House of Hillel."
>
> Said R. Simeon b. Azzai, "I have a tradition from the testimony of the seventy-two elders, on the day on which they seated R. Eleazar b. Azariah in the session, that the Song of Songs and Qohelet do impart uncleanness to hands."
>
> Said R. Aqiba, "Heaven forbid! No Israelite man ever disputed concerning Song of Songs that it imparts uncleanness to hands. For the entire age is not so worthy as the day on which the Song of Songs was given to Israel. For all the scriptures are holy, but the Song of Songs is holiest of all. And if they disputed, they disputed only concerning Qohelet."
>
> Said R. Yohanan b. Joshua the son of R. Aqiba's father-in-law, according to the words of Ben Azzai, "Indeed did they dispute, and indeed did they come to a decision."
>
> MISHNAH-TRACTATE YADAYIM 3:5

Clearly, the Mishnah-passage, ca. 200, records a point at which the status of the Song of Songs is in doubt. By the time of the compilation of Song of Songs Rabbah, that question had been settled. Everybody took for granted that our document is holy for the reason given.

The sages who compiled Song of Songs Rabbah read the Song of Songs as a sequence of statements of urgent love between God and Israel, the holy people. How they convey the intensity of Israel's love of God forms the point of special interest in this document. For it is not in propositions that they choose to speak, but in the medium of symbols. As we noted in Chapter Nine, section 10, in our discussion of words that serve as opaque symbols in "another-matter"-compositions, sages here use language as a repertoire of opaque symbols in the form of words. They set forth sequences of words that connote meanings, elicit emotions, stand for events, form the verbal equivalent of pictures or music or dance or poetry. Through the repertoire of these verbal-symbols and their arrangement and rearrangement, the message the authors wish to convey emerges: not in so many words, but through words nonetheless. Sages chose for their compilation a very brief list of items among many possible candidates. They therefore determined to appeal to a highly restricted list of implicit meanings, calling upon some very few events or persons, repeatedly identifying these as the expressions of God's profound affection for Israel, and Israel's deep love for God. The message of the document comes not so much from stories of what happened or did not happen, assertions of truth or denials of error, but rather from the repetitious rehearsal of sets of symbols.

1.   TRANSLATIONS INTO ENGLISH

The first translation is the excellent one of Maurice Simon, *Song of Songs,* in H. Freedman and Maurice Simon, eds., *Midrash Rabbah* (London, 1939: Soncino Press), Volume IX. The second, and first form-analytical one, is this writer's *Song of Songs Rabbah. An Analytical Translation.* Atlanta, 1990: Scholars Press for Brown Judaic Studies. I.. *Song of Songs Rabbah to Song Chapters One through Three*.and II.. *Song of Songs Rabbah to Song Chapters Four through Eight.*

2.   RHETORIC

The forms that govern the presentation of the document are familiar and easily catalogued:

1.   INTERSECTING-VERSE/BASE-VERSE FORM: the citation of a verse other than one in the document at hand (here: Song of Songs Rabbah) followed by a protracted exposition of that cited verse, leading in the end to a clarification of the base-verse of the document at hand.

2.   COMMENTARY-FORM: citation of a verse clause-by-clause, with attached language, brief or protracted, amplifying that clause.

3.   PROPOSITIONAL-FORM: citation of a verse plus the statement of a proposition, proved by appeal to diverse verses, including the one originally cited.

4.   PARABLE-FORM: parables very commonly begin with attributive language; they nearly always start with, "to what is the matter to be likened?" This may be explicit or implied, e.g., simply, "to [the case of] a king who...." We are supposed to know that "to what may the matter be compared?" stands prior to the initial phrase. Then the author proceeds to set forth the parable. This need not take the form of a long story. It can be a set-piece tableau, e.g., "The matter is comparable to the case of a woman of noble family who had three representatives of her family at hand." The parable always follows a proposition, and the parable may then bear in its wake an explication of its components in terms of the case at hand, again as in the cited instance. And the parable may execute its purpose through a protracted narrative. So what makes a parable unique from all other forms is not the narrative but the presence of an inaugural simile or metaphor.

5.   THE DISPUTE: The dispute-form here follows the model of that in the Talmud of the Land of Israel rather than the Mishnah. The formal requirements are [1] statement of a problem, e.g., a word that will be explained, [2] two or more authorities' names, followed in sequence by [3] the repetition of each name and [4] a proposition assigned to that name. The explication of the propositional language

may be substantial or brief, but the formal requirements of the dispute are always simple: names, then repetition of the names followed by fairly well-balanced sentences, in which propositions held by two or more authorities on the same subject will be contrasted.

6. THE NARRATIVE IN THE FORM OF DIALOGUE: here we have a protracted story, which unfolds through exchange of dialogue. The extrinsic narrative language is simply, "he said to him," "he said to him," and variations thereof. The entire tale is told by means of what is said. Verses of Scripture may or may not occur; they do not define a requirement of the form.

7. THE NARRATIVE EFFECTED THROUGH DESCRIBED ACTION, THAT IS, IN THE FORM OF A STORY OF WHAT PEOPLE DO: the story here depends upon described action, rather than cited speech. In this type of narrative we have a reference to what someone did, and the dialogue is not the principal medium for conveying the action. Rather, what the actors do, not only what they say, proves integral; details extrinsic to speech, e.g., "well-balanced that man had a wife and two sons...," are critical to the unfolding of the tale. The explanation of what is done then forms the burden of the spoken components. The criterion for distinguishing narrative in the form of a dialogue from narrative in the form of described action is the burden placed upon the dialogue. If it explains action, then the action is the centerpiece; if it contains and conveys the action, then the dialogue is the centerpiece.

8. NO FORMAL PATTERN TO BE DISCERNED: a small number of items do not conform to familiar patterns at all.

3. LOGIC OF COHERENT DISCOURSE

The document holds together its individual units of thought in a variety of ways. But the means for holding together those individual units in a large-scale composition is in one logic only, and that is, the logic of fixed association. So there is a mixed logic before us, one serving the compilers in their large-scale organization and composition of the whole document, the other serving the various authorships of the cogent units of sustained but completed discourse that are assembled by the ultimate compilers.

4. TOPICAL PROGRAM

In reading the love-songs of the Song of Songs as the story of the love affair of God and Israel, sages identify implicit meanings that are always few and invariably self-evident; no serious effort goes into demonstrating the fact that God speaks, or Israel speaks; the point of departure is the message and meaning the One or the other means to convey. To take one instance, time and again we shall be told that a certain expression of love in the poetry of the Song of Songs is God's speaking to Israel about [1] the Sea, [2] Sinai, and [3] the world to come; or [1] the first redemption, the one from Egypt; [2] the second redemption, the one from Babylonia; and [3] the third redemption, the one at the end of days. The repertoire of symbols covers Temple and schoolhouse, personal piety and public worship, and other matched pairs and sequences of coherent matters, all of them seen as embedded within the poetry. Here is Scripture's poetry read as metaphor, and the task of the reader is kwell-balanced that for which each image of the poem stands. So Israel's holy life is metaphorized through the poetry of love and beloved, Lover and Israel. Long lists of alternative meanings or interpretations end up saying just one thing, but in different ways. The implicit meanings prove very few indeed. When in Song of Songs Rabbah we have a sequence of items alleged to form a taxon, that is, a set of things that share a common taxic indicator, what we have is a list. The list presents diverse matters that all together share, and therefore also set forth, a single fact or rule or phenomenon. That is why we can list them, in all their distinctive character and specificity, in a common catalogue of "other things" that pertain all together to one thing.

What do the compilers say through their readings of the metaphor of — to take one interesting example — the nut-tree for Israel? First, Israel prospers when it gives scarce resources for the study of the Torah or for carrying out religious duties; second, Israel sins but atones, and Torah is the medium of atonement; third, Israel is identified through carrying out its religious duties, e.g., circumcision; fourth, Israel's leaders had best watch their step; fifth, Israel may be nothing well-balanced but will be in glory in the coming age; sixth, Israel has plenty of room for outsiders but cannot afford to lose a single member. What we have is a repertoire of fundamentals, dealing with Torah and Torah-study, the moral life and atonement, Israel and its holy way of life, Israel and its coming salvation. A sustained survey of these composites shows the contradictory facts that the several composites are heterogeneous, but the components of the composites derive from a rather limited list, essentially scriptural events and personalities, on the one side, and virtues of the Torah's holy way of life, on the other. Here is a survey:

Joseph, righteous men, Moses, and Solomon;
patriarchs as against princes, offerings as against merit, and Israel as against the nations; those who love the king, proselytes, martyrs, penitents;
first, Israel at Sinai; then Israel's loss of God's presence on account of the golden calf; then God's favoring Israel by treating Israel not in accord with the requirements of justice but with mercy;
Dathan and Abiram, the spies, Jeroboam, Solomon's marriage to Pharaoh's daughter, Ahab, Jezebel, Zedekiah;
Israel is feminine, the enemy (Egypt) masculine, but God the father saves Israel the daughter;
Moses and Aaron, the Sanhedrin, the teachers of Scripture and Mishnah, the rabbis;
the disciples; the relationship among disciples, public recitation of teachings of the Torah in the right order; lections of the Torah;
the spoil at the Sea = the Exodus, the Torah, the Tabernacle, the ark;
the patriarchs, Abraham, Isaac, Jacob, then Israel in Egypt, Israel's atonement and God's forgiveness;

the Temple where God and Israel are joined, the Temple is God's resting place, the Temple is the source of Israel's fecundity;

Israel in Egypt, at the Sea, at Sinai, and subjugated by the gentile kingdoms, and how the redemption will come;

Rebecca, those who came forth from Egypt, Israel at Sinai, acts of loving kindness, the kingdoms who well-balanced rule Israel, the coming redemption;

fire above, fire below, meaning heavenly and altar fires; Torah in writing, Torah in memory; fire of Abraham, Moriah, bush, Elijah, Hananiah, Mishael, and Azariah;

the Ten Commandments, show-fringes and phylacteries, recitation of the Shema and the Prayer, the tabernacle and the cloud of the Presence of God, and the mezuzah;

the timing of redemption, the moral condition of those to be redeemed, and the past religious misdeeds of those to be redeemed;

Israel at the sea, Sinai, the Ten Commandments; then the synagogues and school houses; then the redeemer;

the Exodus, the conquest of the Land, the redemption and restoration of Israel to Zion after the destruction of the first Temple, and the final and ultimate salvation;

the Egyptians, Esau and his generals, and, finally, the four kingdoms;

Moses' redemption, the first, to the second redemption in the time of the Babylonians and Daniel;

the palanquin of Solomon: the priestly blessing, the priestly watches, the sanhedrin, and the Israelites coming out of Egypt;

Israel at the sea and forgiveness for sins effected through their passing through the sea; Israel at Sinai; the war with Midian; the crossing of the Jordan and entry into the Land; the house of the sanctuary; the priestly watches; the offerings in the Temple; the sanhedrin; the Day of Atonement;

God redeemed Israel without preparation; the nations of the world will be punished, after Israel is punished; the nations of the world will present Israel as gifts to the royal messiah, and here the base-verse refers to Abraham, Isaac, Jacob, Sihon, Og, Canaanites;

the return to Zion in the time of Ezra, the Exodus from Egypt in the time of Moses;

the patriarchs and with Israel in Egypt, at the Sea, and then before Sinai;

Abraham, Jacob, Moses;

Isaac, Jacob, Esau, Jacob, Joseph, the brothers, Jonathan, David, Saul, man, wife, paramour;

Abraham in the fiery furnace and Shadrach Meshach and Abednego, the Exile in Babylonia, well-balanced with reference to the return to Zion

These components form not a theological system, made up of well-joined propositions and harmonious positions, nor propositions that are demonstrated syllogistically through comparison and contrast. The point is just the opposite; it is to show that many different things really do belong on the same list. That yields not a proposition that the list syllogistically demonstrates. The list yields only itself, but, to be sure, — but then the list invites our exegesis; the connections among these items require exegesis. What this adds up to, then, is not argument for proposition, hence comparison and contrast and rule-making of a philosophical order, but rather a theological structure — comprising well-defined attitudes. Because of the character of Song of Songs Rabbah, the topical program of the document is best portrayed through the actual workings of the "another matter-" compositions.

Part One
PARASHAH ONE

1

Song of Songs Rabbah to
Song of Songs 1:1

1:1   *The Song of Songs, which is Solomon's.*

I:i
1.   A.   "The song of songs":

      B.   This is in line with that which Scripture said through Solomon: "Do you see a man who is diligent in his business? He will stand before kings, he will not stand before mean men" (Prov. 22:29).

      C.   "Do you see a man who is diligent in his business":

      D.   This refers to Joseph: "But one day, when he went into the house to do his work [and none of the men of the house was there in the house, she caught him by his garment, saying, 'Lie with me.' But he left his garment in her hand and fled and got out of the house]" (Gen. 39:10-13).

            E.   R. Judah and R. Nehemiah:

            F.   R. Judah said, "[Following Gen. R; LXXXVII:VII:] It was a festival day for the Nile. [Everybody went to see it, but he went to the household to take up his master's account books]."

            G.   R. Nehemiah said, "It was a day of theater. Everybody went to see it, but he went to the household to take up his master's account books."

                2. A. R. Phineas says in the name of R. Samuel bar Abba, "Whoever serves his master properly goes forth to freedom.

                    B. "Whence do we learn that fact? From the case of Joseph.

                    C. "It was because he served his master properly that he went forth to freedom."

3.   A.   "He will stand before kings":

B.   this refers to Pharaoh: "Then Pharaoh sent and called Joseph and they brought him hastily from the dungeon" (Gen. 41:14).

4.   A.   "...he will not stand before mean men":
B.   this refers to Potiphar, whose eyes the Holy One, blessed be He, darkened [the word for 'darkened' and 'mean men' share the same consonants], and whom he castrated.

5.   A.   Another interpretation of the verse, "Do you see a man who is diligent in his business" (Prov. 22:29):
B.   this refers to our lord, Moses, in the making of the work of the tabernacle.
C.   Therefore: "He will stand before kings":
D.   this refers to Pharaoh: "Rise up early in the morning and stand before Pharaoh" (Ex. 8:16).
E.   "...he will not stand before mean men":
F.   this refers to Jethro.
      G.   Said R. Nehemiah, "[In identifying the king with Pharaoh,] you have made the holy profane.
      H.   "Rather, 'He will stand before kings': this refers to the King of kings of kings, the Holy One, blessed be He: 'And he was there with the Lord forty days' (Ex. 34:28).
      I.   "'...he will not stand before mean men': this refers to Pharaoh: 'And there was thick darkness' (Ex. 10:22)."

6.   A.   Another interpretation of the verse, "Do you see a man who is diligent in his business" (Prov. 22:29):
B.   this refers to those righteous persons who are occupied with the work of the Holy One, blessed be He.
C.   Therefore: "He will stand before kings":
D.   this refers to for they stand firm in the Torah: "By me kings rule" (Prov. 8:15).
E.   "...he will not stand before mean men":
F.   this refers to the wicked: "And their works are in the dark" (Isa. 29:15); "Let their way be dark and slippery" (Ps. 35:6).

7.   A.   Another interpretation of the verse, "Do you see a man who is diligent in his business" (Prov. 22:29):
B.   this refers to this is R. Hanina.
      8.   A.   They say:
      B.   One time he saw people of his village bringing whole-offerings and peace-offerings up [on a pilgrimage to the Temple].
      C.   He said, "All of them are bringing peace-offerings to Jerusalem, but I am not bringing up a thing! What shall I do?"

D. Forthwith he went out to the open fields of his town, the unoccupied area of his town, and there he found a stone. He went and plastered it and polished it and painted it and said, "Lo, I accept upon myself the vow to bring it up to Jerusalem."

E. He sought to hire day-workers, saying to them, "Will you bring this stone up to Jerusalem for me?"

F. They said to him, "Pay us our wage, a hundred gold pieces, and we'll be glad to carry your stone up to Jerusalem for you."

G. He said to them, "Where in the world will I get a hundred gold pieces, or even fifty, to give you?"

H. Since at the time he could not find the funds, they immediately went their way.

I. Immediately the Holy One, blessed be He, arranged for him for fifty angels in the form of men [to meet him]. They said to him, "My lord, give us five selas, and we shall bring your stone to Jerusalem, on condition that you help us with the work."

J. So he put his hand to the work with them, and they found themselves standing in Jerusalem. He wanted to pay them their wage, but he could not find them.

K. The case came to the Chamber of the Hewn Stone [where the high court was in session]. They said to him, "It appears that in the case of our lord, ministering angels have brought the stone up to Jerusalem."

L. Immediately he gave sages that wage for which he had hired the angels.

9. A. Another interpretation of the verse, "Do you see a man who is diligent in his business" (Prov. 22:29):

B. this refers to Solomon son of David.

C. "He will stand before kings."

D. for he was diligent in building the house of the sanctuary: "So he spent seven years in building it" (1 Kgs. 6:38).

10. A. [Supply: "So he spent seven years in building it" (1 Kgs. 6:38),] but a different verse says, "And Solomon was building his own house for thirteen years" (1 Kgs. 7:1),

B. so the building of the house of Solomon was lovelier and more elaborate than the building of the house of the sanctuary.

C. But this is what they said:

D.   In the building of his house he was slothful, in the building of the house of the sanctuary he was diligent and not slothful.

11. A.   Huna in the name of R. Joseph: "All help the king, all the more so do all help out on account of the glory of the King of kings of kings, the Holy One, blessed be He,

B.   "even spirits, demons, ministering angels."

12. A.   Isaac b. R. Judah b. Ezekiel said, "'I have surely built you a house of habitation' (1 Kgs. 8:13): 'I have built what is already built.'"

13. A.   R. Berekhiah said, "'The house that they were building' is not what is said,

B.   "but rather, 'the house in its being built' (1 Kgs. 6:7), which is to say, it was built of itself.

C.   "'It was built of stone made ready at the quarry' (1 Kgs. 6:7):

D.   "what it says is not 'built' but 'it was built,' which is to say, the stones carried themselves and set themselves on the row."

14. A.   Said Rab, "Do not find this astonishing. What is written elsewhere? 'And a stone was brought and laid upon the mouth of the den' (Dan. 6:18).

B.   "Now are there any stones in Babylonia? [Of course not.] But from the land of Israel it flew in a brief moment and came and rested on the mouth of the pit."

15. A.   R. Huna in the name of R. Joseph said [concerning the verse, "And a stone was brought and laid upon the mouth of the den" (Dan. 6:18)], "An angel came down in the form of a lion made of stone and put itself at the mouth of the pit.

B.   "That is in line with this verse: 'My God has sent his angel and has shut the lions mouths' (Dan. 6:23).

C.   "Now do not find it astonishing. If for the honor owing to that righteous man, it is written, 'a certain stone was brought' (Dan. 6:18), for the honoring of the Holy One, blessed be He, how much the more so [will stones be provided in a magical manner].''

16. A. [Resuming where the discussion of 9.D:] "He will stand before kings":
B. before the kings of the Torah he will stand.
C. "...he will not stand before mean men":
D. this refers to a conspiracy of wicked men.

17. A. Said R. Joshua b. Levi, "When they took a vote and decided, **Three kings and four ordinary folk have no share in the world to come [M. San. 10:1],**
B. "they wanted to include Solomon with them.
C. "But an echo came forth and said, 'Do not lay hands on my anointed ones' (Ps. 105:15)."
D. Said R. Judah b. R. Simon, "And not only so, but he was given the place of honor at the head of three genealogical tables: 'And Rehoboam, son of Solomon, reigned in Judah' (1 Kgs. 14:21). [Simon, p. 4: "He was placed at the head of a genealogical tree...." Simon, p. 4, n. 11: "The mention of his name here being superfluous implies that he was a founder of a royal line.]
E. Said R. Yudan b. R. Simon, "Not only so, but the Holy Spirit rested on him, and he said the following three books: Proverbs, the Song of Songs, and Qohelet."

I:ii

1. A. [Supply: "The Song of Songs, which is Solomon's:"] That is in line with this verse: "Instead of your fathers shall be your sons" (Ps. 45:17).
B. You have cases in which a righteous man fathers a righteous man, a wicked man fathers a wicked man, a righteous man fathers a wicked man, and a wicked man fathers a righteous man.
C. And all of them derive from a verse of Scripture and also from a proverb and a popular saying.

2. A. That a righteous man fathers a righteous man can be shown in a verse of Scripture, a proverb, and a popular saying:
B. In Scripture: "Instead of your fathers shall be your sons" (Ps. 45:17).
C. In a proverb: "A scion proves the value of the fig tree."

3. A. That a wicked man fathers a wicked man can be shown in a verse of Scripture, a proverb, and a popular saying:

B. In Scripture: "And behold you have risen up in your fathers' place, a brood of sinful men" (Num. 32:14).

C. In a proverb: "As says the proverb of the ancients, Out of the wicked comes forth wickedness" (1 Sam. 24:14).

D. In a popular saying: "What does the beetle bear? Insects worse than itself" [following Simon, p. 5].

4. A. That a righteous man fathers a wicked man can be shown in a verse of Scripture, a proverb, and a popular saying:

B. In Scripture: "Let thistles grow instead of wheat" (Job 31:40).

C. In a proverb: "They father those who are not like them, they raise those who are not similar to them."

5. A. That a wicked man fathers a righteous man can be shown in a verse of Scripture, a proverb, and a popular saying:

B. In Scripture: "Instead of the thorn shall come up the cypress" (Isa. 55:13).

C. In a proverb: "The thorn produces the rose."

6. A. Truly, Solomon was king, son of a king, sage son of a sage, righteous man, son of a righteous man, noble son of a noble.

B. You find that everything that is written concerning this one [David] is written concerning that one [Solomon].

C. David ruled for forty years, and this one ruled for forty years.

D. David ruled over Israel and Judah, and his son ruled over Israel and Judah.

E. His father built the foundations and he built the main structure [of the Temple].

F. His father ruled from one end of the world to the other, and this one ruled from one end of the world to the other.

G. David wrote books, and Solomon wrote books.

H. David said songs, and Solomon said songs.

I. David spoke about the vanity of things, and Solomon spoke about the vanity of things.

J. David said important statements, and Solomon said important statements.

K. David said proverbs, and Solomon said proverbs.

L. David praised [God] with a passage starting with "then," and Solomon praised [God] with a passage starting with "then."

M. David built an altar, and Solomon built an altar.

N. David made an offering, and Solomon made an offering.

O. David brought up the ark, and Solomon brought up the ark.

P. David ruled for forty years: "And the days that David ruled over Israel were forty years" (1 Kgs. 2:11); and this one ruled for forty years: "And Solomon reigned in Jerusalem over all Israel forty years" (2 Chr. 9:30).

Q. David ruled over Israel and Judah, and his son ruled over Israel and Judah: "The Lord, the God of Israel, chose me out of all the house of my father to be king over Israel for ever, for he has chosen Judah to be prince" (1 Chr. 28:4); "Judah and Israel were many" (1 Kgs. 4:20).

R. David [his father] built the foundations and Solomon built the main structure [of the Temple]: "The David the king stood up upon his feet and said...I had made ready for the building" (1 Chr. 28:2); "I have surely built you a house of habitation" (1 Kgs. 8:13).

S. [Omitted: His father ruled from one end of the world to the other, and this one ruled from one end of the world to the other.]

T. David wrote books, for the Psalms bear his name, and Solomon wrote books, specifically, Proverbs, Qohelet, and the Song of Songs.

U. David spoke about the vanity of things, and Solomon spoke about the vanity of things: "Surely every man at his best estate is altogether vanity" (Ps. 39:6); "Vanity of vanities, says Qoheleth, vanity of vanities, all is vanity" (Qoh. 1:2).

V. David said important statements, and Solomon said important statements: "Now these are the last words of David" (2 Sam. 23:1); "The words of Qoheleth, son of David, king in Jerusalem" (Qoh. 1:1).

W. David said proverbs, and Solomon said proverbs: "As says the proverb of the ancients, out of the wicked comes forth wickedness" (1 Sam. 24:14); "The proverbs of Solomon, son of David, king of Israel" (Prov. 1:1).

X. David praised [God] with a passage starting with "then," and Solomon praised [God] with a passage starting with "then": "Then was our mouth filled with laughter and our tongue with singing, then they said among the nations" (Ps. 126:2); "Then said Solomon, the Lord has said" (1 Kgs. 8:12).

Y. David brought up the ark, and Solomon brought up the ark: "So David and the elders of Israel...went to bring up the ark" (1 Chr. 15:25); "Then Solomon assembled the elders of Israel to bring up the ark" (1 Kgs. 8:1).

Z. David said songs, and Solomon said songs: "And David spoke unto the Lord the words of this song" (2 Sam. 22:1); "The Song of Songs which is Solomon's" (Song 1:1).

7. A. R. Simon in the name of R. Jonathan of Bet Gubrin in the name of R. Joshua b. Levi said, "Since you are comparing him [to his father], compare him in every aspect.

B.   "Just as his father was forgiven for all his transgressions, 'The Lord
      has put away your sin, you will not die' (2 Sam. 12;13),
C.   "so he too was treated in the same way.
D.   "And not only so, but the Holy Spirit rested on him, and Solomon
      spoke the books of Proverbs, Qohelet, and the Song of Songs."

I:iii
1. A.   Another interpretation of "The Song of Songs":
    B.   This is in line with the following verse of Scripture: "The heart of the
          wise teaches his mouth [and adds learning to his lips]" (Prov. 16:23).
    C.   The heart of the wise man is full of wisdom, so who guides him, and
          who makes his mouth wise for him? [Simon, p. 7: "who endows him
          with the power to make intelligent and orderly use of his wisdom?"]
    D.   "His mouth": it is his mouth that makes him wise, his mouth that
          teaches him [Simon: what he is].
2. A.   "...and adds learning to his lips":
    B.   When he brings forth words of Torah from his heart, [by that very
          act] he adds to the lessons learned from the Torah.
          C.   They made a comparison: to what is this matter to be
                compared?
          D.   To a jar full of precious stones and pearls, tightly sealed,
                set in a corner, concerning the contents of which no one
                is aware.
          E.   Someone came along and emptied it. Then everybody
                knew what is in it.
          F.   So the heart of Solomon was full of wisdom, but no one
                knew what was in it.
          G.   When the Holy Spirit rested on him, so he set forth three
                books, everybody knew his wisdom.
3. A.   "...and adds learning to his lips":
    B.   The learning that he added to the words of Torah exalted him:
    C.   "And I applied my heart to seek and to explore by wisdom" (Qoh.
          1:13).
          4.   A.   [Supply: "And I applied my heart to seek and to explore
                      by wisdom" (Qoh. 1:13):]
                B.   What is the meaning of the clause, "to explore by
                      wisdom"?
                C.   He became an explorer of wisdom: "And they explored
                      the land" (Num. 13:21).
                D.   If there was someone who read Scripture well, he went to
                      him.
                E.   If there was someone who repeated Mishnah-sayings well,
                      he went to him,

          F.   for it is said, "and to explore by wisdom" (Qoh. 1:13).

5.   A.   Another interpretation of the phrase, "And I applied my heart to seek and to explore by wisdom" (Qoh. 1:13):

          B.   The letters in the word "to explore" may yield the word "to leave over."

          C.   When a poet is making an acrostic poem, sometimes he finishes [the alphabet], and sometimes he does not.

          D.   [Simon, p. 8:] But Solomon made alphabetical poems with five extra letters in addition: "And his poem was a thousand and five" (1 Kgs. 5:12), meaning, "what was left over from the alphabet was five."

6.   A.   And it was not only words of Torah alone that he explored, but everything that was done under the sun,

       B.   for example, how to sweeten mustard or lupines.

       C.   Said to him the Holy One, blessed be He, "After words of Torah you have ventured, by your life, I will not withhold your reward. Lo, I shall bring to rest on you the Holy Spirit."

       D.   Forthwith the Holy Spirit rested on him, and he recited these three books: Proverbs, Qohelet, and Song of Songs.

I:iv

1.   A.   Another interpretation of "The Song of Songs":

       B.   This is in line with the following verse of Scripture: "And more so because Qohelet was wise; [he also taught the people knowledge, yes, he pondered and sought out and set in order many proverbs]" (Qoh. 12:9):

       C.   If any other person had said them, you would have had to pay attention and listen to these things. All the more so, since Solomon said them.

       D.   If he had made them up from his own mind, you you would have had to pay attention and listen to these things. All the more so, since Solomon said them through the Holy Spirit.

2.   A.   "And more so because Qohelet was wise; he also taught the people knowledge, yes, he pondered and sought out and set in order many proverbs" (Qoh. 12:9):

       B.   "He pondered" words of the Torah, and "he sought out" words of the Torah.

       C.   He made "handles" for the Torah. [This is spelled out at 4.A-C below.]

       D.   For you find that before Solomon came along, there was no parable [Hebrew: *dugma*, e.g., paradigm].

          3.   A.   R. Nahman said two things [in this connection].

                B.   R. Nahman said, "[The matter may be compared] to the case of a huge palace that had many doors, so whoever came in would wander from the path to the entry.

C. "A smart fellow came along and took a skein of string
    and hung the string on the way to the entry, so everybody
    came and went following the path laid out by the skein.

D. "So too, until Solomon came along, no person could
    comprehend the words of the Torah. But when Solomon
    came along, everyone began to make sense of the Torah."

E. R. Nahman said the matter in yet another way: "[The
    matter may be compared] to the case of a reed marsh that
    no one could enter. A smart fellow came along and took
    a scythe and cut the reeds, so everybody began to go in
    and come out by chopping down the reeds.

F. "So was Solomon."

4. A. Said R. Yosé, "[The matter may be compared] to the case
        of a basket full of produce but lacking a handle so no one
        could lift it up.

    B. "A smart fellow came along and made handles for it, so
        people began to carry it about holding on to the handles.

    C. "So too, until Solomon came along, no person could
        comprehend the words of the Torah. But when Solomon
        came along, everyone began to make sense of the Torah."

5. A. Said R. Shila, "[The matter may be compared] to the case
        of a big jug full of boiling water but lacking a handle so
        no one could lift it up.

    B. "A smart fellow came along and made handles for it, so
        people began to carry it about holding on to the handles.

    C. [Supply: "So too, until Solomon came along, no person
        could comprehend the words of the Torah. But when
        Solomon came along, everyone began to make sense of
        the Torah."]

6. A. Said R. Hanina, "[The matter may be compared] to the
        case of a deep well full of water, and the water was cold,
        sweet, and good, but no one could drink from it.

    B. "A smart fellow came along and provided a rope joined
        with another rope, a cord joined with another cord,
        sufficiently long so people could draw water from the well
        and drink it, and then everybody began to draw and drink.

    C. "So from one thing to the next, from one proverb to the
        next, Solomon penetrated into the secret of the Torah.

    D. "For it is written, 'The proverbs of Solomon, son of David,
        king of Israel, to know wisdom and instruction' (Prov.
        1:1).

    E. "By means of the proverbs of Solomon, he mastered the
        words of the Torah."

7. A. And rabbis say, "Let a parable not be despised in your view, for it is through the parable that a person can master the words of the Torah.

B. "The matter me be compared to the case of a king who lost gold in his house or pearls. Is it not through a wick that is worth a penny that he finds it again?

C. "So let a parable not be despised in your view, for it is through the parable that a person can master the words of the Torah.

D. "You may know that that is so, for lo, Solomon through parables mastered the smallest details of the Torah."

8. A. [Supply: "And more so because Qohelet was wise; he also taught the people knowledge, yes, he pondered and sought out and set in order many proverbs]" (Qoh. 12:9):] Said R. Yudan, "This serves to teach you that whoever speaks words of the Torah in public acquires such merit that the Holy Spirit comes to rest upon him.

B. "And from whom do you learn that fact? From the case of Solomon.

C. "For it is because he spoke words of the Torah in public, he acquired such merit that the Holy Spirit came to rest upon him.

D. "So he wrote three books: Proverbs, Qohelet, and the Song of Songs."

I:v

1. A. R. Phineas b. Yair commenced by citing this verse: "'If you seek it like silver [and search for it as for hidden treasures, then you will understand the fear of the Lord and find the knowledge of God]' (Prov. 2:4-5):

B. "If you seek words of the Torah like hidden treasures, the Holy One, blessed be He, will not withhold your reward.

C. "The matter may be compared to the case of a person, who, if he should lose a penny or a pin in his house, will light any number of candles, any number of wicks, until he finds them.

D. "Now the matter yields an argument *a fortiori:*

E. "If to find these, which are useful only in the here and now of this world, a person will light any number of candles, any number of wicks, until he finds them, as to words of Torah, which concern the life of the world to come as much as this world, do you not have to search for them like treasures?

F. "Thus: 'If you seek it like silver [and search for it as for hidden treasures, then you will understand the fear of the Lord and find the knowledge of God]' (Prov. 2:4-5)."

2. A. Said R. Eleazar, "In all my days nobody ever got to the schoolhouse before me, and I never left anyone there when I went out.

B. "One time, however, I got up early and found manure-carriers and straw-carriers out already, and I recited this verse: 'If you seek it like silver [and search for it as for hidden treasures, then you will understand the fear of the Lord and find the knowledge of God]' (Prov. 2:4-5).

C. "Yet we for our part do not seek it even like manure and straw. [Simon, p. 11, n. 2: We do not rise so early to seek it as the farm laborers do to seek manure and straw.]"

3. A. In this connection R. Phineas b. Yair would say, "Promptness leads to [hygienic] cleanliness, cleanliness to [cultic] cleanness, cleanness to holiness, holiness to humility, humility to fear of sin, fear of sin to true piety, true piety to the Holy Spirit, the Holy Spirit to the resurrection of the dead, the resurrection of the dead to Elijah the prophet [bringing the Day of Judgment]" [M. Sot. 9:15].

B. "Promptness leads to [hygienic] cleanliness": "And when he made an end of atoning for the holy place" (Lev. 16:20).

C. "...cleanliness to [cultic] cleanness": "And the priest shall make atonement for her, and she shall be clean" (Lev. 12:8).

D. "...cleanness to holiness": "And he shall purify it and make it holy" (Lev. 16:9).

E. "...holiness to humility": "For thus says the High and Lofty One, who inhabits eternity, whose name is holy, 'I dwell in the high and holy place, with the one who is of a contrite and humble spirit'" (Isa. 57:15).

F. "...humility to fear of sin": "The reward of humility is the fear of the Lord" (Prov. 22:4).

G. "...fear of sin to true piety": "Then you spoke in a vision to your saints" (Ps. 89:20).

H. "...true piety to the Holy Spirit": "Then you spoke in a vision to your saints" (Ps. 89:20).

I. "...the Holy Spirit to the resurrection of the dead": "And I will put my spirit in you and you shall live" (Ez. 37:14).

J. "...the resurrection of the dead to Elijah the prophet of blessed memory": "Behold I will send you Elijah the prophet" (Mal. 3:23).

4. A. Said R. Mattena, "That which wisdom made a crown for her head, humility put on as a shoe for her foot.

B. "That which wisdom made a crown for her head: 'the fear of the Lord is the beginning of wisdom' (Ps. 111:10),

C. "humility put on as a shoe for her foot: 'The fear of the Lord is the heel of humility' (Prov. 22:4)."

5. A. The resurrection of the dead will come about through the prophet Elijah of blessed memory:

B. "then you will understand the fear of the Lord and find the knowledge of God"(Prov. 2:5) –

C. this refers to the Holy Spirit.

6. A. R. Simon in the name of R. Simeon b. Halafta: "The matter may be compared to a councillor who was a big man in the court of a king.

B. "The king said to him, 'Ask what I should give to you.'

C. "Thought the councillor, 'If I ask for silver and gold, he will give it to me; precious stones and pearls he will give to me.'

D. "He thought, 'Lo, I shall ask for the daughter of the king, and everything else will come along too.'

E. "So: 'In Gibeon the Lord appeared to Solomon in a dream by night, and God said, Ask what I shall give you' (1 Kgs. 3:5).

F. "Thought Solomon, 'If I ask for silver and gold, precious stones and pearls he will give them to me. Lo, I shall ask for wisdom, and everything else will come along too.'

G. "That is in line with this verse: 'Give your servant therefore an understanding heart' (1 Kgs. 3:9).

H. "Said to him the Holy One, blessed be He, 'Solomon, wisdom is what you have asked for yourself, and you did not ask for wealth and property and the lives of your enemies. By your life, wisdom and knowledge are given to you, and thereby I will give you also riches and possessions.'

7. A. "Forthwith: 'Solomon woke up and lo, it was a dream' (1 Kgs. 3:15)."

   B. Said R. Isaac, "The dream stood solidly: if an ass brayed, he knew why it brayed, if a bird chirped, he knew why it chirped."

8. A. Forthwith: "He came to Jerusalem and stood before the ark of the covenant of the Lord and offered up whole-offerings, peace-offerings, and made a feast for all his servants" (1 Kgs. 3:15):

   B. Said R. Eleazar, "On this basis we learn that people are to make a banquet at the conclusion of a cycle of the Torah."

9. A. [Supply: "And more so because Qohelet was wise; he also taught the people knowledge, yes, he pondered and sought out and set in order many proverbs]" (Qoh. 12:9):] Said R. Yudan, "This serves to teach you that whoever speaks words of the Torah in public acquires such merit that the Holy Spirit comes to rest upon him.

   B. "And from whom do you learn that fact? From the case of Solomon.

   C. "For it is because he spoke words of the Torah in public, he acquired such merit that the Holy Spirit came to rest upon him.

   D. "So he wrote three books: Proverbs, Qohelet, and the Song of Songs."

I:vi

1. A. Another interpretation of "The Song of Songs":

   B. R. Aibu and R. Judah:

   C. R. Aibu said, "'Song' – lo, one. 'Songs' – two. Lo, there are three in all."

   D. R. Judah bar Simon said, "'Song of Songs' all together adds up to one."

   E. Then as to the other two songs, how do you deal with them?

   F. "A song of ascent of Solomon" (Ps. 127) is one, and "A psalm, a song at the dedication of the house of David" (Ps. 30) is the other.

   G. People suppose that David said them.

        H. But you assign them to David [in the same way in which] it is said, "Like the tower of David is your neck" (Song 4:4).

        I. In the case of "Song of Songs" [better: Ps. 30] too, Solomon said it but assigned it to David.

2.   A. When you find occasion, you may say that all of the events affecting that man came in groups of threes.

    B. Solomon ascended to the throne in three stages.

    C. Of the first stage it is written, "For he had dominion over all the region on this side of the river" (1 Kgs. 5:4).

    D. Of the second stage: "And Solomon ruled" (1 Kgs. 5:1).

    E. Of the third stage: "Then Solomon sat on the throne of the Lord as king" (1 Chr. 29:23).

        3. A. [As to the verse, "Then Solomon sat on the throne of the Lord as king" (1 Chr. 29:23):] said R. Isaac, "Now is it really possible for someone to sit on the throne of the Lord,

            B. "of whom it is written: 'For the Lord your God is a devouring fire' (Dt. 4:24); 'A fiery stream issued and came forth' (Dan. 7:10); 'his throne was fiery flames' (Dan. 7:9)?

            C. "Yet you say, "Then Solomon sat on the throne of the Lord as king" (1 Chr. 29:23)!

            D. "But [the statement serves to validate the following analogy:] just as the throne of the Holy One, blessed be He, rules from one end of the world to the other, so the throne of Solomon rules from one end of the earth to the other.

            E. "Just as the throne of the Lord reaches judgment without witnesses and prior admonition, so the throne of Solomon reaches judgment without witnesses and prior admonition.

            F. "And what case was that? It was the case involving the two whores: 'Then came there two women' (1 Kgs. 3:16)."

              4. A. [Supply: "Then came there two women" (1 Kgs. 3:16):] who were they?

                 B. Rab said, "They were spirits."

                 C. Rabbis said, "They were co-wives of a deceased childless brother-in-law."

                 D. R. Simon in the name of R. Joshua b. Levi said, "They were really whores."

              5. A. [Resuming 3.F:] "And he produced a judgment concerning them without witnesses and prior admonition."

6.   A.   [Resuming 2.E:] Solomon went down by three stages.

     B.   The first descent was that, after he had been a great king, ruling from one end of the world to another, his dominion was reduced, and he ruled as king only over Israel: "The Proverbs of Solomon, son of David, king of Israel" (Prov. 1:1).

     C.   The second descent was that, after he had been king over Israel, his dominion was reduced, and he was king only over Jerusalem: "I Qohelet have been king over Israel in Jerusalem" (Qoh. 1:12).

     D.   The third descent was that, after he had been king over Jerusalem, his dominion was reduced, and he was king only over his own house: "Behold it is the litter of Solomon! About it are sixty mighty men of the might men of Israel, all girt with swords and expert in war, each with his sword at his thigh, against alarms by night" (Song 3:7-8).

     E.   But even over his own bed he did not really rule, for he was afraid of spirits.

7.   A.   He saw three ages [Simon: "he lived three lives"].

     B.   R. Yudan and R. Hunia:

     C.   R. Yudan said, "He was king, a commoner, then king; a sage, a fool, and then a sage; rich, poor, then rich.

     D.   "What verse of Scripture suggests so? 'All things I have seen in the days of my vanity' (Qoh. 7:15).

     E.   "Someone does not rehearse his sufferings unless he is again at ease."

     F.   R. Hunia said, "He was commoner, king, and commoner; fool, sage, and fool; poor, rich, then poor.

     G.   "What verse of Scripture suggests so? 'I Qohelet have been king over Israel' (Qoh. 1:12).

     H.   "'I was' – 'I was when I was, but now I am not any more.'"

8.   A.   He committed three transgressions.

     B.   He accumulated too many horses, he accumulated too many wives, he accumulated too much silver and gold: "And the king made silver in Jerusalem as stones" (2 Chr. 9:27).

          9.   A.   [With reference to the verse, "And the king made silver in Jerusalem as stones" (2 Chr. 9:27):] And were they not stolen?

               B.   Said R. Yosé b. R. Hanina, "They were stones of ten cubits and stones of eight cubits."

               C.   R. Simeon b. Yohai repeated on Tannaite authority: "Even the weights in the time of Solomon were made of gold: 'Silver was thought worthless in the time of Solomon' (1 Kgs. 10:21)."

10. A.   [Resuming 8.B:] He accumulated too many wives: "Now king Solomon loved many foreign women, besides the daughter of

Pharaoh...of the nations concerning which the Lord said to the children of Israel, you shall not go among them, nor shall they come among you...Solomon did cleave to them in love" (1 Kgs. 11:1-2).

B. R. Joshua b. Levi said, "It was on the count of 'you shall not marry them' (Dt. 7:3)."

C. R. Simeon b. Yohai says, "'In love,' meaning, it was actually harlot-love."

D. R. Eliezer, son of R. Yosé the Galilean, says, "It is written, 'Nevertheless even him did the foreign women cause to sin' (Neh. 13:26).

E. "This teaches that he would have sexual relations with them when they were menstruating, but they did not inform him."

F. R. Yosé b. Halapta says, "'In love' meaning, to make them beloved, that is, to draw them near, to convert them and to bring them under the wings of the Presence of God."

G. It turns out that R. Joshua b. Levi, R. Simeon b. Yohai, and R. Eliezer, son of R. Yosé the Galilean, held one position, while R. Yosé b. Halapta differs with all three of them.

11. A. Three adversaries fought against him:

B. "And the Lord raised up an adversary to Solomon, Hadad the Edomite" (1 Kgs. 11:14);

C. "And God raised up another adversary to him, Rezon, son of Eliada" (1 Kgs. 11:23).

D. "And he was an adversary to Israel all the days of Solomon" (1 Kgs. 11:23).

12. A. [Resuming 8.B:] He accumulated too many horses:

B. "And a chariot came up and went out of Egypt for six hundred shekels of silver, and a horse for a hundred and fifty" (1 Kgs. 10:29).

13. A. He said three sets of proverbs:

B. "The proverbs of Solomon, son of David, king of Israel" (Prov. 1:1);

C. "the proverbs of Solomon: a wise son makes a happy father" (Prov. 10:1);

D. "These also are proverbs of Solomon, which the staff of Hezekiah, king of Judah, copied out" ()Prov. 25:1).

14. A. He said three "vanities":

B. "Vanity of vanities, says Qohelet, all is vanity" (Qoh. 1:1).

C. "Vanity" – one; "vanities" – two; lo, three in all.

15. A. He said three songs:

B. "Song" – one; "Songs" – two; lo, three in all.

16. A. He was called by three names: Yedidiah [2 Sam. 12:25], Solomon, and Qohelet.

B.   R. Joshua b. Levi said, "These are three; then Agur, Jakeh, Lemuel, and Ithiel – seven in all."

C.   Said R. Samuel b. R. Nahman, "The main names that belong to him are Yedidiah, Solomon, and Qohclct."

  D.   But R. Samuel b. R. Nahman concedes that the four in addition applied as well and he was called by those names too.

  E.   So they require explanation.

  F.   Agur: he gathered words of Torah [and the word for gather uses the same consonants as the name].

  G.   Jakeh: [Simon, p. 17:] the son who vomited it out for a time [and the words for vomit and the name use the same consonants], like a dish that was filled and then emptied. So too, Solomon studied Torah for a time and then forgot it.

  H.   Lemuel: for he spoke with God with all his heart. He said, "I can accumulate [many women] and not sin."

  I.   Ithiel: "God is with me, and I can prevail," [for] the name "Ithiel" divided into its two clauses reads, "with me is God," so I can prevail.

17. A.   He wrote three books: Proverbs, Qohelet, and Song of Songs.

  B.   Which of them did he write first of all?

  C.   R. Hiyya the Elder and R. Jonathan:

  D.   R. Hiyya the Elder said, "He wrote Proverbs first, then Song of Songs, and finally Qohelet."

  E.   He brings evidence for that position from the following verse of Scripture: "And he spoke three thousand proverbs" (1 Kgs. 5:12) – the book of Proverbs; 'and his songs were a thousand and five' (1 Kgs. 5:12) – that is the Song of songs. And Qohelet he wrote later on."

  F.   There is a statement on Tannaite authority attributed to R. Hiyya the Elder that differs from this view. The statement maintains that all three of them he wrote at the same time, while this statement takes the view that he wrote each one by itself.

  G.   R. Hiyya the Elder repeated on Tannaite authority, "Only in the old age of Solomon did the Holy Spirit rest on him, and he said three books: Proverbs, Qohelet, and the Song of Songs."

  H.   And R. Jonathan said, "He wrote Song of Songs first, then Proverbs, finally Qohelet."

  I.   R. Jonathan brings evidence for that position from the natural course of life: "When a man is young, he composes songs; when he grows up, he speaks in proverbs; when he gets old, he speaks of vanities."

J. R. Yannai, father in law of R. Ammi, said, "All concur that he wrote Qohelet last of all."

18. A. R. Eliezer b. R. Abinah in the name of R. Aha, and Rabbis:

B. R. Eliezer b. R. Abinah in the name of R. Aha said, "'And he spoke three thousand proverbs' (1 Kgs. 5:12) with a proverb for each one; 'And his songs were a thousand and five' (1 Kgs. 5:12) with a thousand and five reasons for each statement."

C. Rabbis said, "'And he spoke three thousand proverbs' (1 Kgs. 5:12) on each verse; 'And his songs were a thousand and five' (1 Kgs. 5:12) a thousand and five reasons for each proverb.

D. "What is written is not, 'and his proverbs were,' but only, 'and his songs were,' and 'the songs of the proverb' bears the sense of 'the reason for each thing.'"

19. A. [With reference to the verse, "And he spoke three thousand proverbs. And his songs were a thousand and five" (1 Kgs. 5:12)], said R. Samuel b. R. Nahman, "We have reviewed the entire book of Proverbs, and we find written in it only nine hundred fifteen verses,

B. "and yet you say, 'And he spoke three thousand proverbs'?

C. "But you have no verse on which there are not two or three meanings [or applications];

D. "for example: 'as an earring of gold and an ornament of fine gold' (Prov. 25:12); 'as a ring of gold in a swine's snout, so is a fair woman that turns aside from discretion' (Prov. 11:22); 'Glorify not yourself in the presence of the king, and do not stand in the place of great men' (Prov. 25:6).

E. "And it is not necessary to say, do not sit.

F. "'Do not sit' – and it is not necessary to say, do not speak. [Here is an instance in which a single statement bears three meanings.]"

20.A. We have learned in the Mishnah: [All sacred scriptures impart uncleanness to hands. The Song of Songs and Qohelet impart uncleanness to hands. R. Judah says, "The Song of Songs imparts uncleanness to hands, but as to Qohelet there is dispute." R. Yosé says, "Qohelet does not impart uncleanness to hands, but as to Song of Songs there is dispute." Rabbi Simeon says, "Qohelet is among the lenient rulings of the

House of Shammai and strict rulings of the House of Hillel." Said R. Simeon b. Azzai, "I have a tradition from the testimony of the seventy-two elders, on the day on which they seated R. Eleazar b. Azariah in the session, that the Song of Songs and Qohelet do impart uncleanness to hands."].

B. Said R. Aqiba, "Heaven forbid! No Israelite man ever disputed concerning Song of Songs that it imparts uncleanness to hands. For the entire age is not so worthy as the day on which the Song of Songs was given to Israel For all the scriptures are holy, but the Song of Songs is holiest of all. And if they disputed, they disputed only concerning Qohelet."

C. Said R. Yohanan b. Joshua the son of R. Aqiba's father-in-law, according to the words of Ben Azzai, "Indeed did they dispute, and indeed did they come to a decision" [M. Yadayim 3:5G-S].

21.   A.   R. Eleazar b. Azariah offered a parable: "The matter may be compared to the case of a man who took a seah of wheat to a baker, saying to him, 'Make for me from it flour and bake one cake of the best quality.'

       B.   "So all of the wisdom of Solomon produced for Israel as fine flour only the Song of Songs.

I:vii

1.   A.   "The Song of Songs":
       B.   the best of songs, the most excellent of songs, the finest of songs.
       C.   "Let us recite songs and praise the One who has made us a a theme of song in the world: 'And they shall shout aloud the songs of the Temple' (Amos 8:3), that is, praise of the Temple."

2.   A.   Another interpretation of "The Song of Songs":
       B.   the best of songs, the most excellent of songs, the finest of songs.
       C.   "Let us recite songs and praise the One who has made us a remnant for the world: 'The Lord alone shall lead him [Simon: in solitude]' (Dt. 32:12)."

       3.   A.   R. Yohanan in the name of R. Aha in the name of R. Simeon b. Abba: "Let us recite songs and praise for the One who will one day cause the Holy Spirit to come to rest upon us.

              B.   "Let us say before him many songs."

       4.   A.   In all other songs, either He praises them, or they praise him.

B. In the Song of Moses, they praise him, saying, "This is my God and I will glorify him" (Ex. 15:2).

C. In the Song of Moses, he praises them: "He made him ride on the high places of the earth" (Dt. 32:13).

D. Here, they praise him and he praises them.

E He praises them: "Behold, you are beautiful, my love; behold, you are beautiful; your eyes are doves."

F. They praise him: "Behold, you are beautiful, my beloved, truly lovely" (Song 1:15-16).

5. A. R. Simeon in the name of R. Hanin of Sepphoris said, "['The Song of Songs'] means a double song."

    B. R. Simon said, "Doubled and redoubled."

6. A. R. Levi said, "[The numerical value of the letters in the word for song] corresponds to the life-span of the patriarchs and the Ten Commandments.

    B. "The numerical value of those letters is five hundred ten. [Abraham lived 175 years, Isaac 180, Jacob, 147, a total of 502, plus 10 for the Ten Commandments].

    C. "Now should you object that there are two extra, deduct the years of famine [one in Abraham's, one in Isaac's lifetime], since these do not count."

7. A. Another interpretation [of "The Song of Songs, which is Solomon's]":

    B. R. Yudan and R. Levi in the name of R. Yohanan: "In every passage in this scroll in which you find the words, 'King Solomon,' the intent is actually King Solomon.

    C. "And whenever the text says, 'the king,' it means the Holy One, blessed be He."

    D. And rabbis say, "Wherever you find 'King Solomon,' the reference is to the King who is the master of peace. When it speaks of 'the king' it refers to the Community of Israel."

2

Song of Songs Rabbah to
Song of Songs 1:2

1:2   *O that you would kiss me with the kisses of your mouth!*
       For your love is better than wine.

II:I

1.   A.   "O that you would kiss me with the kisses of your mouth! [For your love is better than wine]":

      B.   In what connection was this statement made?

      C.   R. Hinena b. R. Pappa said, "It was stated at the sea: '[I compare you, my love,] to a mare of Pharaoh's chariots' (Song 1:9)."

      D.   R. Yuda b. R. Simon said, "It was stated at Sinai: 'The Song of Songs' (Song 1:1) – the song that was song by the singers: 'The singers go before, the minstrels follow after' (Ps. 68:26)."

         2.   A.   It was taught on Tannaite authority in the name of R. Nathan, "The Holy One, blessed be He, in the glory of his greatness said it: 'The Song of Songs that is Solomon's' (Song 1:1),

             B.   "[meaning,] that belongs to the King to whom peace belongs."

3.   A.   Rabban Gamaliel says, "The ministering angels said it: 'the Song of Songs' (Song 1:1) –

      B.   "the song that the princes on high said."

4.   A.   R. Yohanan said, "It was said at Sinai: 'O that you would kiss me with the kisses of your mouth!' (Song 1:2)."

5.   A.   R. Meir says, "It was said in connection with the tent of meeting."

      B.   And he brings evidence from the following verse: "Awake, O north wind, and come, O south wind! Blow upon my garden, let its fragrance be wafted abroad. Let my beloved come to his garden, and eat its choicest fruits" (Song 4:16).

      C.   "Awake, O north wind": this refers to the burnt-offerings, which were slaughtered at the north side of the altar.

      D.   "...and come, O south wind": this refers to the peace-offerings, which were slaughtered at the south side of the altar.

      E.   "Blow upon my garden": this refers to the tent of meeting.

      F.   "...let its fragrance be wafted abroad": this refers to the incense-offering.

G. "Let my beloved come to his garden": this refers to the Presence of God.

H. "...and eat its choicest fruits": this refers to the offerings.

6. A. Rabbis say, "It was said in connection with the house of the ages [the Temple itself]."

B. And they bring evidence from the same verse: "Awake, O north wind, and come, O south wind! Blow upon my garden, let its fragrance be wafted abroad. Let my beloved come to his garden, and eat its choicest fruits" (Song 4:16).

C. "Awake, O north wind": this refers to the burnt-offerings, which were slaughtered at the north side of the altar.

D. "and come, O south wind": this refers to the peace-offerings, which were slaughtered at the south side of the altar.

E. "Blow upon my garden": this refers to the house of the ages.

F. "...let its fragrance be wafted abroad": this refers to the incense-offering.

G. "Let my beloved come to his garden": this refers to the Presence of God.

H. "...and eat its choicest fruits": this refers to the offerings.

I. The Rabbis furthermore maintain that all the other verses also refer to the house of the ages.

J. Said R. Aha, "The verse that refers to the Temple is the following: 'King Solomon made himself a palanquin, from the wood of Lebanon. He made its posts of silver, its back of gold, its seat of purple; it was lovingly wrought within by the daughters of Jerusalem'(Song 3:9-10)."

K. Rabbis treat these as the intersecting verses for the verse, 'And it came to pass on the day that Moses had made an end of setting up the tabernacle' (Num. 7:1)."

7. A. In the opinion of R. Hinena [1.C], who said that the verse was stated on the occasion of the Sea, [the sense of the verse, "O that you would kiss me with the kisses of your mouth"] is, "may he bring to rest upon us the Holy Spirit, so that we may say before him many songs."

B. In the opinion of Rabban Gamaliel, who said that the verse was stated by the ministering angels, [the sense of the verse, "O that you would kiss me with the kisses of your mouth"] is, "may he give us the kisses that he gave to his sons."

C.   In the opinion of R. Meir, who said that the verse was stated in connection with the tent of meeting, [the sense of the verse, "O that you would kiss me with the kisses of your mouth"] is, "May he send fire down to us and so accept his offerings."

D.   In the opinion of R. Yohanan, who said that the verse was stated in connection with Sinai, [the sense of the verse, "O that you would kiss me with the kisses of your mouth"] is, "May he cause kisses to issue for us from his mouth."

E.   "That is why it is written, 'O that you would kiss me with the kisses of your mouth.'"

II.ii

1.   A.   Another interpretation of the verse, "O that you would kiss me with the kisses of your mouth":

B.   Said R. Yohanan, "An angel would carry forth the Word [the Ten Commandments] from before the Holy One, blessed be He, word by word, going about to every Israelite and saying to him, 'Do you accept upon yourself the authority of this Word? There are so and so many rules that pertain to it, so and so many penalties that pertain to it, so and so many decrees that pertain to it, and so are the religious duties, the lenient aspects, the stringent aspects, that apply to it. There also is a reward that accrues in connection with it.'

C.   "And the Israelite would say, 'Yes.'

D.   "And the other would go and say to him again, 'Do you accept the divinity of the Holy One, blessed be He?'

E.   "And the Israelite would say, 'Yes, yes.'

F.   "Then he would kiss him on his mouth.

G.   "That is in line with this verse: 'To you it has been shown, that you might know' (Dt. 4:25) – that is, by an angel."

H.   Rabbis say, "It was the Word itself that made the rounds of the Israelites one by one, saying to each one, 'Do you accept me upon yourself? There are so and so many rules that pertain to me, so and so many penalties that pertain to me, so and so many decrees that pertain to me, and so are the religious duties, the lenient aspects, the stringent aspects, that apply to me. There also is a reward that accrues in connection with me.'

I.   "And the Israelite would say, 'Yes.' [Delete the words that can be translated, 'for Adqulain son of Hadimah'].

J.   "So he taught him the Torah.

K.   "That is in line with this verse: 'Lest you forget the things your eyes saw' (Dt. 4:9) – how the Word spoke with you."

2. A. Another explanation of the phrase, "Lest you forget the things your eyes saw" (Dt. 4:9):

   B. The Israelites heard two acts of speech from the mouth of the Holy One, blessed be He.

      3. A. [Reverting to No. 1:] R. Joshua b. Levi said, "The scriptural foundation for the position of rabbis is that after all the commandments, it then is written, 'You speak with us, and we will hear' (Ex. 20:16)."

         B. How does R. Joshua b. Levi explain this verse?

         C. He rejects the view that temporal order does not pertain to the Torah.

         D. Or perhaps the statement, "You speak with us and we will hear" applies only after every two or three of the Ten Commandments.

            4. A. R. Azariah and R. Judah b. R. Simon in the name of R. Joshua b. Levi took his position. They said, "It is written, 'Moses commanded us the Torah' (Dt. 33:4).

               B. "In the entire Torah there are six hundred thirteen commandments. The numerical value of the letters in the word 'Torah' is only six hundred eleven. These are the ones that Moses spoke to us.

               C. "But 'I [am the Lord your God]' and 'You will not have [other gods besides me]' (Ex. 20:1-2) we have heard not from the mouth of Moses but from the Mouth of the Holy One, blessed be He.

               D. "That is in line with this verse: 'O that you would kiss me with the kisses of your mouth.'"

5. A. How did the Word issue forth from the mouth of the Holy One, blessed be He?

   B. R. Simeon b. Yohai and Rabbis:

   C. R. Simeon b. Yohai says, "It teaches that the Word came forth from the right hand of the Holy One, blessed be He, to the left hand of the Israelites. It then made the round and circumambulated the camp of Israel, a journey of eighteen miles by eighteen miles, and then went and returned from the right hand of Israel to the left hand of the Holy One, blessed be He.

   D. "The Holy One, blessed be He, received it in his right hand and incised it on the tablets, and the sound went from one end of the world to the other: 'The voice of the Lord hews out flames of fire' (Ps. 29:7)."

   E. Rabbis say, "But it there a consideration of 'left' above? And is it not written, 'Your right hand, O Lord, is glorious in power, your right hand, O Lord' (Ex. 15:6)?

F.   "But the Word came forth from the mouth of the Holy One, blessed
       be He, from his right hand to the right hand of Israel. It then made
       the round and circumambulated the camp of Israel, a journey of
       eighteen miles by eighteen miles, and then went and returned from
       the right hand of Israel to the right hand of the Holy One, blessed be
       He.

G.   "The Holy One, blessed be He, received it in his right hand and incised
       it on the tablets, and the sound went from one end of the world to the
       other: 'The voice of the Lord hews out flames of fire' (Ps. 29:7)."

6.   A.   Said R. Berekhiah, "R. Helbo repeated to me the tradition
              that the Word itself was inscribed on its own, and when it
              was inscribed, and the sound went from one end of the
              world to the other: 'The voice of the Lord hews out flames
              of fire' (Ps. 29:7).

       B.   "I said to R. Helbo, 'And lo, it is written, "written with
              the finger of God" (Ex. 31:18).'

       C.   "He said to me, 'Strangler! Are you thinking of strangling
              me?'

       D.   "I said to him, 'And what is the sense of this verse: "tables
              of stone, written with the finger of God" (Ex. 31:18)?'

       E.   "He said to me, 'It is like a disciple who is writing, with
              the master's hand guiding his hand.'"

7.   A.   R. Joshua b. Levi and Rabbis:

       B.   R. Joshua b. Levi says, "Two Words [two of the Ten Commandments]
              did the Israelites hear from the mouth of the Holy One, blessed be
              He: 'I' and 'you will not have other gods, besides me' (Ex. 20:1-2),
              as it is said, 'O that you would kiss me with kisses of your mouth,'
              some, but not all of the kisses [commandments]."

       C.   Rabbis say, "All of the Words did the Israelites hear from the mouth
              of the Holy One, blessed be He."

       D.   R. Joshua of Sikhnin in the name of R. Levi: "The
              scriptural basis for the position of sages is the following
              verse of Scripture: 'And they said to Moses, Speak with
              us, and we will hear' (Ex. 20:16)."

       E.   How does R. Joshua b. Levi interpret the verse?

       F.   He differs, for considerations of temporal order do not
              apply in the Torah.

       G.   Or perhaps the statement, "You speak with us and we will
              hear" applies only after every two or three of the Ten
              Commandments.

8.   A.   R. Azariah and R. Judah b. R. Simon in the name
              of R. Joshua b. Levi took his position. They said,

"It is written, 'Moses commanded us the Torah' (Dt. 33:4).

B. "In the entire Torah there are six hundred thirteen commandments. The numerical value of the letters in the word 'Torah' is only six hundred eleven. These are the ones that Moses spoke to us.

C. "But 'I [am the Lord your God]' and 'You will not have [other gods besides me]' (Ex. 20:1-2) we have heard not from the mouth of Moses but from the Mouth of the Holy One, blessed be He.

D. "That is in line with this verse: 'O that you would kiss me with the kisses of your mouth.'"

9. A. R. Yohanan interpreted the verse ["O that you would kiss me with the kisses of your mouth"] to speak of the Israelites when they went up to Mount Sinai:

B. "The matter may be compared to the case of a king who wanted to marry a woman, daughter of good parents and noble family. He sent to her a messenger to speak with her. She said, 'I am not worthy to be his serving girl. But I want to hear it from his own mouth.'

C. "When that messenger got back to the king, his face was full of smiles, but what he said was not grasped by the king.

D. "The king, who was astute, said, 'This one is full of smiles. It would appear that she has agreed. But what he says is not to be understood by me. It appears that she has said, 'I want to hear it from his own mouth.'

E. "So the Israelites are the daughter of good parents. The messenger is Moses. The king is the Holy One, blessed be He.

F. "At that time: 'And Moses reported the words of the people to the Lord' (Ex. 19:8).

G. "Then why say, 'And Moses told the words of the people to the Lord' (Ex. 19:9)?

H. "Since it says, 'Lo, I come to you in a thick cloud, so that the people may hear when I speak to you, and may also believe you forever' (Ex. 19:9), therefore, 'And Moses told the words of the people to the Lord' (Ex. 19:9).

I. "He said to him, 'This is what they have asked for.'

J. "He said to him, 'They tell a child what he wants to hear.'"

10. A. R. Phineas in the name of R. Levi said, "There is a proverb that people say: 'One who has been bitten by a snake is afraid even of a rope.'

B. "So said Moses, 'Yesterday, when I said, 'But behold, they will not believe me' (Ex. 4:1), I got what was coming to me on their account. [He was struck by leprosy (Simon, p. 25, n. 3).] Now what am I going to do for them?'

11.   A.   It was taught on Tannaite authority by R. Simeon b. Yohai, "This is what they asked.

      B.   "They said, 'We want to see the glory of our King.'"

12.   A.   R. Phineas in the name of R. Levi: "It was perfectly obvious before the Holy One, blessed be He, that the Israelites were going to exchange his glory for another: 'They exchanged their glory for the likeness of an ox that eats grass' (Ps. 106:20).

      B.   "Therefore, [Simon, p. 25: he left them no excuse for saying] so that they might not say, 'If he had shown us his glory and greatness, we should certainly have believed in him, but not that his glory and greatness has not been shown to us, we do not believe in him.'

      C.   "This confirms the following: 'And enter not into judgment with your servant' (Ps. 143:2)."

13.   A.   R. Yudan in the name of R. Judah b. R. Simon, R. Judah, and R. Nehemiah:

      B.   R. Judah says, "When the Israelites heard, 'I am the Lord your God' (Ex. 20:1), the study of the Torah was fixed in their hearts, and they would study and not forget.

      C.   "They came to Moses saying, 'Our lord, Moses, you serve as intermediary, the messenger between us [and God]: "You speak with us, and we will hear" (Ex. 20:16), "...now therefore why should we die" (Dt. 5:22). Who gains if we perish?'

      D.   "Then they would study and forget what they have learned.

      E.   "They said, 'Just as Moses is mortal and passes on, so his learning passes away.'

      F.   "Then they came again to Moses, saying to him, 'Our lord, Moses, would that he would reveal it to us a second time.' 'O that you would kiss me with the kisses of your mouth!' Would that the learning of Torah would be set in our hearts as it was before.'

      G.   "He said to them, 'That cannot be now, but it will be in the age to come.'

      H.   "For it is said, 'I will put my Torah in their inner part, and on their heart I shall write it' (Jer. 31:33)."

      I.   R. Nehemiah said, "When the Israelites heard the word, 'You will not have other gods besides me,' the impulse to do evil was uprooted from their hearts.

      J.   "They came to Moses and said to him, 'Our lord, Moses, you serve as intermediary, the messenger between us [and God]: "You speak with us, and we will hear" (Ex. 20:16), "...now therefore why should we die" (Dt. 5:22). Who gains if we perish?'

K.   "Forthwith the impulse to do evil came back.

L.   "Then they came again to Moses, saying to him, 'Our lord, Moses, would that he would reveal it to us a second time.' 'O that you would kiss me with the kisses of your mouth!'

M.   "He said to them, 'That cannot be now, but it will be in the age to come.'

N.   "For it is said, 'And I will take away the stony heart out of your flesh' (Ez. 36:26).'"

14.   A.   R. Azariah, and some say R. Eliezer and R. Yosé b. R. Hanina and rabbis:

B.   R. Eliezer says, "The matter may be compared to the case of a king who had a wine cellar.

C.   "The first guest came to him first, and he mixed a cup for him and gave it to him.

D.   "A second came and he mixed a cup for him and gave it to him.

E.   "When the son of the king came, he gave him the whole cellar.

F.   "So the First Man was commanded in respect to seven commandments.

G.   "That is in line with this verse: 'And the Lord God commanded the man, saying, You may freely eat of every tree of the garden, [but of the tree of the knowledge of good and evil you shall not eat, for in the day that you eat of it you shall die]' (Gen. 2:16)."

15. A.   ["And the Lord God commanded the man, saying, 'You may freely eat of every tree of the garden, [but of the tree of the knowledge of good and evil you shall not eat, for in the day that you eat of it you shall die]'" (Gen. 2:16).]

B.   [Gen. R. XVI:VI.1B adds:] R. Levi said, "He made him responsible to keep six commandments.

C.   "He commanded him against idolatry, in line with this verse: 'Because he willingly walked after idols' (Hos. 5:11).

D.   "'The Lord' indicates a commandment against blasphemy, in line with this verse: 'And he who blasphemes the name of the Lord' (Lev. 24:16).

E.   "'God' indicates a commandment concerning setting up courts [and a judiciary]: 'You shall not revile the judges' [in the verse at hand, 'God'] (Ex. 22:27).

F.   "'...the man' refers to the prohibition of murder: 'Whoever sheds man's blood' (Gen. 9:6).

G.   "'...saying' refers to the prohibition of fornication: 'Saying, "If a man put away his wife"' (Jer. 3:1).

H.   "'Of every tree you may eat' (Gen. 2:16) indicates that he commanded him concerning theft. [There are things one may take, and there are things one may not take.]"

16. A.   [Continuing Eliezer's statement, 14:G:] "As to Noah, a further commandment was assigned to him, not eating a limb cut from a living animal: 'Only flesh with the life thereof which is the blood thereof' (Gen. 9:4).

B.   "As to Abraham, a further commandment was assigned to him, circumcision.

C.   "Isaac devoted the eighth day to that rite.

D.   "As to Jacob, a further commandment was assigned to him, the prohibition of the sinew of the thigh-vein: 'Therefore the children of Israel do not eat the sinew of the thigh-vein' (Gen. 32:33).

E.   "As to Judah, a further commandment was assigned to him, levirate marriage: 'And Judah said to Onan, Go into your brother's wife and perform the duty of a husband's brother for her' (Gen. 38:8).

F.   "The Israelites, by contrast, made their own all of the religious duties, positive and negative alike."

17. A.   R. Yosé b. R. Hanina and rabbis say, "The matter may be compared to the case of a king who was divvying up rations to his legions through his generals, officers, and commanders.

B.   "But when the turn of his son came, he gave him his rations with his own hand."

18. A.   R. Isaac says, "The matter may be compared to a king who was eating sweetmeats,

B.   "And when the turn of his son came, he gave him his rations with his own hand."

19. A.   Rabbis say, "The matter may be compared to the case of a king who was eating meat.

B.   "And when the turn of his son came, he gave him his rations with his own hand."

C. And some say, "He took it out of his mouth and gave it to him: 'For the Lord gives wisdom, out of his mouth comes knowledge and discernment' (Prov. 2:6)."

20. A. R. Abbahu, and some say the following in the name of R. Judah, and R. Nehemiah:

B. R. Nehemiah said, "[The matter of 'O that you would kiss me with the kisses of your mouth!' may be compared to] two colleagues who were occupied with teachings of the law. This one states a general principle of law, and that one states a general principle of law.

C. "Said the Holy One, blessed be He, 'Their source is through my power.' [Simon, p. 28: 'Their source comes from me.']

D. R. Judah said, "Even as to the breath that comes forth from one's mouth, as you say, 'But Job does open his mouth with a breath' (Job 35:16), said the Holy One, blessed be He, 'Their source is through my power.' [Simon, p. 28: 'Their source comes from me.']

E. Rabbis say, "The souls of these are going to be taken with a kiss."

21. A. Said R. Azariah, "We find that the soul of Aaron was taken away only with a kiss: 'And Aaron the priest went up to Mount Hor at the mouth of the Lord and died there' (Num. 33:38).

B. "How do we know the same in the case of the soul of Moses? 'So Moses the servant of the Lord died there...according to the mouth of the Lord' (Dt. 34:5).

C. "How do we know the same in the case of the soul of Miriam? 'And Miriam died there' (Num. 30:1). And just as 'there' in the former passage means, 'by the mouth of the Lord,' so here too the fact is the same.

D. "But it would have been inappropriate to say it explicitly.

E. "How do we know the same in the case of the soul of all the righteous? 'O that you would kiss me with the kisses of your mouth!'

F. "[The sense is,] 'If you have occupied yourself with teachings of the Torah, so that your lips are [Simon, p. 28:] well armed with them, then, at the end, everyone will kiss you on your mouth.'"

II:iii

1. A. Another explanation of the verse, "O that you would kiss me with the kisses of your mouth! [For your love is better than wine]":

B. "Let him arm me, purify me, make me cleave to him."

C. "Let him arm me": "They were armed with bows and could use both the right hand and the left" (1 Chr. 12:2).

2. A. Said R. Simeon b. R. Nahman, "The words of Torah are to be compared to weapons.

B.   "Just as weapons protect their owners in wartime, so words of Torah protect those who works sufficiently hard at learning them."

C.   R. Hana b. R. Aha brings proof from the following verse for the same proposition: "'Let the high praises of God be in their mouth and a double-edged sword in their hand' (Ps. 149:6):

D.   "Just as a sword consumes on both its edges, so the Torah gives life in this world and life in the world to come."

3.   A.   R. Judah, R. Nehemiah, and rabbis:

B.   R. Judah says, "The Torah, which was said with one mouth, was said with many mouths."

C.   R. Nehemiah said, "Two Torahs were stated, one by mouth, one in writing."

D.   Rabbis say, "It is because they make a decree on creatures above and they do it, on creatures below and they do it." [Simon, p. 29: "[The Torah is said to have many mouths] because its students impose their will on the beings of the upper world and on the beings of the lower world."]

E.   R. Joshua of Sikhnin in the name of R. Levi said, "The scriptural verse that supports the position of rabbis is as follows: 'For they were princes of holiness and princes of God' (1 Chr. 24:5).

F.   "'...princes of holiness': these are the ministering angels, thus: 'Therefore I have profaned the princes of the sanctuary' (Isa. 43:28).

G.   "'...and princes of God': this refers to Israel, thus, 'I said, "You are godlike beings"' (Ps. 82:6).

H.   "'...they make a decree on creatures above and they do it, on creatures below and they do it': for they carry out their deeds in a state of cultic cleanness."

II:iv

1.   A.   Another explanation of the verse, "O that you would kiss me with the kisses of your mouth! [For your love is better than wine]":

B.   "Let him purify me, make me cleave to him, let him kiss me."

C.   "Let him purify me": like a man who joins together ["kisses"] the water in two cisterns to one another and makes them cleave together [and so forms of them a valid immersion-pool].

D.   That is in line with the usage in the following verse: "Like the joining of cisterns he joins it" (Isa. 33:4).

II:v

1.   A.   Another explanation of the verse, "O that you would kiss me with the kisses of your mouth":

       B.   "Let him kiss me, let him make me cleave to him."

       C.   That is in line with the usage in this verse: "The noise of the wings of the living creatures as they touched one another" (Ez. 3:13).

2.   A.   Another explanation of the verse, "O that you would kiss me [with the kisses of your mouth]":

       B.   Let him make for me the sound of kissing with his mouth.

II:vi

1.   A.   "For your love is better than wine": There we have learned in the Mishnah [following the version in the Mishnah, which differs slightly from the version before us:] **Said R. Judah, "R. Ishmael asked R. Joshua as they were going along the road.**

       B.   **"He said to him, 'On what account did they prohibit cheese made by gentiles?'**

       C.   **"He said to him, 'Because they curdle it with rennet from carrion.'**

       D.   **"He said to him, 'And is not the rennet from a whole-offering subject to a more stringent rule than rennet from carrion, and yet they have said, 'A priest who is not squeamish sucks it out raw?' [That is not deemed an act of sacrilege, even though the priests have no right to any part of a whole-offering; hence the rennet is deemed null. Why then take account of rennet in the present circumstance, which is, after all, of considerably less weight than the sin of sacrilege?]"**

       E.   **For R. Simeon b. Laqish said, "They treated it as one who drinks from a dirty cup. While, on the one side, one may derive no benefit from such a cup that belongs to the cult, yet one also is not liable for having violated the rule against sacrilege in making use of that cup."**

       F.   **[Lacking in Song:] (But they did not concur with him and ruled, "It is not available for [the priests'] benefit, while it also is not subject to the laws of sacrilege.")**

       G.   **[Lacking in Song:] [Judah resumes his narrative:] "He went and said to him, 'Because they curdle it with rennet of calves sacrificed to idols.'"**

       H.   **[Lacking in Song:] "He said to him, 'If so, then why have they not also extended the prohibition affecting it to the matter of deriving benefit from it?'**

       I.   **"He moved him on to another subject.**

J. "He said to him, 'Ishmael, my brother, how do you read the verse:
"For your [masculine] love is better than wine," or, "Your
[feminine] love is better than wine" (Song 1:2)?'

K. "He said to him, '"For your [feminine] love is better than wine."'"

L. "He said to him, 'The matter is not so. For its neighbor teaches
concerning it, "Your [masculine] ointments have a goodly
fragrance"' (Song 1:3)" [M. Abodah Zarah 2:5A-K].

M. But why did he not tell him the reason [H, instead of just
changing the subject, I]?

N. Said R. Jonathan, "It is because it was only recently that
they had made the ruling, and R. Ishmael was junior."

2. A. R. Simeon b. Halafta and R. Haggai in the name of R.
Samuel b. R. Nahman: "It is written, 'The lambs will be
for your clothing' (Prov. 27:26).

B. "What is actually written may be read 'hidden,' yielding
the meaning, 'when your disciples are junior, you should
head from them words of Torah. When they grow up and
become disciples of sages, you may reveal to them the
secrets of the Torah.'"

3. A. R. Simeon b. Yohai taught on Tannaite authority: "'Now
these are the ordinances which you shall set before them'
(Ex. 21:1).

B. "[Since the consonants in 'set' may yield 'treasure,' we
interpret in this way:] just as a treasure is not shown to
any one who comes along, so is the case with teachings
of the Torah."

4. A. R. Huna raised the question, and R. Hama b. Uqba
presented the same as an objection [to 1.M's response to
1.H:] "If his intention was only to put him off, he should
have put him off with one of the five equivalent points of
unclarity in the Torah, which are [Simon, p. 31:] 'uplifting,
cursed, tomorrow, almond-shaped, and arise.'

B. "['Uplifting':] do we read 'If you do well, will it not be
lifted up? (Gen. 4:7), or 'It is incurring sin if you do not
do well' (Gen. 4:7)?" [That is another example of a point
of unclarity in Scripture. He did not have to choose the
one he chose. The others are not specified here.]"

C. Said R. Tanhuma, "I have another [a sixth]: 'The sons of
Jacob came in from the field when they heard it' (Gen.
34:7), or, 'When they heard it, the men were grieved' (Gen.
34:7-8) [so where is the break between the two
sentences?]"

5.   A.   Said R. Isaac, "It is written, 'And me did the Lord command' (Dt. 4:14):

      B.   "'There are matters that he said to me, all by myself, and there are matters that he said to me to say to his children.'"

6.   A.   [Following Simon, p. 31, n. 2, the point of reference in what follows is our base verse, "O that you would kiss me with the kisses of your mouth! For your love is better than wine"]: Said R. Ila, "There are matters about which one's lips are sealed. [Simon, p. 31, n. 2: It was for this reason that he put him off with the verse, because 'let him kiss me' may also mean, 'let him seal my lips,' and thus he hinted by this quotation that not everything is to be explained.]

    B.   "How so? One verse of Scripture says, 'Your word have I laid up in my heart, that I might not sin against you' (Ps. 119:11), while another verse says, 'With my lips have I told all the ordinances of your mouth' (Ps. 119:13). How hold the two together?

    C.   "So long as Ira the Jairite was the master of David, he observed the verse, 'Your word have I laid up in my heart, that I might not sin against you' (Ps. 119:11), but after he died, then he followed this verse: 'With my lips have I told all the ordinances of your mouth' (Ps. 119:13)."

II:vii

1.   A.   "For your love is better than wine":

    B.   Words of Torah complement one another, friends of one another, close to one another,

    C.   in line with the usage [of the consonants that are translated "love"] in the following verse: "or his uncle or his uncle's son" (Lev. 25:49).

      2.   A.   [Supply: water removes uncleanness, when the water is of the correct classification:] "But a fountain or cistern wherein is a gathering of water" (Lev. 11:36).

         B.   Water imparts susceptibility to uncleanness: "If water be put on seed" (Lev. 11:38). [The point of the juxtaposition is that while water can remove uncleanness, water can also impart susceptibility to uncleanness. The relationship of the two verses shows how words of Torah "complement one another, friends of one another, close to one another."]

         3.   A.   Simeon b. R. Abba in the name of R. Yohanan: "Words of scribes are as precious as words of the Torah.

            B.   "What is the scriptural basis for that view? [Following Simon:] 'And the roof of your mouth like the best wine' [Simon, p. 32, n. 3: The roof of the mouth is taken as a symbol of the Oral Torah and wine as a symbol of the written Torah.]"

C. Colleagues in the name of R. Yohanan: "Words of scribes are more precious than words of Torah: 'For your love is better than wine' (Song 1:2).

D. "If one says, 'there is no requirement as to phylacteries,' so as to violate the requirements of the explicit words of the torah, he is exempt from liability.

E. "If he says, 'There is a requirement that the phylacteries contain five [not four] compartments,' intending thereby to add to the requirements of the teachings of the scribes, by contrast, he is liable to a penalty."

4. A. R. Abba b. R. Kahana in the name of R. Judah b. Pazzi derived the same lesson from the following:

B. Said R. Tarfon, "I was coming along the road [in the evening] and reclined to recite the Shema as required by the House of Shammai. And [in doing so] I placed myself in danger of [being attacked by] bandits." [They said to him, "You are yourself responsible [for what might have befallen you], for you violated the words of the House of Hillel."] [M. Berakhot 1:3G-H].

C. You see that had he not recited the Shema at all, he would have violated a positive commandment alone. Now that he has recited the Shema, he has become liable for his life.

D. That proves that Words of scribes are more precious than words of Torah.

5. A. R. Hanina b. R. Aha in the name of R. Tanhum b. R. Aha said, "They are subject to more stringent penalties than the words of the Torah and of the prophets.

B. "It is written, 'Do not preach, they preach' (Mic. 2:6). [Simon, p. 32, n.

9: implying that prophecy can be interrupted, but not so the teaching of the sages.]

C. "[The relationship of teachings of scribes and prophets] yields the following simile: the matter may be compared to the case of a king who sent his agents to a town. Concerning one of them he wrote, 'If he shows you my seal and signature, believe him, and if not, do not believe him,' and concerning the other of them he wrote, 'Even if he does not show you my seal and signature, believe him.'

D. "So in connection with teachings of prophecy: 'If there arise in your midst a prophet...and he gives you a sign' (Dt. 13:2).

E. "But as to words of scribes: 'According to the Torah that they will teach you' (Dt. 17:11).

F. "What is written is not, 'according to the Torah that the Torah will teach you,' but 'according to the Torah that they will teach you.'

G. "What is written is not, 'according to the judgment that it will tell you,' but, '...that they shall tell you.'

H. "Further: 'You shall not turn aside from the sentence that they shall declare to you to either the right hand or to the left' (Dt. 17:11):

I. "If they tell you that the right hand is right and the left hand is left, obey; and even if they tell you that the right hand is left and the left hand is right!'"

II:viii

1. A. Another explanation of the verse, "For your love is better than wine":

   B. Words of the Torah are compared to water, wine, oil, honey, and milk.

2. A. To water: "Ho, everyone who thirsts come for water" (Isa. 55:1).

B.   Just as water is from one end of the world to the other, "To him who spread forth the earth above the waters" (Ps. 136:6), so the Torah is from one end of the world to the other, "The measure thereof is longer than the earth" (Job 11:9).

C.   Just as water is life for the world, "A fountain of gardens, a well of living waters" (Song 4:15), so the Torah is life for the world, "For they are life to those who find them and health for all their flesh" (Prov. 4:22); "Come, buy and eat" (Isa. 55:1).

D.   Just as water is from heaven, "At the sound of his giving a multitude of waters in the heavens" (Jer. 10:13), so the Torah is from heaven, "I have talked with you from heaven" (Ex. 20:19).

E.   Just as water [when it rains] is with loud thunder, "The voice of the Lord is upon the water" (Ps. 29:3), so the Torah is with loud thunder, "And it came to pass on the third day, when it was morning, that there were thunderings and lightnings" (Ex. 19:16).

F.   Just as water restores the soul, "But God cleaves the hollow place which was in Levi and water came out, and when he had drunk, he revived" (Judges 15:19), so the Torah [restores the soul], "The Torah of the Lord is perfect, restoring the soul" (Ps. 19:8).

G.   Just as water purifies a person from uncleanness, "And I will sprinkle clean water upon you, and you will be clean" (Ez. 36:25), so the Torah cleans a person of uncleanness, "The words of the Lord are pure" (Ps. 12:7).

H.   Just as water cleans the body, "He shall bathe himself in water" (Lev. 17:15), so the Torah cleans the body, "Your word is purifying to the uttermost" (Ps. 119:140).

I.   Just as water covers over the nakedness of the sea, "As the waters cover the sea" (Isa. 11:9), so the Torah covers the nakedness of Israel, "Love covers all transgressions" (Prov. 10:12).

J.   Just as water comes down in drops but turns into rivers, so the Torah – a person learns two laws today, two tomorrow, until he becomes an overflowing river.

K.   Just as water, if one is not thirsty, has no sweetness in it, so the Torah, if one does not labor at it, has no sweetness in it.

L.   Just as water leaves the height and flows to a low place, so the Torah leaves one who is arrogant on account of [his knowledge of] it and cleaves to one who is humble on account of [his knowledge of] it.

M.   Just as water does not keep well in utensils of silver and gold but only in the most humble of utensils, so the Torah does not stay well except in the one who treats himself as a clay pot.

N.   Just as with water, a great man is not ashamed to say to an unimportant person, "Give me a drink of water," so as to words of Torah, the great man is not ashamed to say to an unimportant person, "Teach me a chapter," or "a verse," or even "a single letter."

O.   Just as with water, when one does not know how to swim in it, in the end he will be swallowed up, so words of Torah, if one does not know how to swim in them and to give instruction in accord with them, in the end he will be swallowed up.

    P.   Said R. Hanina of Caesarea, "Just as water is drawn not only for gardens and orchards, but also for baths and privies, shall I say that that is so also for words of the Torah?

    Q.   "Scripture says, 'For the ways of the Lord are right' (Hos. 14:10)."

    R.   Said R. Hama b. Uqba, "Just as water makes plants grow, so words of the Torah make everyone who works in them sufficiently grow.

        S.   Then [may one say,] just as water becomes rancid and smelly in a vessel, so words of the Torah are the same way? Scripture says that the Torah is like wine. Just as with wine, so long as it ages in the bottle, it improves, so words of the Torah, so long as they age in the body of a person, they improve in stature.

        T.   Then [may one say,] just as water is not to be discerned in the body, so is the case with words of the Torah? Scripture says that the Torah is like wine. Just as with wine. its presence is discerned when it is in the body, so words of the Torah are discerned when they are in the body.

        U.   [For] people hint and point with the finger, saying, "This is a disciple of a sage."

        V.   Then [may one say,] just as water does not make one happy, so is the case with words of the Torah? Scripture says that the Torah is like wine. Just as wine "makes the heart of man glad" (Ps. 104:15), so words of the Torah make the heart happy, "The precepts of the Lord are right, rejoicing the heart" (Ps. 19:9).

        W.   Then [may one say,] just as wine sometimes is bad for the head and the body, so is the case with words of the Torah? Scripture compares words of the Torah to oil. Just as oil is pleasing for the head and body, so words of the Torah are pleasing for the head and body: "Your word is a lamp to my feet" (Ps. 119:105).

X. May one then say, just as oil is bitter to begin with, and sweet only at the end, so is it the case also with words of Torah? Scripture states, "Honey and milk" (Song 4:11). Just as they are sweet, so words of the Torah are sweet: "Sweeter than honey" (Ps. 19:11).

Y. May one then say, just as honey has wax cells [that cannot be eaten], so words of the Torah are the same? Scripture says, "...milk" (Song 4:11). Just as milk is pure, so words of the Torah are pure: "Gold and glass cannot equal it" (Job 28:17).

Z. May one then say, just as milk is insipid, so words of the Torah are the same? Scripture states, "Honey and milk" (Song 4:11). Just as honey and milk, when they are stirred together, do not do any harm to the body, so words of the Torah: "It shall be health to your navel" (Prov. 3:8); "For they are life to those who find them" (Prov. 4:22).

II:ix

1. A. Another explanation of the verse, "For your love is better":
    B. This refers to the patriarchs.
    C. "...than wine":
    D. this refers to the princes.
2. A. Another explanation of the verse, "For your love is better":
    B. This refers to the the offerings..
    C. "...than wine":
    D. this refers to the libations.
    3. A. Said R. Hanina, "If when the Israelites came to that awful deed, Moses had known how precious were the offerings, he would have offered all of the offerings that are catalogued in the Torah.
        B. "Instead he ran to the merit of the patriarchs: 'Remember Abraham, Isaac, and Israel, your servants' (Ex. 32:13)."
4. A. Another explanation of the verse, "For your love is better":
    B. This refers to Israel.
    C. "...than wine":
    D. this refers to the gentiles.
    E. [For the numerical value of the letters that make up the word for wine] is seventy,

F.　teaching you that the Israelites are more precious before the Holy One, blessed be He, than all of the nations."

3

Song of Songs Rabbah to Song of Songs 1:3

1:3　　*Your anointing oils are fragrant,*
your name is oil poured out;
therefore the maidens love you.

III:i

1.　A.　"Your anointing oils are fragrant":

　　B.　R. Yannai son of R. Simeon: "All the songs that the patriarchs said before you were fragrances, but as to us, 'your name is oil poured out.

　　C.　"It is like a man who pours out what is in his jar into the jar of his fellow. [Simon, p. 36, n. 2: our hymns are to theirs as the actual ointment to the mere fragrance.]

　　D.　"All of the religious duties that the patriarchs did before you were fragrances, but as to us, 'your name is oil poured out.'

　　E.　"[These are] two hundred forty-eight religious actions of commission and three hundred sixty-five religious actions of omission."

　　2.　A.　R. Eliezer, R. Joshua, and R. Aqiba:

　　　　B.　R. Eliezer says, "If all the seas were ink, and all the reeds were pens, and the heaven and the earth were scrolls, and all people were scribes, they would not be sufficient to write down the Torah that I have learned, but I have taken away from it only so much as a person who dips the point of his pen in the sea."

　　　　C.　R. Joshua says, "If all the seas were ink, and all the reeds were pens, and the heaven and the earth were scrolls, and all people were scribes, they would not be sufficient to write down the words of Torah that I have learned, but I have taken away from it only so much as a person who dips the point of his pen in the sea."

　　　　D.　R. Aqiba says, "As for me, I do not have the strength to say what my lords have said, but my lords have taken away something from it, while for my part, I have taken away no more than one who smells an etrog. The one who takes the scent enjoys it, but the etrog is not diminished;

E. "and like one who fills his jug from a stream, or like one who lights a lamp from another lamp."

3. A. One time R. Aqiba delayed coming to the house of study. He came and sat down outside. The question was raised, "Is this the law?"

B. They said, "The law is outside."

C. Again a question was raised.

D. They said, "The law is outside."

E. Again a question was raised.

F. They said, "Aqiba is outside. Make a place for him."

G. He came and sat down at the feet of R. Eliezer.

4. A. Now the house of study of R. Eliezer was set up like an arena, and a stone there was designed there for him to sit on.

B. One time R. Joshua came in and began kissing that stone.

C. He said, "This stone is like Mount Sinai, and this one who sat on it is like the ark of the covenant."

III:ii

1. A. Another interpretation of the verse, "Your anointing oils are fragrant, your name is oil poured out; therefore the maidens love you":

B. R. Aha in the name of R. Tanhum b. R. Hiyya: "There are two oils, the oil used to anoint into the priesthood, and the oil used to anoint for the kingship."

C. Rabbis say, "There are two Torahs, the Torah that is in writing and the Torah that is memorized."

2. A. Said R. Yudan "'...your name is oil poured out': Your name is exalted over all who occupy themselves with the oil of the Torah."

B. This is the position of R. Yudan, who said, "'And the yoke shall be destroyed by reason of oil' (Isa. 10:27) [means], the yoke of Sennacherib will be destroyed on account of Hezekiah and his company, who were occupied with the oil of the Torah."

III:iii

1. A. Another interpretation of the verse, "your name is oil poured out":

   B. just as olive oil is bitter in the beginning but ends up sweet, so "though your beginning was small, yet your end shall greatly increase" (Job. 8:7).

   C. Just as oil is improved only by crushing in the press, so Israel accomplishes repentance only on account of suffering.

   D. Just as oil does not mix with other liquids, so Israel does not mix with the nations of the world: "Neither shall you make marriages with them" (Dt. 7:3).

   E. Just as oil poured into a full cup does not overflow with other liquids [not mixing with them, it overflows on its own], so words of Torah does not flow with trivial words.

   F. Just as, with oil, if you have a full cup of oil in hand, and into it falls a drop of water, a drop of oil exudes on its account, so if a word of the Torah goes into the heart, correspondingly a word of trivial nonsense goes forth.

   G. If a word of trivial nonsense goes into the heart, correspondingly a word of the Torah goes forth.

   H. Just as oil brings light into the world, so Israel is the light of the world: "Nations shall walk at your light" (Isa. 60:3).

   I. Just as oil is above all other liquids, so Israel is above all the nations: "And the Lord your God will set you on high" (Dt. 28:1).

   J. Just as oil does not produce an echo [when poured], so Israel does not produce resonance in this world, but in the world to come: "And brought down you shall speak out of the ground" (Isa. 29:4).

III:iv

1. A. [Supply: Another interpretation of the verse, "Your anointing oils are fragrant, your name is oil poured out; therefore the maidens love you":]

   B. R. Yohanan interpreted the verse to speak of Abraham.

2. A. [Genesis Rabbah XXXIX:II.1: R. Berekhiah commenced [discourse by citing the following verse of Scripture]: "Your ointments have a good smell" (Song 1:3).]

   B. "When the Holy One, blessed be He, said to him, 'Leave your land and your birthplace' (Gen. 12:1), what was he like? He was like a flask of myrrh sealed with a tight lid and lying in the corner. The fragrance of that vial does not waft upward. But when someone came and moved it from its place, then its fragrance spreads upward.

   C. "So said the Holy One, blessed be He, 'Abraham, many good deeds do you have to your credit, many religious duties do you have to your credit. Move yourself about from place to place, so that your name may be made great in the world: "Go out" (Gen. 12:1).'

D.   "Written thereafter is the following: 'And I will make of you a great nation' (Gen. 12:2)."

3.   A.   "...therefore the maidens love you":

B.   Said to him the Holy One, blessed be He, "Here are many worlds for you" [the words for maidens and worlds share the same consonants].

C.   For it is written, "And Abram took Sarai his wife, and Lot his brother's son, and all their possessions which they had gathered, and the soul that they had made..." (Gen. 12:5).

4.   A.   [Supply, as at Genesis Rabbah XXXIX:XIV.1:] "And Abram took Sarai his wife, and Lot his brother's son, and all their possessions which they had gathered, and the soul that they had made..." (Gen. 12:5):

B.   [Genesis Rabbah XXXIX:XIV.1 attributed the following to R. Eleazar in the name of R. Yosé b. Zimra:] "If all of the nations of the world should come together to try to create a single mosquito, they could not [put a soul into it, and yet you say, 'And the soul that they had made'?] [They could not have created souls.] But this refers to proselytes whom Abraham and Sarah had made. Therefore it is said, 'and the soul that they had made' (Gen. 12:5)."

5.   A.   Said R. Huniah, "Abraham converted the men and Sarah the women."

B.   And what is the sense of the statement, "the souls that they had made in Haran" (Gen. 12:5)?

C.   This teaches that our father, Abraham, would bring them home and feed them and give them drink and treat them with love and so draw them near and convert them and bring them under the wings of the Presence of God.

D.   This serves to teach you that whoever brings a gentile close [to the worship of the true God] is as if he had created him anew. [Simon, p. 39: had created him and formed him and molded him.]

6.   A.   Said R. Berekhiah, "Said the Israelites before the Holy One, blessed be He, 'Lord of the world, Since you bring light to the world, your name is exalted in the world.

B.   "'And what is the light? It is redemption.

    C. "'For when you bring us light, many proselytes come and convert and are added to us, for instance, Jethro and Rahab.

    D. "'Jethro heard and came, Rahab heard and came.'"

7. A. Said R. Hanina, "When the Holy One, blessed be He, did a miracle for Hananiah, Mishael, and Azariah, many gentiles came and converted: 'When he sees his children, the work of my hands, in the midst of them, they shall sanctify my name' (Isa. 29:23), and then, 'They also that err in spirit shall come to understanding' (Isa. 29:23)."

III:v

1. A. Another interpretation of the verse, "therefore the maidens love you":

    B. It is because you gave us the spoil of Egypt, the spoil of the [Egyptian army at] the sea, the spoil of Sihon and Og, the spoil of the thirty-one kings [of Canaan] that we love you.

2. A. Another interpretation of the verse, "therefore the maidens love you":

    B. It is because you hid from them the day of death and the day of consolation that they love you [the words for "hid" and "maidens" use the same consonants].

3. A. Another interpretation of the verse, "therefore the maidens love you":

    B. It is with youthful energy and vigor.

4. A. Another interpretation of the verse, "therefore the maidens love you":

    B. This refers to those who repent.

5. A. Another interpretation of the verse, "therefore the maidens love you":

    B. This refers to the third group in the following: "And I will bring the third part through the fire and will refine them as silver is refined" (Zech. 13:9).

6. A. Another interpretation of the verse, "therefore the maidens love you":

    B. This refers to the proselytes: "O Lord, I have heard the report of you and am afraid, O Lord, revive your work in the midst of the years" (Hab. 3:2).

7. A. Another interpretation of the verse, "therefore the maidens love you":

    B. This refers to the generation that lived through the repression [in the time of Hadrian, after the war of Bar Kokhba]: "For your sake we are killed all day long, we are accounted as sheep for slaughter" (Ps. 44:23).

8. A. Another interpretation of the verse, "therefore the maidens love you":

B.   This refers to the Israelites: "But because the Lord loved you and because he would keep the oath" (Dt. 7:8).

9.   A.   Another interpretation of the verse, "therefore the maidens love you":

B.   This refers to the fact that you hid from them the reward that is coming to the righteous.

C.   For said R. Berekhiah and R. Helbo, "The Holy One, blessed be He, is going to be the lord of the dance for the righteous in the age to come.

D.   "What verse of Scripture indicates it? 'Mark well her ramparts' (Ps. 48:14). Now the word for 'ramparts' is written to be read 'dance.'

E.   "The righteous will be on one side, and the righteous on the other, and the Holy One, blessed be He will be in the middle, and they will dance before him with zest [which uses the same consonants as the word for 'maidens'].

F.   "And they will gesture to one another with their fingers, saying, 'For this is God, our God, for ever and ever. He will guide us eternally' (Ps. 48:15)."

G.   What is the meaning of the word translated "eternally" [which uses the same consonants as the word for 'maidens']? It means, "in two worlds he will guide us," in this world and in the world to come.

10. A.   Another interpretation of the verse, "He will guide us eternally" (Ps. 48:15):

B.   with energy and vigor.

11.   A.   Another interpretation of the verse, "therefore the maidens love you":

B.   like those maidens of whom Scripture says, "In the midst of damsels playing upon timbrels" (Ps. 68:26).

12.   A.   Another interpretation of the verse, "therefore the maidens love you":

B.   Aqilas translated, "athnasia," meaning, a world in which there is no death.

C.   And they will gesture to one another with their fingers, saying, "For this is God, our God, for ever and ever. He will guide us eternally" (Ps. 48:15)."

D.   He will guide us in two worlds: "For the Lord your God will bless you" (Dt. 15:6), and in the world to come, "And the Lord will guide you continually" (Isa. 58:11).

4

Song of Songs Rabbah to Song of Songs 1:4

1:4   *Draw me after you, let us make haste.*
The king has brought me into his chambers.
We will exult and rejoice in you;
we will extol your love more than wine;
rightly do they love you.

IV:i

1. A. "Draw me after you, let us make haste. The king has brought me into his chambers. We will exult and rejoice in you; we will extol your love more than wine; rightly do they love you":

    B. Said R. Meir, "When the Israelites stood before Mount Sinai to receive the Torah, said to them the Holy One, blessed be He, 'Shall I really give you the Torah? Bring me good sureties [Simon: guarantors] that you will keep it, and then I shall give it to you.'

    C. "They said to him, 'Lord of the ages, our fathers are our sureties for us.'

    D. "He said to them, 'Your fathers themselves require sureties.'

    E. "To what is the matter comparable? To someone who went to borrow money from the king. He said to him, 'Bring me a surety, and I shall lend to you.'

    F. "He went and brought him a surety. He said to him, 'Your surety has to have a surety.'

    G. "He went and brought him another surety. He said to him, 'Your surety has to have a surety.'

    H. "When he had brought him yet a third surety, he said to him, 'You should know that it is on this one's account that I am lending to you.'

    I. "So when the Israelites stood to receive the Torah, he said to them, 'Shall I really give you my Torah? Bring me good sureties that you will keep it, and then I shall give it to you.'

    J. "They said to him, 'Lord of the ages, our fathers are our sureties for us.'

    K. "Said to them the Holy One, blessed be He, 'As to your fathers, I have my complaints with them.

    L. "'As to Abraham, I have my complaint against him, for he said, "How shall I know that I shall inherit it?" (Gen. 15:8).

M.   "'As to Isaac, I have my complaint against him, for he loved Esau, while I hated him: 'But Esau I hated' (Mal. 1:3).

N.   "'As to Jacob, I have my complaint against him, for he said, 'My way is hid from the Lord' (Isa. 40:27).

O.   "'Bring me good sureties, and then I shall give it to you.'

P.   "They said to him, 'Lord of the world, our prophets will be our sureties.

Q.   "He said to them, 'I have my complaints against them: 'And the shepherds transgressed against me' (Jer. 2:8); 'Your prophets have been like foxes in ruins' (Ez. 13:4).

R.   "'Bring me good sureties, and then I shall give it to you.'

S.   "They said to him, 'Lo, our children will be our sureties for us.'

T.   "Said to them the Holy One, blessed be He, 'Lo, these are certainly good sureties. On their account I shall give it to you.'

U.   "That is in line with the following verse of Scripture: 'Out of the mouth of babes and sucklings you have founded strength' (Ps. 8:3).

V.   "'Strength' bears the sole meaning of Torah: 'The Lord will give strength to his people' (Ps. 29:11).

W.   "Now when the debtor has to pay up and cannot pay, who is seized? Is it not the surety? That is in line with this verse: 'Seeing that you have forgotten the Torah of your God, I also will forget your children' (Hos. 4:6)."

X.   Said R. Aha, "'I also': it is as if I also am subject to forgetting. [God speaks:] 'Who will see in the Torah before me, "Blessed is the Lord who is to be blessed"? Is it not the youngsters?'"

Y.   [Reverting to Meir's exposition, W:] "It is on account of the weakness of the Torah among you that your children are seized: 'For your faithlessness I have smitten your children' (Jer. 2:30)."

Z.   [The printed text repeats:] "'I also': it is as if I also am subject to forgetting. [God speaks:] 'Who will see in the Torah before me, "Blessed is the Lord who is to be blessed"?'"

AA.   [Reverting to Y:] "Therefore a parent has to introduce one's child to the Torah and to educate the child in learning, so that the child will live a long time in the world: "For by me your days shall be multiplied" (Prov. 9:11).

IV:ii

1.   A.   [Supply: "Draw me after you, let us make haste]":

      B.   R. Yohanan, R. Joshua b. Levi, and Rabbis:

C.   R. Yohanan said, "Because you brought us into a good and spacious land, 'after you let us make haste,' to a good land which is called 'a dwelling place.'"

D.   R. Joshua b. Levi said, "Because you have given us a good and large land which is called 'a dwelling place,' 'after you let us make haste.'"

E.   Rabbis said, "Because you have brought your Presence to dwell in our midst, since it is written, 'And let them make me a sanctuary' (Ex. 25:8), 'after you let us make haste.'"

2.   A.   And rabbis say further, "Because you have taken away your Presence from our midst, 'after you let us make haste.'

     B.   "You should know that that is the case, for all of the sorrows that came upon them on account of the deed involving the golden calf did not bring them to mourning.

     C.   "But when Moses said to them, 'For I will not go up in the midst of you' (Ex. 33:3), then forthwith, 'And when the people heard these evil tidings, they mourned' (Ex. 33:4)."

      3.   A.   [Expanding the foregoing,] R. Simeon b. Yohai taught, "The weapon that he had given to the Israelites at Horeb, on which the Ineffable Name of God was incised, when they sinned in the deed of the golden calf, was taken away from them."

         B.   How was it taken away from them?

         C.   R. Aibu and rabbis:

         D.   R. Aibu said, "On its own, the name peeled off."

         E.   And rabbis said, "An angel descended and peeled it off."

      4.   A.   [Continuing Simeon b. Yohai, A:] "Said the Israelites before the Holy One, blessed be He, 'Lord of the age, does a woman adorn herself for anyone other than her husband?' [We do not need any ornament any more now that you have left us.]'"

5.   A.   Said R. Joshua b. Levi, "The Israelites greatly desired the Presence of God:

     B.   "'[Awake, O north wind, and come, O south wind! Blow upon my garden, let its fragrance be wafted abroad.] Let my beloved come to his garden, [and eat its choicest fruits]' (Song 4:16).

     C.   "'...to his garden': 'to his bridal chamber.'"

IV:iii

1.   A.   [Supply: "Draw me after you, let us make haste":]

     B.   R. Yudan and R. Azariah:

C.   R. Yudan said, "Said the Congregation of Israel before the Holy One, blessed be He, 'Because you have treated my neighbors [a word that uses the same consonants as 'draw me'] in accord with the strict requirements of justice, and me in accord with the requirements of mercy, 'after you, let us make haste.'"

2.   A.   For said R. Berekhiah in the name of R. Eleazar, "[Genesis Rabbah XXVIII:V.1:] "From the face of the ground" (Gen. 6:7), Said R. Abba bar Kahana,] "What was done by the ten tribes was not done by the generation of the Flood.

    B.   "With respect to the generation of the Flood, it is written, 'And every imagination of the thoughts of his heart was only evil all day' (Gen. 6:5).

    C.   "With regard to the ten tribes: 'Woe to them that devise iniquity and work evil upon their beds' (Mic. 2:1) which is to say, even by night. And how do we know that they did it by day as well? 'When the morning is light, they execute it' (Mic. 2:1).

    D.   "Nonetheless, of those [of the generation of the Flood] not a remnant was left, while of these [the ten tribes] a remnant was left.

        E.   [Genesis Rabbah XXVIII:V.1:] "It was on account of the merit of the righteous men and righteous women who were destined to emerge from [the ten tribes that a remnant was spared].

        F.   [Genesis Rabbah XXVIII:V.1:] "That is in line with this verse: 'And behold there shall be left a remnant therein that shall be brought forth, both sons and daughters' (Ez. 14:22), that is, on account of the merit of the righteous men and righteous women, the men and women prophets, who were destined to emerge from [the ten tribes a remnant was spared]."

3.   A.   Said R. Hanina, "Things were said concerning the cities of the sea that were not said concerning the generation of the Flood: 'Woe to the inhabitants of the seacoast, the nation of the Cherethites' (Zeph. 2:5), indicating by their name [consonants that bear the meaning of extirpation] that they were suitable to be annihilated.

        B.   [Genesis Rabbah XXVIII:V.1:] "On account of what merit do they endure? It is on account of the merit of a singular gentile, who fears heaven, that the Holy One, blessed be He, receives from their hand [that he spares them while having destroyed Sodom and the generation of the Flood]. [There are some good among them.]"

C. [Genesis Rabbah XXVIII:V.1:] "The nation of the Cherethites" (Zeph. 2:5): Some explain the name in a positive sense, that is," a nation that enters into a covenant [with God]."

D. [Genesis Rabbah XXVIII:V.1:] R. Levi interpreted the verse to speak in a favorable sense: "'Woe to the inhabitants of the seacoast, the nation of the Cherethites' (Zeph. 2:5)': 'Woe to the nation that has made a covenant,' in line with this usage: 'and made a covenant with him' (Neh. 9:8)."

4. A. R. Joshua b. R. Nehemiah in the name of R. Aha said, "What was said concerning the tribes of Judah and Benjamin was never said concerning Sodom.

B. "In respect to Sodom, it is written, 'And yes, their sin is exceedingly grievous' (Gen. 18:20), but with regard to the tribes of Judah and Benjamin: 'The iniquity of the house of Israel and Judah is *most* exceedingly great' (Ez. 9:9).

C. [Gen. R. continues:] "Nonetheless, of those [of the generation of the Flood] not a remnant was left, while of these [the two tribes] a remnant was left.

D. [Gen. R. continues:] "As to Sodom, 'that was overthrown in a moment' (Lam. 4:6), they never put forth their hands to carry out religious duties, 'Hands therein accepted no duties' (Lam. 4:6), in the line with what R. Tanhuma said, 'No hand joined another hand [to help one another.' [The people did not help one another to carry out their religious duties.]

E. [Gen. R. continues:] "But in regard to the others [of Judah and Benjamin], they extended hands to one another in carrying out religious duties: 'The hands of women full of compassion have sodden their own children and provided the mourner's meal' (Lam. 4:10)."

F. R. Tanhuma said, "We have yet another verse of Scripture in this matter: 'For the iniquity of the daughter of my people is greater than the sin of Sodom' (Lam. 4:6)."

G. Said R. Tanhuma, "They did not assist one another; they did not put out their hands to carry out their religious obligations; but these put out their hands to carry out their religious obligations: 'The hands of women full of compassion' (Lam. 4:6).

H. "Why so? 'So that 'they should have food in the destruction of the daughter of my people' (Lam. 4:6)."

5.   A.   [As to the verse, "Draw me after you, let us make haste":] said R. Azariah, "Said the Congregation of Israel before the Holy One, blessed be He, 'Because you have given me the spoil of my neighbors, 'after you let us make haste.'

B.   "For it is said, 'But every woman shall ask of her neighbor' (Ex. 11:2).

C.   "'It is because you gave us the spoil of Egypt, the spoil of the [Egyptian army at] the sea, the spoil of Sihon and Og, the spoil of the thirty-one kings [of Canaan] that 'after you let us make haste.'"

6.   A.   Another explanation of the verse, "Draw me after you, let us make haste":

B.   "We shall make haste because you have incited against me my wicked neighbors."

C.   Said R. Abun, "It is comparable to the case of a king who was angry with a royal lady, and so aroused against her her wicked neighbors.

D.   "She began to cry out, 'My lord, King, save me.'

E.   "So the Israelites: 'The Zidonians also and the Amalekites and the Maonites did oppress you, and you cried to me and I saved you out of their hand' (Judges 10:12)."

7.   A.   Another explanation of the verse, "Draw me after you, let us make haste":

B.   "Endanger me, and 'after you let us make haste.'"

8.   A.   Another explanation of the verse, "Draw me after you, let us make haste":

B.   Impoverish me and "after you, let us make haste."

C.   That is in line with what R. Aha said, "When a Jew has to eat carobs, he repents."

D.   That is also in line with what R. Aqiba says, "Poverty is as appropriate to a daughter of Jacob as a red streak on the neck of a white horse."

9.   A.   Another explanation of the verse, "Draw me after you, let us make haste":

B.   "Take a pledge from me, and 'after you, let us make haste.'

C. "For the great pledge that you have taken from me, 'after you, let us make haste.'"

    D. That is in line with what R. Menahema said in the name of R. Yohanan, "It is written, 'We have given a pledge to you' (Neh. 1:7):

    E. "This refers to the first catastrophe [the destruction of the first Temple] and the second catastrophe.

    F. "For these have been taken as pledges only on our account."

10. A. R. Berekhiah in the name of R. Judah b. R. Ilai: "It is written, 'And Moses led Israel onward from the Red Sea' (Ex. 15:22):

B. "He led them on from the sin committed at the sea.

C. "They said to him, 'Moses, our lord, where are you leading us?'

D. "He said to them, 'To Elim, from Elim to Alush, from Alush to Marah, from Marah to Rephidim, from Rephidim to Sinai.'

E. "They said to him, 'Indeed, wherever you go and lead us, we are with you.'

F. "The matter is comparable to the case of one who went and married a woman from a village. He said to her, 'Arise and come with me.'

G. "She said to him, 'From here to where?'

H. "He said to her, 'From here to Tiberias, from Tiberias to the Tannery, from the Tannery to the Upper Market, from the Upper Market to the Lower Market.'

I. "She said to him, 'Wherever you go and take me, I shall go with you.'

J. "So said the Israelites, 'My soul cleaves to you' (Ps. 63:9)."

K. Said R. Yosé b. R. Iqa, "And lo, a verse of Scripture itself proclaims the same point: 'Draw me, after you let us make haste.'

L. "If it is from one verse of Scripture to another verse of Scripture, if it is from one passage of the Mishnah to another passage of the Mishnah, if it is from one passage of the Talmud to another passage of the Talmud, if it is from one passage of the Tosefta to another passage of the Tosefta, if it is from one aspect of narrative to another aspect of narrative."

IV:iv

1. A. "The king has brought me into his chambers":

    B. We have learned in Tannaite tradition:

    C. Four entered paradise: Ben Azzai and Ben Zoma, Elisha b. Abbuyah and R. Aqiba.

    D. Ben Azzai gazed and was afflicted: "Have you found honey? Eat so much as is enough for you" (Prov. 25:16).

E. Ben Zoma gazed and died, and concerning him it is said in Scripture, "Precious in the sight of the Lord is the death of his saints" (Ps. 116:15).
F. Elisha ben Abbuyah made cuttings among the plantings.
2. A. How did he make cuttings among the plantings?
   B. When he would enter synagogues and school houses and see youngsters succeeding in the Torah, he would say about them a word, and they would be stopped.
   C. In his regard it is said in Scripture, "Do not let your mouth bring your flesh into guilt" (Qoh. 5:5).
3. A. [Continuing 1.E:] R. Aqiba went in whole and came out whole.
   B. And he said, "It is not because I am greater than my colleagues, but this have sages taught in the Mishnah:
   C. "**'Your deeds will draw you near, or your deeds will put you out'** [M. Ed. 5:7]."
   D. And in his regard it is said in Scripture, "The king has brought me into his chambers."
4. A. R. Yannai said, "The Torah had to be expounded only from the passage, 'This month shall be to you' (Ex. 12:2) [at which point the laws commence].
   B. "And on what account did the Holy One, blessed be He, reveal to Israel what was on the first day and what was on the second, on to the sixth? It was by reason of the merit gained when they said, 'All that the Lord has spoken we shall do and we shall obey' (Ex. 24:7).
   C. "Forthwith the rest was revealed to them."
5. A. R. Berekhiah said, "It is written, 'And he told you his covenant [which he commanded you to perform, even the ten words]' (Dt. 4:13).
   B. "[Since the word for covenant and the word for creation contained the same letters, it is to be interpreted:] 'And he told you his book of Genesis, which is the beginning of the creation of the world.'

C. "'which he commanded you to perform, even the ten words' (Dt. 4:13): this refers to the Ten Commandments.

D. "Ten for Scripture, ten for Talmud."

6. A. And whence was Elihu son of Barachel the Buzite to come and reveal to the Israelites the innermost mysteries of Behemoth and Leviathan,

B. and whence was Ezekiel to come and reveal to them the innermost secrets of the divine chariot?

C. But that is in line with the following verse of Scripture: "The king has brought me into his chambers."

IV:v

1. A. "We will exult and rejoice in you":

B. The Israelites are described with ten expressions of joy:

C. rejoicing, joy, gladness, song, breaking forth, crying aloud, exultation, great rejoicing, gaiety, and shouting.

D. rejoicing: "Rejoice greatly, O daughter of Zion" (Zech. 9:9).

E. joy: "I will greatly rejoice in the Lord" (Isa. 61:10).

F. gladness: "Be glad with Jerusalem" (Isa. 66:10).

G. song: "Sing and rejoice, O daughter of Zion" (Zech. 2:14).

H. breaking forth: "Break forth into singing and cry aloud" (Isa. 54:1).

I. crying aloud: "Cry aloud and shout" (Isa. 12:6).

J. exultation: "My heart exults in the Lord" (1 Sam. 2:1).

K. great rejoicing: My heart greatly rejoices and with my soul I will praise him" (Ps. 28:7).

L. gaiety: "And the children of Israel kept the dedication with gaiety" (Ezra 6:16).

M. And shouting: "Shout to the Lord all the earth": (Ps. 98:4).

N. Some exclude shouting and include dancing: "Dismay dances before him" (Job 41:14),

O. [Simon] leaping like a stranded fish.

2. A. Another interpretation of the verse, "We will exult and rejoice in you":

B. There we have learned on Tannaite authority: If one has married a woman and lived with her for ten years and not produced offspring, he has not got the right to stop trying.

C. Said R. Idi, "There was the case of a woman in Sidon, who lived with her husband for ten years and did not produce offspring.

D. They came before R. Simeon b. Yohai and wanted to be parted from one another.

E. He said to them, "By your lives! Just as you were joined to one another with eating and drinking, so you will separate from one another only with eating and drinking."

F. They followed his counsel and made themselves a festival and made a great banquet and drank too much.

G. When his mind was at ease, he said to her, "My daughter, see anything good that I have in the house! Take it and go to your father's house!"

H. What did she do? After he fell asleep, she made gestures to her servants and serving women and said to them, "Take him in the bed and pick him up and bring him to my father's house."

I. Around midnight he woke up from his sleep. When the wine wore off, he said to her, "My daughter, where am I now?"

J. She said to him, "In my father's house."

K. He said to her, "What am I doing in your father's house?"

L. She said to him, "Did you not say to me last night, 'See anything good that I have in the house! Take it and go to your father's house!' But I have nothing in the world so good as you!"

M. They went to R. Simeon b. Yohai, and he stood and prayed for them, and they were answered [and given offspring].

N. This serves to teach you that just as the Holy One, blessed be He, answers the prayers of barren women, so righteous persons have the power to answer the prayers of barren women.

O. And does this not yield a proposition a fortiori: if a mortal person, on account of saying to another mortal, "I have nothing in the world

so good as you!" has prayers answered, the
Israelites, who every single day await the
salvation of the Holy One, blessed be He,
saying, "We have nothing in the world so good
as you!" – how much the more so

P. Thus":We will exult and rejoice in you."

3. A. The matter [of the situation of the Israelites] may
be compared to the case of a noble lady, whose
husband, the king, and whose sons and sons-in-
law went overseas. They came and told her, "Your
sons are coming home."

B. She said, "What difference does it make to me?
Let my daughters-in-law rejoice."

C. When her sons-in-law came home, they said to her,
"Your sons-in-law are coming."

D. So she said, "What difference does it make to me?
Let my daughters rejoice."

E. When they told her, "The king, your husband, is
coming," she said, "This is the occasion for whole-
hearted rejoicing, waves upon waves of joy!"

F. So in the age to come the prophets will come and
say to Jerusalem, "Your sons come from afar" (Isa.
60:4), and she will say, "What difference does that
make to me?"

G. And when they say, "And your daughters are borne
on the side" (Isa. 60:4), she will say, "What
difference does that make to me?"

H. But when they said to her, "Lo, your king comes
to you, he is triumphant and victorious" Zech. 9:9),
she will say, "This is the occasion for whole-hearted
rejoicing!"

I. For so it is written, "Rejoice greatly, O daughter of
Zion" (Zech. 9:9); "Sing and rejoice, O daughter
of Zion" (Zech. 2:14).

J. Then she will say, "I will greatly rejoice in the Lord,
my soul shall be joyful in my God" (Isa. 61:10).

IV:vi

1. A. Another interpretation of the verse, "We will exult and rejoice in
you; [we will extol your love more than wine; rightly do they love
you]":

B.   R. Abin commenced discourse by citing the following verse of Scripture: "This is the day that the Lord has made. We will rejoice and be glad in it" (Ps. 118:24).

C.   Said R. Abin, "We do not know in what to rejoice [since "in it" may be read "in him"], whether in the day or in the Holy One, blessed be He.

D.   "Came Solomon and spelled the matter out: 'We will exult and rejoice in you' – in the Holy One, blessed be He.

E.   "'...in you': in your salvation.

F.   "'...in you': in your Torah.

G.   "'...in you': in reverence for you."

2.   A.   Said R. Isaac, "[Supply: We will exult and rejoice in you':]

B.   "'...in you': in the twenty-two letters [the numerical value of the word 'in you' being twenty-two] which you wrote for us in the Torah,

C.   "for the B is two, the K [of the Hebrew word 'in you'] stands for twenty, hence twenty-two."

IV:vii

1.   A.   "...we will extol your love more than wine; [rightly do they love you]":

B.   More than the wine of the Torah:

C.   for instance, the laws of Passover on Passover, the laws of Pentecost on Pentecost, the laws of the Festival [of Tabernacles] on the Festival.

2.   A.   Another matter concerning the verse, "we will extol your love more than wine; [rightly do they love you]":

B.   more than the wine of the patriarchs:

C.   The first Man – what did he do before you?

D.   Who did deeds before you like Abraham?

E.   Who did deeds before you like Isaac?

F.   Who did deeds before you like Jacob? [Simon, p. 50, n. 4: "We will make mention of the love the Patriarchs bore for you; then their merit will stand us in good stead too."]

IV:viii

1.   A.   "...rightly do they love you":

B.   How upright is their love for you!

C.   How powerful is their love for you!

2.   A.   Said R. Aibi, "With formidable right did our patriarchs act before you in everything that they did."

3.   A.   Said R. Hanin, "'Because you have done this thing' (Gen. 22:16):

B.   "This was the tenth trial, and you call it merely 'a thing'?

C. "Lo, if he had not accepted that thing, he would have lost and been deprived of [the merit of] all the earlier deeds.

D. "Thus: 'rightly do they love you.'"

5

Song of Songs Rabbah to
Song of Songs 1:5

1:5 *I am very dark, but comely,*
O daughters of Jerusalem,
like the tents of Kedar,
like the curtains of Solomon.

V:i

1. A. "I am very dark, but comely, [O daughters of Jerusalem, like the tents of Kedar, like the curtains of Solomon]" (Song 1:5):

    B. "I am dark" in my deeds.

    C. "But comely" in the deeds of my forebears.

2. A. "I am very dark, but comely":

    B. Said the Community of Israel, "'I am dark' in my view, 'but comely' before my Creator."

    C. For it is written, "Are you not as the children of the Ethiopians to Me, O children of Israel, says the Lord" (Amos 9:7):

    D. "as the children of the Ethiopians" – in your sight.

    E. But "to Me, O children of Israel, says the Lord."

3. A. Another interpretation of the verse, "I am very dark": in Egypt.

    B. "...but comely": in Egypt.

    C. "I am very dark" in Egypt: "But they rebelled against me and would not hearken to me" (Ez. 20:8).

    D. "...but comely" in Egypt: with the blood of the Passover-offering and circumcision, "And when I passed by you and saw you wallowing in your blood, I said to you, In your blood live" Ez. 16:6) – in the blood of the Passover.

    E. "I said to you, In your blood live" Ez. 16:6) – in the blood of the circumcision.

4. A. Another interpretation of the verse, "I am very dark": at the sea, "They were rebellious at the sea, even the Red Sea" (Ps. 106:7).

    B. "...but comely": at the sea, "This is my God and I will be comely for him" (Ex. 15:2) [following Simon's rendering of the verse].

5. A. "I am very dark": at Marah, "And the people murmured against Moses, saying, What shall we drink" Ex. 15:24).

    B. "...but comely": at Marah, "And he cried to the Lord and the Lord showed him a tree, and he cast it into the waters and the waters were made sweet" (Ex. 15:25).

6. A. "I am very dark": at Rephidim, "And the name of the place was called Massah and Meribah" (Ex. 17:7).

    B. "...but comely": at Rephidim, "And Moses built an altar and called it by the name 'the Lord is my banner' (Ex. 17:15).

7. A. "I am very dark": at Horeb, "And they made a calf at Horeb" (Ps. 106:19).

    B. "...but comely": at Horeb, "And they said, All that the Lord has spoken we will do and obey" (Ex. 24:7).

8. A. "I am very dark": in the wilderness, ""How often did they rebel against him in the wilderness" (Ps. 78:40).

    B. "...but comely": in the wilderness at the setting up of the tabernacle, "And on the day that the tabernacle was set up" (Num. 9:15).

9. A. "I am very dark": in the deed of the spies, "And they spread an evil report of the land" (Num. 13:32).

    B. "...but comely": in the deed of Joshua and Caleb, "Save for Caleb, the son of Jephunneh the Kenizzite" (Num. 32:12).

10. A. "I am very dark": at Shittim, "And Israel abode at Shittim and the people began to commit harlotry with the daughters of Moab" (Num. 25:1).

    B. "...but comely": at Shittim, "Then arose Phinehas and wrought judgment" (Ps. 106:30).

11. A. "I am very dark": through Achan, "But the children of Israel committed a trespass concerning the devoted thing" (Josh. 7:1).

    B. "...but comely": through Joshua, "And Joshua said to Achan, My son, give I pray you glory" (Josh. 7:19).

12. A. "I am very dark": through the kings of Israel.

    B. "...but comely": through the kings of Judah.

    C. If with my dark ones that I had, it was such that "I am comely," all the more so with my prophets.

V:ii

1. A. "I am very dark":

    B. Scripture speaks of Ahab: "And it came to pass when Ahab heard those words that he tore his clothing and put sackcloth upon his flesh and fasted and went softly" (1 Kgs. 21:27).

        2. A. How long did he afflict himself?

B. R. Joshua b. Levi said, "For three hours. If he was accustomed to eat his meal at the third hour of the day, he ate it at the sixth, and if he was accustomed to eat at the sixth, he ate at the ninth."

3. A. And he lay in sackcloth and went softly" (1 Kgs. 21:27):

B. R. Joshua b. Levi said, "He went barefoot."

4. A. As to Jehorum, what is written?

B. "And the people look, and behold, he had sackcloth within, upon his flesh" (1 Kgs. 6:30):

5. A. [As to the verse, "I am very dark, but comely," R. Levi b. R. Haita gave three interpretations:

B. "'I am very dark': all the days of the week.

C. "'...but comely': on the Sabbath.

D. "'I am very dark': all the days of the year.

E. "'...but comely': on the Day of Atonement.

F. "'I am very dark': among the Ten Tribes.

G. "'...but comely': in the tribe of Judah and Benjamin.

H. "'I am very dark': in this world.

I. "'...but comely': in the world to come."

V:iii

1. A. "O daughters of Jerusalem":

B. Rabbis say, "Do not read the letters that spell out "daughters of Jerusalem" as given, but rather, as "builders of Jerusalem" [since the same consonants can yield that other reading].

C. This refers to the great sanhedrin of Israel, which goes into session and clarifies every question and matter of judgment. ["Builders" and "clarify" have the same consonants.]

2. A. Another interpretation of the phrase, "O daughters of Jerusalem":

B. Said R. Yohanan, "Jerusalem is destined to be made the metropolitan capital of all cities and draw people to her in streams to do her honor.

C. "That is in line with the following passage of Scripture: 'Ashdod, its towns [using the letters that spell out the word for daughters] and villages, Gaza, its towns and its villages until Lesha' (Josh. 15:47)."

D. That is the view, then, of R. Yohanan.

E. For R. Yohanan said, "It is written, 'I will give them to you for daughters, but not because of your covenant' (Ez. 16:61).

F. "What is the sense of 'daughters'? It means towns.

G. "What is the sense of, 'but not because of your covenant'? 'Not on account of your contract, but as a gift from me.'"

3.   A. R. Bibi in the name of R. Reuben said, "'Sing, O barren one' (Isa. 54:1).

      B. "Now is there a song to celebrate barrenness?

      C. "But 'sing O barren one' for you have not born children for Gehenna."

4.   A. R. Berekhiah in the name of R. Samuel b. R. Nahman said, "The Israelites are compared to a woman.

      B. "Just as an unmarried women receives a tenth part of the property of her father and takes her leave [for her husband's house when she gets married], so the Israelites inherited the land of the seven peoples, who form a tenth part of the seventy nations of the world.

      C. "And because the Israelites inherited in the status of a woman, they said a song in the feminine form of that word, as in the following: 'Then sang Moses and the children of Israel this song [given in the feminine form] unto the Lord' (Ex. 15:1).

      D. "But in the age to come they are destined to inherit like a man, who inherits all of the property of his father.

      E. "That is in line with this verse of Scripture: 'From the east side to the west side: Judah, one portion...Dan one, Asher one...' (Ez. 48:7), and so throughout.

      F. "Then they will say a song in the masculine form of that word, as in the following: 'Sing to the Lord a new song' (Ps. 96:1).

      G. "The word 'song' is given not in its feminine form but in its masculine form."

5.   A. R. Berekhiah and R. Joshua b. Levi: "Why are the Israelites compared to a woman?

      B. "Just as a woman takes up a burden and puts it down [that is, becomes pregnant and gives birth], takes up a burden and puts it down, then takes up a burden and puts it down and then takes up no further burden,

      C. "so the Israelites are subjugated and then redeemed, subjugated and then redeemed, but in the end are redeemed and will never again be subjugated.

D. "In this world, since their anguish is like the anguish of a woman in childbirth, they say the song before him using the feminine form of the word for song,

E. "but in the age to come, because their anguish will no longer be the anguish of a woman in childbirth, they will say their song using the masculine form of the word for song:

F. "'In that day this song [in the masculine form of the word] will be sung' (Isa. 26:1)."

V:iv

1. A. "...like the tents of Kedar, [like the curtains of Solomon]" (Song 1:5):

B. Just as the tents of Kedar, while they appear from the outside to be ugly, black, and tattered, on the inside are made up of precious stones and pearls,

C. so disciples of sages, while they appear in this world to be ugly and black, inside they contain Torah, Scripture, Mishnah, Midrash, laws, Talmud, Tosefta, and lore.

D. Might one say just as the tents of Kedar do not need to be cleaned, so is the case with Israel?

E. Scripture says, "like the curtains of Solomon."

F. Just as the curtains of Solomon get dirty and are cleaned and then get dirty and are cleaned again, so the Israelites, even though they are dirty with sins all the days of the year, the Day of Atonement comes and makes atonement for them:

G. "For on this day shall atonement be made for you, to cleanse you" (Lev 16:30); "Though your sins be as scarlet, they shall be white as snow" (Isa. 1:18).

H. Might one say just as tents of Kedar are moved about from place to place, so is the case with Israel?

I. Scripture says, "like the curtains of Solomon."

J. They are like the tents of Him to whom peace belongs, the One at whose word the world came into being,

K. for from the moment that he stretched [his tents] forth, they never again moved from their place.

2. A. R. Eliezer b. Jacob taught on Tannaite authority, "A tent that shall not be removed' (Isa. 33:20):

B. "the word for 'removed' means, shall not go forth and shall not stir."

3. A. Just as in the case of the tents of Kedar, the yoke of no creature is upon them,

B. so in the case of the Israelites in the age to come, the yoke of no creature will be upon them.

4.   A.   R. Hiyya taught on Tannaite authority, "'And I made you
            go upright' (Lev. 26:13):
      B.   "'upright' means standing erect, fearful of no creature."
      5.   A.   R. Yudan said, "[Israel] is like Joseph:
            B.   "Just as Joseph was sold to the tents of Kedar, 'And
                  they sold Joseph to the Ishmaelites' (Gen. 37:28),
                  and afterward bought those who had bought him,
                  'So Joseph bought all the land of Egypt' (Gen.
                  47:20),
            C.   "so the Israelites, 'will take their captors captive'
                  (Isa. 14:2)."

6

Song of Songs Rabbah to
Song of Songs 1:6

*1:6   Do not gaze at me because I am swarthy,
        because the sun has scorched me.
        My mother's sons were angry with me,
        they made me keeper of the vineyards;
        but my own vineyard I have not kept!*

VI:i
1.   A.   "Do not gaze at me because I am swarthy":
      B.   R. Simon commenced discourse by citing the following verse of
            Scripture: "'Do not slander a servant to his master' (Prov. 30:10).
      C.   "The Israelites are called servants: 'For to me the children of Israel
            are servants' (Lev. 25:55).
      D.   "The prophets are called servants: 'But he reveals his counsel to his
            servants the prophets' (Amos 3:7).
      E.   "Thus said the Community of Israel to the prophets, "'Do not gaze at
            me because I am swarthy."
      F.   "'None among my sons rejoiced more than Moses, but because he
            said, "Listen, please, you rebels" (Num. 20:10), he suffered the decree
            not to enter the land.'"
      2.   A.   Another interpretation: "'None among my sons rejoiced
                  more than Isaiah, but because he said, "And I dwell in the
                  midst of a people of unclean lips" (Num. 6:5), God said

to him, "Isaiah, you can say of yourself, "Because I am a man of unclean lips" (Isa. 6:5), but can you say, "And in the midst of a people of unclean lips I dwell" (Isa. 6:5)?'

B. "Note what is written there: 'Then flew to me one of the seraphim with a glowing stone in his hand' (Isa. 6:6)."

3. A. [Supply: "Then flew to me one of the seraphim with a glowing stone in his hand" (Isa. 6:6):]

B. [As to the meaning of the word for glowing stone, since its consonants may be read differently,] said R. Samuel, "The word for glowing stone yields the meaning, break the mouth.

C. "'...break the mouth' of the one who has defamed my children."

4. A. Along these same lines:

B. It is written concerning Elijah, "And he said, I have been very jealous for the Lord, the god of hosts, for the children of Israel have forsaken your covenant" (1 Kgs. 19:14).

C. Said to him the Holy One, blessed be He, "'...my covenant,' yes, but it is 'your covenant'?"

D. "They have thrown down your altars" (1 Kgs. 19:14).

E. He said to him, "They are my altars, are they your altars?"

F. "They have slain your prophets with the sword" (1 Kgs. 19:14).

G. He said to him, "They are my prophets, are they your prophets? What business is it of yours!"

H. "And I, even I alone am left, and they seek my life to take it away" (1 Kgs. 19:14).

I. Note what is written there: "And he looked and behold there was at his head a cake baked on hot stones" (1 Kgs. 19:6).

5. A. What is the meaning of "hot stones"?

B. [As to the meaning of the word for hot stones, since its consonants may be read differently,] said R. Samuel, "The word for hot stone yields the meaning, break the mouth.

C. "'...break the mouth' of the one who has defamed my children."

6. A. R. Yohanan derives the same proposition from the following:

B. "'The burden of Damascus. Behold Damascus...the cities of Aroer are forsaken' (Isa. 17:1, 2)."

7. A. How come this one deals with Damascus but makes mention of Aroer?

   B. Is not Aroer in the boundaries of Moab?

   C. Now in Damascus were three hundred sixty five temples of idolatry, corresponding to the days of the solar year, and they would worship each one on its day, and they had one day on which all of them would be worshipped at once.

   D. And the Israelites made of all of them a single entity and worshipped them: "And the children of Israel continued to do that which was evil in the sight of the Lord and served the Baalim and the Ashtarot and the gods of Aram and Nidon and Moab" (Judges 10:6). [Simon, p. 57, n. 1: Thus Aram (Damascus) and Moab (Aroer) are mentioned together and for that reason they are coupled in the present verse too.]"

8. A. [Continuing 6.B:] "Now at that moment at which Elijah spoke ill of the Israelites, the Holy One, blessed be He, said to him, 'Elijah, instead of accusing these, come and accuse those!'

   B. "That is in line with this verse: 'Go, return on your way to the wilderness of Damascus' (1 Kgs. 19:15)."

9. A. R. Abbahu and R. Simeon b. Laqish were going to enter the city of Caesarea. Said R. Abbahu to R. Simeon b. Laqish, "How can we go into a city full of cursing and blaspheming?"

   B. R. Simeon b. Laqish got off his ass, took some dirt, and put it into the mouth [of Abbahu].

   C. [Abbahu] said to him, "What's going on?"

   D. [Simeon b. Laqish] said to him, "The Holy One, blessed be He, does not take pleasure in one who defames Israel."

VI:ii

1. A. "...because the sun has scorched me":
   B. Said R. Abba b. R. Kahana in the name of R. Hiyya the Elder, "It is written, 'Said R. Abba b. R. Kahana in the name of R. Hiyya the Elder, "It is written, 'For my people have committed two evils' (Jer. 2:13).
   C. "Lo, they neglected many.
   D. "This teaches that they did one that was as bad as two.
   E. "For they worship an idol and turn their backsides toward the house of the sanctuary: 'And he brought me into the inner court of the Lord's house and behold...twenty-five men with their backs toward the Temple of the Lord...and they bowed down toward the sun, toward the east' (Ez. 8:16).
      F. "The use of 'bow down' is the same as in the passage, 'Because their corruption [using some of the same consonants] is in them, there is a blemish in them' (Lev. 22:25)."
2. A. Another interpretation of the verse, "because the sun has scorched me":
   B. It is because I kept stables of horses for the sun:
   C. "And he took away the horses that the kings of Judah had given to the sun at the entrance of the house of the Lord" (2 Kgs. 23:11).
3. A. [Supply: "because the sun has scorched me":]
   B. R. Isaac interpreted the verse to speak of the wars of Midian:
   C. "You find that when the Israelites went to war against Midian, then went in in pairs to a woman. One of them would blacken her face, the other stripped her of her jewelry [to make her repulsive and so prevent themselves from having sexual relations with her].
   D. "But she would say to them, 'Are we too not among the creatures of the Holy One, blessed be He, that you treat us in such a way!'
   E. "And the Israelites would reply, 'Is it not enough for you that we got what was coming to us through you? 'And the Lord said to Moses, Take all the chiefs of the people and hang them up to the Lord in the face of the sun' (Num. 25:4)."
      F. R. Aibu said, "How had they sinned? It was because 'they had joined themselves to Baal Peor' (Num. 25:3)."
5. A. And said R. Isaac, "There was the case of a local noblewoman who had an Ethiopian slave-girl, who went down to draw water from the well with her friend.

B.   "She said to her friend, 'My friend, tomorrow my master is going to divorce his wife and take me as his wife.'

C.   "The other said to her, 'Why?'

D.   "'It is because he saw her hands dirty.'

E.   "She said to her, 'You big fool! Let your ears hear what your mouth is saying. Now if concerning his wife, who is most precious to him, you say that because he saw her hands dirty one time, he wants to divorce her, you, who are entirely dirty, scorched from the day of your birth, how much the more so!'

F.   "So too, since the nations of the world taunt the Israelites, saying, 'This nation has exchanged its glory [for nought],' as in the verse, 'They exchanged their glory for an ox that eats grass' (Ps. 106:20),

G.   "the Israelites reply to them, 'Now if we who are in that condition for an hour and have incurred liability on that account, as for you, how much the more so!'

H.   "And not only so, but the Israelites say to the nations of the world, 'We shall say to you to what we are to be compared:

I.   "It is to a prince who went forth to the wilderness around the town, and the sun beat on his head so that his face was darkened. He came back to the town, and with a bit of water and a bit of bathing in the bath houses, his body turned white and regained its beauty, just as before.

J.   "'So it is with me [the Israelites continue]. If the worship of idols has scorched us, truly you are scorched from your mother's womb!

K.   "'While you are yet in your mother's womb, you served idols, for when a woman is pregnant, she goes into the house of her idol and bows down and worships the idol – both she and her child.'"

VI:iii

1.   A.   "My mother's sons were angry with me":

B.   R. Meir and R. Yosé:

C.   R. Meir says, "'My mother's sons': the sons of my nation [which word uses the same consonants], that is Dathan and Abiram.

D.   "'...were angry with me': attacked me, filled with wrath the judge who [ruled] against me.

E.   "'...they made me keeper of the vineyards': while he brought justice among the daughters of Jethro, could he not bring justice between me and my brothers in Egypt?

F.   "Thus: 'but my own vineyard I have not kept.'"

G.   R. Yosé says, "'My mother's sons': 'the sons of my nation [which word uses the same consonants], that is the spies.'

H.   "'...were angry with me': 'attacked me, filled with wrath the judge who [ruled] against me.

I. "'...they made me keeper of the vineyards': 'it was because I delayed in the wilderness for forty-two journeys, I did not have the privilege of entering the land of Israel.'

J. "Thus: 'but my own vineyard I have not kept.'"

2. A. Another interpretation:

B. "My mother's sons": the sons of my nation [which word uses the same consonants], that is, Jeroboam b. Nebat.

C. "...were angry with me": attacked me, filled with wrath the judge who [ruled] against me.

D. "...they made me keeper of the vineyards": the task of guarding the two golden calves of Jeroboam [1 Kgs. 12:28].

E. "...but my own vineyard I have not kept": "I did not keep the watch of the priests and Levites."

F. Thus: "but my own vineyard I have not kept."

3. A. Said R. Levi, "On the day on which Solomon was married to the daughter of Pharaoh Neccho, Michael, the great prince, descended from heaven, and he stuck a large reed into the sea, so that mud came up on either side, and the place was like a marsh. And that was the site of Rome.

B. "On the day on which Jeroboam b. Nebat set up the two golden calves, two huts were built in Rome.

C. "And they would build them, but the huts would fall down, build and see the collapse. But there was a sage there, by the name of Abba Qolon. He said to them, 'If you do not bring water from the Euphrates river and mix it with the clay, the building will not stand.'

D. "They said to him, 'Who will do it?'

E. "He said to them, 'I.'

F. "He dressed up like a wine-porter, going into a town and out of a town, into a province and out of a province, until he got there. When he reached there, he went and took water from the Euphrates. They kneaded it into mud and built with it, and the building stood.

G. "From that time they would say, 'Any town that does not have an Abba Qolon cannot be called a town.'

H. "And they called Rome Babylon."

I. On the day on which Elijah, of blessed memory, was taken away, a king arose in Edom: "And there was no king in Edom, a deputy was king" (1 Kgs. 22:48).

4. A. Another explanation: "My mother's sons were angry with me": the sons of my nation [which word uses the same consonants]. This refers to Ahab.

B.   "...were angry with me": attacked me, filled with wrath the judge who [ruled] against me.

C.   "...they made me keeper of the vineyards": "They made me provide dainties for and feed Zedekiah b. Canaanah and his allies."

D.   But I had one true prophet there, Micaiah, and he ordered them to "feed him with little bread and little water" (1 Kgs. 22:27), thus: "but my own vineyard I have not kept."

5.   A.   Another explanation: "My mother's sons": the sons of my nation [which word uses the same consonants]. This refers to Jezebel.

B.   "...were angry with me": attacked me, filled with wrath the judge who [ruled] against me.

C.   "...they made me keeper of the vineyards": She was providing dainties for and feeding the prophets of Baal and Asherah.

D.   But to Elijah, of blessed memory, who was the true prophet, she sent word, "If I do not make your life as the life of one of them by tomorrow" (1 Kgs. 19:2). Thus: "but my own vineyard I have not kept."

6.   A.   Another explanation: "My mother's sons": that is Zedekiah the king.

B.   "...were angry with me": attacked me, filled with wrath the judge who [ruled] against me.

C.   "...they made me keeper of the vineyards": This is because he gave dainties to Pashhur b. Malkiah and his colleagues.

D.   One true prophet I had, namely, Jeremiah, about whom it is written, "And they gave him daily a loaf of bread out of the bakers' street" (Jer. 37:21).

E.   What is the meaning of "the bakers' street"?

F.   Said R. Isaac, "This is coarse bread, sold outside of the confectioner's shop, and it is blacker than coarse barley bread.

G.   Thus: "but my own vineyard I have not kept."

7.   A.   R. Hiyya in the name of R. Yohanan: "Said the Community of Israel before the Holy One, blessed be He, 'Because I did not observe the law about giving a single dough-offering in the proper manner in the land of Israel, lo, I keep the law concerning setting aside two dough-offerings in Syria [Simon, p. 61, n. 3: one for the priest and one to be burnt, out of doubt.]

B.   "I was hoping that I might receive the reward for setting aside two, but I receive the reward for only one of them."

C.   R. Abbah in the name of R. Yohanan: "Said the Community of Israel before the Holy One, blessed be He, 'Because I did not observe the law of keeping a single day holy as the festival in the proper manner in the land of Israel, lo, I keep the law concerning keeping two successive days holy as the festival applicable to the Exiles, outside of the land.

D. "I was hoping that I might receive the reward for setting aside two, but I receive the reward for only one of them."

E. R. Yohanan cited concerning them the following verse: "Wherefore I gave them also statutes that were not good" (Ez. 20:25).

7

Song of Songs Rabbah to Song of Songs 1:7

1:7   *Tell me, you whom my soul loves,*
where you pasture your flock,
where you make it lie down at noon;
for why should I be like one who wanders
beside the flocks of your companions?

VII:i

1. A. "Tell me, you whom my soul loves, [where you pasture your flock, where you make it lie down at noon; for why should I be like one who wanders beside the flocks of your companions?]"

    B. R. Judah b. R. Simon interpreted the verse to speak of Moses:

    C. "When the Holy One, blessed be He, said to him, 'Come now, therefore, and I will send you to Pharaoh,' (Ex. 3:10),

    D. "he said to him, 'Lord of the world, "Through me, O Lord" (Ex. 4:13) Can all these things be done? How can I bear all of these vast populations? How many nursing mothers are there among them, how many pregnant women, how many infants! How much good food have you provided for the pregnant women among them? How much parched corn and nuts have you given for the children among them?'

    E. "Where is this matter made explicit? [It is in the exposition of the following verse:]

    F. "'Tell me, you whom my soul loves': 'the nation that my soul loves, the nation for which I have given my life.'

G.   "'...where you pasture your flock': 'in the sunny season.'

H.   "'...where you make it lie down at noon': 'in the rainy season.'"

2.   A.   "...for why should I be like one who wanders [Hebrew: veils herself] beside the flocks of your companions":

        B.   R. Helbo in the name of R. Huna said, "'Do not let me be like a mourner, who covers his lip and weeps.'

        C.   "That is in line with the following usage: 'And he shall cover his upper lip' (Lev. 13:45)."

3.   A.   Another explanation for the verse, "for why should I be like one who wanders [Hebrew: veils herself] [besides the flocks of your companions]":

        B.   "So that I may not be like a shepherd whose flock is attacked and ravaged by wolves, and he merely folds his garment and escapes.

        C.   [That interpretation of the letters of the word translated "wanders/veils herself"] is in accord with the following usage: "And he shall fold up the land of Egypt" (Jer. 43:12).

4.   A.   "...beside the flocks of your companions":

        B.   [Moses speaks, continuing from 1.H:] "When I go to your companions [the patriarchs], and they ask me about their flocks, what am I going to answer them?"

5.   A.   [Supply: "Tell me, you whom my soul loves, where you pasture your flock, where you make it lie down at noon; for why should I be like one who wanders besides the flocks of your companions?]"

        B.   R. Berekhiah interpreted the verse in light of the following: "Let the Lord, the God of the spirits of all flesh, set a man over the congregation" (Num. 27:16).

        C.   "[Moses] said before him, 'Lord of the world, since you are going to remove me from the world, kindly inform me exactly who will be the shepherds that you will appoint over your children.'

        D.   "Where is the matter made explicit? [It is in the exposition of the following verse:]

        E.   "'Tell me, you whom my soul loves': 'the nation for which I have given my life,'

        F.   "'...where you pasture your flock': 'in the time of the pagan kingdoms?'

        G.   "'...where you make it lie down at noon': 'in the subjugation of the pagan nations?'"

        H.   "...for why should I be like one who wanders [Hebrew: veils herself] beside the flocks of your companions":

I.   R. Azariah said, "[The letters used in the word 'for why'] may be read, 'so that I may not be made as nothing in the eyes of your companions as they pasture their flocks.'

J.   "'It would be a profanation of heaven that your children should be afflicted while the flocks of your companions should be prospering.'"

K.   Said R. Yudan b. R. Simon, "It is so that the nations of the world may not say you have erred in the attribute of justice.

L.   "He knew that he wanted to slaughter them in the wilderness, and he slaughtered them in the wilderness: 'Therefore he has slain them in the wilderness' (Num. 14:16)."

M.   Rabbis say, "It is so that your children should not see that they suffer great affliction and so turn away from following you and cleave to 'the flocks of your companions':

N.   "'Shall the seat of wickedness be your companion' (Ps. 94:20)."

O.   [Continuing Berekhiah, G:] "At that moment, said the Holy One, blessed be He, to Moses, 'Moses, you say to me, "where you pasture your flock, where you make it lie down at noon"! By your life, if you do not know, in the end you will know: "If you do not know, O fairest among women, [follow in the tracks of the flock, and pasture your kids beside the shepherds' tents]' (Song 1:8).

8

Song of Songs Rabbah to Song of Songs 1:8

1:8   *If you do not know,*
O fairest among women,
follow in the tracks of the flock,
and pasture your kids
beside the shepherds' tents.

VIII.i

1.   A.   Another interpretation of the verse, "If you do not know, O fairest among women, [follow in the tracks of the flock, and pasture your kids beside the shepherds' tents]":

B.   "Fairest among women" – fairest among the prophets,
C.   most eminent among the prophets.
   2.   A.   Said R. Yosé b. R. Jeremiah, "How come the prophets are compared to women?
     B.   "It is to tell you, just as a woman is not ashamed to demand what her house needs from her husband,
     C.   "so the prophets are not ashamed to demand the needs of the Israelites from their Father who is in heaven."
3.   A.   "...follow in the tracks of the flock":
B.   R. Eliezer, R. Aqiba, and rabbis:
C.   R. Eliezer says, "From the cakes that the Israelites had taken along from Egypt they eat for thirty-one days."
     D.   For said R. Shila, "Sixty-two meals, you may know, the Israelites had from these cakes."
E.   [Resuming C:] "[From this you may know] what I am going to do for them in the end, at the conclusion.
F.   "That is in line with this verse: 'There shall be provision of grain in the land' (Ps. 72:16)." [Simon, p. 64, n. 3: This was the answer to Moses' doubts about providing for Israel in the desert: since I caused a miracle whereby one cake lasted so long, you may rest assured that I can provide for all their wants – in the wilderness and in the Messianic era.]
G.   R. Aqiba says, "From the way in which I surrounded them with clouds of glory, in line with this verse, 'And the Lord went before them by day...the pillar of cloud departed not by day' (Ex. 13:21, 22), you may know what I am going to do for them in the end, at the conclusion.
H.   "That is in line with this verse: 'And there shall be a pavilion for shade in the daytime' (Isa. 4:6)."
I.   Rabbis say, "'From the way in which I fed them in the wilderness [which was through manna,] sweeter than milk and honey, you may know what I am going to do for them in the end, at the conclusion.'
J.   "That is in line with this verse: 'And it shall come to pass in that day that the mountains shall drop down sweet wine' (Joel 4:18)."

VIII:ii

1.   A.   Another interpretation of the verse, "follow in the tracks of the flock, [and pasture your kids beside the shepherds' tents]":
B.   [God] said to him, "In the end the entire flock will go forth [to death], but you will go forth at the end."
C.   And it is not that Moses tarried, but when the Israelites were busy with the spoil [of Egypt], Moses was busy with the religious duty involving the bones of Joseph.

D.   That is in line with this verse: "And Moses took the bones of Joseph with him" (Ex. 13:19).

2.   A.   Another interpretation of the verse, follow in the tracks of the flock, [and pasture your kids beside the shepherds' tents]":

B.   [God] said to him, "In the end the generation will die, and you will be no different from them."

3.   A.   How come this came about?

B.   R. Samuel b. R. Nahman said, "It was on account of the bush."

C.   For said R. Samuel b. R. Nahman, "All the seven days at the bush, the Holy One, blessed be He, was enticing Moses to go on his mission to Egypt:

D.   "'And Moses said to the Lord, Oh Lord, I am not a man of words, neither in the yesterday nor the day before nor since you have spoken to your servant' (Ex. 4:10).

E.   "Lo, that statement encompasses six days, and the day on which the conversation took place makes seven in all.

F.   "And at the end, to the Holy One, blessed be He, he said, '"Send, I pray you, by the hand of the one whom you will send"' (Ex. 4:10).

G.   "Said to him the Holy One, blessed be He, 'By your life, I shall bind this up for you in your garment. [I shall exact a penalty from you for your conduct here.]'"

4.   A.   And when did the Holy One, blessed be He, exact that penalty?

B.   R. Berekhiah, R. Helbo, and R. Levi:

C.   One said, "During all the seven days of the consecration [of the priesthood], he served as high priest, thinking that the office was his. At the end it was said to him, 'It is not yours, it is Aaron's, your brother's!' 'And it came to pass on the eighth day that Moses called Aaron' (Lev. 9:1)."

D.   R. Helbo said, "All the seven days of Adar [forty years after the exodus,] Moses was appealing and begging before the Holy One, blessed be He, to let him enter the land. At the end he said to him, 'But you will not cross this Jordan' (Dt. 3:27).

5.   A.   "...and pasture your kids":

B.   He said to him, "The kids will enter the land, the old goats won't."

6.   A.   "...beside the shepherds' tents":

B.   Said to him the Holy One, blessed be He, "I shall tell you how long you will take care of my people: 'beside the shepherds' tents.'

C.   "[Since the words for shepherds and wicked use the same consonants, the meaning is this:] "up to these thorns, that is, until you reach the land of the evil and wicked, that is, Sihon and Og."

9

Song of Songs Rabbah to Song of Songs 1:9

1:9   *I compare you, my love,*
       to a mare of Pharaoh's chariots.

IX:i

1.   A.   "I compare you, my love, to a mare of Pharaoh's chariots":
      B.   R. Pappias interpreted the verse, "'But he is at one with himself, and who can turn him' (Job 23:13):
      C.   "He judges on his own everyone who passes through the world, and none can answer the rulings of the One who spoke and brought the world into being."
      D.   Said to him R. Aqiba, "It would have been enough for you, Pappias, [not to claim that he rules all alone, which is not true, but only] to say that none can answer the rulings of the One who spoke and brought the world into being. For all is done in truth, and all is done in justice.
      E.   "For so it is written, 'I saw the Lord sitting upon a throne high and lifted up' (Isa. 6:1)."
            F.   Said R. Simon, "It is the throne that distinguishes between life and death."
      G.   [Continuing E:] "'And all the host of heaven were standing by him on his right hand and on his left' (1 Kgs. 22:19).
      H.   "Now is there such a thing as left on high? And is not everything on the right? 'Your right hand, O Lord, glorious in power, your right hand, O Lord, dashes in pieces the enemy' (Ex. 15:6).
      I.   "Why then does Scripture refer to 'his right hand and his left'?
      J.   "But these favor the right, those the left, meaning, these favor acquittal, those a verdict of guilty."
            2.   A.   R. Yohanan in the name of R. Aha derived proof for the same proposition [that God does not judge all by himself] from the following: "And the word was true, even a great host' (Dan. 10:1).

    B. "True is the ruling when a great host is formed."

3. A. That [same proposition, namely, that God does not judge all by himself] is in line with this verse: "But the Lord God is true" (Jer. 10:10).

    B. What is the meaning of the word "true"?

    C. Said R. Ibun, "It means that he is the living God and eternal king."

    D. Said R. Eleazar, "Every passage in which it is said, 'and the Lord' refers to him and his court.

    E. "And the generative analogy governing all of them is as follows: 'And the Lord has spoken evil concerning you' (1 Kgs. 22:23). [Here there is an explicit reference to the host of heaven standing by him, as at 1 Kgs. 22:19: 'And all the host of heaven were standing by him on his right hand and on his left.']

    F. "That is the generative analogy governing all of them."

4. A. Now how does R. Eleazar interpret this verse of Scripture that is cited by R. Pappias, "But he is at one with himself, and who can turn him'" (Job 23:13)?

    B. He alone seals the fate of all those who pass through the world, and no other creature seals the document with him.

5. A. What is the seal of the Holy One, blessed be He?

    B. R. Bibi in the name of R. Reuben said, "It is truth: 'Howbeit I will declare to you that which is inscribed in the writing of truth' (Dan. 10:21).

    C. "If 'truth' why then 'writing,' and if 'writing,' then why 'truth'? [Simon, p. 67, n. 4: (truth is) something written, but not necessarily decided upon].

    D. "But until the document is sealed, it is merely written. When it has been sealed, then the decree is a judgment of truth."

6. A. Said R. Simeon b. Laqish, "And why is it 'truth'?

        B.   "Since the Hebrew word for truth consists of the letters A, M, and T, the word bears the A at the head of the alphabet, the M in the middle, and the T at the end.

        C.   "This then conveys the message, 'I am the first and I am the Last and besides me there is no god' (Isa. 44:6).

        D.   "'I am the first': 'I did not receive my dominion from anybody else.'

        E.   "'I am the last': 'I am not going to give it over to anybody else, there being no other.'

        F.   "'...and besides me there is no god': 'I have no second.'"

7.   A.   [=Genesis Rabbah XXI:V.1] [Concerning the verse, "Behold, the man has become like one of us" (Gen. 3:22),] R. Pappias interpreted the verse as follows: "'Behold, the man has become like one of us' means, like the unique one of the world."

      B.   Said to him R. Aqiba, "That is enough from you, Pappias."

      C.   He said to him, "Then how do you interpret the word, 'like one of us'?"

      D.   He said to him, "Like one of the ministering angels."

      E.   And sages say, "Not in accord with the position of this one, nor in accord with the position of that one. But it teaches the following:

      F.   "The Holy One, blessed be He, set before him two paths, life and death, and he chose the 'other path,' [that of heresy, hence death] and he abandoned the path of life." [Freedman, Genesis Rabbah, p. 175, n. 1: That which God did not wish him to choose, that is, death. "Behold the man has become as one who knows good and evil of himself, of his own free will, and thereby has himself chosen the path of death."]

8.   A.   R. Pappias interpreted the verse, "'Thus they exchanged their glory for the likeness of an ox that eats grass' (Ps. 106:20).

      B.   "Shall I infer that it speaks of the ox that is on high? Scripture says, 'that eats grass.'"

    C.   Said to him R. Aqiba, "That's enough for you, Pappias."

    D.   He said to him, "And how do you interpret the language, 'Thus they exchanged their glory for the likeness of an ox that eats grass' (Ps. 106:20)?"

    E.   "Might it mean, like an ordinary ox? Scripture says, 'that eats grass.'

    F.   "Now as a matter of fact, you have nothing so degraded or disgusting as an ox when it is eating grass."

    9. A. R. Yudan in the name of R. Aha said, "The magicians of Egypt did their enchantments, so that it appeared to be dancing before them.

        B. "That sense of the letters translated dancing occurs in this verse: 'Damascus has gotten weak, she turns around to flee, and trembling [using the same consonants] has seized her' (Jer. 49:24)."

10.   A.   R. Pappias interpreted the verse, "'I compare you, my love, to a mare of Pharaoh's chariots':

       B.   "What is written is, 'at my rejoicing' [since the same letters translated 'to a mare' can be given vowels to make the word read, 'at my rejoicing].'

       C.   "Said the Holy One, blessed be He, 'Just as I rejoiced at the fall of the Egyptians at the sea, so I would have rejoiced to destroy the Israelites. But what saved them?

       D.   "'It was "at their right hand and at their left"' (Ex. 14:22: 'And the waters were a wall to them at their right hand and at their left').

       E.   "That is, it was on account of the merit of the Torah, that they were destined to receive from the right hand of the Holy One, blessed be He, as it is said, 'At his right hand was a fiery law to them' (Dt. 33:2).

       F.   "'...and at their left': this refers to the mezuzah.

       G.   "Another explanation of 'at their right hand and at their left':

       H.   "'at their right hand': this is the recitation of the Shema.

       I.   "'...and at their left': this is the Prayer Said Standing."

       J.   Said to him R. Aqiba, "That is enough from you, Pappias! In every other passage in which the word 'rejoicing' appears, it is written with a sin, but here with a samekh [two different letters with an S-sound]."

       K.   He said to him, "And how do you interpret, 'I compare you, my love, to a mare of Pharaoh's chariots'?"

       L.   [Aqiba said to him,] "Pharaoh rode on a male horse, and, as it were, the Holy One, blessed be He, appeared to him on a male horse: 'And he rode upon a cherub and flew' (Ps. 18:11).

       M.   "Said Pharaoh, 'In a battle this male horse can kill its master. Now I'm going to ride on a female horse': ''I compare you, my love, to a mare of Pharaoh's chariots.'

N.   "Then Pharaoh went and mounted a red horse, a white horse, a black horse, so the Holy One, blessed be He, as it were, revealed himself on a red, white, and black horse too: 'You have trodden the sea with your horses' (Hab. 3:15), that is, horses of various kinds.

O.   "The wicked Pharaoh came forth wearing a breastplate and helmet, so the Holy One, blessed be He, as it were, revealed himself wearing a breastplate and helmet: 'And he put on righteousness as a coat of mail' (Isa. 59:17).

P.   "The former brought forth naphtha [for chemical warfare], so the Holy One, blessed be He, as it were, did the same: 'his thick clouds passed with hailstones and coals of fire' (Ps. 18:13).

Q.   "He brought forth catapult stones, so the Holy One, blessed be He, as it were, did the same: 'And the Lord sent forth thunder and hail' (Ex. 19:23).

R.   "He produced swords and lances, so the Holy One, blessed be He, as it were, did the same: 'He shot forth lightnings' (Ps. 18:15).

S.   "He brought forth arrows, so the Holy One, blessed be He, as it were, did the same: 'And he sent out his arrows' (Ps. 18:15)."

T.   Said R. Levi, "'He sent out his arrows and scattered them' (Ps. 18:15): the arrows scattered them.

U.   "'...and he shot forth lightnings and discomfited them': this teaches that they threw them into confusion.

V.   "He confused them, frightened them, and took away their standards, so that they did not know what they were doing."

W.   [Reverting to S and Aqiba's exposition:] "Pharaoh came forth in full armor, so the Holy One, blessed be He, as it were, did the same: 'The Lord will go forth as a mighty man' (Isa. 42:13).

X.   "He thundered with his voice, so the Holy One, blessed be He, as it were, did the same: 'The Lord thundered down from heaven' (2 Sam. 22:14).

Y.   "He made his voice loud, so the Holy One, blessed be He, as it were, did the same: 'And the Most High gave forth his voice' (2 Sam. 22:14).

Z.   "Pharaoh came forth in fury, so the Holy One, blessed be He, as it were, did the same: 'You march through the earth in indication' (Hab. 3:12).

AA. "'...with a bow.' So, as it were: 'You uncover fully your bow' (Hab. 3:9).

BB. "'...with shield and buckler.' So, as it were: 'Take hold of shield and buckler' (Hab. 3:9).

CC. "'...with flashing spear.' So, as it were: 'at the shining of your glittering spear' (Hab. 3:11)."

11. A. R. Berekhiah in the name of R. Samuel b. R. Nahman: "When Pharaoh had used up all his weapons, the Holy One, blessed be He, began to exalt himself over him.

   B. "He said to him, 'Wicked one! Do you have the winds? Do you have the cherubim? Do you have wings?'

12. A. And whence did the Holy One, blessed be He, launch them?

   B. Said R. Yudan, "It was from between the wheels of his chariot.

   C. "The Holy One, blessed be He, loosened them and threw them onto the sea."

13. A. Said R. Hanina b. R. Papa, "A mortal who rides on his burden is on something tangible.

   B. "But the Holy One, blessed be He, is not that way.

   C. "He carries his chariot and rides on that which is ineffable: 'And he rode upon a cherub and did fly, yes, he swooped down on the wings of the wind' (Ps. 18:11)."

14. A. [Supply: "And he rode upon a cherub and did fly, yes, he swopped down on the wings of the wind" (Ps. 18:11):]

   B. One version says, "he swooped," and another version reads, "he was seen" (2 Sam. 22:11) [both versions using some of the same consonants but exchanging the D and R, which are similar in appearance].

   C. How are the two versions to be reconciled?

   D. Said R. Aha, "On this basis we learn that the Holy One, blessed be He, had other worlds, and he went forth to make his appearance in them too."

IX:ii

1. A. "I compare you, my love, [to a mare of Pharaoh's chariots]":

   B. Said R. Eliezer, "The matter may be compared to the case of a princess who was kidnapped, and her father was ready to redeem her.

C.   "But she gave indications to the kidnappers, saying to them, 'I am yours, I belong to you, and I am going after you.'

D.   "Said her father to her, 'What are you thinking? Is it that I do not have the power to redeem you? I would have you hold your peace [using the same word as 'compare you'], yes, be silent.'

E.   "So when the Israelites were encamped at the sea, 'and the Egyptians pursued after them and overtook them in camp by the sea' (Ex. 14:9),

F.   "the Israelites, fearful, gave indicates to the Egyptians, saying to them, 'We are yours, we belong to you, and we are going after you.'

G.   "Said to them the Holy One, blessed be He, 'What are you thinking? Is it that I do not have the power to redeem you?

H.   "For the word 'I have compared you' [bears consonants that yield the meaning,] 'I made you silent.'

I.   "Thus: 'The Lord will fight for you, and you will hold your peace' (Ex. 14:14)."

2.   A.   Another explanation of the verse, "I compare you, my love, to a mare of Pharaoh's chariots":

B.   Rabbis say, "Since the Israelites were like mares and the wicked Egyptians like males in heat,

C.   "they ran after them until they sunk down in the sea."

D.   Said R. Simon, "God forbid that the Israelites should be compared to mares!

E.   "But the waves of the ocean appeared like mares, and the Egyptians were like stallions in heat, so they ran after them until they sunk down in the sea.

F.   "The Egyptian said to his horse, 'Yesterday I tried to lead you to the Nile, and you would not follow me, but now you are drowning me in the sea.

G.   "And the horse said to its rider, 'He has thrown me in the sea' (Ex. 14:10) – [the several consonants being read as individual words, altogether] meaning, see what is in the sea. An orgy [so Simon] has been made ready for you in the sea."

3.   A.   R. Ishmael taught on Tannaite authority, "'And the Lord overthrew the Egyptians in the midst of the sea' (Ex. 14:27):

B.   "this teaches that the horse threw its rider up, and he came down with the horse on top."

C.   Said R. Levi, "It is like turning a dish over, so that what is at the bottom is on top, and what is on top is on the bottom."

IX:iii

1.   A.   "[I compare you,] my love, [to a mare of Pharaoh's chariots]":

B. What is the meaning of "my love"?

C. Said R. Jonathan, "The one who feeds me, those who feed me two daily whole-offerings each day: 'The one lamb shall you offer in the morning' (Num. 28:4)."

  2. A. For said R. Judah b. R. Simon, "The Israelites would offer two daily whole-offerings every day, one in the morning, one at dusk.

  B. "The one offered in the morning was presented for the transgressions that had been done overnight, and the one at dusk for the transgressions that had been done through the day.

  C. "So no one would ever spend the night in Jerusalem subject to transgression that he might have done [since day and night these were expiated]: 'Righteousness lodged in her' (Isa. 1:21)."

3. A. Another explanation of "I compare you, my love, [to a mare of Pharaoh's chariots]":

B. Rabbis say, "The shepherds of my world, who have accepted my Torah.

C. "For had you not accepted it, I should have made my world revert to formlessness and void."

  4. A. For said R. Hanina in the name of R. Aha, "'When the earth and all the inhabitants thereof are dissolved, I myself establish the pillars of it, selah' (Ps. 75:4).

  B. "Were it not that the Israelites had stood at Mount Sinai and said, 'We shall do and we shall obey' (Ex. 24:7), the world would have melted and reverted to formlessness and void.

  C. "And who laid the foundations for the world? 'When the earth and all the inhabitants thereof are dissolved, I myself establish the pillars of it, selah' (Ps. 75:4).

  D. "This is as if to say, 'on account of 'I am the Lord your God' (Ex. 20:1), 'I myself establish the pillars of it, selah' (Ps. 75:4)."

10

Song of Songs Rabbah to
Song of Songs 1:10

1:10   *Your cheeks are comely with ornaments,*
        your neck with strings of jewels.

X:i

1. A. "Your cheeks are comely with ornaments":
    B. just as the cheeks are created only for speech, so Moses and Aaron were created only for speech.
    C. "...your neck with strings [of jewels]":
    D. [since the words for jewels and the word for strings use the same consonants, the sense is,] with the two Torahs, the Torah that is in writing and the Torah that is in memory.

2. A. Another interpretation of "[your neck] with strings [of jewels]":
    B. with many Torahs: "This is the Torah of the burnt-offering" (Lev. 6:2); "this is the Torah of the sin-offering" (Lev. 7:1); "this is the Torah of the peace-offering" (Lev. 7:11); "this is the Torah when a man shall die in a tent" (Num. 19:14).

3. A. Another explanation of "with strings":
    B. with two ornaments [a word using the same consonants],
    C. with two brothers, speaking of Moses and of Aaron,
    D. who treat each other with a gracious demeanor.
    E. This one took pleasure in the achievements of that one, and that one took pleasure in the achievements of this one.

    4. A. Said R. Phineas, "'And he shall be your spokesman to the people, and it shall come to pass that he shall serve you as a mouth, and you shall serve him as God (Ex. 4:16).
        B. "['Mouth':] means, public interpreter.
        C. "'...and you shall serve him as God': was Moses turned into Aaron's idol, that you say, 'and you shall serve him as God' (Ex. 4:16)?
        D. "But this is what the Holy One, blessed be He, said to Moses, 'Moses, just as reverence for me is upon you, so reverence for you will be upon your brother.'
        E. "But he did not act in that way.

F. "Rather: 'Moses and Aaron went and gathered together all the elders of the children of Israel. And Aaron spoke all the words' (Ex. 4:29-30).

G. "He put shoulder to shoulder, for even now this one took pleasure in the achievements of that one, and that one took pleasure in the achievements of this one.

H. "And whence in Scripture do we know that Aaron took pleasure in the achievements of Moses?

I. "'And also, behold, he comes to meet you, and when he sees you, he will be glad in his heart' (Ex. 4:14).'"

5. A. Taught on Tannaite authority R. Simeon b. Yohai, "The heart that rejoiced for the achievements of Moses his brother will don the Urim and Thummim:

B. "'And you shall put on the breastplate of judgment the Urim and the Thummim, and they shall be upon Aaron's heart' (Ex. 28:30)."

6. A. [Continuing 4.I:] "And how do we know from Scripture that Moses took pleasure in the achievements of Aaron?

B. "'Like the precious oil upon the head, coming down upon the beard; Aaron's beard' (Ps. 133:2)."

7. A. [Supply: "Like the precious oil upon the head, coming down upon the beard; Aaron's beard" (Ps. 133:2):]

B. Said R. Aha, "Now did Aaron have two beards, that Scripture says, 'upon the beard; Aaron's beard'?

C. "But when Moses saw the anointing oil dripping down Aaron's beard, it seemed to him as thought it were dripping down his own beard, and he took pleasure, thus: 'upon the beard; Aaron's beard.'"

X:ii

1. A. "...your neck with strings of jewels":

B. This refers to the seventy members of the sanhedrin who were strung out after them [Moses and Aaron] like a string of pearls.

2. A. Another explanation of the phrase, "your neck with strings of jewels":

B. This refers to this refers to those who teach Scripture and repeat Mishnah, instructing children in good faith.

C. "...your neck with strings of jewels" refers to children.

3. A. Another explanation of the verse, "Your cheeks are comely with ornaments":

B.   This refers to the rabbis.

C.   "...your neck with strings of jewels":

D.   This refers to the disciples, who strain their necks to hear the teachings of the Torah from their mouth,

E.   like someone who has never heard teachings of the Torah in his entire life.

4.   A.   Another explanation of the verse, "Your cheeks are comely with ornaments":

B.   when they pronounce the law with one another, for instance, R. Abba b. R. Qomi and his colleagues.

C.   "...your neck with strings of jewels":

D.   When they make connections among teachings of the Torah, then go on and make connections between teachings of the Torah and teachings of the prophets, teachings of the Prophets and teachings of the Writings, and fire flashes around them, then the words rejoice as when they were given from mount Sinai.

E.   For the principal point at which they were given was at Mount Sinai with fire: "And the mountain burned with fire to the heart of heaven" (Dt. 4:11).

5.   A.   Ben Azzai was sitting and expounding, and fire burned all around him.

B.   They went and told R. Aqiba, "My lord, Ben Azzai is sitting and expounding, and fire is burning all around him."

C.   He went to him and said to him, "I have heard that you are expounding, and fire is burning all around you."

D.   He said to him, "True."

E.   He said to him, "Is it possible that you have been occupied with the deepest mysteries of the Chariot?"

F.   He said to him, "Not at all. I was in session and making connections among teachings of the Torah, then going on and making connections between teachings of the Torah and teachings of the prophets, teachings of the Prophets and teachings of the Writings, so fire flashed around them, and the words rejoiced as when they were given from mount Sinai.

G.   "For is not the principal point at which they were given was at Mount Sinai with fire: 'And the mountain burned with fire to the heart of heaven' (Dt. 4:11)?"

6.   A.   R. Abbahu was in session and expounding, and fire burned all around him.

B.   He thought, "Is it possible that I am not making connections among teachings of the Torah as is required for them?"

C. For R. Simeon b. Laqish said, "There are those who know how to make connections among words of Torah, but do not know how to penetrate inside of them, and those who know how to penetrate into the depths of the teachings but do not know how to make connections. But I am expert at both making connections and also getting at the heart of matters."

X:iii

1. A. Another explanation of the verse, "Your cheeks are comely with ornaments":
   B. When people publicly recite teachings of the Torah in their proper turn:
   C. teachings of the laws of Passover on Passover, the laws of Pentecost on Pentecost, the laws of Tabernacles on Tabernacles,
   D. [in line with the meaning of the letters of the word for ornaments as in this verse,] "now when the *turn* of every maiden had come" (Est. 3:12).

2. A. "...your neck with strings of jewels":
   B. R. Levi in the name of R. Hama b. R. Hanina said, "This refers to the lections of the Torah, which are connected to one another, lead on to one another, or leap from one to the other, or exhibit parallels to one another, or are related to one another."
   C. Said R. Menahema, "For example, the following:
   D. "'To these the land shall be divided for an inheritance' (Num. 26:53), followed by, 'Then the daughters of Zelophehad came near' (Num. 27:1); so too: 'The daughters of Zelophehad speak rightly' (Num. 27:7), followed by 'Get you up to this mountain of Abarim' (Num. 27:12).
   E. "What has one thing to do with the next?
   F. "Once the land had been divided, the daughters of Zelophehad came to take their share from Moses, and Moses recused himself from their case: 'And Moses brought their case before the Lord' (Num. 27:5).
   G. "Said to him the Holy One, blessed be He, 'Moses, from their case you recuse yourself, but from my presence you cannot recuse yourself: 'Get you up to this mountain of Abarim.'
   H. "He said before him, 'Lord of the world, since you remove me from the world, at least let me know what sort of leaders you are going to provide for the Israelites!'

I. "Said to him the Holy One, blessed be He, 'Moses, concerning my children you have to have commandments, and concerning the work of my hands do you presume to command me? Instead of giving me instructions concerning my children, give instructions to my children concerning me!'

J. "That is in line with this verse: 'Command the children of Israel and say to them' (Num. 28:2)."

3. A. [Supply: "Command the children of Israel and say to them" (Num. 28:2):]

B. The matter provokes a parable: to what may it be compared?

C. To the case of a queen who was departing from this life. She said to him, "By the life of my lord, the king, I command you concerning my children!"

D. He said to her, "Instead of giving me orders concerning my children, give my children orders concerning me!"

E. So when Moses said before the Holy One, blessed be He, "Lord of the world, since you remove me from the world, at least let me know what sort of leaders you are going to provide for the Israelites!"

F. [Supply: Said to him the Holy One, blessed be He, "Moses, concerning my children you have to have commandments, and concerning the work of my hands do you presume to command me? Instead of giving me instructions concerning my children, give instructions to my children concerning me!" That is in line with this verse: "Command the children of Israel and say to them" (Num. 28:2).

11

Song of Songs Rabbah to Song of Songs 1:11

1:11   *We will make you ornaments of gold,*
        studded with silver.

XI:i

1.   A.   "We will make you ornaments of gold":
     B.   this refers to the spoil at the Sea.
     C.   "...studded with silver":
     D.   this refers to the spoil of Egypt.

2.   A.   Just as there is a difference between silver and gold, so there is greater value assigned to the money gotten at the Sea than the spoil of Egypt.
     B.   For it is said, "And you came with ornaments upon ornaments" (Ez. 16:7):
     C.   "...ornaments" refers to the spoil of Egypt.
     D.   "...upon ornaments" refers to the spoil at the Sea.

3.   A.   Another interpretation of "We will make you ornaments of gold":
     B.   this refers to the Torah, which Onqelos, the nephew of Hadrian, learned.
     C.   "...studded with silver":
     D.   R. Abba b. R. Kahana said, "These are the letters."
     E.   R. Aha said, "These are the words."

4.   A.   Another interpretation of "We will make you ornaments of gold":
     B.   this is the writing.
     C.   "...studded with silver":
     D.   this is the ruled lines.

5.   A.   Another interpretation of "We will make you ornaments of gold":
     B.   this refers to the tabernacle: "And you shall overlay the boards with gold" (Ex. 26:29).
     C.   "...studded with silver":
     D.   "The hooks of the pillars and their fillets shall be silver" (Ex. 27:10).

6.   A.   R. Berekhiah interpreted the verse to speak of the ark:
     B.   "'We will make you ornaments of gold':
     C.   "this refers to the ark, as it is said, 'And you shall overlay it with pure gold' (Ex. 25:11).
     D.   "'...studded with silver':

E.   "this refers to the two pillars that stand before it, which were made of silver, like columns of a balcony."

7.   A.   How was the ark made?

B.   R. Hanina and R. Simeon b. Laqish:

C.   R. Hanina said, "They made three arks, two of gold, one of wood.

D.   "He put the one of wood around the one of gold, and the other one of gold around the one of wood, and covered its upper rims with gold."

E.   "R. Simeon b. Laqish said, "They made one ark and covered it on the inside and on the outside: 'within and without you shall overlay it' (Ex. 25:11)."

F.   How does R. Hanina deal with the verse invoked by R. Simeon b. Laqish?

G.   "Said R. Phineas, "They put an overlay in the spaces between the boards."

8.   A.   Judah, the son of Rabbi says, "'Your cheeks are comely with ornaments':

B.   "this refers to the Torah.

C.   "'...your neck with strings of jewels': this refers to the prophets.

D.   "'We will make you ornaments of gold':

E.   "this refers to the Writings.

F.   "'...studded with silver':

G.   "this refers to the Song of Songs,

H.   " something complete and finished off."

12

Song of Songs Rabbah to Song of Songs 1:12

1:12   *While the king was on his couch,*
my nard gave forth its fragrance.

XII:i

1.   A.   "While the king was on his couch, [my nard gave forth its fragrance]":

B.   R. Meir and R. Judah:

C.   R. Meir says, "'While the king,' the King of kings of kings, the Holy One, blessed be He, 'was on his couch,' in the firmament, ['my nard gave forth its fragrance'], the Israelites gave forth a bad odor, saying to the calf, 'These are your Gods, O Israel' (Ex. 32:4)."

D. Said to him R. Judah, "Enough for you, Meir. The Song of Songs is to be interpreted not to the disadvantage, but only to the glory [of Israel].

E. "For the Song of Songs has been given only for the glory of Israel.

F. "Then what is the meaning of, 'While the king was on his couch, [my nard gave forth its fragrance]'?

G. "'While the king,' the King of kings of kings, the Holy One, blessed be He, 'was on his couch,' in the firmament, ['my nard gave forth its fragrance'], the Israelites gave forth a good fragrance before Mount Sinai, saying, 'All that the Lord has said we will do and obey' (Ex. 24:7)."

H. The position of R. Meir is that "my bad spice" gave its smell.

I. [Simon, verbatim, p. 77:] Only a tradition was brought by Israel from the Babylonian captivity which they transmitted, that God [in writing the Torah] skipped over the incident of the calf and wrote first the construction of the Tabernacle. [Simon, p. 77, n. 4: This remark seems to be inserted in order to show why on R. Meir's theory the account of the calf does not follow immediately on the account of the giving of the Torah, but is separated from it by the description of the Tabernacle.]

2. A. R. Eliezer, R. Aqiba, and R. Berekhiah:

B. R. Eliezer says, "'While the King' of kings of kings, the Holy One, blessed be He, 'was on his couch,' in the firmament, ['my nard gave forth its fragrance'], Mount Sinai was already sending up pillars of smoke: 'And the mountain was burning with fire' (Dt. 4:11)."

C. R. Aqiba says, "'While the King' of kings of kings, the Holy One, blessed be He, 'was on his couch,' in the firmament, ['my nard gave forth its fragrance'], 'already the glory of the Lord abode upon Mount Sinai' (Ex. 24:16)."

D. R. Berekhiah says, "While Moses, who was called king as in the following, 'And there was a king in Jeshurun when the heads of the people were gathered' (Dt. 33:5) 'was at his couch' in the heaven, already 'God spoke all these words' (Ex. 20:1)."

3. A. R. Eliezer b. Jacob and Rabbis:

B. R. Eliezer b. Jacob says, "'While the King' of kings of kings, the Holy One, blessed be He, 'was on his couch,' in the firmament, ['my nard gave forth its fragrance'], Michael, the great prince, had already come down, from heaven and saved Abraham, our father, from the fiery furnace."

C.   And Rabbis say, "The Omnipresent, may he be blessed, came down and saved him personally: 'I am the Lord who brought you out of Ur of the Chaldees' (Gen. 15:7).

      D.   "Then when did Michael come down?

      E.   "It was in the time of Hananiah, Mishael, and Azariah."

      F.   Said R. Tabiyomi, "When Jacob, our father, was still reclining on his couch, the Holy Spirit sparkled upon him and he said to his sons, '"God will be with you"' (Gen. 48:21).

      G.   "He said to them, 'He is destined to bring his Divine Presence to rest among you.'"

4.   A.   Said R. Nahman, "It is written, 'And Israel journeyed with all that he had and came to Beer-sheba' (Gen. 46:1).

      B.   "Where was he going?

      C.   "He went down to cut down the cedars that Abraham, our father, had planted in Beer-sheba: 'And he planted a grove in Beer-sheba' (Gen. 21:33)."

5.   A.   Said R. Levi, "'And the middle bar in the midst of the boards' (Ex. 26:28):

      B.   "The bar was thirty-two cubits.

      C.   "And how at that moment could they get one?

      D.   "This teaches that they had been stored up with them from the time of Jacob, our father: 'And every man with whom was found with him acacia wood' (Ex. 36:24).

      E.   "What is written is not 'was found' but 'was found with him,' meaning, from the beginning."

6.   A.   Said R. Levi b. R. Hiyya, "In Magdala of the Dyers [near Tiberias] they cut them down and took them down with them to Egypt.

      B.   "The wood contained no knots or cracks."

7.   A.   There were some acacia trees in Magdala, and the people treated them as prohibited, on account of the sanctity inhering in the ark.

      B.   They came and asked R. Hanania, associate of the Rabbis, who said to them, "Do not change the custom that you have received from your forebears."

XII:ii

1. A. R. Phineas in the name of R. Hoshaia said, "'While the king,' the King of kings of kings, the Holy One, blessed be He, 'was on his couch,' in the firmament, ['my nard gave forth its fragrance'], he had already anticipated [his descent on Mount Sinai] [Simon, p. 79, n. 4: by enveloping the mountain in flames and smoke],

   B. "thus: 'And it came to pass on the third day, while it was yet morning, that there were thunders...upon the mount' (Ex. 19:16)."

2. A. It may be compared to the case of a king who decreed, "On such and such a day, I shall enter town. The townsfolk slept all night, so when the king came and found them sleeping, he had the trumpets and horns sounded.

   B. The prince of that town woke the people up and brought them forth to receive the king.

   C. The king walked before them until he reached his palace.

   D. Thus the Holy One, blessed be He, anticipated [his descent on Mount Sinai]: "And it came to pass on the third day, while it was yet morning, that there were thunders...upon the mount" (Ex. 19:16).

   E. But prior: "For the third day the Lord will come down in the sight of all the people" (Ex. 19:11).

   F. The Israelites had been sleeping all that night, for the sleep of Pentecost is very pleasant, and the night is brief.

      G. R. Yudan said, "Not a flea bit them."

   H. Came the Holy One, blessed be He, and found them sleeping. So he had the trumpets and horns sounded.

   I. That is in line with this verse: "And it came to pass on the third day, while it was yet morning, that there were thunders...upon the mount" (Ex. 19:16).

   J. Moses woke up the Israelites and brought them forth to receive the King of kings of kings, the Holy One, blessed be He: "And Moses brought the people forth to meet God" (Ex. 19:17).

   K. The Holy One went before them until he came to Mount Sinai: "Now Mount Sinai was entirely in smoke" (Ex. 19:18).

      L. Said R. Isaac, "This is why he criticized them through Isaiah: 'Wherefore when I came was there no man? When I called, there was no one to answer? Is my hand shortened at all, that it cannot redeem' (Isa. 50:2)."

3. A. [Supply: "While the king was on his couch, [my nard gave forth its fragrance]":] Said R. Yudan, "While Hezekiah and his comrades were eating their Passover-offerings in Jerusalem, the Holy One, blessed be He, had already anticipated [their deliverance] on that same night:

B. "'And it came to pass that night that the angel of the Lord went forth and smote in the camp of the Assyrians' (2 Kgs. 19:35)."

4.   A. [Supply: "While the king was on his couch, [my nard gave forth its fragrance]":] Said R. Abbahu, "While Moses and Israel were eating their Passover-offerings in Egypt, the Holy One, blessed be He, had already anticipated [their deliverance] on that same night:

B. "'And it came to pass at midnight that the Lord smote all the firstborn in the land of Egypt' (Ex. 12:29)."

5.   A. Then it is the position of R. Abbahu that "my nard gave forth its fragrance" bears a negative meaning: "my bad spice gave forth its stink," for the smell of the blood was bad, but God brought them a good scent of the spices of paradise.

B. So that made them want to eat.

C. They said to him, "Our lord, Moses, give us something to eat."

D. Said to them Moses, "Thus has the Holy One, blessed be He, said to me, 'No foreigner will eat of it' (Ex. 12:43)."

E. They went and put out the gentiles who were among them, and that made them want to eat.

F. They said to him, "Our lord, Moses, give us something to eat."

G. He said to them, "Thus has the Holy One, blessed be He, said to me, 'And every man's servant, bought for money, when you have circumcised him, shall eat thereof' (Ex. 12:44)."

H. So they went and circumcised their servants, and that made them want to eat.

I. They said to him, "Our lord, Moses, give us something to eat."

J. He said to them, "Thus has the Holy One, blessed be He, said to me, 'No uncircumcised persons shall eat of it' (Ex. 12:48)."

K. Thereupon everyone put his sword on his thigh and circumcised himself.

L. Who circumcised them?

M. R. Berekhiah said, "Moses was circumcising them, Aaron was doing the trimming, and Joshua gave them what to drink."

N. Some say, "Joshua did the circumcising, Aaron did the trimming, and Moses gave them to drink.

O. "So it is written, 'At that time the Lord said to Joshua, Make knives of flint and again circumcise the children of Israel the second time' (Josh. 5:2).

P. "Why a second time? Because he was the one who had done it the first time.

Q. "Forthwith: 'Joshua made knives of flint and circumcised the children of Israel at Gibeat-haaralot' (Josh. 5:3)."

R. What is the meaning of "at Gibeat-haaralot"?

S. Rabbi said, "On this basis we learn that they made it a hill of foreskins."

13

Song of Songs Rabbah to Song of Songs 1:13

1:13   *My beloved is to me a bag of myrrh,*
that lies between my breasts.

XIII:i

1. A.   "My beloved is to me a bag of myrrh, [that lies between my breasts]":

     B.   What is the meaning of "a bag of myrrh"?

     C.   R. Azariah in the name of R. Judah interpreted the verse to speak of Abraham, our father:

     D.   "Just as myrrh is the best of all kinds of spices, so Abraham is the best of all the righteous persons.

     E.   "Just as myrrh's fragrance circulates only when brought near fire, so Abraham's deeds were known only when he was thrown into the fiery furnace. And just as whoever collects myrrh finds that his hands get sore, so Abraham afflicted himself and gave himself pain through suffering."

2. A.   "...that lies between my breasts":

     B.   For he was clasped between the Presence of God and the angel:

     C.   "And when he saw he ran to meet them" (Gen. 18:2):

     D.   "...he saw": the Presence of God.

     E.   "...he ran to meet them": the angel.

14

Song of Songs Rabbah to
Song of Songs 1:14

1:14   *My beloved is to me a cluster of*
         henna blossoms,
         in the vineyards of En-gedi.

XIV:i

1.   A.   "My beloved is to me a cluster of henna blossoms, [in the vineyards of En-gedi]":
      B.   "cluster" refers to Isaac,
      C.   who was bound on the altar like a cluster [Simon, p. 81, n. 4: he was tied to the wood as a large cluster of grapes is tied to a pole].
      D.   "...henna" [also refers to Isaac,]
      E.   who atones for the sins of Israel [the words for henna and atone use the same consonants].

2.   A.   "...in the vineyards of En-gedi":
      B.   this speaks of our father, Jacob,
      C.   who came into his father [Isaac, to steal the birthright] with a pallid face out of fear and shame, and who wore as his cloak the skin of a goat, and so took the blessings which are the eye of the world [the words for eye and goat use the same consonants as En-gedi].

LIV:ii

1.   A.   [Supply: "My beloved is to me a bag of myrrh, that lies between my breasts":]
      B.   R. Hunia in the name of R. Aha: "You have nothing more prized by a woman than a bundle of perfume.
      C.   "Where does she keep it? It is between her breasts."

2.   A.   And said R. Huna in the name of R. Simeon b. Laqish, "Said the community of Israel before the Holy One, blessed be He, 'You have afflicted the Egyptians through their first born, you have embittered their souls,
      B.   "'but as for me, "that lies between my breasts."'
      C.   "How so? An Egyptian would say to an Israelite, 'Hide this firstborn among your children,' and he would take him and hide him, but the angel would enter and smite him.
      D.   "'But as for me, he "lies between my breasts."'"

XIV:iii

1. A. [Supply: "My beloved is to me a cluster of henna blossoms, in the vineyards of En-gedi":}

   B. R. Berekhiah said, "Said the Community of Israel before the Holy One, blessed be He, 'When you pain me, when you distress me, "My beloved is mine [and I am his, he pastures his flock among the lilies]" (Song 2:16).

   C. "'You become my beloved, and you see what man there is in my midst who is so great as can say to the attribute of justice, "Enough," and you take him and make him a pledge on my behalf.'

   D. "So it is written, '[My beloved is to me] a cluster of henna blossoms, [in the vineyards of En-gedi].'"

   2. A. What is the meaning of "a cluster"?

      B. [Reading the letters of the word for cluster yields] a man in who is all:

      C. Scripture, Mishnah, Talmud, Supplements, Lore.

3. A. "...henna blossoms":

   B. who atones for the sins of Israel [the words for henna and atone use the same consonants].

4. A. "...in the vineyards of En-gedi":

   B. this [En-gedi] refers to the patriarchs of the world, who follow after you like kids and receive the blessings which are the eye of the world [the words for eye and kid use the same consonants as En-gedi].

XIV:iv

1. A. [Supply: "My beloved is to me a bag of myrrh, that lies between my breasts. My beloved is to me a cluster of henna blossoms, in the vineyards of En-gedi]":

   B. R. Yohanan interpreted the verse to speak of the kind of incense that was made by the family of Abtinus:

   C. "'...a bag of myrrh': this is one of the eleven spices that comprised that incense."

   2. A. R. Hunia said [why there were eleven], "Scripture states, 'And the Lord said to Moses, Take for you sweet spices' (Ex. 30:34): two; 'stacte and onycha and galbanum' – five; 'sweet spices' – if you say this is only two more, then this has already been said, so [read the phrase in line with the following] 'of each shall there be a like weight,' thus adding five to the former five, ten; 'with pure frankincense' – eleven.

      B. "In this connection, sages made an inquiry and found that there is nothing better for incense than these eleven spices alone."

3.   A.   "...that lies between my breasts":

      B.   [the cloud of incense] was held exactly within the two staves of the
            ark [Simon, p. 83: on the Day of Atonement when burned in the Holy
            of Holies by the High Priest].

4.   A.   "[My beloved is to me] a cluster of henna blossoms":

      B.   which atones for the sins of Israel [the words for henna and atone use
            the same consonants].

      C.   Said R. Isaac, "'Cluster' indicates that [the cloud of incense] would
            spread and ascend to the beams, and then would come down like a
            cluster [that was hanging on the vine].

      D.   "'...henna blossoms' means that it would atone for the sins of Israel
            [the words for henna and atone use the same consonants]."

      5.   A.   And said R. Isaac, "'That the cloud of incense may cover'
                  (Lev. 16:13):

            B.   "We do not know the purpose of this covering.

            C.   "But David came and explained it: 'You have forgiven
                  the iniquity of your people, you have covered all their
                  sin' (Ps. 85:3)."

6.   A.   "...in the vineyards of En-gedi":

      B.   On account of the merit of the undertakings that I made with your
            father, Abraham, between the pieces, as it is said, "On that day the
            Lord made a covenant with Abram saying" (Gen. 15:18).

      C.   The verse, "My beloved is to me a cluster of henna blossoms, in the
            vineyards of En-gedi" speaks of Abraham: "After these things the
            word of the Lord came to Abram in a vision, saying, Fear not Abram"
            (Gen. 15:1).

      7.   A.   [Supply: "After these things the word of the Lord came to
                  Abram in a vision, saying, Fear not Abram" (Gen. 15:1).]

            B.   R. Levi in the name of R. Hama said, "At that time there
                  was a measure of uncertainty.

            C.   "Who felt uncertain?

            D.   "It was Abraham, who felt uncertainty and said before
                  the Holy One, blessed be He, 'Lord of the age, you made
                  a covenant with Abraham that you would not wipe out his
                  seed from the world, and I went and collected good deeds
                  before you, so you gave my covenant precedence over his
                  covenant. Now perhaps someone else is going to come
                  and assemble the merit of religious duties and good deeds
                  more than mine, so the covenant made with him will set
                  aside the covenant made with me!'

            E.   "Said to him the Holy One, blessed be He, "'After these
                  things the word of the Lord came to Abram in a vision,

saying, Fear not Abram, I am your shield" (Gen. 15:1). Out of Noah I did not raise up shields and righteous men, but out of you I shall raise up shields and righteous men. And not only so, but if your children should fall into transgression and wicked actions, I shall discern which great man there is among them who can say to the Attribute of Justice, "Enough!" and I shall take him and treat him as the pledge in their behalf.'

F. "For so it is said, 'a cluster,' [reading the letters of the word for cluster yields] a man in who is all, Scripture, Mishnah, Talmud, Supplements, Lore.

G. "'...henna blossoms': who atones for the sins of Israel [the words for henna and atone use the same consonants].

H. "'...in the vineyards of En-Gedi': I take him as a pledge in their behalf."

8. A. Another explanation of "a cluster [of henna blossoms, in the vineyards of En-gedi]":

B. Ben Nezirah said, "This refers to the Holy One, blessed be He, a man in whom is everything.

C. "'...of henna blossoms': who rejected the nations of the world and acknowledged Israel.

D. "When did he reject the nations of the world? One must say, in the war of Jehoshaphat: 'And it came to pass after this that the children of Moab and the children of Ammon and with them some of the Ammonites came against Jehoshaphat to battle' (2 Chr. 20:1).

E. "You note that the Israelites came in the might of Abraham, while Ammon and Moab came in the might of Lot. These fought those, and these fell at the hand of those, and as for Jehoshaphat, his God aided him so he won.

F. "Thus he rejected the nations of the world.

G. "Now if someone should say to you that Scripture does not speak of Jehoshaphat, say to him:

H. "'Here we find a reference to En-gedi and elsewhere the same: "In Hazazon-tamar, the same is En-gedi" (2 Chr. 20:1). Just as En-gedi in the latter passage speaks of the war of Jehoshaphat, so the reference here means that Scripture speaks of Jehoshaphat.'"

9. A. Said R. Levi b. R. Zechariah, "Now if in connection with this world, it is written concerning the Holy One, blessed be He, 'the Lord your God is a devouring fire, a jealous God' (Dt. 4:24), he rejects the nations of the world and recognizes Israel,

B. "in the age to come, how much the more so!"

15

Song of Songs Rabbah to
Song of Songs 1:15

1:15   *Behold, you are beautiful, my love;*
behold, you are beautiful;
your eyes are doves.

XV:i

1. A. "Behold, you are beautiful, my love; behold, you are beautiful; [your eyes are doves]":

    B. "Behold you are beautiful" in religious deeds,

    C. "Behold you are beautiful" in acts of grace,

    D. "Behold you are beautiful" in carrying out religious obligations of commission,

    E. "Behold you are beautiful" in carrying out religious obligations of omission,

    F. "Behold you are beautiful" in carrying out the religious duties of the home, in separating priestly ration and tithes,

    G. "Behold you are beautiful" in carrying out the religious duties of the field, gleanings, forgotten sheaves, the corner of the field, poor person's tithe, and declaring the field ownerless.

    H. "Behold you are beautiful" in observing the taboo against mixed species.

    I. "Behold you are beautiful" in providing a linen cloak with woolen show-fringes.

    J. "Behold you are beautiful" in [keeping the rules governing] planting,

    K. "Behold you are beautiful" in keeping the taboo on uncircumcised produce,

    L. "Behold you are beautiful" in keeping the laws on produce in the fourth year after the planting of an orchard,

    M. "Behold you are beautiful" in circumcision,

    N. "Behold you are beautiful" in trimming the wound,

    O. "Behold you are beautiful" in reciting the Prayer,

    P. "Behold you are beautiful" in reciting the Shema,

    Q. "Behold you are beautiful" in putting a mezuah on the doorpost of your house,

    R. "Behold you are beautiful" in wearing phylacteries,

S.   "Behold you are beautiful" in building the tabernacle for the Festival of Tabernacles,

T.   "Behold you are beautiful" in taking the palm branch and etrog on the Festival of Tabernacles,

U.   "Behold you are beautiful" in repentance,

V.   "Behold you are beautiful" in good deeds,

W.   "Behold you are beautiful" in this world,

X.   "Behold you are beautiful" in the world to come.

2.   A.   "...your eyes are doves":

B.   "...your eyes" stand for the sanhedrin, which is the eyesight of the community.

C.   That is in line with this verse: "If it is hid from the eyes of the community" (Num. 15:24).

D.   There are two hundred forty-eight limbs in a human being, and all of them function only through eyesight.

E.   So the Israelites can function only in line with their sanhedrin.

3.   A.   "Doves":

B.   Just as a dove is innocent, so the Israelites are [Simon supplies: innocent; just as the dove is beautiful in its movement, so Israel are] beautiful in their movement, when they go up for the pilgrim festivals.

C.   Just as a dove is distinguished, so the Israelites are distinguished: not shaving, in circumcision, in show-fringes.

D.   Just as the dove is modest, so the Israelites are modest.

E.   Just as the dove puts forth its neck for slaughter, so the Israelites: "For your sake are we killed all day long" (Ps. 44:23).

F.   Just as the dove atones for sin, so the Israelites atone for other nations.

G.   For all those seventy bullocks that they offer on the Festival of Tabernacles correspond to the nations of the world, so that the world should not become desolate on their account: "In return for my love they are my adversaries, but I am all prayer" (Ps. 109:4).

H.   Just as the dove, once it recognizes its mate, never again changes him for another, so the Israelites, once they recognized the Holy One, blessed be He, never exchanged him for another.

I.   Just as the dove, when it enters its nest, recognizes its nest and young, fledglings and apertures, so the three rows of the disciples of the sages, when they take their seats before them, knows each one his place.

J.   Just as the dove, even though you take its fledglings from under it, does not ever abandon its cote, so the Israelites, even though the house of the sanctuary was destroyed, never nullified the three annual pilgrim festivals.

K.   Just as the dove renews its brood month by month, so the Israelites every month renew Torah and good deeds.

L. Just as the dove goes far afield but returns to her cote, so do the Israelites: "They shall come trembling as a bird out of Egypt" (Hos. 11:11), this speaks of the generation of the wilderness; "and as a dove out of the land of Assyria" (Hos. 11:11), this speaks of the Ten Tribes.

M. And in both cases: "And I will make them dwell in their houses, says the Lord" (Hos. 11:11).

4. A. Rabbi says, "There is a kind of dove, who, when it is being fed, attracts her fellows, who smell her scent and come to her cote.

B. "So when an elder is in session and expounding, many proselytes convert at that time, for example, Jethro, who heard and came, and Rahab, who heard and came.

C. "Likewise on account of Hananiah, Mishael, and Azariah, many converted: 'For when he sees his children...sanctify my name...they also that err in spirit shall come to understanding' (Isa. 29:23)."

5. A. Rabbi was in session and expounding, but the community's attention wandered, so he wanted to wake them up. He said, "A single woman in Egypt produced six hundred thousand at a single birth."

B. Now there was present a disciple, named R. Ishmael b. R. Yosé, who said to him, "Who was this?"

C. He said to him, "This was Jochebed, who produced Moses, and he was numbered as the equal to six hundred thousand Israelites: 'Then sang Moses and the children of Israel' (Ex. 15:1); 'And the children of Israel did according to all that the Lord has commanded Moses' (Num. 1:54); 'And there has not arisen a prophet in Israel like Moses' (Dt. 34:10)."

6. A. "...your eyes are doves":

B. they are like doves.

C. Your likeness is similar to that of the dove:

D. Just as a dove brought light to the world, so you bring light to the world: "And nations shall walk at your light" (Isa. 60:3).

E. When did a dove bring light to the world?

F. In the time of Noah: "And the dove came in to him in the evening, and lo, in her mouth was an olive leaf, freshly plucked" (Gen. 8:11).

7. A. [Supply: "And the dove came in to him in the evening, and lo, in her mouth was an olive leaf, freshly plucked" (Gen. 8:11):] What is the meaning of "freshly plucked"?]

B. It was killed: "Joseph is without doubt torn in pieces" (Gen. 37:33).

C. Said R. Berekhiah, "Had she not killed it, it would have turned into a great tree."

   8. A. [=Genesis Rabbah **XXX:VI.3:**] Whence did the dove bring the olive branch?

     B. R. Levi [Gen. R.: Abba] said, "She brought it from the young shoots in the Land of Israel."

     C. [Gen. R.: R. Levi said, "She brought it from the mount of Olives,] for the Land of Israel had not been submerged in the flood. That is in line with what the Holy One, blessed be He, said to Ezekiel, 'Son of man, say to her: "You are a land that is not cleaned nor rained upon in the day of indignation"' (Ez.. 22:24)."

     D. R. Yohanan said, "Even millstone cases dissolved in the water of the flood."

     E. R. Tarye [Gen. R.: Birai] said, "The gates of the garden of Eden opened for the dove, and from there she brought it."

     F. Said to him R. Abbahu, "If she had brought it from the garden of Eden, should the dove not have brought something of greater value, such as cinnamon or balsam? But in choosing the olive leaf, the dove gave a signal to Noah, saying to him, 'Noah, better is something bitter from this [source, namely,] the Holy One, blessed be He, than something sweet from you.'"

16

Song of Songs Rabbah to
Song of Songs 1:16

1:16   *Behold, you are beautiful, my beloved,*
         truly lovely.
         Our couch is green...

XVI:i

1.   A.   "Behold, you are beautiful, my beloved, truly lovely. [Our couch is green]":

      B.   R. Abbahu and R. Hanina:

      C.   R. Abbahu said, "He praised her with repetition, but she praised him with plain speech.

      D.   "He praised her with repetition: 'Behold, you are beautiful, my love; behold, you are beautiful; [your eyes are doves]' (Song 1:15). For he he wanted to make himself another nation, he can do it.

      E.   "She praised him with plain speech, 'Behold, you are beautiful, my beloved, truly lovely.'"

      F.   R. Hanina said to him, "She too praised him with repetition: 'Behold, you are beautiful, my beloved, truly lovely.'

      G.   "She said to him, 'Lord of the age, the anger that you bring upon me is pleasant. Why? For you bring me back and carry me to better ways.'" [The words for anger and truly use the same consonants.]

2.   A.   Another explanation of the clause, "Our couch is green":

      B.   This refers to the house of the sanctuary: "With his nurse in his bed chamber, he was hid in the house of the Lord" (2 Kgs. 11:2).

            3.   A.   [Supply: "With his nurse in his bed chamber, he was hid in the house of the Lord" (2 Kgs. 11:2):]

                  B.   What is the meaning of "bed chamber?

                  C.   R. Eleazar and R. Samuel b. R. Nahman:

                  D.   R. Eleazar said, "in the side chambers.

                  E.   R. Samuel b. R. Nahman said, "in the upper chambers."

                  F.   There is no disagreement.

                  G.   One who said "in the side chambers" speaks of the rainy season, and one who said, "in the upper chambers" speaks of the dry season.

4.   A.   Another explanation of the clause, "Our couch is green":

B. R. Azariah in the name of R. Judah b. R. Simon: "The matter is to be compared to the case of a king who went out to the wilderness, and they brought him a short bed. He began to find it uncomfortable and it cramped his limbs.

C. "When they got to town, they brought him a good-sized bed. He began to stretch himself out and loosen his limbs.

D. "So before the house of the sanctuary was built, the Presence of God was cramped in between the two staves of the ark.

E. "When the house of the sanctuary was built, 'and the staves were lengthened' (1 Kgs. 8:8)."

5. A. Another explanation of the clause, "Our couch is green":

B. Just as a bed is made only for comfort, so before the house of the sanctuary was built, the Presence of God was moved from place to place:

C. "But I have walked in a tent and in a tabernacle" (1 Sam. 7:6).

D. After the house of the sanctuary was built, "This is my resting place forever" (Ps. 132:14).

6. A. Another explanation of the clause, "Our couch is green":

B. Just as a bed is made only for comfort, so Israel, before the house of the sanctuary was built, were moved from place to place: "they journeyed and they encamped."

C. Once the house of the sanctuary was built: "And Judah and Israel dwelt safely" (1 Kgs. 5:5).

7. A. Another explanation of the clause, "Our couch is green":

B. Just as a bed is only for sexual propagation, so before the house of the sanctuary was built: "Go, count Israel" (1 Chr. 21:2).

C. Once the house of the sanctuary was built: "Judah and Israel were many, as the sand" (1 Kgs. 4:20).

8. A. Another explanation of the clause, "Our couch is green":

B. Just as a bed is only for sexual propagation, so before the house of the sanctuary was built: "The whole congregation was forty two thousand" (Ezra 2:64).

C. Once the house of the sanctuary was built, they were fruitful and multiplied.

9. A. For R. Yohanan said, "From Gabbata to Antipatris were six hundred thousand villages, and they would count a population twice as numerous as the Israelites who went out of Egypt.

B. "And now if you tried to stick in six hundred thousand reeds, it could not hold them."

C. Said R. Hanina, "The land of Israel has shrunk."

17

Song of Songs Rabbah to
Song of Songs 1:17

1:17   *...the beams of our house are cedar,*
        our rafters are pine.

XVII

1. A. "...the beams of our house are cedar, [our rafters are pine]":
    B. R. Menahama in the name of R. Berekhiah: "The stones on which
        our father, Jacob, slept were turned beneath him into feather beds.
    C. "What sprung from them?
    D. "'...the beams of our house are cedar.'"
2. A. Another interpretation of the phrase, "the beams of our house are
        cedar":
    B. This refers to the righteous men and women, the prophets and
        prophetesses, who came from him.
        3. A. "...our rafters are pine":
            B. Said R. Yohanan, "No one can derive any use of pine.
                Why? Because it bends."
            C. So too is the view of R. Yohanan, for R. Yohanan said, "'I
                am like a leafy cypress tree' (Hos. 14:9): 'I am the one
                who bowed down so as to uproot the desire to serve
                idolatry.'
            D. "'Ephraim shall say, what have I to do with idols' (Hos.
                14:9): 'What have I to do with the impulse to worship
                idols?'
            E. "'As for me I respond' (Hos. 14:9): 'I raise up my voice
                to him.'
            F. "'And look on him' (Hos. 14:9): 'did I not sing a song to
                you?'
            G. "Thus: 'I am the one who bowed down so as to uproot the
                desire to serve idolatry.'"
        4. A. Another explanation of the clause, "our rafters are pine":
            B. the place on which the priests ran was made of pine: "And
                he covered the floor of the house with pine boards" (1
                Kgs.6:15).

5.   A.   Said R. Yohanan, "The Torah thereby teaches good policy: a person should make his ceiling with cedars and his floor with pine wood:

B.   "'the beams of our house are cedar, our rafters are pine.'"

Part Two
PARASHAH TWO

18

Song of Songs Rabbah
to Song of Songs 2:1

2:1   *I am a rose of Sharon,*
       a lily of the valleys.

XVIII.i

1.   A.   "I am a rose of Sharon, [a lily of the valleys]":
      B.   Said the Community of Israel, "I am the one, and I am beloved.
      C.   "I am the one whom the Holy One, blessed be He, loved more than the seventy nations."

2.   A.   "I am a rose of Sharon":
      B.   "For I made for him a shade through Bezalel [the words for shade and Bezalel use the same consonants as the word for rose]: 'And Bezalel made the ark' (Ex. 38:1)."

3.   A.   "...of Sharon":
      B.   "For I said before him a song [which word uses the same consonants as the word for Sharon] through Moses:
      C.   "'Then sang Moses and the children of Israel' (Ex. 15:1)."

4.   A.   Another explanation of the phrase, "I am a rose of Sharon":
      B.   Said the Community of Israel, "I am the one, and I am beloved.
      C.   "I am the one who was hidden in the shadow of Egypt, but in a brief moment the Holy One, blessed be He, brought me together to Raamses, and I blossomed forth in good deeds like a rose, and I said before him this song: 'You shall have a song as in the night when a feast is sanctified' (Isa. 30:29)."

5.   A.   Another explanation of the phrase, "I am a rose of Sharon":
      B.   Said the Community of Israel, "I am the one, and I am beloved.
      C.   "I am the one who was hidden in the shadow of the sea, but in a brief moment I blossomed forth in good deeds like a rose, and I pointed to him with the finger (opposite to me): 'This is my God and I will glorify him' (Ex. 15:2)."

6.   A.   Another explanation of the phrase, "I am a rose of Sharon":

B. Said the Community of Israel, "I am the one, and I am beloved.

C. "I am the one who was hidden in the shadow of Mount Sinai, but in a brief moment I blossomed forth in good deeds like a lily in hand and in heart, and I said before him, 'All that the Lord has said we will do and obey' (Ex. 24:7)."

7. A. Another explanation of the phrase, "I am a rose of Sharon":

B. Said the Community of Israel, "I am the one, and I am beloved.

C. "I am the one who was hidden and downtrodden in the shadow of the kingdoms. But tomorrow, when the Holy One, blessed be He, redeems me from the shadow of the kingdoms, I shall blossom forth like a lily and say before him a new song: 'Sing to the Lord a new song, for he has done marvelous things, his right hand and his holy arm have wrought salvation for him' (Ps. 98:1)."

8. A. R. Berekhiah said, "This verse ["I am a rose of Sharon, a lily of the valleys"] was said by the wilderness.

B. "Said the wilderness, 'I am the wilderness, and I am beloved.

C. "'For all the good things that are in the world are hidden in me: 'I will plant in the wilderness a cedar, an acacia tree' (Isa. 41:19).

D. "'The Holy One, blessed be He, has put them in me so that they may be guarded in me. And when the Holy One, blessed be He, seeks them from me, I shall return to him unimpaired the bailment that he has left with me.'

E. "'And I shall blossom in good deeds and say a song before him: "The wilderness and parched land shall be glad" (Isa. 35:1).'"

9. A. In the name of rabbis they have said, "'This verse ["I am a rose of Sharon, a lily of the valleys"] was said by the land [of Israel].

B. "Said the land, 'I am the land, and I am beloved.

C. "'For all the dead of the world are hidden in me: "Your dead shall live, my dead bodies shall arise" (Isa. 26:19).

D. "'When the Holy One, blessed be He, will ask them from me, I shall restore them to him.

E. "'And I shall blossom in good deeds and say a song before him: "From the uttermost parts of the earth we have heard songs" (Isa. 24:16).'"

XVIII:ii

1. A. [Concerning the verse, "I am a rose of Sharon, a lily of the valleys,"] R. Yudan and R. Eliezer:

B. R. Yudan said, "'I am a rose': does not the word for rose mean the same as the word for lily, and the word for lily the same as the word for rose?

C. "But when it is in the early stages of growth, it is called rose, but when full-grown, lily.

D. "And as to the word for rose, why is it called rose? Because it is hidden in its own shadow [the words for hidden in its own shadow use the letters for the word for rose] [Simon, p. 93, n. 1: its many petals creating a shadow for itself]."

2. A. Said R. Eliezer, "The righteous are compared to the most beautiful of plants, and among the most beautiful of plants, the most beautiful species. The most beautiful of plants is the lily,. and the most beautiful species of that plant is the lily.

B. "And not to the lily of the mountains, which easily withers, but the lily of the valley, which continues to bloom.

C. "But the wicked are compared to the most vile of things, and to the most vile species of that thing.

D. "They are compared to the most vile of things, which is chaff, and not to the chaff of the valley, which has some wetness, but: 'And they shall be chased as the chaff of the mountains before the wind' (Isa. 17:13)."

XVIII:iii

1. A. R. Abba b. Kahana said, "[With reference to 'a lily of the valleys'], said the Community of Israel before the Holy One, blessed be He, 'I am the one, and I am beloved.

B. "'For I am [Simon} plunged into the valley of troubles.

C. "'But when the Holy One, blessed be He, will draw me up from my sorrows, I shall blossom in good deeds like a lily and say before him a song.'

D. "Is it not the one that says, 'Lord in trouble they have sought you' (Isa. 26:3) [Simon, p. 93, n. 3: in consequence of their trouble, having been released therefrom, they have sought thee with song.]"

2. A. Said R. Aha, "[With reference to 'a lily of the valleys'], said the Community of Israel before the Holy One, blessed be He, 'When you look piercingly at me, I shall blossom in good deeds like a lily and say a song:

B. "'"A song of ascents: out of the depths I have called you O Lord" (Ps. 130:1).'"

3. A. Rabbis say, "[With reference to 'a lily of the valleys'], said the Community of Israel before the Holy One, blessed be He, 'I am the one, and I am beloved.

B. "'For I am [Simon} plunged into the valley of Gehenna.

C. "'But he Holy One, blessed be He, will draw me up from the depths: "He brought me up also out of the tumultuous pit" (Ps. 40:3).

D. "'Then I shall blossom forth in good deeds and say a song:

E. "'"And he has put a new song in my mouth" (Ps. 40:4).'"

4. A. The statement of Rabbis accords with the view of R. Eleazar the Modite: "In the age to come the angels in charge of the other nations will come to accuse Israel before the Holy One, blessed be He,

    B. "saying to him, 'Lord of the world, these have worshipped idolatry, and those have worshipped idolatry.

    C. "'These have practiced fornication and those have practiced fornication.

    D. "'These have shed blood and those have shed blood.

    E. "How come these go down to Gehenna, while those do not go down?'

    F. "And the Holy One, blessed be He, will answer them, saying, 'If so, then let all of the nations go to Gehenna with their gods.'

    G. "That is in line with this verse: 'For let all the peoples walk each one in the name of its god' (Mic. 4:5)."

5. A. Said R. Reuben, "If the matter were not expressly written out in Scripture, it would not be possible to say it at all:

    B. "'For in fire will the Lord be judged' (Isa. 66:16).

    C. "What is written is not 'judges' but 'is judged'!

    D. "So too David by the Holy Spirit said, 'Yes, though I walk in the valley of the shadow of death I will fear no evil, for you are with me' (Ps. 23:4) [that is, God is in Gehenna with David]."

6. A. [Supply: "Yes, though I walk in the valley of the shadow of death I will fear no evil, for you are with me; your rod and your staff comfort me; only goodness and mercy shall follow me all the days of my life, and I shall dwell in the house of the Lord forever" (Ps. 23:4-6]:

    B. Another comment on "your road and your staff comfort me":

    C. "your rod" refers to suffering.

    D. "...your staff" refers to the Torah.

    E. "...comfort me": shall I claim, without suffering? No, for Scripture says, "only."

    F. Might one say, "in this world"?

    G. Scripture says, "only goodness and mercy shall follow me all the days of my life, and I shall dwell in the house of the Lord forever."

19

Song of Songs Rabbah
to Song of Songs 2:2

2:2   *As a lily among brambles,*
           so is my love among maidens.

XIX:i

1.   A.   "As a lily among brambles, [so is my love among maidens]":

      B.   R. Isaac interpreted the verse to speak of Rebecca: "'And Isaac was forty years old when he took as his wife Rebecca, daughter of Bethuel, the Aramaean of Paddan-aram, sister of Laban the Aramaean' (Gen. 25:20).

      C.   "Why does Scripture find it necessary to say that she was the sister of Laban the Aramaean? Has not the fact that she was the daughter of Bethuel the Aramaean already been stated? Whey does Scripture find it necessary to say that she was the daughter of Bethuel? Has not the fact that she was the sister of Laban the Aramaean already been stated?

      D.   "It is necessary to indicate that her father was a deceiver, her brother a deceiver, the people of her place where she grew up deceivers.

      E.   "This righteous woman has emerged from their midst. To what may she be compared? To 'a lily among brambles.'"

            F.   R. Phineas in the name of R. Simon: "'And Isaac sent Jacob away, and he went to Paddan-aram, to Laban, son of Bethuel, the Aramaean, brother of Rebecca, mother of Jacob and Esau' (Gen. 28:5).

            G.   "He included them all in the same circle of deception."

2.   A.   R. Eleazar interpreted the same verse to speak of those who came forth from Egypt: "'a lily among brambles':

      B.   "Just as it is difficult to pick a rose among thorns, so it was hard to redeem the Israelites from Egypt.

      C.   "That is in line with the following verse of Scripture: 'Or has God tried to come to take a nation for himself from the midst of another nation' (Dt. 4:34)."

            3.   A.   R. Joshua in the name of R. Hanan: "'A nation from the midst of a people' is not written here, nor 'a people from the midst of a nation,' but 'a nation from the midst of a nation.'"

B. "For the Egyptians were uncircumcised and the Israelites were uncircumcised, the Egyptians grew ceremonial locks and so did the Israelites, the Egyptians wore garments made of mixed species and so did the Israelites.

C. "Therefore by the measure of strict justice, the Israelites ought not to have been redeemed from Egypt."

D. Said R. Samuel b. R. Nahman, "If the Holy One, blessed be He, had not bound himself by an oath, the Israelites would never have been redeemed from Egypt.

E. "'Therefore say to the children of Israel, I am the Lord, and I shall take you out of the burdens of Egypt' (Ex. 6:6).

F. "The language, 'therefore,' can refer only to an oath, as it is said, 'Therefore I take an oath concerning the house of Eli' (1 Sam. 3:14)."

4. A. Said R. Berekhiah, "'You have redeemed your people with your arm' (Ps. 77:6) – with naked power."

    B. Said R. Yudan, "From the phrase, 'to go and take a nation from the midst of another nation' to the phrase 'great terrors' (Dt. 4:34) are seventy-two letters.

    C. "Should you claim that there are more, you should deduct from the count the last reference to 'nation,' which does not count."

    D. R. Abin said, "It was for the sake of his name that he redeemed them, and the name of the Holy One, blessed be He, consists of seventy-two letters."

5. A. R. Azariah in the name of R. Judah in the name of R. Simon [interpreted the cited verse to speak of Israel before Mount Sinai].

    B. ["'a lily among brambles':] The matter may be compared to a king who had an orchard. He planted in it rows upon rows of figs, grapevines, and pomegranates. After a while the king went down to his vineyard and found it filled with thorns and brambles. He brought woodcutters and cut it down. But he found in the orchard a single red rose. He took it and smelled it and regained his serenity and said, 'This rose is worthy that the entire orchard be saved on its account.'

    C. "So too the entire world was created only on account of the Torah. For twenty-six generations the Holy One, blessed be He, looked down upon his world and saw it full of thorns and brambles, for example, the Generation of Enosh, the generation of the Flood, and the Sodomites.

D. "He planned to render the world useless and to destroy it: 'The Lord sat enthroned at the flood' (Ps. 29:10).

E. "But he found in the world a single red rose, Israel, that was destined to stand before Mount Sinai and to say before the Holy One, blessed be He, 'Whatever the Lord has said we shall do and we shall obey' (Ex. 24:7).

F. "Said the Holy One, blessed be He, [Lev. R.:] 'Israel is worthy that the entire world be saved on its account.'" [Song: "for the sake of the Torah and those who study it...."]

6. A. R. Hanan of Sepphoris interpreted the verse to speak of acts of loving kindness [that one may do by helping others carry out their liturgical obligations]:

B. "Ten men entered a synagogue to say their prayers, but they did not know how to say the Shema and go before the ark to recite the Prayer. But there was among them one who did know how to say the Shema and to go before the ark.

C. "Among them, he was 'like a lily among brambles.'

D. "Ten men went in to greet the bride, but did not know how to say the blessings for the bride and groom. But there was among them one who knew how to say the blessing for bride and groom.

E. "Among them, he was 'like a lily among brambles.'

F. Ten went into a house of mourning but did not know how to say the blessing for mourners. But among them one did know how to say the blessing for mourners.

G. "Among them, he was 'like a lily among brambles.'

7. A. R. Eleazar Hisma went to a certain place. The people said to him, "Does my lord know how to recite the Shema's blessings?"

B. He said to them, "No."

C. They said to him, "Does my lord know how to come near to recite the prayer before the ark?"

D. He said to them, "No."

E. They said to him, "Is this R. Eleazar, the man for whom people make such a fuss? It is for nothing that people call you 'my lord!'"

F. His face turned white. He went to R. Aqiba, and he looked sick. He said to him, "What's with you? You look sick."

G. He told the story to him.

H. He said to him, "Does my lord wish to learn?"

I. He said to him, "Yes."

J. After he had learned, he went to the same place. They said to him, "Does my lord know how to recite the Shema's blessings?"

K.   He said to them, "Yes."

L.   They said to him, "Does my lord know how to come near
     to recite the prayer before the ark?"

M.   He said to them, "Yes."

N.   They said to him, "Lo, Eleazar has regained the power of
     speech," and they called him R. Eleazar Hisma [=who
     can speak].

> O.   R. Jonah would teach his disciples even the blessing
>   for bride and groom and even the blessing for
>   mourners, saying to them, "You should be masters
>   in every detail."

8.   A.   R. Huna interpreted the verse to speak of the kingdoms [who now
          rule Israel]:

     B.   "['As a lily among brambles':] just as, when the north wind blows on
          the lily, it bends southward, and a thorn pricks it, and when the south
          wind blows, it bends northward, and a thorn pricks it, and all the
          while, the heart [of its stem[points upward,]

     C.   "so even though Israel is enslaved among the nations of the world by
          surcharges, head taxes, and confiscations, nonetheless their heart
          points upward toward their father in heaven.

     D.   [So did David say,] 'My eyes are always toward the Lord' (Ps. 25:15).

9.   A.   R. Abihu interpreted the cited verse to speak of the coming
          redemption:

     B.   "['As a lily among brambles':] when the lily is among the brambles,
          it is hard for the farmer to pick it, so what does he do? He burns the
          thorns around it and plucks it.

     C.   "So: 'The Lord has commanded concerning Jacob that those who are
          around him should be his enemies' (Lam. 1:17),

          > D.   "for example, Halamo [which is gentile, is enemy] to
          >   Naveh [which is Israelite], Susita to Tiberias, Qastra to
          >   Haifa, Jericho to Nauran, Lud to Ono.

     E.   "That is in line with the following verse of Scripture: 'This is
          Jerusalem. I have est her in the midst of the gentiles' (Ez. 5:5).

     F.   "Tomorrow, when redemption comes to Israel, what will the Holy
          One, blessed be He, do to them? He will bring a flame and burn the
          area around Israel.

     G.   "That is in line with this verse: 'And the peoples will be as burnings
          of lime, as thorns cut down that are burned in fire' (Isa. 33:12).

     H.   "And in the same connection: 'The Lord alone shall lead him' (Dt.
          32:12)."

10. A.   R. Abun said, "Just as a lily wilts so long as the hot spell persists, but
          when the dew falls on it, the lily thrives again,

        B.   "so Israel, so long as the shadow of Esau falls across the world, Israel wilts,

        C.   "but when the shadow of Esau passes from the world, Israel will once more thrive:

        D.   "'I shall be like the dew for Israel. It will blossom as the lily' (Hos. 14:6)."

11.   A.   Just as the lily expires only with its scent, so Israel expires only with religious acts and good deeds.

        B.   Just as the lily is only for the scent, so the righteous were created only for the redemption of Israel.

        C.   Just as the lily is placed on the table of kings at the beginning and end of a meal, so Israel will be in both this world and the world to come.

        D.   Just as it is easy to tell a lily from the thorns, so it is easy to tell the Israelites from the nations of the world.

        E.   That is in line with this verse of Scripture: "All those who see them will recognize them" (Isa. 61:9).

        F.   Just as a lily is made ready for Sabbaths and festivals, so Israel is made ready for the coming redemption.

                G.   R. Berekhiah said, "Said the Holy One, blessed be He, to Moses, 'Go and say to Israel My children, when you were in Egypt, you were like a lily among brambles. Now that you come into the land of Israel, you shall be like a lily among brambles.

                H.   ""Be careful not to do deeds like those of this party or that.""

                I.   "Thus [Moses admonished Israel, saying to them, 'You shall not do as they do in the land of Egypt, where you dwelt, and you shall not do as they do in the land of Canaan, to which I am bringing you. You shall not walk in their statutes'" (Lev. 18:3).

20

Song of Songs Rabbah
to Song of Songs 2:3

2:3   *As an apple tree among the trees of the wood,*
        so is my beloved among young men.
        With great delight I sat in his shadow,
        and his fruit was sweet to my taste.

XX:i

1. A. "As an apple tree among the trees of the wood":
    B. R. Huna and R. Aha in the name of R. Yosé b. Zimra, "Just as in the case of an apple tree, everybody avoids it in extreme heat, since it has no shade in which to sit,
    C. "so the nations of the world fled from sitting in the shade of the Holy One, blessed be He on the day on which the Torah was given.
    D. "Might one suppose that the same was so of Israel?
    E. "Scripture states, 'With great delight I sat in his shadow,'
    F. "'I took delight in him and I sat.'
    G. "'I am the one who desired him, and not the nations of the world.'"
2. A. R. Aha b. R. Zeira made two statements.
    B. "First: an apple produces blossoms before leaves,
    C. "so the Israelites in Egypt declared their faith before they heard the message:
    D. "'And the people believed, and they heard that the Lord had remembered' (Ex. 4:31)."
3. A. R. Aha b. R. Zeira made a second statement:
    B. "Just as an apple produces blossoms before leaves,
    C. "so the Israelites at Mount Sinai undertook to do even before they had heard what they were supposed to do:
    D. "'We will do and we will hear' (Ex. 24:7)."
4. A. R. Azariah made two statements:
    B. "Just as an apple completes the ripening of its fruit only in Sivan,
    C. "so the Israelites gave forth a good fragrance only in Sivan."
5. A. R. Azariah made a second statement:
    B. "Just as in the case of an apple tree, from the moment that it blossoms until its fruit ripens is a span of fifty days,
    C. "so from the time that the Israelites went forth from Egypt until they accepted the Torah was a span of fifty days.

      D.   "When did they receive it?

      E.   "'In the third month after the children of Israel had gone forth' (Ex. 19:1)."

6.   A.   R. Judah b. R. Simon made two statements:

      B.   "Just as an apple costs only a penny, but you can smell its fragrance any number of times,

      C.   "So said Moses to the Israelites, 'If you wish to be redeemed, you may be redeemed for a simple matter.'

      D.   "They may be compared to someone who had sore feet and he went to all the physicians for healing and was not healed. Then he came to one, who said to him, 'If you want to be healed, you can be healed in a simple way. Plaster your feet with bullshit.'

      E.   "So said Moses to the Israelites, 'If you wish to be redeemed, you may be redeemed for a simple matter.'

      F.   "'"And you shall take a bunch of hyssop and dip it"' (Ex. 12:22).

      G.   "They said to him, 'Our lord, Moses, how much does this bundle of hyssop cost? Four or five cents?'

      H.   "He said to them, 'Even a penny. But it will make it possible for you to inherit the spoil of Egypt, the spoil at the Sea, the spoil of Sihon and Og, and the spoil of the thirty-one kings [of Canaan].'

      I.   "The palm-branch [for the Festival of Tabernacles], which costs someone a good dollar, and through which one carries out a variety of religious duties, all the more so!

      J.   "Therefore Moses admonishes Israel, 'And you shall take for yourself on the first day' (Lev. 23:40)."

7.   A.   R. Judah b. R. Simon made another statement:

      B.   "The matter may be compared to the case of a king who had a precious stone and a pearl. His son came along and said to him, 'Give it to me.'

      C.   "He said to him, 'It is yours, it belongs to you, and I give it over to you.'

      D.   "So said the Israelites before the Holy One, blessed be He, '"The Lord is my strength and my song"' (Ex. 15:2).

      E.   "Said to them the Holy One, blessed be He, 'It is yours, it belongs to you, and I give it over to you.'

      F.   "For 'strength' refers only to the Torah: 'The Lord will give strength to his people' (Ps. 29:11). [Simon, p. 100, n. 3: So the Community of Israel said, "I longed for his shadow," i.e. "I longed for the Torah and the Divine protection it affords – and I did indeed sit there, God freely giving it to me, declaring it altogether mine.]

      8.   A.   Said R. Levi, "Three good hopes did the Israelites form at the Sea.

B.   "They hoped for the Torah, they hoped for the standards, and they hoped for the tabernacle.

C.   "They hoped for the Torah: 'With great delight I sat in his shadow.'

D.   "They hoped for the standards: 'with great delight.'

E.   "They hoped for the tabernacle: 'I sat....'

F.   "That is in line with this verse: 'For I have not dwelled in a house since the day that I brought up the children of Israel out of Egypt' (2 Sam. 7:6)."

   9. A.   That accords with the view of R. Menaheman: "'And they went out into the wilderness of Shur' (Ex. 15:22):

      B.   "This teaches that they prophesied in their own regard that they were going to be organized in camps, with standards and rows, like a vineyard."

XX:ii

1.   A.   "...and his fruit was sweet to my taste":

      B.   Said R. Isaac, "This refers to the twelve months that the Israelites spent before Mount Sinai, regaling themselves with teachings of the Torah.

      C.   "What verse of Scripture makes that point? 'and his fruit was sweet to my taste.

      D.   "'...to my taste' it was sweet, but to the taste of the seventy nations of the world it was bitter like wormwood."

   2. A.   [=Leviticus Rabbah I:X:] "Out of the tent of meeting" (Lev. 1:1):

      B.   Said R. Eleazar, "Even though Torah had been given earlier to Israel, at Sinai [Lev. R.: as a fence, restricting their actions], they were liable to punishment on account of violating it only after it had been repeated for them in the tent of meeting.

      C.   "This may be compared to a royal decree that had been written and sealed and brought to the province. The inhabitants of the province became liable to be punished on account of violating the decree only after it had been proclaimed to them in a public meeting in the province.

      D.   "Along these same lines, even though the Torah had been given to Israel at Sinai, they bore liability for punishment on account of violating its commandments only after it had been repeated for them in the tent of meeting.

E. "This is in line with the following verse of Scripture: 'Until I had brought him into my mother's house and into the chamber of my teaching (Song 3:4).

F. "'...into my mother's house' refers to Sinai.

G. "'...and into the chamber of my teaching' refers to the tent of meeting, from which the Israelites were commanded through instruction in the Torah."

3. A. [=Lev. R. I:XI.1:] Said R. Joshua b. Levi, "If the nations of the world had known how valuable the tent of meeting was to them, they would have sheltered it with tents and balustrades.

B. "You note that before the tabernacle was erected, the nations of the world used to hear the sound of God's word and [fearing an earthquake] they would rush out of their dwellings.

C. "That is in line with this verse: 'For who is there of all flesh, who has heard the voice of the living God speaking out of the midst' (Dt. 5:23)."

4. A. [=Lev. R. I:XI.2:] Said R. Simon, "The word of God went forth in two modes, for Israel as life, for the nations of the world as poison.

B. "'...as you have and lived; (Dt. 4:33) – you heard and lived.

C. "for the nations of the world as poison: you hear the voice of God and live, while the nations of the earth hear and die.

D. "'That is in line with this verse: 'Under the apple tree I awakened' (Song 8:5)."

E. "...out of the tent of meeting":

F. R. Hiyya taught, "The sound was cut off from that point and did not go beyond the tent of meeting."

5. A. [=Lev. R. I:XII.1:] Said R. Isaac, "Before the tent of meeting was set up, prophecy was common among the nations of the world. Once the tent of meeting was set up, prophecy disappeared from among them. That is in line with this verse: 'I held it' [the Holy spirit, producing], 'and would not let it go [until I had brought it...into the chamber of her that conceived me' (Song 3:4)."

B. Should you object, "Lo, Balaam later on practiced prophecy –

C. the answer is, "He did so for the good of Israel: 'Who has counted the dust of Jacob (Num. 23:10);

'No one has seen iniquity in Jacob' (Num. 23:21); 'For there is no enchantment with Jacob' (Num. 23:23); 'How goodly are your tents, O Jacob' (Num. 24:5); 'There shall go forth a star out of Jacob' (Num. 24:17); 'and out of Jacob shall one have dominion' (Num. 24:19).

21

Song of Songs Rabbah
to Song of Songs 2:4

2:4   *He brought me to the wine cellar,*
       and his banner over me was love.

XXI:i

1. A. "He brought me to the wine cellar, [and his banner over me was love]":
    B. R. Meir and R. Judah:
    C. R. Meir says, "Said the Congregation of Israel, 'The impulse to do evil took hold of me through wine, and I said to the calf, "These are your gods, Israel" (Ex. 32:4).
    D. "'When wine gets into someone, it mixes up his mind.'"
    E. Said to him R. Judah, "That's enough for you, Meir! People interpret the Song of Songs not in a derogatory way but only in a praiseworthy way [for Israel],
    F. "for the Song of Songs was given only for Israel's praise.
    G. "And what is the meaning of, 'He brought me to the wine cellar'?
    H. "Said the Congregation of Israel, 'The Holy One, blessed be He, "brought me" to the great wine cellar, meaning, to Sinai.
    I. "'["and his banner over me was love]": and he placed over me there banners of the Torah, religious duties, and good deeds.
    J. "'And with great love did I accept them.'"
2. A. R. Abba in the name of R. Isaac said, "Said the Congregation of Israel, 'The Holy One, blessed be He, "brought me" to the great wine cellar, meaning, to Sinai.
    B. "'And he gave me the Torah there, which is interpreted in forty-nine different ways to yield a ruling of cleanness, and in forty-nine different ways to yield a ruling of uncleanness.'

C. "How come? Because the numerical value of the letters in the word for 'and his banner' is forty-nine.

D. "'And with great love did I accept them.'

E. "Thus: 'and his banner over me was love.'"

3. A. R. Jonah said, "In the case of two associates occupied in teachings of law,

B. "with this one citing the generative source of the law, while that one does not cite the generative source of the law [as he reads it], –

C. "said the Holy One, blessed be He, 'and his banner over me was love.'" [Simon, p. 103, n. 4: his array of words is beloved, although they are not in accord with the true law, since his intention is good.]

4. A. Said R. Aha, "An ignorant person who reads the word 'love' as 'enmity,' for instance, 'and you will love' as 'and you will hate' –

B. "said the Holy One, blessed be He, 'His mistake [using the same letters as the word for banner] is beloved to me.'"

5. A. Said R. Issachar, "A child who reads for Moses, 'Muses,' and for Aaron 'Arun,' and for Efron 'Efran' –

B. "said the Holy One, blessed be He, 'His babble [using some of the same letters as the word for banner] is beloved to me.'"

6. A. Said R. Hunia, "In the past if someone would point to an icon [of the king] with his finger, he would be punished, but now, someone can leave his entire hand any number of times upon the name of God [in the scroll] and is not punished.

B. "Said the Holy One, blessed be He, 'His thumb [using the same letters as the word for banner] is beloved to me.'"

7. A. And Rabbis say, "Even in the case of a child who skips the name of God any number of times is not punished.

B. "Not only so, but said the Holy One, blessed be He, 'His omission [using the same letters as the word for banner] is beloved to me.'"

8. A. [Supply: "and his banner over me was love]":

B. Said R. Berekhiah, "Even concerning those banners with which Jacob deceived his father, 'And she put the skins of the kids of the goats upon his hands' (Gen. 27:16),

C.   "the Holy One, blessed be He, said, 'Even on them I shall bring my Presence to rest.'

D.   "Thus: 'And you shall make curtains of goats' hair' (Ex. 26:7).

E.   "Not only so, but further, said the Holy One, blessed be He, 'and his banner over me was love': 'his deceiving of me was beloved.'"

9.   A.   [Supply: "He brought me to the wine cellar, and his banner over me was love]":

B.   R. Joshua of Sikhnin in the name of R. Levi: "Said the Congregation of Israel, 'The Holy One, blessed be He, "brought me" to the great wine cellar, meaning, to Sinai.

C.   "'And there I saw Michael and his banner, Gabriel and his banner, and my eyes saw the arrangements on high, and I loved them.'

D.   "At that moment said the Holy One, blessed be He, to Moses, 'Since it is the wish of my children to encamp by banners [as in heaven], let them encamp by banners: 'Every man with his own banner, according to the ensigns' (Num. 2:2)."

22

Song of Songs Rabbah
to Song of Songs 2:5

2:5   *Sustain me with raisins,*
refresh me with apples;
for I am sick with love.

XXII:i

1.   A.   "Sustain me with raisins, [refresh me with apples; for I am sick with love:]"

B.   [With reference to letters of the word for raisins, we interpret the opening clause:] with two fires, the fire above, the fire below [the heavenly fire, the altar fire].

2.   A.   Another explanation: "Sustain me with raisins":

B.   with two fires, the Torah in Writing, the Torah in Memory.

3.   A.   Another explanation: "Sustain me with raisins":

B.   with many fires, the fore of Abraham, the fire of Moriah, the fire of the bush, the fire of Elijah, and the fire of Hananiah, Mishael, and Azariah.

4.   A.   Another explanation: "Sustain me with raisins":

	B.	This refers to the well-founded laws.
5.	A.	"...refresh me with apples":
	B.	this refers to the lore, the fragrance and taste of which are like apples.
6.	A.	"...for I am sick with love":
	B.	Said the Congregation of Israel before the Holy One, blessed be He, "Lord of the world, all of the illnesses that you bring upon me are so as to make me more beloved to you."
7.	A.	Another interpretation of the phrase, "for I am sick with love":
	B.	Said the Congregation of Israel before the Holy One, blessed be He, "Lord of the world, all of the illnesses that you bring upon me are because I love you."
8.	A.	Another interpretation of the phrase, "for I am sick with love:]"
	B.	"Even though I am sick, I am beloved unto him."

XXII:ii

1. A. It has been taught on Tannaite authority: when a person is not ill, he eats whatever he finds. When he gets sick, he wants to eat all sorts of sweets.

B. Said R. Isaac, "In the past, the Torah was worked out in encompassing principles, [Simon: the main outlines of the Torah were known to all], so people wanted to hear a teaching of the Mishnah or of the Talmud.

C. "Now that the Torah is not worked out in encompassing principles, [Simon: the main outlines of the Torah are not known] people want to hear a teaching of Scripture or a teaching of lore."

D. Said R. Levi, "In the past, when money was available, people wanted to hear a teaching of the Mishnah or law or Talmud.

E. "Now that money is scarce, so that people are sick on account of subjugation, people want to hear only words of blessing and consolation."

2. A. R. Simeon b. Yohai taught on Tannaite authority, "When the Israelites came forth from Egypt, what were they like?

B. "They were comparable to a prince who recovered from an illness.

C. "Said his tutor [to the king], 'Let your son go to school.'

D. "Said the king to him, 'My son has not yet recovered his full color. For he has become pale because of his illness. Let my son take it easy and enjoy himself for three months with food and drink, and then he can go back to school.'

E. "So when the Israelites went forth from Egypt, there were among them those who had been deformed through the slave labor of mortar and bricks.

F. "The ministering angels said to him, 'Lo, the time has come. Give them the Torah.'

G. "Said to them the Holy One, blessed be He, 'My children have not yet recovered their full color on account of the slave labor of mortar and bricks.

H. "'But let my children take it easy for three months at the well and with the quail, and then I will give them the Torah.

I. "'And when is that? "In the third month"' (Ex. 19:1)." [Simon, p. 106, n. 1: Hence now in the third month has the time come for you to 'Sustain me with raisins, refresh me with apples; for I am sick with love.']

3. A. At the end of the repression our masters gathered in Usha, and these are they:

B. R. Judah, R. Nehemiah, R. Meir, R. Yosé, R. Simeon b. Yohai, R. Eliezer b. R. Yosé the Galilean, and R. Eliezer b. Jacob.

C. They sent word to the sages of Galilee and said to them, "Whoever has learned, let him come and teach. And whoever has not learned, let him come and learn."

D. So they met and learned and did what was necessary.

E. Now when it came time to depart, they said, "Is this place, in which we have been received, going to be left empty? [Simon: 'We cannot leave a place where we have been thus entertained without a parting blessing.']

F. They gave the place of honor to R. Judah, who was a local resident. It is not because he was greater than the others in Torah-learning, but it is the residence of a person that endows him with the honor of precedence. [His task, like that of all the others, was to speak in praise of hospitality.]

4. A. R. Judah came forward and interpreted this verse: "'Now Moses used to take the tent and pitch it outside the camp, afar off from the camp. [And it came to pass that everyone who sought the Lord]' (Ex. 33:7):

> B. "Here the word 'afar off' is used, and the same word is used elsewhere: 'Yet there shall be a space afar off between you and it, about two thousand cubits by measure' (Josh. 3:4).
>
> C. "Just as the sense of the word in that latter passage is explicitly two thousand cubits, so here too 'afar off' means two thousand cubits.
>
> D. "[The verse proceeds:] 'And it came to pass that everyone who sought' not Moses but 'every one sought the Lord.'
>
> E. "On this basis we learn that whoever hospitably receives associates is as though he receives the Presence of God.
>
> F. "And you, my brothers, my lords, great authorities of the Torah, who among you has taken the trouble to travel ten mils [a mil being two thousand cubits], or twenty, or thirty, or forty, so as to hear words of the Torah, all the more so that the Holy One, blessed be He, will not hold back your reward in this world and in the coming one!"

> 5. A. R. Nehemiah came forward and interpreted this verse: "'An Ammonite or a Moabite shall not enter into the assembly of the Lord' (Dt. 23:4):
>
> B. "It has been taught, 'Two great nations were excluded from entering the congregation of the Lord.
>
> C. "'Why was this so? "Because they did not meet you with bread and water" (Dt. 23:5).'
>
> D. "Now were the Israelites really in need at that moment? And is it not the fact that all the forty years that the Israelites were in the wilderness, the well would bubble for them and the manna would come down for them and the quail was available to them and the clouds of glory surrounded them and the pillar of cloud traveled before them?
>
> E. "And yet you say, 'Because they did not meet you with bread and water'!"
>
> F. Said R. Eleazar, "It is a matter of proper conduct that one who comes in from a trip is met with food and drink."
>
> G. [Resuming E:] "Come and see how the Holy One, blessed be He, exacted a penalty from those two nations.

H. "It is written in the Torah, 'An Ammonite and a Moabite shall not enter the assembly of the Lord' (Dt. 23:4).

I. "But you, people of Usha, who greeted our lords with your food and your drink and your beds, how much the more so will the Holy One, blessed be He, provide for you a good reward!"

6. A. R. Meir came forward and interpreted this verse: "'Now there dwelled an old prophet in Bethel' (1 Kgs. 13:11):

B. "And who was it? This was Amaziah, priest of Bethel [Amos 7:10]."

C. Said to him R. Yosé, "Meir, you're making scrambled eggs! Who was he really? He was Jonathan son of Gershom son of Moses: 'Jonathan, son of Gershom, son of Manasseh' (Judges 18:30).

D. "Now the N in the name Manasseh is suspended, indicating that if he attained merit, he would be deemed the son of Moses, and if not, then he would be deemed the son of Manasseh [2 Kgs. 21]."

E. Associates asked before R. Samuel b. R. Nahman, saying to him, "How come a priest for an idol lived all those years?"

F. He said to them, "It was because he was stingy with the idol. [Simon: he tried to discourage idolatry.]

G. "How so? [Cf. Gen. R. XXXVIII:XIII.1: Said R. Hiyya (in explanation of how Haran died in his father's presence) "Terah was an idol manufacturer. Once he went off on a trip and put Abraham in charge of the store. Someone would come in and want to buy an idol.] If someone came to worship the idol, he would say to him, 'How old are you?'

H. "He would say, 'Forty or fifty or sixty or seventy or eighty years old.'

I. "He would, 'Woe to that man, who is forty or fifty or sixty or seventy or eighty years old and this idol was made only five or twelve years ago, and you are going to abandon your God and worship it? That is a come-down!"

J. "So the man would be ashamed and go his way.

K. "A smart-ass came and said this to him, 'Then why do you stay here and serve it?'

L. "He said to him, 'I collect my salary and blind its eye.'

M. "When David heard about this, he sent word to him and brought him and said to him, 'Are you really the grandson of that righteous man and are worshipping idolatry?'

N. "He said to him, 'Indeed, I have a tradition from the household of my father's father: "Sell yourself for idolatry, but do not fall into need from other people!"'

O. "He said to him, 'God forbid! That is not the point. But: "Sell yourself to work that is alien to you, but do not fall into need from other people!"'

P. "Since David saw that he loved money, he went and made him secretary of the treasury.

Q. "They say that when David died, he reverted to his corruption: 'And he said to him, I also am a prophet as you are...he lied to him' (1 Kgs. 13:18).

R. "What is the meaning of 'lied'?

S. "He deceived him.

T. "And what was the deceit?

U. "He fed him food in a spirit of deceit [Simon, p. 108, n. 7: by his lies he persuaded him to accept his hospitality, notwithstanding that he had been ordered strictly to eat nothing in that place].

V. "'And it came to pass, as they sat at the table, that the word of the Lord came to the prophet who brought him back' (1 Kgs. 13:20).

W. "Now this yields an argument *a fortiori:*

X. "If this one, who lied to him and fed him food in a spirit of deceit, had the merit that the Holy Spirit would come to rest upon him, you, our brothers, people of Usha, who have received our lords with food in a spirit of sincerity and drink and a bed, how much the more so will the Holy One, blessed be He, provide for you a good reward!"

7. A. R. Yosé came forward and interpreted this verse:

"'And the ark of the Lord remained in the house of Obed-edom the Gittite...and it was told to king David, saying, The Lord has blessed the house of Obed-edom and all that belongs to him' (2 Sam. 6:11f.):

B. "How come? It was because of the ark of God.

C. "And how did he bless him?

D. "With children: 'Ammiel the sixth, Issachar the seventh' (1 Chr. 26:5); 'all these were of the children of Obed-edom, they and their children' (1 Chr. 26:5).

E. "They say: he had eight sons and eight daughters-in-law, and every one of them had two children each month.

F. "How did this work?

G. "She was unclean for seven days [of her menstrual period], then clean for seven days, and then she gave birth, then unclean for seven days [of her menstrual period], then clean for seven days, and then she gave birth, this sixteen per month, forty-eight in three months, and with six of his own, there were fifty-four, and the initial eight bring the count to sixty-two: 'Sixty-two of Obed-edom' (1 Chr. 26:5)."

  H. Colleagues asked before R. Yohanan, saying to him, "What is the meaning of this statement: 'Peullethai the eighty, for God blessed him" (1 Chr. 26:55)?

  I. He said to them, "[Referring to the letters in the name of Peullethai, which can yield the following meaning:] 'He did a great service for the Torah."

J. [Reverting to G:] "And what was the great service that he performed for the Torah?

K. "He would light before the ark a single candle in the morning, and a single candle at dusk.

L. "Now this yields an argument *a fortiori:* if because he lit a single candle before the ark of God, which neither eats nor drinks nor speaks, but merely contains the two tablets of stone, he acquired the merit of being blessed on account of the honor paid to it,

M. "you, our brothers, people of Usha, how much the more so!"

8. A. R. Simeon b. Yohai came forward and interpreted this verse: "'And it fell on a day that Elisha passed to Shunem, where there was an important woman, and she insisted that he eat bread' (2 Kgs. 4:8)."

B. Said to him R. Judah b. R. Simon, "Merely because it is written of her that 'she insisted that he eat bread' did she gain the merit that her son be resurrected?"

C. R. Yudan in the name of R. Zeira and R. Yohanan in the name of R. Simeon b. Yohai said, "Great is supporting the poor, for it brings about the resurrection of the dead not in its appointed time."

D. [Reverting to B, supply: said to him R. Simeon b. Yohai,] "The women of Zarephath, because she fed Elijah, had the merit that her son was resurrected from the dead.

E. "The Shunammite woman, because she fed Elisha, had the merit that her son was resurrected from the dead."

F. Said R. Judah b. R. Ilai, "Even candles and even wicks did Elijah bring from place to place, so as not to impose bother upon people."

G. R. Judah b. R. Simon said, "Now did he really eat her food? And is it not the fact that both she and he ate his food [and not hers]? 'And she and he...ate' (1 Kgs. 17:15) – so what is written is he and she [Simon, p. 110, n. 2: which implies that he was the principal, the food being his].

H. "But because she welcomed him in a cordial way and served him, she had the merit of having her son resurrected from the dead.

I. "Now you, people of Usha, who have accorded such grace to us, all the more so!"

9. A. R. Eliezer b. R. Yosé the Galilaean came forward and interpreted this verse: "'And Saul said to the Kenites, Go, depart, leave the Amalekites, lest I destroy you with them, for you showed kindness to all the children of Israel when they came up out of Egypt' (1 Sam. 15:6):

B. "Now did Jethro show kindness to all Israel? But is it the fact that Jethro showed kindness only with Moses alone?"

C. Said R. Eleazar, "Jethro surely showed kindness to Moses: 'Call him that he may eat bread' (Ex. 2:20)."

D. Said R. Simon, "That is not so, but he gave him food only for pay: 'And moreover he drew water for us' (Ex. 2:19)."

E. R. Judah, R. Nehemiah, and rabbis:

F. R. Judah said, "'...he drew water for us' and for our parents."

G. R. Nehemiah said, "'...he drew water for us' and for our shepherds."

H. Rabbis said, "'...he drew water for us' on account of the merit accrued by our fathers. He drew water for the shepherds so as to keep the peace among them."

I. [Reverting to B, Eliezer b. R. Yosé continues,] "And yet you say that Jethro showed kindness to all Israel?

J. "But this serves to teach you that whoever shows kindness to a single one of the eminent persons of Israel is credited as though he had done it for all Israel.

K. "Now you, our brothers, people of Usha, how much the more so!"

10. A. R. Eliezer b. Jacob came forward and interpreted this verse: "'And Moses and the priests the Levites spoke to all Israel, saying, Keep silence and hear, O Israel: this day you have become a people' (Dt. 27:9):

B. "Now was that the day on which they received the Torah? And had they not received it forty years earlier, and yet you say, 'this day'!

C. "This teaches that once Moses repeated the Torah to them and they received it cordially, it was credited to them as though they had received it that very day from Sinai.

D. "That is why it is said, 'this day you have become a people' (Dt. 27:9).

E. "Now you, our brothers, people of Usha, who have received our lords so cordially – how much the more so!"

23

Song of Songs Rabbah
to Song of Songs 2:6

2:6   *O that his left hand were under my head,*
        and that his right hand embraced me!

XXIII:i

1. A. "O that his left hand were under my head":
    B. this refers to the first tablets.
    C. "...and that his right hand embraced me":
    D. this refers to the second tablets.
2. A. Another interpretation of the verse, "O that his left hand were under my head":
    B. this refers to the show-fringes.
    C. "...and that his right hand embraced me":
    D. this refers to the phylacteries.
3   A. Another interpretation of the verse, "O that his left hand were under my head":
    B. this refers to the recitation of the *Shema*.
    C. "...and that his right hand embraced me":
    D. this refers to the Prayer.
4   A. Another interpretation of the verse, "O that his left hand were under my head":
    B. this refers to the tabernacle.
    C. "...and that his right hand embraced me":
    D. this refers to the cloud of the Presence of God in the world to come: "The sun shall no longer be your light by day nor for brightness will the moon give light to you" (Isa. 60:19). Then what gives light to you? "The Lord shall be your everlasting light" (Isa. 60:20).
5   A. Another interpretation of the verse, "O that his left hand were under my head":
    B. this refers to the mezuzah.
        6. A. It has been taught on Tannaite authority by R. Simeon b. Yohai, "'And you shall write them on the doorposts of your house' (Dt. 6:9).
            B. "[Since the words for house and coming use the same consonants,] 'when you come into your house from the

street [you should have the mezuzah on the doorpost that you will see at your right, so it is affixed on the right doorpost as one enters the house]."

7.   A.   Said R. Yohanan, "'And you shall set the table outside the veil and the candlestick...toward the south' (Ex. 26:35). [That is, the candlestick is to be set on the left of someone entering from the east (Simon, p. 112, n. 3)].

      B.   "And is that not the way? For does a person not put the candlestick down at the left, so that it will not impede his right hand?

      C.   "[And, with reference to the verse, 'O that his left hand were under my head, and that his right hand embraced me,"] does not a man put his left hand under the head and caress with the right?"

8.   A.   Said R. Aha, "R. Yohanan derives the evidence from this verse: 'to love the Lord your God...and to cleave to him' (Dt. 11:22).

      B.   "And what is this cleaving? It is with 'his left hand under my head.'"

24

Song of Songs Rabbah
to Song of Songs 2:7

2:7   *I adjure you, O daughters of Jerusalem,*
       by the gazelles or the hinds of the field,
       that you not stir up nor awaken love
       until it please.

XXIV:i

1.   A.   "I adjure you, O daughters of Jerusalem, [by the gazelles or the hinds of the field, that you not stir up nor awaken love until it please]":

      B.   By what did he impose the oath? [That is, By what did God impose an oath upon Israel]?

      C.   R. Eliezer says, "He imposed the oath by heaven and earth.

      D.   "'...by the gazelles': [since the word for gazelle and the word for host use the same consonants], it was by the host above and by the host below, by two hosts. That is, by the hosts.

2.   A.   "...or the hinds of the field":

B. this is the beasts of the field: "For you shall be in league with the stones of the field, and the beasts of the field shall be at peace with you" (Job 5:23).

3. A. R. Hanina b. R. Pappa and R. Judah b. R. Simon:

B. R. Hanina said, "He imposed the oath by the patriarchs and matriarchs.

C. "For 'by the gazelles,' [since the word for gazelle and the word for will use the same consonants], it was by the patriarchs, who carried out my will, and through whom I accomplished my will.

D. "'...or the hinds of the field,' [since the word hind occurs here and in the verse to be cited,] it was by the tribal progenitors, in line with the usage of the word for hind in this verse: 'Naphtali is a hind let loose' (Gen. 49:21)."

E. R. Judah b. R. Simon said, "He imposed the oath upon them by the circumcision, since the word for 'gazelles' refers to the host that bears a sign.

F. "And it was by 'the hinds of the field' because they pour out their blood for the sanctification of my Name like the blood of a deer or a hind."

4. A. Rabbis said, "He imposed the oath upon them by the generation of the repression, specifically:

B. "'by the hosts that carried out my will in the world, and through whom I carried out my will.

C. "And it was by 'the hinds of the field' because they pour out their blood for the sanctification of my Name like the blood of a deer or a hind: 'For your sake we are killed all day long' (Ps. 44:23)."

5. A. Said R. Hiyya b. R. Abba, "If someone should say to me, 'Give your life for the sanctification of the Name of the Holy One, blessed be He, I should readily give it up, on condition that he kill me immediately.

B. "But in the generation of the repression, I should not have been able to bear the torment.

C. "For what did they do in the generation of the repression?

D. "They would bring iron discs and make them white-hot in fire, and then put them under the armpits and took away their lives through them.

E. "They would bring needles of reeds and put them under their fingernails and remove their lives through them.

F. "That is in line with what David said, 'To you, O Lord, do I lift up my soul' (Ps. 25:1),

G. "that is written, 'I give up,' which is to say, they gave up their souls for the sanctification of the Name of the Holy One, blessed be He.'"

6. A. Said R. Hoshaiah, "Said the Holy One, blessed be
    He, to Israel, 'Wait for me, and I shall make you
    like the host above.'"

7. A. R. Yudan in the name of R. Meir: "Said the Holy
    One, blessed be He, to Israel, 'If you keep my oath,
    I shall make you like the host above,

    B. "and if not, I shall make you like the host below."

XXIV:ii

1. A. R. Yosé b. R. Hanina said, "The two oaths [Song 2:7: 'I adjure you, O
       daughters of Jerusalem,' and Song 3:5, 'I adjure you, O daughters of
       Jerusalem, by the gazelles or the hinds of the field'] apply, one to
       Israel, the other to the nations of the world.

    B. "The oath is imposed upon Israel that they not rebel against the yoke
       of the kingdoms.

    C. "And the oath is imposed upon the kingdoms that they not make the
       yoke too hard for Israel.

    D. "For if they make the yoke too hard on Israel, they will force the end
       to come before its appointed time."

    2. A. Said R. Levi, "It is written, 'Behold a king shall reign in
        righteousness' (Isa. 32:1).

        B. "The Holy One, blessed be He, does not place a tyrannical
        king over his nation before he [Simon] first exacts their
        debt and completely liquidates it. [Simon, p. 114, n. 5:
        The setting up of a tyrant is a sign that God is now about
        to liquidate Israel's debt, i.e., punish Israel for all their
        sins, so that the redemption may come all the sooner.]"

    3. A. R. Abbahu in the name of R. Tanhum said, "What did the
        Israelite officials say to Pharaoh? 'There is no straw given
        to your servants...but the fault is in your own people' (Ex.
        5:16).

        B. "'You sin against your people, and you sin against your
        nation, and through your own actions your kingdom will
        be taken away from you and given to another nation.'"

4. A. R. Helbo says, "There are four oaths that are mentioned here [Song
       2:7, 'I adjure you, O daughters of Jerusalem,' Song 3:5, 'I adjure
       you, O daughters of Jerusalem, by the gazelles or the hinds of the
       field,' Song 5:8, 'I adjure you, O daughters of Jerusalem, if you find
       my beloved, that you tell him I am sick with love,' Song 8:4, 'I adjure
       you, O daughters of Jerusalem, that you not stir up nor awaken love
       until it please'], specifically,

B. "he imposed an oath on Israel not to rebel against the kingdoms and not to force the end [before its time[, not to reveal its mysteries to the nations of the world, and not to go up from the exile by force.

C. "For if so [that they go up from the exile by force], then why should the royal messiah come to gather together the exiles of Israel?"

5. A. R. Onia said, "The four oaths he imposed upon them corresponded to the four generations that forced the end before its time and stumbled in the effort.

   B. "And what are they?

   C. "Once in the days of Amram, once in the days of Dinai, once in the days of Kosiba, and once in the days of Shutelah son of Abraham: 'The children of Ephraim were as archers handling the bow' (Ps. 78:9)."

   D. Some say, "One in the days of Amram, once in the generation of the repression, once in the days of the son of Kosiba, and once in in the days of Shutelah son of Abraham: 'The children of Ephraim were as archers handling the bow' (Ps. 78:9)."

   E. "For they were reckoning the hour from the time that the Holy One, blessed be He, made the decree when he speak with our father, Abraham, between the pieces [Gen. 15:13-17], but the time actually commenced from the moment at which Isaac was born.

   F. "[Basing their actions upon this erroneous reckoning,] they assembled and went forth to battle and many of them fell slain.

   G. "How come? 'Because they did not believe in the Lord and did not trust in his salvation' (Ps. 78:9),

   H. "but they forced the end and violated the oath."

XXIV:iii

1. A. "...that you not stir up nor awaken love until it please":

   B. R. Yudan and R. Berekhiah:

   C. R. Yudan said, "It is the love ['nor awaken love'] that Isaac had for Esau: 'Now Isaac loved Esau' (Gen. 25:8).

   D. "What is then the sense of, 'until it please'?

   E. "Until the pleasure of the old man has been done."

2. A. R. Berekhiah said, "It is the love that the Holy One, blessed be He, had for Israel: 'I have lord you, says the Lord' (Mal. 1:2).

   B. "What is then the sense of, 'until it please'?

   C. "The 'it' refers to the dominion of heaven, and bears this meaning: 'until the Attribute of Justice will be pleased on its own.'

D.   "'[But then,] I shall bring it with great thunders, and I shall not delay.'
E.   "That is why it is written, 'until it please.'"

25

Song of Songs Rabbah
to Song of Songs 2:8

2:8   *The voice of my beloved!*
       Behold he comes,
       leaping upon the mountains,
       bounding over the hills.

XXV:i

1.   A.   "The voice of my beloved! Behold he comes [leaping upon the mountains, bounding over the hills]":
      B.   R. Judah and R. Nehemiah and Rabbis:
      C.   R. Judah says, "'The voice of my beloved! Behold he comes': this refers to Moses.
      D.   "When he came and said to the Israelites, 'In this month you will be redeemed,' they said to him, 'Our lord, Moses, how are we going to be redeemed? And did not the Holy One, blessed be He, say to Abraham, "And they shall work them and torment them for four hundred years" (Gen. 15:13), and now we have in hand only two hundred and ten years!'
      E.   "He said to them, 'Since he wants to redeem you, he is not going to pay attention to these reckonings of yours.
      F.   "'But: "leaping upon the mountains, bounding over the hills." The reference here to mountains and hills in fact alludes to calculations and specified times. "He leaps" over reckonings, calculations, and specified times.
      G.   "'And in this month you are to be redeemed: "This month is the beginning of months" (Ex. 12:1).'"
2.   A.   R. Nehemiah says, "'The voice of my beloved! Behold he comes': this refers to Moses.
      B.   "When he came and said to the Israelites, 'In this month you will be redeemed,' they said to him, 'Our lord, Moses, how are we going to be redeemed? We have no good deeds to our credit.'

	C.	"He said to them, 'Since he wants to redeem you, he is not going to pay attention to bad deeds.'
	D.	"'And to what does he pay attention? To the righteous people among you and to their deeds,
	E.	"'for example, Amram and his court.
	F.	"''leaping upon the mountains, bounding over the hills": mountains refers only to courts, in line with this usage: "I will depart and go down upon the mountains" (Judges 11:37).
	G.	"'And in this month you are to be redeemed: "This month is the beginning of months" (Ex. 12:1).'"
3.	A.	Rabbis say, "'The voice of my beloved! Behold he comes': this refers to Moses.
	B.	"When he came and said to the Israelites, 'In this month you will be redeemed,' they said to him, 'Our lord, Moses, how are we going to be redeemed? And the whole of Egypt is made filthy by our own worship of idols!'
	C.	"He said to them, 'Since he wants to redeem you, he is not going to pay attention to your worship of idols.
	D.	"'Rather, "leaping upon the mountains, bounding over the hills": mountains and hills refer only to idolatry, in line with this usage: "They sacrifice on the tops of the mountains and offer upon the hills" (Hos. 4:13).
	E.	"'And in this month you are to be redeemed: "This month is the beginning of months" (Ex. 12:1).'"
4.	A.	R. Yudan and R. Hunia:
	B.	R. Yudan in the name of R. Eliezer son of R. Yosé the Galilean, and R. Hunia in the name of R. Eliezer b. Jacob say, "'The voice of my beloved! Behold he comes': this refers to the royal messiah.
	C.	"When he says to the Israelites, 'In this month you are to be redeemed, they will say to him, 'How are we going to be redeemed? And has not the Holy One, blessed be He, taken an oath that he would subjugate us among the seventy nations.'"
	D.	"Now he will reply to them in two ways.
	E.	"He will say to them, 'If one of you is taken into exile to Barbary and one to Sarmatia, it is as though all of you had gone into exile.
	F.	"'And not only so, but this state conscripts troops from all of the world and from every nation, so that if one Samaritan or one Barbarian comes and subjugates you, it is as though his entire nation had ruled over you and as if you were subjugated by all the seventy nations.
	G.	"'In this month you are to be redeemed: "This month is the beginning of months" (Ex. 12:1).'"

26

Song of Songs Rabbah
to Song of Songs 2:9

2:9   *My beloved is like a gazelle,*
        or a young stag.
        Behold, there he stands
        behind our wall,
        gazing in at the windows,
        looking through the lattice.
[2:10 *My beloved speaks and says to me,*
        "Arise, my love, my fair one,
        and come away..."]

XXVI:i

1. A. "My beloved is like a gazelle":
    B. Said R. Isaac, "Said the Congregation of Israel before the Holy One, blessed be He, 'Lord of the world, you have said to us, "My love, my love." You are the one who says, "My love, my love" to us first.' [Simon, p. 118: *Dew* is an exclamation of affection. Jastrow: Thou art sighing for us first, instead of our aspiring for Thee.]
2. A. "My beloved is like a gazelle":
    B. Just as a gazelle leaps from mountain to mountain, hill to hill, tree to tree, thicket to thicket, fence to fence,
    C. so the Holy One, blessed be He, lept from Egypt to the sea, from the sea to Sinai, from Sinai to the age to come.
    D. In Egypt they saw him: "For I will go through the land of Egypt" (Ex. 12:12).
    E. At the sea they saw him: "And Israel saw the great hand" (Ex. 14:31); "This is my God and I will glorify him" (Ex. 15:2).
    F. At Sinai they saw him: "The Lord spoke with you face to face in the mountain" (Dt. 5:4); "The Lord comes from Sinai" (Dt. 33:2).
3. A. "...or a young stag":
    B. R. Yosé b. R. Hanina said, "Meaning, like young deer."
4. A. "Behold, there he stands behind our wall":
    B. behind our wall at Sinai: "For on the third day the Lord will come down" (Ex. 19:11).
5. A. "...gazing in at the windows":

B. "And the Lord came down upon mount Sinai, at the top of the mountain" (Ex. 19:11).

6. A. "...looking through the lattice":

B. "And God spoke all these words" (Ex. 20:1).

7. A. "My beloved speaks and says to me, ['Arise, my love, my fair one, and come away] (Song 2:10)'":

B. What did he say to me?

C. "I am the Lord your God" (Ex. 20:2).

XXVI:ii

1. A. Another explanation of the verses, "My beloved is like a gazelle":

B. Said the Community of Israel before the Holy One, blessed be He, "Lord of the world, you have said to us, "My love, my love." You are the one who says, "My love, my love" to us first.' [Simon, p. 118: *Dew* is an exclamation of affection. Jastrow: Thou art sighing for us first, instead of our aspiring for Thee.]

2. A. "My beloved is like a gazelle":

B. Just as a gazelle leaps from mountain to mountain, hill to hill, tree to tree, thicket to thicket, fence to fence,

C. so the Holy One, blessed be He, leaps from synagogue to synagogue, school house to school house.

D. All this why? So as to bestow blessing upon Israel.

E. And on account of what merit?

F. It is for the merit accruing to Abraham: "And the Lord appeared to him by the terebinths of Mamre and he was sitting" (Gen. 18:1).

3. A. R. Berekhiah in the name of R. Simeon b. Laqish: "While read as 'sitting,' the word is written as, 'sat.'

B. "Abraham intended to stand up. Said to him the Holy One, blessed be He, 'Remain seated, Abraham. You provide a model for your children. Just as you sit while I stand, so your children will be when they enter the synagogue and the school house and recite the Shema: they will sit, while my Glory will stand among them.

C. "What verse of Scripture indicates it? 'God stands in the congregation of God' (Ps. 82:1)."

4. A. [Supply: "God stands in the congregation of God" (Ps. 82:1):]

B. R. Haggai in the name of R. Isaac said, "What is written here is not, 'God is standing,' but rather, 'God stands.'

               C.   "What is the meaning of 'God stands'?
               D.   "It is, 'ready to attention,' as it says: 'And present yourself there to me on the top of the mount' (Ex. 34:2); 'And it shall come to pass that before they call, I will answer' (Isa. 65:24)."
       5.   A.   Rabbi in the name of R. Hanina: "Upon the occasion of every expression of praise with which the Israelites praise the Holy One, blessed be He, the Holy One, blessed be He, sits among them:

B.   "'You are holy, enthroned upon the praises of Israel' (Ps. 22;4)."

6. A.   "...or a young stag":

B.   R. Yosé b. R. Hanina said, "Meaning, like young deer."

7. A.   "Behold, there he stands behind our wall":

B.   behind the walls of the synagogues and schoolhouses.

8. A.   "...gazing in at the windows":

B.   from between the shoulders of the priests.

9. A.   "...looking through the lattice":

B.   from between the fingers of the priests.

10. A.   "My beloved speaks and says to me":

B.   What did he say to me?

C.   "The Lord bless you and keep you" (Num. 6:24).

XXVI:iii

1. A.   Another explanation of the verse, "My beloved is like a gazelle":

B.   Said the Community of Israel before the Holy One, blessed be He, "Lord of the world, you have said to us, "My love, my love." You are the one who says, "My love, my love" to us first.' [Simon, p. 118: *Dew* is an exclamation of affection. Jastrow: Thou art sighing for us first, instead of our aspiring for Thee.]

2. A.   "...or a young stag":

B.   Just as a stag appears and then disappears, appears and then disappears,

C.   so the first redeemer [Moses] came but then disappeared and then reappeared.

   3. A.   How long did he disappear?

     B.   R. Tanhuma said, "Three months: 'And they met Moses and Aaron' (Ex. 5:20)."

     C.   Judah b. Rabbi said, "Intermittently."

     D.   So the final redeemer will appear to them and then disappear from sight.

      E.   And how long will he disappear from them?

F. Forty-five days: "And from the time that the continual burnt-offering shall be taken away and the detestable thing that causes abomination be set up, there shall be a thousand and two hundred ninety days" (Dan. 12:11); "Happy is he who waits and comes to the thousand three hundred and thirty-five days" (Dan. 12:13).

G. What are the additional days?

H. R. Yohanan, the laundry-woman's son, said in the name of R. Jonah, "These are the forty-five days on which he will disappear from them."

I. In those days the Israelites will pick saltwort and juniper roots for food: "They pluck saltwort with wormwood and the roots of the broom are their food" (Job 30:3).

J. Where will he lead them?

K. Some say, "To the wilderness of Judah."

L. Some say, "To the wilderness of Sihon and Og."

M. Those who say, "To the wilderness of Judah," cite the following: "I will yet again make you dwell in tents as in the days of the appointed season" (Hos. 12:10).

N. Those who say, "To the wilderness of Sihon and Og cite the following: "Therefore behold I will allure her and bring her into the wilderness and speak tenderly to her. And I will give her vineyards from there" (Hos. 2:16-17).

O. And whoever believes in him and follows him and waits for him will live.

P. But whoever does not believe in him and follow him and wait for him but goes over to the nations of the world in the end will be killed by them.

Q. Said R. Isaac b. R. Merion, "In the end of the forty-five days [H-I above], he will reappear to them and bring down manna for them.

R.   "For 'there is nothing new under the sun.'"

4.   A.   "...or a young stag":
     B.   meaning, like young deer.
5.   A.   "Behold, there he stands behind our wall":
     B.   behind the Western Wall of the house of the sanctuary.
     C.   Why so?
     D.   Because the Holy One, blessed be He, took an oath to him that it would never be destroyed.
     E.   And the Priests' Gate and the Huldah gate will never be destroyed before the Holy One, blessed be He, will restore them.
6.   A.   "...gazing in at the windows":
     B.   through the merit of the matriarchs.
7.   A.   "My beloved speaks and says to me":
     B.   What did he say to me?
     C.   "This month shall be for you the beginning of the months" (Ex. 12:2).

27

Song of Songs Rabbah
to Song of Songs 2:10

2:10   *My beloved speaks and says to me,*
       "Arise, my love, my fair one,
       and come away..."

XXVII:i

1.   A.   Another interpretation of the verse, "My beloved speaks and says to me":
     B.   R. Azariah said, "Are not 'speaking' and 'saying' the same thing?
     C.   "But 'he spoke to me' through Moses, and 'said to me' through Aaron."
2.   A.   What did he say to me?
     B.   "Arise, my love, my fair one":
     C.   "Arise" means, "get up."
3.   A.   Another interpretation of "arise my love":
     B.   "Arise, daughter of Abraham," of whom it is written, "Get you up out of your country and from your kin" (Gen. 12:1).
4.   A.   "Arise, my love, my fair one":

B. Daughter of Isaac, who became my friend and beautified me on the altar.

5. A. "...and come away":

    B. Daughter of Jacob, who obeyed his father and mother: "And Jacob obeyed his father and his mother and went away to Paddan-aram" (Gen. 28:7).

28

Song of Songs Rabbah
to Song of Songs 2:11

2:11   *"...for lo, the winter is past,*
        the rain is over and gone."

XXVIII:i

1. A. "...for lo, the winter is past":

    B. this refers to the four hundred years that were decreed for our ancestors in Egypt.

    C. "...the rain is over and gone":

    D. this refers to the two hundred and ten years [of actual duress].

2. A. [Supply: "for lo, the winter is past, the rain is over and gone":]

    B. are not winter and rain the same thing?

        C. Said R. Tanhuma, "The principal duress [of winter] is the rain.

        D. "So the principal subjugation of the Israelites in Egypt took place in the eighty-six years from the time of the birth of Miriam."

            3. A. The explanation [of her name] is that it was on that account that she was called "Miriam,"

                B. on account of the fact that "they made their lives bitter" (Ex. 1:14),

                C. for the name Miriam bears the meaning of bitterness.

29

Song of Songs Rabbah
to Song of Songs 2:12

2:12   *"The flowers appear on the earth,*
        the time of singing has come,
        and the voice of the turtledove is heard in our land."

XXIX:i

1. A. "The flowers appear on the earth":
    B. the conquerors [a word that uses some of the same consonants as the word flowers] appear on the earth.
    C. To whom does this refer?
    D. to Moses and Aaron: "And the Lord spoke to Moses and Aaron in the land of Egypt, saying" (Ex. 12:1).
2. A. "...the time of singing has come":
    B. The time has come for Israel to be redeemed.
    C. The time has come for the foreskin to be cut off [a word that uses the same consonants as singing].
    D. The time has come for the Canaanites to be cut off.
    E. The time has come for their idolatry to be uprooted: "And against all the gods of Egypt I will execute judgments" (Ex. 12:12).
    F. The time has come for the sea to have its waters cleaved in two: "And the waters were divided" (Ex. 14:21).
    G. The time has come for the Song [at the sea] to be said: "Then sang Moses" (Ex. 15:1).
        3. A. R. Tanhuma said, "The time has come for songs should be made for the Holy One, blessed be He: 'The Lord is my strength and my song' (Ex. 15:2),
            B. "meaning, 'the songs of the Lord [are my strength].'"
        4. A. [Supply (Simon, p. 122, n. 5:) "the time has come for the Torah to be given":]
            B. Said R. Bibi, "'Your statutes have been my songs' (Ps. 119:54)."
        5. A. "...and the voice of the turtledove is heard in our land":
            B. Said R. Yohanan, "'The voice of the good pioneer is heard in our land' [the words for turtledove and pioneer or explorer using the same consonants].

C. "This refers to Moses when he said, 'And Moses, says, thus says the Lord, at about midnight' (Ex. 11:4)."

30

Song of Songs Rabbah
to Song of Songs 2:13

2:13 *"The fig tree puts forth its figs,
and the vines are in blossom;
they give forth fragrance.
"Arise, my love, my fair one,
and come away."*

XXX:i

1. A. "The fig tree puts forth its figs":
   B. this refers to the Israelite sinners who perished during the three days of darkness: "And there was thick darkness...they did not see one another" (Ex. 10:22-23).
   C. "...and the vines are in blossom; they give forth fragrance":
   D. this refers to the survivors, who repented and were redeemed.
   E. Moses came along to them and said to them, "All this good fragrance is wafted about you, and yet you sit here!
   F. "'Arise, my love, my fair one, and come away.'"

XXX:ii

1. A. Another comment on the verses, "My beloved speaks and says to me, ['Arise, my love, my fair one, and come away, for lo, the winter is past, the rain is over and gone. The flowers appear on the earth, the time of singing has come, and the voice of the turtledove is heard in our land. The fig tree puts forth its figs, and the vines are in blossom; they give forth fragrance. Arise, my love, my fair one, and come away]'" (Song 2:10-13):
   B. "My beloved speaks and says to me":
   C. R. Azariah said, "Are not 'speaking' and 'saying' the same thing?
   D. "But 'he spoke to me' through Moses, and 'said to me' through Aaron."
2. A. What did he say to me? "Arise, my love, my fair one, and come away, for lo, the winter is past":
   B. This refers to the forty years that the Israelites spent in the wilderness.

3.   A.   "the rain is over and gone":

      B.   This refers to the thirty-eight years that the Israelites were as though excommunicated in the wilderness.

            C.   For the Word did not speak with Moses until that entire generation had perished: "And the days in which we came from Kadesh-barnea...moreover the hand of the Lord was against them...so it came to pass that when all the men of war were consumed...the Lord spoke to me saying" (Dt. 2:14-17).

4.   A.   "The flowers appear on the earth":

      B.   the conquerors appear on the earth,

      C.   that is, the princes: "Each prince on his day" (Num. 7:11).

5.   A.   "...the time of singing has come":

      B.   The time for the foreskin to be removed.

      C.   The time for the Canaanites to be cut off.

      D.   The time for the land of Israel to be split up: "Unto these the land shall be divided" (Num. 26:53).

6.   A.   "...and the voice of the turtledove is heard in our land":

      B.   Said R. Yohanan, "'The voice of the good pioneer is heard in our land' [the words for turtledove and pioneer or explorer using the same consonants].

      C.   "This refers to Joshua when he said, 'Pass in the midst of the camp.'"

7.   A.   "The fig tree puts forth its figs":

      B.   this refers to the baskets of first fruits.

8.   A.   "...and the vines are in blossom; they give forth fragrance":

      B.   this refers to drink-offerings.

XXX:iii

1.   A.   Another reading of the verse, "My beloved speaks and says to me":

      B.   He "spoke to me" through Daniel,

      C.   and "said to me" through Ezra.

      D.   And what did he say to me?

2.   A.   "Arise, my love, my fair one, and come away, for lo, the winter is past":

      B.   this refers to the seventy years that the Israelites spent in Exile.

3.   A.   "...the rain is over and gone":

      B.   this is the fifty-two years between the time that the first Temple was destroyed and the kingdom of the Chaldaeans was uprooted.

            C.   But were they not seventy years?

            D.   Said R. Levi, "Subtract from them the eighteen years that an echo was circulated and saying to Nebuchadnezzar, 'Bad servant! Go up and destroy the house of your Master, for the children of your Master have not obeyed him.'"

4. A. "The flowers appear on the earth":
    B. For example, Mordecai and his colleagues, Ezra and his colleagues.
5. A. "...the time of singing has come":
    B. The time for the foreskin to be removed.
    C. The time for the wicked to be broken: "The Lord has broken off the staff of the wicked" (Isa. 14:5),
    D. the time for the Babylonians to be destroyed,
    E. the time for the Temple to be rebuilt: "And saviors shall come up on Mount Zion" (Obad. 1:21); "The glory of this latter house shall be greater than that of the former" (Hag. 2:9).
6. A. "...and the voice of the turtledove is heard in our land":
    B. Said R. Yohanan, "'The voice of the good pioneer is heard in our land' [the words for turtledove and pioneer or explorer using the same consonants].
    C. "This refers to Cyrus: 'Thus says Cyrus, king of Persia...all the kingdoms of the earth...whoever there is among you of all his people...let him go up...and build the house of the Lord' (Ezra 1:2-3)."
7. A. "The fig tree puts forth its figs":
    B. this refers to the baskets of first-fruits.
8. A. "...and the vines are in blossom; they give forth fragrance":
    B. this refers to drink-offerings.

XXX:iv

1. A. Another explanation of the verse, "My beloved speaks and says to me":
    B. He "spoke" through Elijah,
    C. and "said to me" through the Messiah.
    D. What did he say to me?
2. A. "Arise, my love, my fair one, and come away, for lo, the winter is past":
    B. Said R. Azariah, "'...for lo, the winter is past': this refers to the kingdom of the Cutheans [Samaritans], which deceives [the words for winter and deceive use some of the same consonants] the world and misleads it through its lies: 'If your brother, son of your mother...entices you' (Dt. 13:7)."
3. A. "...the rain is over and gone":
    B. this refers to the subjugation.
4. A. "The flowers appear on the earth":
    B. the conquerors appear on the earth.
        C. Who are they?
        D. R. Berekhiah in the name of R. Isaac: "It is written, 'And the Lord showed me four craftsmen' (Zech. 2:3),

E.   "and who are they? Elijah, the royal Messiah, the
     Melchizedek, and the military Messiah."
5.   A.   "...the time of singing has come":
     B.   The time for the Israelites to be redeemed has come,
     C.   the time for the foreskin to be removed.
     D.   The time for kingdom of the Cutheans to perish,
     E.   the time for the kingdom of Heaven to be revealed: "and the Lord
          shall be king over all the earth" (Zech. 14:9).
6.   A.   "...and the voice of the turtledove is heard in our land":
     B.   What is this? It is the voice of the royal Messiah,
     C.   proclaiming, "How beautiful upon the mountains are the feet of the
          messenger of good tidings" (Isa. 52:7).
7.   A.   "The fig tree puts forth its figs":
     B.   Said R. Hiyya b. R. Abba, "Close to the days of the Messiah a great
          pestilence will come to the world, and the wicked will perish."
8.   A.   "...and the vines are in blossom; they give forth fragrance":
     B.   this speaks of those who will remain, concerning whom it is said,
          "And it shall come to pass that he who is left in Zion and he who
          remains in Jerusalem" (Isa. 4:3).
          9.   A.   Said R. Yohanan, [B. Sanhedrin 97A: Our Rabbis have
                    taught on Tannaite authority]:
               B.   "The seven year cycle in which the son of David will come:
               C.   "As to the first one, the following verse of Scripture will
                    be fulfilled: 'And I will cause it to rain upon one city and
                    not upon another' (Amos 4:7).
               D.   "As to the second year, the arrows of famine will be sent
                    forth.
               E.   "As to the third, there will be a great famine, in which
                    men, women, and children will die, pious men and
                    wonder-workers alike, and the Torah will be forgotten in
                    Israel.
               F.   "As to the fourth year, there will be plenty which is no
                    plenty.
               G.   "As to the fifth year, there will be great prosperity, and
                    people will eat, drink, and rejoice, and the Torah will be
                    restored to those that study it.
               H.   "As to the sixth year, there will be rumors.
               I.   "As to the seventh year, there will be wars.
               J.   "As to the end of the seventh year [the eighth year], the
                    son of David will come."
                    K.   Said Abbayye, "Lo, how many septenates have
                         passed like that one, and yet he has not come."

10. A. The Messiah will come only in the conditions described in that which was said by R. Simeon b. Laqish:

    B. **[M. Sot. 9:15AA-GG:] R. Judah says, "In the generation in which the son of David will come, the gathering place will be for prostitution, Galilee will be laid waste, Gablan will be made desolate, and the men of the frontier will go about from town to town, and none will take pity on them; and the wisdom of scribes will putrefy; and those who fear sin will be rejected; and the truth will be herded away.**

    C   **"And the generation will be brazen-faced like a dog.**

        D. "How do we know that truth will be abandoned?

        E. "For it is said, 'And the truth will be herded away [and he who departs from evil makes himself a prey' (Isa. 59:15)."

        F. And where does truth go?

        G. The school of R. Yannai said, "It will be divided into herds and herds, each going its way.

11. A. Rabbis say, "In the generation in which the son of David will come, the sages of the generation will die,

    B. "and the eyes of those who remain will grow dim because of sorrow and anguish,

    C. "and much trouble and many evils will come upon the community.

    D. "Harsh decrees will be renewed and sent forth.

    E. "Before the first has been carried out, another will come and add to it."

12. A. Said R. Nehorai, "In the generation in which the son of David will come, the youth will humiliate the elders,

    B. "the elders will stand up before the youth.

    C. "'The daughter rises up against her mother, the daughter-in-law against her mother-in-law, a man's enemies are the men of his own house' (Mic. 7:6).

D. "And a son will not be ashamed before his father."

13. A. R. Nehemiah says, "Before the days of the Messiah poverty will increase, there will be inflation, while the vine will give its fruit, the wine will sour.

B. "The entire kingdom will turn to heresy.

C. "And there will be no reproof."

14. A. Said R. Abba b. Kahana, "The son of David will come only in a generation the leadership of which is in the hands of dogs."

15. A. Said R. Levi, "The son of David will come only in a generation the leadership of which is impudent and liable to annihilation."

16. A. Said R. Yannai, "If you see one generation after another cursing and blaspheming, expect the Messiah:

B. "'Wherewith your enemies have taunted, O Lord, wherewith your enemies have taunted the footsteps of your anointed' (Ps. 89:52); then 'Blessed be the Lord forevermore, amen and amen' (Ps. 89:53)."

31

Song of Songs Rabbah
to Song of Songs 2:14

2:14   *"O my dove, in the clefts of the rock,*
in the covert of the cliff,
"let me see your face,
let me hear your voice,
"for your voice is sweet,
and your face is comely"

XXXI:i

1. A. "O my dove, in the clefts of the rock, [in the covert of the cliff, let me see your face, let me hear your voice, for your voice is sweet, and your face is comely]":

B. What is the meaning of "my dove, in the clefts of the rock"?

C. Said R. Yohanan, "Said the Holy One, blessed be He, 'I call Israel a dove: "And Ephraim has become like a silly dove, without understanding" (Hos. 7:11).

	D.	"'To me they are like a dove, but to the nations of the world they are like wild beasts: "Judah is a lion's whelp" (Gen. 49:9); "Naphtali is a hind let loose" (Gen. 49:21); "Dan shall be a serpent in the way" (Gen. 49:17); "Benjamin is a wolf that ravages" (Gen. 49:27).'
	E.	"For the nations of the world make war on Israel and say to Israel, 'What do you want with the Sabbath and with circumcision?'
	F.	"And the Holy One, blessed be He, strengthens Israel and before the nations of the world they become like wild beasts so as to subdue them before the Holy One, blessed be He, and before Israel.
	G.	"But as to the Holy One, blessed be He, they are like a dove that is without guile, and they obey him: 'And the people believed, and when heard that the Lord had remembered' (Ex. 4:31)."

2. A. [Supply: "And the people believed, and when heard that the Lord had remembered" (Ex. 4:31):]

B. Said the Holy One, blessed be He, to Moses, "Moses, are you standing and crying out? I have already heard Israel and their cry: 'Wherefore do you cry out to me' (Ex. 14:25).

C. "The children of Israel do not need you."

3. A. [Reverting to 1.G:] "Therefore said the Holy One, blessed be He, "'...my dove, in the clefts of the rock.'""

4. A. Said R. Judah b. R. Simon, Yohanan, "Said the Holy One, blessed be He, 'To me they are like a dove, but to the nations of the world they are as cunning as snakes.'

B. "Thus: 'Shadrach, Meshach and Abed-nego answered and said to the king, O Nebuchadnezzar' (Dan. 3:16).

C. "If 'to the king' then why 'Nebuchadnezzar,' and if 'Nebuchadnezzar,' then why 'king'?

D. "But this is what they said to him: 'If it is for the purposes of taxes, head-taxes, crop-taxes, or corvée, you are king over us: "to the king, Nebuchadnezzar."

E. "'But if it is for this matter [of worshipping an idol] that you tell us to bow down to your idol, you are simply Nebuchadnezzar, and your name is Nebuchadnezzar, you are a mere man, and we regard you as no more than a dog.

F. "'[The name Nebuchadnezzar yields letters with this sense:] 'bark like a dog, bubble with rage like a pot, chirp like a cricket.'

G. "Forthwith he barked like a dog, boiled like a pot, and chirped like a cricket."

5. A. "I advise you, obey the command of the king" (Qoh. 8:2):

B. Said R. Levi, "'I obey the command of the King of kings of kings,

C. "'the command that instructed at Sinai, "I am the Lord your God" (Ex. 20:2).

D. "'And with special reference to the statement of the oath of God (Qoh. 8:2): "You shall not take the name of the Lord your god in vain" (Ex. 20:7).'"

6. A. It was taught on Tannaite authority by the house of R. Ishmael, "When the Israelites went forth from Egypt, to what were they to be compared?

B. "To a dove that fled from a hawk and flew into the cleft of a rock and found a serpent hidden there.

C. "It went in but could not, because the snake was hidden there, and it tried to go backward but could not, because the hawk was standing outside.

D. "What did the dove do? It began to cry out and beat its wings, so that the owner of the dovecote should hear and come and save it.

E. "That is what the Israelites were like at the sea.

F. "To go down into the sea they could not do, because the sea had not yet been split before them.

G. "To retreat they could not do, because Pharaoh was already drawing near.

H. "So what did they do?

I. "'And they were afraid, and the children of Israel cried out to the Lord' (Ex. 14:10).

J. "Forthwith: 'Thus the Lord saved Israel that day' (Ex. 14:30)."

7. A. R. Judah in the name of R. Hama of Kefar Tehumin: "The matter may be compared to the king who had an only daughter and wanted to listen to her converse.

B. "What did he do?

C. "He circulated an announcement and said, 'Let everybody assemble in the piazza.'

D. "When they had come forth, what did he do? He made a gesture to his servants, and they suddenly fell on her like thugs.

E. "She began to cry out, 'Father, father, save me.'

F. "He said, 'Had I not treated you in this way, you would not have cried out and said, "Father, save me."'

G. "So when the Israelites were in Egypt, the Egyptians enslaved them, and they begin to cry out and look upward to the Holy One, blessed be He: 'And it came to pass in the course of those many days that the king of Egypt died, and the children of Israel signed by reason of the bondage, and they cried' (Ex. 2:23).

H. "Forthwith: 'And God heard their groaning' (Ex. 2:24).

I. "The Holy One, blessed be He, heard their prayer and brought them out with am mighty hand and with an outstretched arm.

J. "But the Holy One, blessed be He, wanted to listen to their voice, and they did not want it.

K. "What did the Holy One, blessed be He, do?

L. "He hardened Pharaoh's heart and he pursued after them: 'And the Lord hardened the heart of Pharaoh, king of Egypt, and he pursued' (Ex. 14:8); 'And Pharaoh brought near' (Ex. 14:10)."

8. A. [Supply: "And Pharaoh brought near" (Ex. 14:10):]

B. What is the meaning of "brought near"?

C. He brought the Israelites near to repentance.

9. A. [Continuing 7.L:] "When they saw them, they raised their eyes to the Holy One, blessed be He: 'The children of Israel lifted up their eyes, and behold, the Egyptians were marching after them, and they were much afraid, and the children of Israel cried out to the Lord' (Ex. 14:10).

B. "This was in the same way that they had cried out in Egypt.

C. "Now when the Holy One, blessed be He, heard, he said to them, 'If I had not treated you in this way, I should not have heard your voice.

D. "It is in connection with that moment that he said, 'O my dove, in the clefts of the rock.'

E. "What is says is not 'let me hear a voice,' but 'let me hear your voice.'

F. "For 'I have already heard it in Egypt.'

G. "And when the children of Israel cried out before the Holy One, blessed be He, forthwith: 'thus the Lord saved Israel that day' (Ex. 14:30).

XXXI:ii

1. A. [Supply: "my dove, in the clefts of the rock, in the covert of the cliff, let me see your face, let me hear your voice, for your voice is sweet, and your face is comely":

B. R. Eleazar interpreted the verse to speak of Israel when it stood at the sea:

C. "'...my dove, in the clefts of the rock, in the covert of the cliff': for they were hidden in the recess of the sea.

D.   "'...let me see your face': 'Stand still and see the salvation of the Lord' (Ex. 14:13).

E.   "'...let me hear your voice': that is, the song, 'Then sang Moses' (Ex. 15:1).

F.   "'...for your voice is sweet': this refers to the song.

G.   "'...and your face is comely': for the Israelites were making a gesture of glorification with their finger and saying, 'This is my God and I will glorify him' (Ex. 15:2)."

2.   A.   R. Aqiba interpreted the verse to speak of Israel when it stood at Mount Sinai:

    B.   "'...my dove, in the clefts of the rock, in the covert of the cliff': for they were hidden in the recess of the Sinai.

    C.   "'...let me see your face': 'And all the people saw the thundering' (Ex. 20:15).

    D.   "'...let me hear your voice': this is the voice that was before the Ten Commandments: 'All that the Lord has spoken we shall do and obey' (Ex. 24:7).

    E.   "'...for your voice is sweet': this is the voice after the Ten Commandments: 'And the Lord heard the voice of your words...and said...they have said well all that they have spoken' (Dt. 5:25)."

3.   A.   [Supply: "And the Lord heard the voice of your words...and said...they have said well all that they have spoken" (Dt. 5:25):]

    B.   What is the meaning of "they have said well all that they have spoken"?

    C.   Hiyya b. R. Ada and Bar Qappara:

    D.   One said, "It was like the act of trimming [which uses the same consonants as the word well] in the trimming of the lamps."

    E.   The other said, "It was like the act of preparation in the preparation of the incense."

4.   A.   [Continuing 2.E:] "'...and your face is comely': 'And when the people saw it, they trembled and stood afar off' (Ex. 20:15)."

5.   A.   R. Yosé the Galilean interpreted the verse to speak of the [subjugation of Israel to the] kingdoms:

    B.   "'...my dove, in the clefts of the rock, in the covert of the cliff': they were hidden in the shadow of the kingdoms.

    C.   "'...let me see your face': this refers to study.

    D.   "'...let me hear your voice': this refers to a good deed."

6.   A.   Now they took a vote one time in the upper room of Aris in Lydda saying, "What is the more important? Study or deed?"

    B. R. Tarfon says, "Greater is deed."

    C. R. Aqiba says, "Greater is study."

    D. They voted and reached the decision that study is the greater, since it brings about deed.

7.   A. [Continuing 5.D:] "'...for your voice is sweet': this refers to study.

    B. "'...and your face is comely': this refers to deed."

8.   A. R. Huna and R. Aha in the name of R. Aha b. Hanina, following the theory of R. Meir, interpreted the verse to speak of the tent of meeting:

    B. "'...my dove, in the clefts of the rock, in the covert of the cliff': for they were shadowed in the shade of the tent of meeting.

    C. "'...let me see your face': 'And the congregation was assembled at the door of the tent of meeting' (Lev. 8:4).

    D. "'...let me hear your voice': 'And when all the people saw it, they shouted' (Lev. 9:24).

    E. "Since they saw something new, therefore they proclaimed a new song.

    F. "'...for your voice is sweet': this refers to the song.

    G. "'...and your face is comely': 'And all the congregation drew near and stood before the Lord' (Lev. 9:5)."

        9.   A. Said R. Tanhuma, "They [R. Huna and R. Aha in the name of R. Aha b. Hanina] in the theory of R. Meir, interpreted it to refer to the tent of meeting. I will will interpret it, in line with the position of rabbis, [who hold that it speaks of] the eternal house [the temple]:

            B. "'...my dove, in the clefts of the rock, in the covert of the cliff': for they were shadowed in the shade of the eternal house.

            C. "'...let me see your face': 'Then Solomon assembled' (1 Kgs. 8:1).

            D. "'...let me hear your voice': 'It came even to pass, when the trumpeters and singers were as one' (2 Chr. 5:13)."

            10.A. R. Abin in the name of R. Abba, the Priest, son of Daliah: "It is written, 'And all the people answered together' (Ex. 19:8), but also, 'And all the people answered with one voice and said' (Ex. 24:3).

              B. "To what point did [the merit accomplished through] that voice endure to their credit?

              C. "Up to: 'It came even to pass, when the trumpeters and singers were as one' (2 Chr. 5:13)."

11.   A. [Resuming from 9.D:] "'for your voice is sweet': this refers to the song[s sung in the temple rite].

    B. "'...and your face is comely': this speaks of the offerings: 'And Solomon offered for the sacrifice of peace-offerings' (1 Kgs. 8:63)."

12. A. [Supply: "And King Solomon offered the sacrifice of the oxen, twenty-two thousand" (2 Chr. 7:5)]:
     B. What are these oxen?
     C. "The four wagons and the eight oxen" (Num. 7:8).
13. A. R. Elijah interpreted the verse to speak of the pilgrims who come up to celebrate the festivals:
     B. "'...my dove, in the clefts of the rock, in the covert of the cliff': these are the pilgrims who come up for the festivals: 'Three times in a year will all your males be seen' (Dt. 16:16).
     C. "'...let me hear your voice': this refers to the recitation of the Hallel-psalms [Ps. 113-188] in a beautiful choir.
     D. "When the Israelites recite the Hallel-psalms, their voice rises on high.
     E. "There is this proverb: 'Keep Passover in the house, and for Hallel break the roof.'
     F. "'...for your voice is sweet': this refers to the song.
     G. "'...and your face is comely': this refers to the priestly blessing."

XXXI:iii

1. A. Said R. Iudah b. R. Simon in the name of R. Simeon b. Eleazar, "Why was Rebekkah childless [for so long]?
    B. "It was so that the nations of the world should not say, 'Our prayer has borne fruit.'
    C. "For they said to her, '"Our sister, be the mother of thousands of ten thousands" (Gen. 24:60.'
    D. "[Therefore she did not bear] until Isaac prayed in her behalf, and then she was visited [and got pregnant].
    E. "'And Isaac entreated the Lord for his wife' (Gen. 25:21)."
2. A. R. Azariah in the name of R. Hanina b. R. Pappa said, "Why were the matriarchs childless [for so long]?
    B. "It was so that they should not put on airs towards their husbands by reason of their beauty."
3. A. R. Huna and R. Jeremiah in the name of R. Hiyya b. R. Abba said, "Why were the matriarchs childless [for so long]?
    B. "It was so that the greater part of their lives should be spent without servitude."
4. A. R. Hunai in the name of R. Meir: "Why were the matriarchs childless [for so long]?
    B. "It was so that their husbands should have a long time to enjoy their beauty.
    C. "For when a woman gets pregnant, she gets fat and clumsy.

      D.   "You may know that that is the fact, for all the years that our matriarch, Sarah, was barren, she dwelt in her house like a bride in her bridal bower.

      E.   "But when she got pregnant, her appearance changed: 'In pain you shall bring forth children' (Gen. 3:16)."

5.   A.   R. Levi in the name of R. Shila of Kefar Tamarta and R. Helbo in the name of R. Yohanan: "Why were the matriarchs childless [for so long]?

      B.   "It was because the Holy One, blessed be He, craved to hear their pleading.

      C.   "He said to them, 'My dove, I shall tell you how come I have kept you barren. It was because I craved to hear your pleading.'

      D.   "'...for your voice is sweet, and your face is comely.'"

32

Song of Songs Rabbah
to Song of Songs 2:15

2:15   *"Catch us the foxes,*
the little foxes,
that spoil the vineyards,
for our vineyards are in blossom."

XXXII:i

1.   A.   "Catch us the foxes, the little foxes, [that spoil the vineyards, for our vineyards are in blossom]":

      B.   When the other kingdoms are assigned metaphors, the metaphors pertain only to fire: "And I will set my face against them, out of the fire they have come fourth, and the fire shall devour them" (Ez. 15:7).

      C.   But when the Egyptians are assigned a metaphor, it is only that which is consumed by fire: "They are quenched as a wick" (Isa. 43:17).

      D.   When the other kingdoms are assigned metaphors, the metaphors pertain only to silver and gold: "As for that image, its head was of fine gold" (Dan. 2:32).

      E.   But when the Egyptians are assigned a metaphor, it is only lead: "They sank as lead" (Ex. 15:10).

F.   When the other kingdoms are assigned metaphors, the metaphors pertain only to cedars: "Behold, the Assyrian was a cedar in Lebanon" (Ez. 31:3); "The tree that you saw, which grew" (Gen. 4:17); 'Yet I destroyed the Amorite before them, whose height was like that of cedars" (Amos 2:9).

G.   But when the Egyptians are assigned a metaphor, it is only stubble: "It consumes them like stubble" (Ex. 15:7).

H.   When the other kingdoms are assigned metaphors, the metaphors pertain only to beasts of pray: "And four great beasts came up from the sea, different from one another" (Dan. 7:3); "The first was like a lion" (Dan. 7:4).

I.   But when the Egyptians are assigned a metaphor, it is only foxes: "Catch us the foxes, the little foxes."

J.   [What follows is at 6.F and does not make sense here:] Guard them in the river.

2. A.   Said R. Eleazar b. R. Simeon, "The Egyptians were clever, so they are given the metaphor of foxes.

B.   "Just as a fox looks over its shoulder, so the Egyptians looked over their shoulders.

C.   "They were saying, 'Now how shall we impose death upon them?

D.   "'Shall we put them to death with fire? But has it not already been said, "For my fire will the Lord contend" (Isa. 66:16).

E.   "'Shall we put them to death with the sword? "And by his sword with all flesh" (Isa. 66:16).

F.   "'Let us put them to death with water, for the Holy One, blessed be He, has sworn that he will not again bring a flood on the earth: "For this is as the waters of Noah to me" (Isa. 54:9).'

G.   "Said the Holy One, blessed be He, to them, 'By yours lives! Each one of you shall a drag into the flood: "He shall drag them to the power of the sword, they shall be a portion for foxes" (Ps. 63:11).'

H.   "'He shall drag them to the power of the sword': this refers to the wicked, whom he dragged onto the dry bottom of the sea.' [Simon, p. 135, n. 7: Before the water returned. Thus he did not bring a flood upon them, but led them to the flood.]

I.   "'...they shall be a portion for foxes': Said the Holy One, blessed be He, 'This portion will be reserved for the foxes.'"

3. A.   Said R. Berekhiah, "The word for foxes is written out with all its vowels the first time, but the second time not.

B.   "This refers to the foxes who went down to the bed of the sea."

4. A.   Said R. Tanhuma in the name of R. Judah b. R. Simon, "It is written, 'He who makes a way in the sea' (Isa. 63:16).

B. "This is no big deal.

C. "'And a path in the mighty waters' (Isa. 63:16).

D. "This too is no big deal.

E. "But what really takes effort?

F. "'Who brings forth the chariot and horse, the army and the power' (Isa. 63:16)."

5. A. [Supply: "He who makes a way in the sea, and a path in the mighty waters, who brings forth the chariot and horse, the army and the power" (Isa. 63:16):]

B. Said R. Yudan, "They entered in this order like the wild beasts at the games followed by the common spectator first and then by the nobility."

6. A. Said R. Hanan, "What did the proper and modest Israelite women do [when Pharaoh decreed death to the males]?

B. "They would take them and hide them in holes.

C. "So the wicked Egyptians would take their little babies and bring them into the Israelites' houses and pinch them, so the babies would cry.

D. "Then the Israelite baby would hear the voice of the other crying, and would cry with him.

E. "And they would then take them and throw them into the river.

F. "Thus: 'Catch us the foxes, the little foxes,' and guard them to throw them into the river."

G. And how many infants were there that they threw into the river?

H. Ten thousand: "Ten thousand, even as the growth of the field" (Ez. 16:7).

I. And R. Levi said, "Six hundred thousand, for so said Moses, 'The people, among whom I am, are six hundred thousand men on foot' (Num. 11:21)."

7. A. Now what did the Egyptians do?

B. They would bring their children from the schools and send them into the Israelites' bath houses, where they would see which Israelite woman was pregnant.

C. They would then make a note of them and go back and tell their fathers, "Thus and so has three months to go, thus and so, four months, thus and so, five months."

D. When the time had run out, they would take the babes from their breasts and cast them in the river: "Catch us the foxes, the little foxes."

E. What is written is not "seize," or "kill," but "catch,' meaning that they guarded them for the river.

XXXII:ii

1. A. [Supply: "Catch us the foxes, the little foxes":]
    B. R. Yudan and R. Berekhiah:
    C. R. Yudan said, "'the little foxes' are Esau and his generals: 'Behold, I make you little among the nations' (Obad. 1:2)."
    2. A. [=Gen. R. LXV:XI.1-2, with reference to Gen. 27:1: "When Isaac was old, and his eyes were dim, so that he could not see, he called Esau, his older son" – thus, "he called Esau his greater son."] Said R. Eleazar b. R. Simeon, "The matter may be compared to the case of a town that was collecting a bodyguard for the king. There was a woman there, whose son was a dwarf. She called him 'Tall-swift' [Freedman]. She said, 'My son is "Tall-swift," so why do you not take him?'
        B. "They said to her, 'If in your eyes he is "Tall-swift," in our eyes he is the smallest of dwarfs.'
        C. "So his father called him 'great': '...he called Esau his great son.'
        D. "So too his mother called him 'great': 'Then Rebecca took the best garments of Esau, her great son.'
        E. "Said the Holy One, blessed be He, to them, 'If in your eyes he is great, in my eyes he is small: 'Behold, I make you small among the nations' (Obad. 1:2) [speaking of Edom/Esau/Rome]."
    3. A. [Genesis Rabbah's version:] Said R. Abbahu said R. Berekhiah, [Song: "And even if he is great, then:] "In accord with the size of the ox is the stature of the slaughterer.
        B. "That is in line with the following verse: 'For the Lord has a sacrifice in Bozrah, and a great slaughter in the land of Edom' (Isa. 34:6)."
        C. [Genesis Rabbah's version concludes:] Said R. Berekhiah, "The sense is, 'There will be a great slaughterer in the land of Edom. [Freedman, p. 587, n. 2: Since Esau is called great, his slaughterer, God, will likewise be great.]"
4. A. "[Catch us the foxes, the little foxes,] that spoil the vineyards, [for our vineyards are in blossom]":
    B. "that spoil the vineyards" refers to Israel: "For the vineyard of the Lord of hosts is the house of Israel" (Isa. 5:7).
5. A. "...for our vineyards are in blossom":
    B. "There is no cluster to eat, nor first-ripe fig which my soul desires" (Mic. 7:1).

6. A.   R. Berekhiah said, "'the little foxes': these are the four kingdoms:
    B.   "'There are four things that are little upon the earth' (Prov. 30:24).
    C.   "'...that spoil the vineyards': this refers to Israel: 'For the vineyard of the Lord of hosts is the house of Israel' (Isa. 5:7).
    D.   "'...for our vineyards are in blossom':
    E.   "Who is responsible that our vineyards are [Simon: merely] budding?
    F.   "'And I sought for a man among them, who should make up the hedge...but I found none' (Ez. 22:30),
    G.   "except for Noah, Daniel, and Job."

33

Song of Songs Rabbah
to Song of Songs 2:16

2:16   *My beloved is mine and I am his,*
       he pastures his flock among the lilies.

XXXIII:i

1. A.   "My beloved is mine and I am his":
    B.   To me he is God, and to him I am the nation:
    C.   To me he is God: "I am the Lord your God" (Ex. 20:2).
    D.   and to him I am people and nation: "Attend to me, my people, and give ear to me, my nation" (Isa. 51:4).
2. A.   To me he is father, and to him I am son:
    B.   to me he is father: "For you are our father" (Isa. 63:6); "For I have become father to Israel" (Jer. 31:9).
    C.   and to him I am son: "Israel is my son, my firstborn" (Ex. 4:22); "You are children of the Lord" (Dt. 14:1).
3. A.   To me he is shepherd: "Give ear, shepherd of Israel" (Ps. 80:2).
    B.   To him I am flock: "And you, my sheep, the sheep of my pasture" (Ez. 34:31).
4. A.   To me he is guard: "He who guards Israel does not slumber nor sleep" (Ps. 121:4).
    B.   To him I am vineyard: "For the vineyard of the Lord of hosts is the house of Israel" (Isa. 5:7).
5. A.   He is for me against those who challenge me, and I am for him against those who spite him.

B.   He is for me against those who challenge me, for he hit the firstborn: "For I will go through the land of Egypt" (Ex. 12:12); "And it came to pass at midnight that the Lord smote all the firstborn" (Ex. 12:29).

C.   and I am for him against those who spite him, for I sacrificed [the lamb, which is] the god of Egypt.

D.   And thus: "And against all the Gods of Egypt I will execute judgments" (Ex. 12:12), and I sacrificed them to him: "Lo, if we sacrifice the abomination of the Egyptians before their eyes" (Ex. 12:22); "They shall take to them every man a lamb, according to their fathers' houses" (Ex. 12:3).

6.   A.   He said to me, "Let not the mingled wine [which stands for the sanhedrin] be lacking": "Your navel is a rounded bowl, that never lacks mixed wine."

B.   And I said to him, "You are my beloved, let your kindness never be lacking": "The Lord is my shepherd, I shall not want" (Ps. 23:1).

7.   A.   Said R. Judah b. R. Ilai, "He is my song, and I am his song.

B.   "He praised me, and I praised him.

C.   "He called me, 'my sister, my beloved, my perfect one, my dove,'

D.   "and I said to him, 'This is my beloved and my friend.'

E.   "He said to me, 'Behold, you are beautiful, my love; behold, you are beautiful; your eyes are doves' (Song 1:15),

F.   "and I said to him, 'Behold, you are beautiful, my beloved, truly lovely' (Song 1:16).

G.   "He said to me, 'Happy are you, Israel, who is like you' (Dt. 33:29),

H.   "and I said to him, 'Who is like you, Lord, among the mighty' (Ex. 15:11).

I.   "He said to me, 'And who is like your people, Israel, a nation unique on earth' (2 Sam. 7:23).

J.   "And I declare his uniqueness twice a day: 'Hear Israel the Lord our God the Lord is unique' (Dt. 6:4)."

8.   A.   And when there is something that I need, I ask it only from his hand: "And it came to pass in the course of those many days that the king of Egypt died...and God heard their groaning...and God saw the children of Israel" (Ex. 2:23ff).

B.   And when there is something that he needs, he asks it only from me and from my hand: "Speak to all the congregation of Israel, saying to them" (Ex. 12:3).

C.   And when there is something that I need, I ask it only from his hand: "And when Pharaoh drew near, the children of Israel lifted up their eyes" (Ex. 14:10).

D.   And when there is something that he needs, he asks it only from me and from my hand: "Speak to the children of Israel that they take for me an offering" (Ex. 25:2).

E.   When I had trouble, I asked help only from him: "And the children of Israel cried to the Lord, for he had nine hundred chariots of iron, and he greatly oppressed the children of Israel" (Judges 4:3).

9.   A.   [Supply: "And the children of Israel cried to the Lord, for he had nine hundred chariots of iron, and he greatly oppressed the children of Israel" (Judges 4:3):]

B.   What is the meaning of "greatly"?

C.   With insults and blasphemy.

10.   A.   [Resuming from 8.E:] And when there is something that he needs, he asks it only from me: "And let them make me a sanctuary" (Ex. 25:8).

XXXIII:ii

1.   A.   "...he pastures his flock among the lilies":

B.   R. Yohanan was punished with suffering from gallstones for three years and a half.

C.   R. Hanina came up to visit him. He said to him, "How're you doing?"

D.   He said to him, "I have more than I can bear."

E.   He said to him, "Don't say that. But say, 'The faithful God.'"

F.   When the pain got severe, he would say, "Faithful God," and when the pain became greater than he could bear, R. Hanina would come in to him and say something over him, and he restored his soul.

G.   After some time R. Hanina became ill, and R. Yohanan came up to visit him. He said to him, "How're you doing?"

H   He said to him, "How hard is suffering."

I.   He said to him, "Yes, but the reward is still greater."

J.   He said to him, "I don't want either them or their reward."

K.   He said to him, "Why don't you say that word that you said over me and restored my soul?"

L.   He said to him, "When I was up and about, I served as a pledge for others, but now that I am within, I don't need anybody else to serve as a pledge for me."

M.   He said to him, "It is written, 'he pastures his flock among the lilies':

N.   "the rod of the Holy One, blessed be He, draws near only to people whose hearts are as soft as lilies."

2. A. Said R. Eleazar, "The matter may be compared to the case
        of a householder who had two cows, one strong, the other
        weak.
    B. "On which one does he place the burden? Is it not on the
        strong one?
    C. "Thus the Holy One, blessed be He, does not impose trials
        upon the wicked. Why not? Because they cannot endure:
        'But the wicked are like the troubled sea' (Isa. 57:20).
    D. "Upon whom does he impose trials? Upon the righteous:
        'The Lord tries the righteous' (Ps. 11:5); 'And it came to
        pass after these things that god tried Abraham' (Gen. 22:1);
        'And it came to pass after these things that his master's
        wife cast her eyes on Joseph' (Gen. 39:7)."
3. A. Said R. Yosé b. R. Hanina, "A flax-beater, when his flax
        is hard, does not beat it very much. Why? Because it will
        burst.
    B. "But if it is good flax, the more he beats it, the more it
        improves.
    C. "Thus the Holy One, blessed be He, does not impose trials
        upon the wicked, because they cannot endure.
    D. "But he imposes trials upon the righteous: 'The Lord tries
        the righteous' (Ps. 11:5)."
4. A. Said R. Yohanan, "The potter, when he tests his furnace,
        does not test it with weak jars.
    B. "Why not? Because when he hits them, they will break.
    C. "With what does he test his furnace? With strong jars, for
        even though he strikes them many times, they will not be
        broken.
    D. "Thus the Holy One, blessed be He, does not impose trials
        upon the wicked. Upon whom does he impose trials?
        Upon the righteous: 'The Lord tries the righteous' (Ps.
        11:5)."

34

Song of Songs Rabbah
to Song of Songs 2:17

2:17   *Until the day breathes*
        and the shadows flee,
        turn my beloved, be like a gazelle,
        or a young stag upon rugged mountains.

XXXIV:i
1. A.   "Until the day breathes":
    B.   R. Yudan and R. Berekhiah:
    C.   R. Yudan said, "[The meaning of 'until the day breathes' is that God says to Israel,] 'Until I bring a breathing space into the night of the kingdoms.
    D.   "'Did I not bring a breathing space into the night of the Egyptians, for there were to be four hundred years but I made them into only two hundred and ten.'
    E.   "'...and the shadows flee':
    F.   "[God continues,] 'Did I not remove from them two harsh shadows, the mud and the bricks?'"
        2. A.   R. Helbo said, "'And also that nation' (Gen. 15:14): that refers to the Egyptians but also the four kingdoms."
            B.   R. Yudan said, "[For four hundred years they would suffer] the condition of aliens, servitude, and affliction in a land that was not theirs, even when it offered hospitality."
3. A.   [Reverting to 1.F, Yudan continues,] "'...turn my beloved, be like a gazelle': [God says to Israel,] 'In the end I shall transform for you the Attribute of Strict Justice into the Attribute of Mercy,
    B.   "and hasten your redemption like [following Simon's emendation, dropping the word 'blood'] the gazelle or young hart.'"
        4. A.   "...or a young stag [upon rugged mountains]":
            B.   R. Yosé b. R. Hanina said, "Like a young deer."
5. A.   [Reverting to 3.B, Yudan continues:] "upon rugged mountains":
    B.   "On account of the merit of the stipulations that I made with your patriarch, Abraham, between the pieces [the words for rugged and pieces using the same consonants]: 'In that day the Lord made a covenant with Abram, saying' (Gen. 15:18)."

6.   A.   R. Berekhiah said, "'Until the day breathes': That is, 'until I make the day blaze,' as in these usages: 'I will blow upon you with the fire of my wrath' (Ez. 21:36), 'to blow the fire upon it' (Ez. 22:20).

      B.   "And what is the sense of, 'and the shadows flee'?

      C.   "This refers to the shadows of anguish and sighing.

      D.   "'...turn my beloved, be like a gazelle': [God says to Israel,] 'In the end I shall transform for you the Attribute of Strict Justice into the Attribute of Mercy, and hasten your redemption like the gazelle or young hart.

      E.   "'...or a young stag': a young deer."

7.   A.   "...upon rugged mountains":

      B.   R. Yudan said, "It is so that the kingdoms will receive the punishment for their rapacity."

      C.   Said R. Levi b. R. Haitah, "When the kingdom falls towards the thorn."

      D.   R. Berekhiah said, "Said the Holy One, blessed be He, 'Even if I held against them only what they did in Bethar [a word that uses the same consonants as rugged], my judgment will be executed on them."

            8.   A.   And what did they do in Bethar?

                  B.   Said R. Yohanan, "Caesar Hadrian killed in Bethar four hundred myriads of thousands of people."

Part Three
PARASHAH THREE

35

Song of Songs Rabbah
to Song of Songs 3:1

3:1   *Upon my bed by night*
       I sought him whom my soul loves;
       I sought him, but found him not;
       I called him, but he gave no answer.

XXXV:I

1.   A.   "Upon my bed by night":
      B.   Said R. Abba b. R. Kahana, "What is the meaning of the phrase, 'Upon my bed by night'?
      C.   "It means, 'in my sickness,' in line with the following usage: 'And he does not die, but stays in bed' (Ex. 21:18)."

2.   A.   Said R. Levi, "Said the Community of Israel before the Holy One, blessed be He, 'Lord of the world, in the past, you would give light for me between one night and the next night,
      B.   "'between the night of Egypt and the night of Babylonia, between the night of Babylonia and the night of Media, between the night of Media and the night of Greece, between the night of Greece and the night of Edom.
      C.   "'Now that I have fallen asleep neglectful of the Torah and the religious duties, one night flows into the next.'"

3.   A.   "Upon my bed by night":
      B.   Said R. Alexandri, "'When I fell asleep [neglectful] of the Torah and religious duties, one night flowed into the next.'
      C.   "'Upon my bed by night': that is, 'nights have come.'" [Simon, p. 143, n. 3: A play on words based on the plural form, nights, implying that trouble follows on trouble, because I remain on my bed, asleep and heedless of my duties.]

4.   A.   Another interpretation of the verse, "Upon my bed by night":

B.   this refers to the night of Egypt.
C.   "I sought him whom my soul loves":
D.   this refers to Moses.
E.   "I sought him, but found him not, I called him, but he gave no answer."

36

Song of Songs Rabbah
to Song of Songs 3:2

3:2   *"I will rise now and go about the city,*
       in the streets and in the squares;
       I will seek him whom my soul loves."
       I sought him but found him not.

XXXVI:ı
1.   A.   "I will rise now and go about the city, in the streets and in the squares":
     B.   that is, in cities and towns.
     C.   "...I will seek him whom my soul loves":
     D.   that is Moses.
     E.   "...I sought him but found him not."

37

Song of Songs Rabbah
to Song of Songs 3:3

3:3   *The watchmen found me,*
       as they went about in the city.
       "Have you seen him whom my soul loves?"

XXXVII:i
1.   A.   "The watchmen found me":
     B.   this refers to the tribe of Levi: "Go to and fro from gate to gate" (Ex. 32:27).
     C.   "Have you seen him whom my soul loves":
     D.   this refers to Moses.

38

Song of Songs Rabbah
to Song of Songs 3:4

3:4 *Scarcely had I passed them,*
when I found him whom my soul loves.
I held him and would not let him go
until I had brought him into my mother's house,
and into the chamber of her that conceived me.

XXXVIII:i

1. A. "Scarcely had I passed them, when I found him whom my soul loves":
   B. this refers to Moses.
   C. "I held him and would not let him go until I had brought him into my mother's house":
   D. this refers to Sinai.
   E. "...and into the chamber of her that conceived me":
   F. this refers to the tent of meeting.
   > G. For it was from then that the Israelites became liable for transgressing their instructions. [The words for "conceive" and "instruction" use the same consonants.]

XXXVIII:ii

1. A. Another explanation of the verses, "Upon my bed by night I sought him whom my soul loves; I sought him, but found him not; I called him, but he gave no answer. 'I will rise now and go about the city, in the streets and in the squares; I will seek him whom my soul loves.' I sought him but found him not. The watchmen found me, as they went about in the city. 'Have you seen him whom my soul loves?' Scarcely had I passed them, when I found him whom my soul loves. I held him and would not let him go until I had brought him into my mother's house, and into the chamber of her that conceived me":
   B. "Upon my bed by night":
   C. this refers to the night of Babylon.
   D. "...I sought him whom my soul loves":
   E. this refers to Daniel.
   F. "...I sought him, but found him not."
   G. "I will rise now and go about the city, in the streets and in the squares":
   H. in the towns and cities.

I.   "...I will seek him whom my soul loves":

J.   this refers to Daniel.

K.   "I sought him but found him not."

L.   "The watchmen found me, as they went about in the city":

M.   these are the Chaldeans.

N.   "Have you seen him whom my soul loves":

O.   this is Daniel.

2.   A.   So where had he gone?

    B.   One authority said, "To keep a fast."

    C.   The other authority said, "To keep a feast."

    D.   The authority who said, "To keep a fast," explained that he had gone to seek mercy on account of the destruction of the house of the sanctuary: "Now, therefore, O our God, listen to the prayer of your servant" (Dan. (9:17).

    E.   The authority who said, "To keep a feast," explained that it was to read the writing given to Belshazzar, "*Mene, mene, tekel upharsin*" (Dan. 5:25).

3.   A.   [Supply: "*Mene, mene, tekel upharsin*" (Dan. 5:25):]

    B.   R. Hiyya the Elder and R. Simeon b. Halafta:

    C.   R. Hiyya the Elder said, "What he saw were the letters in this order: MMTUS NNQFE EELRN. [Simon, p. 144, n. 3: By combining the first letters of each word one gets MNE, the second likewise, the third gives TKL, and UPHRSN consists of the rest.]"

    D.   R. Simeon b. Halafta said, "What he saw were the letters in this way: YTS YTS ASK PGHMT. [Simon, p. 144, n. 4: The words were written in the code that places the first letter of the alphabet with the last, the second with the penultimate, and so on.]"

    E.   Rabbis say, "It was in this form: ENM ENM LKT NSRFU [each word of the inscription reversed]."

    F.   R. Meir says, "He saw it just as it is given in the text: *Mene, mene, tekel upharsin.*

    G.   "*Mene:* 'God has numbered your kingdom and brought it to an end.'

    H.   "*Tekel:* 'you are weighed in the balance.'

    I.   "*Peres:* 'your kingdom is divided' (Dan. 5:26-28)." [This resumes at No. 27.]

4.   A.   At that time the Israelites gathered together with Daniel and said to him, "Our lord, Daniel, all of the bad and harsh prophecies that Jeremiah made have come upon us. But the one good prophecy that he made for us, 'For after

seven years are accomplished for Babylon, I will remember you and do my good word for you, bringing you back to this place' (Jer. 29:10), has not yet come about!"

B. He said to them, "Bring me the book of Isaiah."

C. He begin proclaiming it until he got to this verse: "The burden of the wilderness of the sea. As whirlwinds in the South sweeping on" (Isa. 21:1).

    5. A. [Supply: "The burden of the wilderness of the sea. As whirlwinds in the South sweeping on" (Isa. 21:1):]

        B. if "sea" then whence "wilderness"? And if "wilderness," whence "sea"?

        C. But this refers to the four kingdoms, which are given the analogies of the wild beasts:

        D. "four great beasts coming out of the sea, different from one another" (Dan. 7:3).

    6. A. [Supply: "different from one another" (Dan. 7:3):]

        B. R. Hanina said R. Yohanan [said], "'Different from one another':

        C. "that is, the blows that they give are different from one another."

    7. A. [Supply: "different from one another" (Dan. 7:3):]

        B. If you enjoy sufficient merit, it will emerge from the sea, but if not, it will come out of the forest.

        C. The animal that comes up from the sea is not violent, but the one that comes up out of the forest is violent.

        D. So if you have sufficient merit, the nations will not rule over you.

    8. A. Along these same lines: "The boar out of the wood ravages it" (Ps. 80:14):

        B. The *ayin* is suspended in the word for "wood," meaning this: If you enjoy sufficient merit, it will come from the river, and if not, from the forest.

C. The animal that comes up from the river is not violent, but the one that comes up out of the forest is violent.

9. A. "The burden of the wilderness of the sea":
    B. If you enjoy sufficient merit, it will emerge from the sea, but if not, it will come out of the forest. [I follow Simon's emended text.]

10. A. "As whirlwinds in the South sweeping on" (Isa. 21:1):
    B. Said R. Levi, "Said R. Levi, "You have no more harsh whirlwind than the one that comes from the North and goes up and works havoc among the inhabitants of the South.
    C. "And who is this? It is Nebuchadnezzar, who came up from the north and destroyed the house of the sanctuary, which is situated in the south."

11. A. "It comes from the wilderness" (Isa. 21:1):
    B. Whence did he come?
    C. R. Hanina said, "He came via the desolate wilderness: 'It comes from the wilderness, from a dreadful land' (Isa. 21:1)."

12. A. "A grievous vision is declared to me: (Isa. 21:1):
    B. [=Gen. R. XLIV:VI.1, which begins: "After these things the word of the Lord came to Abram in a vision" (Gen. 15:1):] Prophecy is called by ten names:
    C. prophecy, vision, exhortation, speech, saying, command, burden, parable, metaphor, and enigma.
    D. And which of them is the most weighty?
    E. R. Eleazar said, "It is vision, as it is said, 'A weighty vision is declared to me' (Isa. 21:2)."
    F. R. Yohanan said, "It is speech, as it is said, 'The man, the lord of the land, spoke weightily with us' (Gen. 42:30)."
    G. Rabbis say, "It is the burden, as it is said, 'As a heavy burden' (Ps. 38:5)."

13. A. "The treacherous dealer deals treacherously, and the spoiler spoils. Go up, Elam, besiege, Media" (Isa. 21:2):
    B. The troubles brought by Elam have already been hidden [by those that came from others].

14. A. "...besiege, Media" (Isa. 21:2):
    B. The trouble to be brought by Media has already been formed. [Simon, p. 146, n. 5: A double play on words:

Elam is connected with the word for hidden or eclipsed, besiege is connected with the word for prepared, in existence, also with the word for trouble.]

15. A. "All the sighing thereof I have made to cease" (Isa. 21:2):
    B. All the sighing on account of Babylon.

16. A. "Therefore my loins are filled with convulsion" (Isa. 21:1):
    B. Said R. Simeon b. Gamaliel, "It is because they smelled some of the stench of the trouble that the kingdoms were bringing, that our ancestors became captious to begin with.
    C. "Thus: 'And they journeyed from Mount Hor...to compass the land of Edom, and the soul of the people became captious because of the way' (Num. 21:1)."
      17.A. Jeremiah said, "We get our bread at the peril of our lives" (Lam. 5:9).
        B. Daniel said, "My spirit was pained in the midst of my body" (Dan. 7:15).
        C. "Isaiah said, "Therefore my loins are filled with convulsion (Isa. 21:3).""

18. A. [Supply: "Therefore my loins are seized with convulsion, I am gripped by pangs like a woman in travail, too anguished to hear, too frightened to see" (Isa. 21:3)]
    B. "Therefore my loins are seized with convulsion":
    C. "We, who are swallowed up in their intestines for so many days, so many years, so many end-times, so many periods – what shall we say?"
    D. "I am gripped by pangs like a woman in travail, too anguished to hear, too frightened to see."
    E. "...too anguished to hear":
    F. the sound of the blasphemy and offense of the wicked: "But you have lifted yourself up against the Lord of heaven and they have brought the vessels of his house" (Dan. 5:23).
    G. "...too frightened to see."
    H. the prosperity of the wicked one: "Belshazzar, the king, made a great feast" (Dan. 5:1).
      19.A. [Supply: "Belshazzar, the king, made a great feast" (Dan. 5:1):]
        B. What is the meaning of "great"?
        C. R. Hama b. R. Hanina said, "It means, 'Greater than the one for his God.'
        D. "He said to them, 'How much was the sheaf of first grain that you offered sifted?'

E. "They said to him, 'It was sifted through a sieve thirteen times.'

F. "He said to them, 'Mine is sifted fourteen times.'"

20. A. "My mind is confused, [I shudder in panic, my night of pleasure he has turned to terror]" (Isa. 21:4):

B. "My mind is confused":

C. this speaks of the court, which erred by one day in its calculations [of when the sheaf of first grain was brought].

21. A. "...I shudder in panic":

B. R. Phineas in the name of R. Joshua said, "' You have regaled yourself from my cup.'"

22. A. Another interpretation of the phrase, "I shudder in panic":

B. the mouth that speaks mockery.

23. A. Another interpretation of the phrase, "I shudder in panic":

B. it is because Israel has presumed to mock.

24. A. "...my night of pleasure he has turned to terror" (Isa. 21:4):

B. "The night that I had yearned for as occasion of redemption has been turned to terror."

25. A. "They set the table, [they light the lamps, rise up you princes, grease the shield]" (Isa. 21:5):

B. "They set the table":

C. they arrange the table.

26. A. "...they light the lamps":

B. they put up the lamp and light its branches.

27. A. "...rise up you princes":

B. this refers to Cyrus and Darius.

28. A. "...grease the shield":

B. take over the government.

27. A. Said Darius to Cyrus, "You rule before me."

B. Cyrus said to Darius, "Not so, for did not Daniel state, '*peres:* your kingdom is divided and given to Media and Persia' (Dan. 5:28) – Media first, then Persia.

C. "Accordingly, you rule before me."

D. Now when that wicked man Belshazzar] heard this [that Darius and Cyrus were going to take over the government,] he summoned his troops, saying, "Against every nation and kingdom that has rebelled against me let us march."

E. Said to him the Holy One, blessed be He, "Wicked one! Have you sent for everybody, or have you sent for me? By your life! Your downfall will come from no other place but from me!"

F. That is in line with this verse: "For neither from the east nor from the west...for God is judge, he puts down one and raises up another" (Ps. 75:7-8).

G. "He puts down" Belshazzar, and "raises up" Cyrus and Darius.

29. A. Cyrus and Darius were the gatekeepers of Belshazzar.

B. When he had heard about these writings, he said to them, "Whoever makes an appearance here tonight, even if he says to you, 'I am the king,' cut off his head."

C. Now it is not the way of kings to leave their privy inside their chamber; rather [they put it] outside their chamber.

D. All that night he had loose bowels.

E. When he went outside, they did not realize it, but when he came back, they spied him out. They said to him, "Who goes there!"

F. He said to them, "It is I, the king."

G. They said to him, "And has not the king himself given orders as follows: 'Whoever makes an appearance here tonight, even if he says to you, "I am the king," cut off his head'?"

H. What did they do? They took a branch of the candelabrum and broke his skull.

I. That is in line with this verse: "In that night Belshazzar the Chaldean king was slain" (Dan. 5:30).

30. A. What time was it that he was killed?

B. R. Eleazar and R. Samuel b. R. Nahman:

C. R. Eleazar said, "When sleep is sweet [at the beginning]."

D. R. Samuel said, "[When the light is such that one can tell the difference] between a wolf and a dog."

E. But they really do not differ.

F. The one who said, "When sleep is sweet [at the beginning]," maintains that he writhed the entire day [emended to: night, to daybreak], to make up the full length of his reign].

G.   And one who said, "[When the light is
such that one can tell the difference]
between a wolf and a dog," says that he
was drowsy all night to make up the full
length of his reign].

31. A.   Said R. Benjamin b. Levi, "At an interval no
greater than that between one cup and the next
did one kingdom enter while the other expired:
'For in the hand of the Lord there is a cup,
with foaming wine, and he pours out of it' (Ps.
75:9).

      B.   "Therefore the prophet spites [Babylon],
saying, 'Come down and sit in the dust, O
virgin daughter of Babylon' (Isa. 47:1)."

32. A.   [Supply: "Come down and sit in the dust,
O virgin daughter of Babylon" (Isa.
47:1):]

      B.   That is to say, measure for measure.

      C.   Elsewhere: "They sit on the ground and
keep silence, the elders of the daughter
of Zion" (Lam. 2:10),

      D.   and here: "Come down and sit in the dust,
O virgin daughter of Babylon [without a
throne]" (Isa. 47:1).

33. A.   Said R. Hunia, "This is what Jerusalem
said to the daughter of Babylon: 'You old
whore! What do you think of yourself?
Is it that you are a virgin?

      B.   "You are an old woman."

34. A.   "...sit in the dust without a throne" (Isa.
47:1):

      B.   The merit that sustained that throne has
been exhausted.

      C.   And what was that merit?

      D.   "At that time Merodach Baladan, the son
of Baladan, sent" (Isa. 39:1).

35. A.   [Spelling out the story to which
allusion has just now been made:] he
was a sun-worshipper, and he would
ordinarily eat at the sixth hour and
sleep to the ninth hour.

B. But, in the time of Hezekiah, king of Judah, when the sun reversed its course, he slept through it and woke up and found it was dawn.

C. He wanted to kill his guards. He accused them, "You let me sleep all day and all night long."

D. They said to him, "It was the day that returned [the sun having reversed its course]."

E. He said to them, "And what god reversed it?"

F. They said to him, "It was the God of Hezekiah who reversed it."

G. He said to them, "Then is there a god greater than mine?"

H. They said to him, "The God of Hezekiah is greater than yours."

I. Forthwith he sent letters and a present to Hezekiah: "At that time Merodach-baladan, son of Baladan, king of Babylonia, sent letters and a present to Hezekiah [for he had heard that he had been sick and recovered]" (Isa. 39:1).

J. And what was written in them?

K. He wrote him, "Peace to King Hezekiah, peace to the city of Jerusalem, peace to the Great God!"

L. But when the letters had been sent, his mind was at ease, and he said, "I did not do it right, for I greeted Hezekiah before his God."

M. Forthwith he arose and took three steps and retrieved the letter and wrote another instead, in which he said, "Peace to the great God, peace to the city of Jerusalem, peace to King Hezekiah.'"

N. Said the Holy One, blessed be He, "You have risen from your throne and taken three steps in order to pay honor to me. By your life, I shall raise up from you three cosmopolitan kings, who will rule from one end of the world to the other."

O. And who are they? Nebuchadnezzar, Evil-Merodach, and Belshazzar.

P. But when they went and blasphemed, the Holy One, blessed be He, crushed their eggs out of the world [exterminated them] and set up others in their place.

36. A. "And Hezekiah was happy about them and showed them his treasure house" (Isa. 39:2):

B. What is the meaning of "his treasure house"?

C. Said R. Immi, "It was the spoil that he had taken from Sennacherib, the booty that he had swiped from Sennacherib."

D. R. Yohanan said, "He showed them a weapon that could swallow a weapon. [Simon: one kind of weapon better than another]."

E. R. Simeon b. Laqish said, "Houses made of ivory poured out of wax he showed them."

F. R. Judah says, "Honey as hard as stone he showed to them [amber]."

G. And R. Levi said, "[He said to them,] 'With this [ark of the covenant] we make war and conquer.'"

37. A. "Grasp the handmill and grind meal; [remove your veil, strip off your train, bear your leg, wade through the rivers; your nakedness shall be uncovered and your shame shall be exposed]" (Isa. 47:2-3):

B. Said R. Joshua b. Levi, "Everybody grinds wheat, and you say, 'Grasp the handmill and grind meal'? [Who grinds meal?]

C. "This is what Jerusalem said to the daughter of Babylon, 'If it were not that from above they made war against me, could you have overcome me? Had he not sent fire into my bones, could you have overcome me?

D. "'You have ground ground meal, you have killed a dead lion, you have burned down a burned-out house.'"

38. A. Another matter concerning the verse, "Grasp the handmill and grind meal; [remove your veil, strip off your train, bear your leg, wade through the rivers; your nakedness shall be uncovered and your shame shall be exposed; I will take vengeance, and let no man intercede. Our redeemer, Lord of hosts is his name, is the Holy One of Israel]" (Isa. 47:2-4):

B. In the past, others would grind for you, now ""Grasp the handmill and grind meal."

39. A. "...remove your veil":

B. give up your separateness.

C. This refers to the king, who had been located within seven screens.

40. A. "...strip off your train":

B. breast the oncoming river.

41. A. "...wade through the rivers":

B. In the past, you would cross in gold and silver carriages, now "bear your leg, wade through the rivers."

42. A. "...your nakedness shall be uncovered":
    B. measure for measure.
43. A. Just as elsewhere, "All those who honored her despise her, because they have seen her nakedness" (Lam. 1:8),
    B. so here: "your shame shall be exposed."
44. A. [Supply: "I will take vengeance, and let no man intercede. Our redeemer, Lord of hosts is his name, is the Holy One of Israel" (Isa. 47:4):]
    B. Said R. Joshua b. Levi, "Said the Holy One, blessed be He, 'I am going to bring punishment upon the daughter of Babylonia, and even if Daniel should pray for mercy for her, saying, "And break off your sins by almsgiving"'(Dan. 4:24), I shall not listen to him.'
    C. "Why not? 'I will take vengeance, and let no man intercede. Our redeemer, Lord of hosts is his name, is the Holy One of Israel.'"

39

Song of Songs Rabbah
to Song of Songs 3:5

3:5   *I adjure you, O daughters of Jerusalem,*
       by the gazelles or the hinds of the field,
       that you not stir up nor awaken love
       until it please.

40

Song of Songs Rabbah
to Song of Songs 3:6

3:6   *What is that coming up from the wilderness,*
       like a column of smoke,
       perfumed with myrrh and frankincense,
       with all the fragrant powders of the merchant?

XL:i

1. A. "What is that coming up from the wilderness":
    B. The ascent [of Israel] was from the wilderness, the decline is from the wilderness.
    C. the death is from the wilderness: "In this wilderness they shall be consumed and there they shall die" (Num. 14:35).
2. A. The Torah came from the wilderness, the tabernacle came from the wilderness, the sanhedrin came from the wilderness, the priesthood came from the wilderness, the Levitical caste came from the wilderness, the monarchy came from the wilderness:
    B. "And you shall be to me a kingdom of priests" (Ex. 19:6).
    C. So all the good gifts that the Holy One, blessed be He, gave to Israel are from the wilderness.
    D. Said R. Simeon b. Yohai, "In the wilderness they took on the burden [of the priestly garb], in the wilderness they took off the same burden.
    E. Prophecy is from the wilderness.
    F. Thus the ascent was from the wilderness.
3. A. "...like a column of smoke":
    B. Said R. Eleazar in the name of R. Yosé b. Zimra, "When the Israelites were wandering from stage to stage, the pillar of cloud would come down, and the pillar of fire would spring up,
    C. "and the smoke of the woodpile would go up like two darts of fire, between the two staves of the ark, burning from before them snakes, scorpions, and adders.
    D. "And the nations of the world would see and say, 'These are divinities, their deeds are only with fire.'
    E. "So fear of the Israelites fell upon them, terror and trembling: 'Terror and dread shall fall upon them' (Ex. 15:16).
    F. "The verse does not say 'has fallen' but 'shall fall,' meaning, from now on."

4.   A.   "...perfumed with myrrh":
     B.   This refers to our father, Abraham.
     C.   Just as myrrh is the best of all spices, so our father Abraham was the first of all the righteous.
     D.   Just as the hands of anyone who picks up myrrh smart, so our father, Abraham, would punish and castigate himself with suffering.
     E.   Just as myrrh emits its fragrance only in fire, so Abraham revealed his good deeds only in the fiery furnace.

5.   A.   "...and frankincense":
     B.   this refers to our father, Isaac.
     C.   For he was offered up upon the altar like a handful of frankincense.

6.   A.   "...with all the fragrant powders of the merchant":
     B.   this refers to our father, Jacob.
     C.   For his bed [offspring] was whole before him [the Holy One, blessed be He], and no blemish was found among them.

     7.   A.   Said R. Tanhuma, "Just as the peddler's box has all kinds of spices, so the priesthood is from Jacob,
          B.   "the Levitical caste and the monarchy likewise are from Jacob.
          C.   "As to Isaac, our father Abraham gave him everything he had: 'Abraham gave all that he had to Isaac' (Gen. 25:5).
          D.   "But the profits of Jacob came only from the dirt beneath his feet."

     8.   A.   R. Yudan made two statements.
          B.   R. Yudan said, "All of the profits that the Israelites make and all their success in this world are on account of the merit of that dirt of our father Jacob."
          C.   R. Yudan made another statement: "All of the trade that the Israelites make and all their success in this world are on account of the merit of that dirt of our father Jacob."

     9.   A.   R. Azariah made two statements.
          B.   R. Azariah said, "All of the wars that the Israelites make and win in this world are on account of the merit of that dirt of our father Jacob."
          C.   R. Azariah made another statement: "All of the Torah that the Israelites carry out in this world is on account of the merit of our father, Jacob."

     10. A.   R. Berekhiah and R. Simon in the name of R. Abbahu: "That dust did the Holy One, blessed be He, take and put under his throne of glory:
          B.   "'The Lord in the whirlwind and in the storm is his way and the clouds are the dust of his feet' (Nah. 1:3)."

11. A. R. Berekhiah in the name of R. Helbo said, "'And a man wrestled there with him' (Gen. 32:25):

    B. "From these words we do not know who ended up in the power of whom, the angel in the power of Jacob or Jacob in the power of the angel [for the word 'wrestle' uses the letters for the word for dirt. So the sense is that he was covered with dust.]

    C. "But from the following, 'And he said, let me go, for the day breaks' (Gen. 32:27), the answer becomes clear.

    D. "Said the angel to Jacob, 'Let me go, for my turn to give praises has come.'

    E. "It follows that the angel ended up in the power of our father, Jacob."

12. A. In what form did he make his appearance to him?

    B. R. Hama b. R. Hanina said, "He appeared to him in the form of the angel that served the wicked Esau: 'For since I have seen your face as one sees the face of a god' (Gen. 33:10).

    C. "He said to him, 'Your face is like the face of your guardian angel.'"

    D. "The matter may be compared to a king who had a savage dog and a tame lion. What did the king do?

    E. "The king would take his lion and sick him against the son, saying, 'If the dog comes to have a fight with the son, he will say to the dog, "The lion cannot have a fight with me, are you going to make out in a fight with me?"'

    F. "So if the nations come to have a fight with Israel, the Holy One, blessed be He, says to them, 'Your angelic prince could not stand up to Israel, and as to you, how much the more so!'"

13. A. R. Huna said, "He appeared to him in the form of a shepherd.

B. "This one had flocks and that one had flocks, this one had camels and that one had camels.

C. "He said to him, 'Bring yours across, and I shall bring mine across.

D. "Jacob brought his flock across, and then he checked to see whether he had forgotten anything behind. [Gen. R. LXXVII:I.2 adds:] Forthwith: 'And a man wrestled with him until the breaking of the day.'"

14. A. R. Hiyya the Elder, R. Simeon b. Rabbi, and Rabban Simeon b. Gamaliel were occupied in trading in silk in the area of Tyre. When they had gone out, they said, "Let us go and take up the example of our ancestor and see if we have left anything behind."

B. They went back and discovered that they had forgotten a bale of silk.

C. They said to him, "Where did this example come to you?"

D. They said, "It is from our father, Jacob, who went back, 'and a man wrestled with him until the breaking of the day.'"

15. A. Rabbis say, "He appeared to him in the guise of a bandit chief.

B. "This one had flocks and that one had flocks, this one had camels and that one had camels.

C. "He said to him, 'Bring mine across, and I shall bring yours across.'

D. "The angel brought our father Jacob's flock across in a flash, and then Jacob brought some across, came back, and found more to bring across, and came back and found still more to cross over.

E. [Gen. R. LXXVII:II.3:] "He said to him, 'You are a sorcerer.'"

F. Said R. Phineas, "When he realized this, he took a piece of wool and put it down his throat and said, 'Sorcerer, sorcerer, magicians do not succeed by night.'"

G. Said R. Huna, "At the end, he [the angel] said to him, "'Should I not tell him with whom he is involved?'

H. "What did he do? He took his finger and stuck it into the ground and the ground began to produce fire.

I. "He said to him, 'From this do you expect to frighten me? The whole of me is made up of such a substance: "And the house of Jacob shall be a fire" (Obad. 1:18).'"

16. A. Said R. Hanina b. R. Isaac, "Said the Holy One, blessed be He, to the angelic guardian of Esau, 'Why are you going up against him? He comes against you with five charms in hand, his own merit, the merit of his father, the merit of his mother, the merit of his grandfather, and the merit of his grandmother.

B. "'Take your measure against him, for you cannot withstand him even on the count of his own merit alone.'

C. "Forthwith: 'He saw that he could not prevail against him' (Gen. 32:6)."

17. A. Said R. Levi, "He saw through the Presence of God that he could not prevail against him.

B. "The matter may be compared to an athlete who was wrestling with a prince. He looked up and saw the king standing over him. He let himself be thrown.

C. "So when the angel saw the Presence of God standing above Jacob, he let himself be thrown beneath him: 'He saw that he did not prevail against him.'"

D. Said R. Levi, "He saw through the Presence of God that he could not prevail against him."

18. A. "...he touched the hollow of his thigh, [and Jacob's thigh was put out of joint as he wrestled with him]" (Gen. 32:25):

       B. He touched the righteous men and women, prophets and prophetess, who are destined to arise from him and his children.

       C. And who were these? For example, the generation that would survive the repression [after the war against Hadrian].

19. A. "...and Jacob's thigh was put out of joint as he wrestled with him" (Gen. 32:25):

      B. R. Eliezer and R Berekhiah:

      C. R. Eliezer said, "He flattened it."

      D. Berekhiah in the name of R. Assi said, "He cut it open like a fish."

      E. R. Nahman b. R. Jacob said, "He separated it, as in this verse: 'Then if my soul was separated [using the same word as 'put out of joint] from her' (Ez. 23:18)."

20. A. "...perfumed with myrrh and frankincense, with all the fragrant powders of the merchant":

    B. R. Yohanan interpreted the verse to speak of the incense of the house of Abtinas.

    C. This was one of the eleven kinds of incense that they would put into it.

21. A. R. Huna interpreted the verse ["perfumed with myrrh and frankincense, with all the fragrant powders of the merchant"] in light of the following:

    B. "'And the Lord said to Moses, take for yourself sweet spices stacte and onycha and galbanum sweet spices' (Ex. 30:34):

    C. "'sweet spices': two.

    D. "'...stacte and onycha and galbanum: now we have five.

    E. "'...sweet spices': this cannot mean only two, since we have said spices, thus 'of each shall there be a light weight' means five, matching the other five, ten in all.

    F. "'...with pure frankincense': this eleven."

22. A. [Supply: "'And the Lord said to Moses, take for yourself sweet spices stacte and onycha and galbanum sweet spices' (Ex. 30:34):]

    B. In this connection sages investigated and came up with the fact that suitable for the incense are only these eleven spices.

23.A. It has been taught on Tannaite authority [with reference to the following passage of the Mishnah:

But these were remembered dishonorably: the members of the household of Garmu did not want to teach others how to make the show bread; the members of the household of Abtinas did not want to teach others how to make the incense; Hygras b. Levi knew a lesson of singing but did not want to teach it to anyone else; Ben Qamsaw did not want to teach others how to write (M. Yoma 3:11A-E):

B. [In the version of T. Kippurim 2:6-7, 2:5, 2:8 verbatim, omitting reference to variations in Song of Song Rabbah:] The members of the house of Abtinas were experts in preparing the incense for producing smoke, and they did not want to teach others how to do so.

C. Sages sent and brought experts from Alexandria, in Egypt, who knew how to concoct spices in much the same way.

D. But they were not experts in making the smoke ascend [in the way in which it ascended for the others].

E. The smoke coming from the incense of the house of Abtina would ascend straight as a stick up to the beams and afterward would scatter in all directions as it came down. But that of the Alexandrians would scatter as it came down forthwith.

F. Now when the sages realized this, they said, "The Omnipresent has created the world only for his own glory: 'The Lord has made everything for his own purpose' (Prov. 16:4) [so we might as well pay the tariff]."

G. Sages sent to [the members of the house of Abtinas], but they declined to come until the sages doubled their wages.

H. "They had been receiving twelve manehs every day, and now they went and got twenty-four," the words of R. Meir.

I. R. Judah says, "They had been getting twenty-four every day. Now they went and got forty-eight."

J. Sages said to them, "Now why were you unwilling to teach others?"

K. They said to them, "The members of father's house knew that the Temple is destined for destruction, and they did not want to teach others their art, so that people would not burn incense before an idol in the same way in which they burn incense before the Omnipresent."

L. And in this matter, they are remembered for Good: a woman of their household never went out wearing perfume at any time,

M. and not only so, but when they would marry into their household a woman from some other place, they made an agreement that she not put on perfume,

N. so that people should not say, "Their women are putting on perfume made up from the preparation of the incense for the Temple."

O. This they did to carry out the following verse, "And you shall be clear before the Lord and before Israel" (Num. 32:22).

24. A. Said R. Aqiba, "Simeon b. Luga told me, 'A certain child of the sons of their sons and I were gathering grass in the field. Then I saw him laugh and cry.

B. "'I said to him, "Why did you cry?"

C. "'He said to me, "Because of the glory of father's house, which has gone into exile."

D. "'I said to him, "Then why did you laugh?"

E. "'He said to me, "At the end of it all, in time to come, the Holy One, blessed be He, is going to make his descendants rejoice. [Song of Songs Rabbah's version: Because it is stored away and kept for the righteous in the time to come, and because in the end he will make his children rejoice – may it speedily come.]"

F. "'I said to him, "Why? [What did you see that made you think of this?]"

G. "'He said to me, "A smoke-raiser in front of me [made me laugh]."

H. "'I said to him, "Show it to me."

I. "'He said to me, "We are subject to an oath not to show it to anyone at all."'"

J. "They say that not many days passed before that child died."

K. Said R. Yohanan b. Nuri, "One time I was going along the way and an old man came across me, with a scroll in his hand containing a list of spices. I said to him, 'What is that you have in your hand?

L. "He said to me, 'I am a member of the house of Abtinas. At the beginning, when the house of father was discreet, they would give their scrolls containing the prescriptions for frankincense only to one another. Now take it, but be careful about it, since it is a scroll containing a recipe for spices.'

M. "When I came and reported the matter before R. Aqiba, he said to me, 'From now on it is forbidden to speak ill of these people again.'"

25. A. The members of the house of Garmu were experts in making show bread and they did not want to teach others how to make it.

B. Sages sent and brought experts from Alexandria, in Egypt, who were expert in similar matters but were not experts in removing it from the oven.

C. The members of the house of Garmu would heat the oven on the outside, and the loaf of bread would be removed on its own on the inside.

D. The experts from Alexandria did not do so.

E. And some say that this made it get moldy.

F. And when the sages learned of the matter, they said, "The Holy One, blessed be He, has created the world only for his own glory: 'Everyone that is called by my name and whom I have created for my glory' (Isa. 43:7) [so we might as well pay the tariff]."

G. They sent for them, but they would not come until they doubled their former salary.

H. "They had been receiving twelve manehs every day, and now they went and got twenty-four," the words of R. Meir.

I. R. Judah says, "They had been getting twenty-four every day. Now they went and got forty-eight."

J. Sages said to them, "Now why were you unwilling to teach others?"

K. They said to them, "The member of father's house knew that the Temple was going to be destroyed, and they did not want to teach others how to do it, so that they should not be able to do it before an idol in the way in which it is done before the Omnipresent."

L. And on account of this next matter they are remembered with honor:

M. For a piece of clean bread was never found in the hands of their sons or daughters under any circumstances, so that people might not be able to say about them, "They are nourished from the show bread of the Temple."

N. This was meant to carry out the following verse: "You shall be clean before the Lord and before Israel."

26. A. All the others found an answer, but Ben Qamsar did not find an answer to what they said.

B. They said to them, "Why do you not wish to teach?"

C. They kept silent and did not reply.

D. Because they wanted to increase their own glory and diminish the glory owing to heaven, therefore their own glory was diminished, while the glory of heaven was increased.

E. Not only so, but they have no issue or descendant in Israel.

F. To the others applies the verse, "The memory of the righteous is for a blessing," but with regard to these, "But the name of the wicked shall rot" (Prov. 10:7).

27. A. On this basis, Ben Azzai said, "Yours do they give back to you,

B. "by your name they will call you,

C. "in your place they will seat you.

D. "There is no forgetting before the Omnipresent,

E. "and no man can touch what is designated for his fellow."

28. A. Hugram b. Levi knew a certain mode of singing, but he did not want to teach it to others.

B. They say of Hugram b. Levi that when he opened his mouth to sing, he would put one

thumb into his mouth and the other into the
ground, with his fingers between his
moustaches, and raise his voice in song.

C. And he could imitate the sound of every kind of
musical instrument.

D. So his fellow Levites willy-nilly would turn
around to look at him.

29. A. Phineas was the dresser.

B. He once helped a general to dress and got a fee.

XL:ii

1. A.   "What is that coming up from the wilderness":

B.   The passage speaks of Elisheba, daughter of Amminadab [and wife
of Aaron].

C.   They say: Elisheba, daughter of Amminadab witnessed five occasions
for rejoicing on a single day.

D.   She witnessed her brother-in-law as king, her brother as prince, her
husband as his priest, her two sons as prefects of the priesthood, and
Phineas, her grandson as priest anointed for war.

E.   But when her two sons entered [the sanctuary] to make an offering,
they emerged burned, so her joy was turned to mourning.

F.   Forthwith she turned into pillars of smoke [thus: "What is that coming
up from the wilderness like a column of smoke"].

2. A.   When R. Eleazar b. R. Simeon died, his generation recited
in his regard: "What is that coming up from the wilderness
like a column of smoke, perfumed with myrrh and
frankincense, with all the fragrant powders of the
merchant."

B.   Why "with all the fragrant powders of the merchant"?

C.   For R. Eleazar b. R. Simeon was learned in Scripture,
Mishnah, liturgy, and poetry.

41

Song of Songs Rabbah
to Song of Songs 3:7-8

3:7   *Behold it is the litter of Solomon!*
About it are sixty mighty men
of the mighty men of Israel,
3:8   *all girt with swords*
and expert in war,
each with his sword at his thigh,
against alarms by night.

XLI:i

1.   A.   "Behold it is the litter of Solomon! About it are sixty mighty men of the mighty men of Israel [all girt with swords and expert in war, each with his sword at his thigh, against alarms by night] (Song 3:8)":
    B.   R. Bibi in the name of R. Eleazar b. R. Yosé interpreted the verse to speak of the priestly blessing:
    C.   "'Behold it is the litter': behold it is the clans [a word that uses the same letters as litter]: 'the oaths of the tribes' (Hab. 3:9).
    D.   "'...of Solomon': of the king to whom peace belongs.
    E.   "'About it are sixty mighty men': this refers to the sixty letters that make up the words for the priestly blessing.
    F.   "'...of the mighty men of Israel': for they [the blessings] strengthen Israel.
2.   A.   "'...all girt with swords [and expert in war, each with his sword at his thigh, against alarms by night]'":
    B.   Said R. Azariah, "These are blessed through the strength [of the Divine Name]: 'The Lord bless you...the Lord make his face to shine...the Lord lift up' (Num. 6:24-6).
    C.   "'...and expert in war': for they make war against all manner of visitations that there are in the world.
    D.   "'...each with his sword at his thigh against alarms by night': for if someone sees in his dream a sword cutting into his thigh, what is he to do?
    E.   "Let him go to the synagogue and recite the Shema and say the Prayer and listen to the blessing of the priests, answering after them, 'Amen,' and nothing bad will happen to him.

F.   "Therefore Scripture admonishes the sons of Aaron: 'In this way you shall bless the children of Israel' (Num. 6:23)."

3. A.   R. Simlai interpreted the verse to speak of the priestly watches [who take turns in conducting the actual rite in the Temple, through the year in sequence]:

B.   "'Behold it is the litter': behold it is the clans [a word that uses the same letters as litter]: 'the oaths of the tribes' (Hab. 3:9).

C.   "'...of Solomon': of the king to whom peace belongs."

D.   "'About it are sixty mighty men': this refers to the twenty-four priestly watches, the twenty-four Levitical watches, and the twelve divisions [1 Chr. 27].

E.   "'...of the mighty men of Israel': who guard Israel.

4. A.   "...all girt with swords [and expert in war, each with his sword at his thigh, against alarms by night]":

B.   Said R. Zeira and R. Judah in the name of Samuel, "This refers to the disciples of sages who teach the priests how to conduct the slaughter of the sacrificial beast and the laws governing the tossing of the blood, the receiving of the blood, and the taking up of the handful of the meal-offering."

C.   R. Isaac in the name of R. Ammi said, "This refers to those who examine the blemishes on the beasts that have been declared holy and who receive their salary from the Temple treasury."

5. A.   R. Gidul b. R. Benjamin in the name of R. Yosé: "There were two judges of civil cases in Jerusalem, and they would take their salary from the Temple treasury."

B.   Samuel said, "Women would weave the curtain [for the Most Holy Place], and they would take their salary from the Temple treasury."

C.   R. Huna said, "From the fund for the upkeep of the building."

D.   The latter regarded the curtain as classified with the building, the former as classified with the offerings.

6. A.   "'...and expert in war': for they would teach the priests how to conduct the liturgy.

B.   "'...each with his sword at his thigh, against alarms by night': for they would admonish them at the time that they conducted the slaughter of the sacrificial animal not to render any of the sacrifices an abomination [by forming the improper intention to eat their share of the beast at the wrong time, that is, too late, or to toss the blood at the wrong place], and not to invalidate any of the offerings through leaving over the meat for too long."

7. A.   R. Yohanan interpreted the verse to speak of the Sanhedrin:

B. "'Behold it is the litter': behold it is the clans [a word that uses the same letters as litter]: 'the oaths of the tribes' (Hab. 3:9).

C. "'...of Solomon': of the king to whom peace belongs.

D. "'About it are sixty mighty men': this refers to the sixty men of the people of the land: 'And sixty men of the people of the land who were found in the city' (2 Kgs. 25:19).

E. "'...of the mighty men of Israel': this refers to the eleven men cited here, 'And the captain of the guard took Seraiah, chief priest, and Zephaniah, second priest, and the three keepers of the door, and out of the city he took an officer [and five men of those who had access to the king' (2 Kgs. 25:18)."

8. A. "...he took an officer":

B. This refers to the head of the court.

C. And why is he called "an officer"?

D. Because he officiates over the law [the words for officer and officiate or adjudicate use the same consonants].

9. A. "...and five men of those who had access to the king" (2 Kgs. 25:18):

B. lo, eleven in all.

C. And when Jeremiah says, "seven" (Jer. 52:25), the intent is to add to the count the two scribes of the judges, who sit in their presence.

10. A. [Continuing 7.E:] "of the mighty men of Israel': they acquit the Israelites through strength [Simon: of argument]."

11. A. "...all girt with swords":

B. R. Meir and R. Yosé:

C. R. Meir says, "For all of them were as sharp as a sword in the study of the law, so that if a case should come to them, the law should not be unclear to them."

D. R. Yosé says, "In the time of reaching a judgment, all of them would give and take in argument concerning how to produce a judgment, subject to the fear of the punishment of Gehenna [should they err]."

E. R. Menahem, son-in-law of R. Eleazar b. R. Abona in the name of R. Jacob b. R. Abina: "If a woman comes before you to the school house to ask you a question concerning the determination of the blood on her rag [that is, whether it is menstrual blood or of some other sort] and concerning her status as a menstruant, you should regard her as though she herself had come forth from your loins and not look upon her, but should be subject to the fear of the punishment of Gehenna."

12. A. Rabbis interpret the verse to speak of the Israelites who came forth from Egypt:

B. "'Behold it is the litter': behold it is the clans [a word that uses the same letters as litter]: 'the oaths of the tribes' (Hab. 3:9).

C. "'...of Solomon': of the king to whom peace belongs.

D. "'About it are sixty mighty men': this refers to the sixty myriads who came forth from Egypt from the age of twenty years and onward.

E. "'...of the mighty men of Israel': this refers to the sixty myriads who came forth from Egypt from the age of twenty years and below.

F. "'...all girt with swords and expert in war, each with his sword at his thigh, [against alarms by night]':

G. "For when Moses said to them, 'Thus has the Holy One, blessed be He, said to me in one word: "No uncircumcised person shall eat of it" (Ex. 12:48), forthwith each one of them took his sword on his thigh and circumcised himself."

13. A. Who circumcised them?

B. R. Berekhiah said, "Moses was circumcising them, Aaron was doing the trimming, and Joshua gave them to drink."

C. Some say, "Joshua did the circumcising, Aaron did the trimming, and Moses gave them to drink."

D. "So it is written, 'At that time the Lord said to Joshua, Make knives of flint and again circumcise the children of Israel the second time' (Josh. 5:2).

E. "Why a second time? Because he was the one who had done it the first time.

F. "Forthwith: 'Joshua made knives of flint and circumcised the children of Israel at Gibeat-haaralot' (Josh. 5:3)."

G. What is the meaning of "at Gibeat-haaralot"?

H. R. Levi said, "On this basis we learn that they made it a hill of foreskins."

XLI:ii

1. A. It has been taught on Tannaite authority:

B. Before someone sins, he is paid awe and fear, and creatures fear him. But once he has sinned, he is subject to awe and fear, and he fears others.

C. You may know that this is so, for so said Rabbi, "Before the First Man sinned, he heard the sound of the Divine Speech while standing on his feet, and he was not afraid.

D. "But once he had sinned, when he heard the sound of the Divine Speech, he was afraid and he hid: 'I heard your voice and I was afraid' (Gen. 3:10); 'And the man and his wife hid themselves' (Gen. 3:8)."

2.   A.   Said R. Aibu, "At that moment Adam's stature was diminished and reduced to a hundred cubits."

3.   A.   R. Levi said, "Before the First Man sinned, he heard the sound of the Divine Speech in a mild way.

      B.   "But once he had sinned, when he heard the sound of the Divine Speech, it was fierce [Simon: it came to him like a fierce wild thing].

      C.   "Before the Israelites sinned, they saw seven fiery partitions pressing on one another, but they were not afraid nor did they tremble or concern themselves.

      D.   "But once they had sinned, even upon the face of the mediator [Moses] they could not gaze: 'The skin of Moses's face sent forth beams' (Ex. 34:35); 'And they were afraid to come near him' (Ex. 34:30)."

      4.   A.   R. Phineas and R. Abun in the name of R. Hanin said, "Even the mediator himself felt with them [the impact of] that transgression.

           B.   "Of the period before the Israelites sinned what is written? 'Kings of armies flee, they flee' (Ps. 68:13)."

           5.   A.   [Supply: "'Kings of armies flee, they flee" (Ps. 68:13):]

                B.   R. Aibu said, "What is written here is not 'angels of armies flee,' but 'kings of armies flee,' meaning, kings of the angels.

                C.   "Who might they be?

                D.   "This refers to Michael and Gabriel.

                E.   "For they could not gave upon the face of Moses.

                F.   "But once they had sinned, even upon the face of the quite ordinary angels they could not gaze: 'For I was afraid of the anger and displeasure' (Dt. 9:19)."

6.   A.   [Continuing the discourse left off at 3.D:] "Concerning the time before that tragic event [involving Bath Sheba] happened to David, it is written, 'The Lord is my light and my salvation, whom shall I fear' (Ps. 27:1).

      B.   "But afterward [Ahitophel could say], 'I will come upon him while he is weary and weak-handed and I will frighten him' (2 Sam. 17:2).

      C.   "Before Solomon sinned, he ruled male and female singers: 'I got myself male and female singers and the delights of mortals' (Qoh. 2:8), baths, and male and female demons who used to heat them.

D. "But once he had sinned, he appointed for himself sixty mighty men of the mighty men of Israel and set them up to guard his bed: 'Behold it is the litter of Solomon! About it are sixty mighty men of the mighty men of Israel all girt with swords and expert in war, each with his sword at his thigh, against alarms by night,'

E. "because he feared the spirits."

42

Song of Songs Rabbah to Song of Songs 3:9

3:9 *King Solomon made himself a palanquin,*
from the wood of Lebanon.

XLII:i

1. A. "King Solomon made himself a palanquin, [from the wood of Lebanon]":

    B. R. Azariah in the name of R. Judah b. R. Simon interpreted the verse to speak of the tabernacle:

    C. "'palanquin' refers to the tabernacle.

2. A. Said R. Judah b. R. Ilai, "The matter may be compared to the case of a king who had a little daughter. Before she reached maturity and produced the signs of puberty, he would see her in the marketplace and speak with her quite publicly, whether in an alleyway or in a courtyard.

    B. "After she grew up and produced the signs of puberty, the king said, 'It is not becoming for my daughter that I should speak with her in public. So make her a pavilion, and when I have to speak with her, I shall speak with her in the pavilion.

    C. "So: 'When Israel was a child, then I loved him' (Hos. 11:1).

    D. "In Egypt they saw him in public: 'For the Lord will pass through to smite the Egyptians' (Ex. 12:23).

    E. "At the Sea they saw him in public: 'And Israel saw the great work' (Ex. 14:31).

F.   "...and the children pointed at him with their finger, saying, 'This is my God and I will glorify him' (Ex. 15:2).

G.   "At Sinai they saw him face to face: 'And he said, the Lord came from Sinai' (Dt. 33:2).

H.   "When the Israelites stood at Mount Sinai and received the Torah and said, 'All that the Lord has spoken we shall do and obey' (Dt. 24:7), so becoming for him a nation complete in all ways,

I.   "then said the Holy One, blessed be He, 'It is not becoming for my children for me to speak with them in public. Make me a tabernacle, and when I have to speak with them, I shall speak with them from within the tabernacle: 'But when Moses went in before the Lord that he might speak with him' (Ex. 34:34).''

3.   A.   "King Solomon made himself a palanquin":

       B.   he is the king whose name is peace.

       C.   "...from the wood of Lebanon":

       D.   "And you shall make the boards for the tabernacle of acacia-wood, standing up" (Ex. 26:15).

43

Song of Songs Rabbah
to Song of Songs 3:10

[3:9   *King Solomon made himself a palanquin,*
         from the wood of Lebanon.]
3:10   *He made its posts of silver,*
         its back of gold, its seat of purple;
         it was lovingly wrought within
         by the daughters of Jerusalem.

XLIII:i

1.   A.   "He made its posts of silver":

       B.   this speaks of the pillars: "The hooks of the pillars and their fillets shall be of silver" (Ex. 27:10).

       C.   "...its back of gold:

       D.   "And you shall overlay the boards with gold" (Ex 26:29).

       E.   "...its seat of purple":

       F.   "And you shall make a veil of blue and purple" (Ex. 26:31).

2.   A.   "...it was lovingly wrought within by the daughters of Jerusalem":

B.   R. Yudan said, "This refers to the merit attained through the Torah and the merit attained through the righteous who occupy themselves with it."

C.   R. Azariah in the name of R. Judah in the name of R. Simon said, "This refers to the Presence of God.

   3.   A.   One verse of Scripture says, "So that the priests could not stand to minister by reason of the cloud, for the glory of the Lord filled the house of the Lord" (1 Kgs. 8:11).

       B.   And another verse of Scripture says, "And the court was full of the brightness of the Lord's glory" (Ez. 10:4).

       C.   IIow arc thcsc two verses to be harmonized?

       D.   R. Joshua of Sikhnin in the name of R. Levi: "To what is the tent of meeting comparable? To a cave open to the sea.

       E.   "When the sea becomes stormy, it fills the cave.

       F.   "The cave is filled, but the sea is undiminished.

       G.   "So the tent of meeting was filled with the splendor of the Presence of God, while the world was undiminished of the Presence of God."

   4.   A.   When did the Presence of God come to rest on the world?

       B.   On the day on which the tabernacle was raised up: "And it came to pass on the day that Moses had made an end" (Num. 7:1).

XLIII:ii

1.   A.   [Supply: "King Solomon made himself a palanquin, from the wood of Lebanon. He made its posts of silver, its back of gold, its seat of purple; it was lovingly wrought within by the daughters of Jerusalem":]

B.   R. Yudan b. R. Ilai interpreted the verses to speak of the ark:

C.   "'...a palanquin': this is the ark."

   2.   A.   [Supply: "a palanquin":]

       B.   What is a palanquin?

       C.   A litter.

       3.   A.   The matter may be compared to the case of a king who had an only daughter, who was beautiful, pious, and gracious.

          B.   Said the king to his staff, "my daughter is beautiful, pious, and gracious, and yet you do not make her a litter? Make her a litter, for it is better that the beauty of my daughter should appear from within a litter."

C. So said the Holy One, blessed be He, "My Torah is beautiful, pious, and gracious, and yet you do not make an ark for it?

D. "It is better that the beauty of my Torah should appear from within the ark."

4. A. [Reverting to 1.C:] "'King Solomon made himself': the king to whom peace belongs.

B. "'...from the wood of Lebanon': 'And Bezalel made the ark of acacia-wood' (Ex. 37:1).

C. "'He made its posts of silver': these are the two pillars that stand within the ark, which were made of silver.

D. "'...its back of gold': 'and he overlaid it with pure gold' (Ex. 37:2)."

5. A. "...its seat of purple':

B. R. Tanhuma says, "This is the veil that adjoined it."

C. R. Bibi said, "This refers to the ark-cover, for the gold of the ark-cover was like purple."

6. A. "...it was lovingly wrought within by the daughters of Jerusalem":

B. R. Yudan said, "This refers to the merit accruing to the Torah and those who study it."

C. R. Azariah said in the name of R. Yudah in the name of R. Simon, "This refers to the Presence of God."

7. A. Said R. Abba b. Kahana, "'And there I will meet with you' (Ex. 25:22):

B. "This serves to teach you that even what is on the other side of the ark cover the space was not empty of the Presence of God."

8. A. A gentile asked R. Joshua b. Qorha, "Why did the Holy One, blessed be He, speak from within the bush and not from any other tree?"

B. He said to him, "Had he spoke with him from the midst of a carob or a sycamore, you would have asked the same thing, and would I have had to answer you?

C. "Nonetheless, to turn you away with nothing is not possible.

D. "It serves to teach you that there is no place in the world that is empty of the Presence of God,

E. "for even from within the bush did he speak with him."

XLIII:iii

1. A. [Supply: "King Solomon made himself a palanquin, from the wood of Lebanon. He made its posts of silver, its back of gold, its seat of purple; it was lovingly wrought within by the daughters of Jerusalem":]

    B. Another interpretation of "a palanquin":

    C. this refers to the house of the sanctuary.

    D. "King Solomon made himself":

    E. this refers in fact to Solomon.

    F. "...from the wood of Lebanon":

    G. "And we will cut wood out of Lebanon" (2 Chr. 2:15).

    H. "He made its posts of silver":

    I. "And he set up the pillars of the porch of the Temple" (1 Kgs. 7:21).

    J. "...its back of gold":

        K. So we have learned on Tannaite authority: The entire house was overlaid with gold, except the backs of the doors.

            L. Said R. Isaac, "That teaching on Tannaite authority applies to the second building, but as to the first building, even the back parts of the doors were covered with gold."

2. A. We have learned: Seven kinds of gold were in it: good gold, pure gold, chased gold, beaten gold, gold of *mufaz*, refined gold, gold of *parvayim*.

    B. Good gold: that is meant literally, "And the gold of that land is good" (Gen. 2:12).

    C. In this regard R. Isaac said, "It is good to have in the house, good to take on a trip."

    D. Pure gold: for they would put it into the furnace and come out undiminished.

        E. R. Judah in the name of R. Ammi: "A thousand bars of gold did Solomon put into the furnace a thousand time, until they yielded a single bar."

        F. But lo, said R. Yosé b,. R. Judah on Tannaite authority, "There was the case that the candlestick of the Temple was heavier than that of the wilderness by the weight of one Gordian *denarius*, and it was passed through the furnace eighty times, until it lost the excess."

        G. But to begin with it lost dross, and thereafter it lacked only the smallest volume.

    H. beaten gold:

I. for it was drawn out like wax.

J. Hadrian had an egg's bulk of it.

K. Diocletian had a Gordian *denarius's* volume of it.

L. This government today has none of it and never had any of it.

M. chased gold: it bears that name because it made all the goldsmiths shut up their shops.

N. Lo, it is written, "Seven thousand talents of refined silver, with which to overlay the walls of the houses" (1 Chr. 29:4):

O. now was it silver? And was it not gold? And why call it silver?

P. It was to shame everyone who owned gold.

Q. And from it were made all of the utensils, the basins, pots, shovels, snuffers, bowls, forks, spoons, censers, and *potot.*

R. R. Isaac of Magdala said, "'*Potot'* are pivots."

S. R. Sima said, "It refers to a cup under the hinge."

T. This teaches you that the sanctuary was not lacking even the most minor thing.

U. Gold of *mufaz:*

V. R. Patriqi, brother of R. Derosah in the name of R. Abba b. R. Bunah said, "It was like sulphur flaring upon in the fire."

W. R. Abun said, "It is so called by reason of the country in which it originates, which is Ufaz."

X. Refined gold:

Y. The household of R. Yannai and the household of R. Yudan b. R. Simeon:

Z. The household of R. Yannai said, "They cut it into the size of olives and feed it to ostriches, and they defecate it in refined condition."

AA. The household of R. Yudan b. R. Simeon said, "They buried it in dung for seven years and it would come out refined."

BB. Gold of *parvayim:*

CC. R. Simeon b. Laqish said, "It was red, like the blood of a bullock."

DD. Some say, "It produces fruit."

EE. For when Solomon built the house of the sanctuary, he made with it every kind of tree, and when the trees produced fruit, the ones in the Temple did too, and the fruit would drop from the trees and be gathered and was saved for the upkeep of the Temple.

FF. But when Manasseh set up an idol in the Temple, all the trees withered: "And the flower of Lebanon languishes" (Nah. 1:4).

GG. But in the age to come, the Holy One, blessed be He, will bring them back: "It shall blossom abundantly and rejoice, even with joy and singing" (Isa. 35:2).

3. A. "...its seat of purple":
   B. "And he made the veil of blue and purple and crimson and fine linen" (2 Chr. 3:14).
4. A. "...it was lovingly wrought within by the daughters of Jerusalem":
   B. R. Yudan said, "This refers to the merit attained through the Torah and the merit attained through the righteous who occupy themselves with it."
   C. R. Azariah in the name of R. Judah in the name of R. Simon said, "This refers to the Presence of God."

XLIII:iv

1. A. [Supply: "King Solomon made himself a palanquin, from the wood of Lebanon. He made its posts of silver, its back of gold, its seat of purple; it was lovingly wrought within by the daughters of Jerusalem":]
   B. Another interpretation of "a palanquin":
   C. this refers to the world.
   D. "King Solomon made himself":
   E. the king to whom peace belongs.
   F. "...from the wood of Lebanon":
   G. for [the world] was built out of the house of the Most Holy Place down below.
   2. A. For we have learned on Tannaite authority:
      B. When the ark was removed [after 586], there remained there a stone from the days of the earlier prophets, called foundation-stone *[Shetiyyah]*.
      C. Why was it called foundation-stone *[Shetiyyah]?*
      D. For upon it the world was based [the word based uses the same consonants as the word for foundation, *Shetiyyah].*
      E. That is in line with this verse: "Out of Zion the perfection of beauty God has shined forth" (Ps. 50:2).

3.   A.   "He made its posts of silver":
      B.   this refers to the chain of genealogies.
      C.   "...its back of gold":
      D.   this speaks of the produce of the earth and of the true, which are exchanged for gold
      E.   "...its seat of purple":
      F.   "Who rides upon heaven as your help" (Dt. 33:26).
      G.   "...it was lovingly wrought within by the daughters of Jerusalem":
      H.   R. Yudan said, "This refers to the merit attained through the Torah and the merit attained through the righteous who occupy themselves with it."
      I.   R. Azariah in the name of R. Judah in the name of R. Simon said, "This refers to the Presence of God."

XLIII:v

1.   A.   [Supply: "King Solomon made himself a palanquin, from the wood of Lebanon. He made its posts of silver, its back of gold, its seat of purple; it was lovingly wrought within by the daughters of Jerusalem":]
      B.   Another interpretation of "a palanquin":
      C.   this refers to the throne of glory.
      D.   "King Solomon made himself":
      E.   the king to whom peace belongs.
      F.   "...from the wood of Lebanon":
      G.   this is the House of the Most Holy Place above, which is directly opposite the House of the Most Holy Place down below,
      H.   as in the following usage: "The place...for you to dwell in" (Ex. 15:17),
      I.   that is, directly opposite your dwelling place [above].
      J.   "He made its posts of silver":
      K.   "The pillars of heaven tremble" (Job 26:11).
      L.   "...its back of gold":
      M.   this refers to teachings of the Torah: "More to be desired are they then gold, yes, than much fine gold" (Ps. 19:11).
      N.   "...its seat of purple":
      O.   "To him who rides upon the heaven of heavens, which are of old" (Ps. 68:34).
      P.   "...it was lovingly wrought within by the daughters of Jerusalem":
            Q.   R. Berekhiah and R. Bun in the name of R. Abbahu: "There are four proud [creatures]:
            R.   "The pride of birds is the eagle.
            S.   "The pride of domesticated beasts is the ox.
            T.   "The pride of wild beasts is the lion.

U. "The pride of them all is man.

V. "And all of them did the Holy One, blessed be He, take and engrave on the throne of glory: 'The Lord has established his throne in the heavens and his kingdom rules over all' (Ps. 103:19).

W. "Because 'The Lord has established his throne in the heavens,' therefore: 'his kingdom rules over all.'"

44

Song of Songs Rabbah
to Song of Songs 3:11

3:11 *Go forth, O daughters of Zion,*
and behold King Solomon,
with the crown with which his mother crowned him
on the day of his wedding,
on the day of the gladness of his heart.

XLIV:i

1. A. "Go forth, O daughters of Zion":
    B. the daughters who are distinguished for me by the mode of hair, circumcision, and show-fringes. [The words for distinguished and Zion use the same consonants.]

2. A. "...and behold King Solomon":
    B. the king who created his creatures in wholeness [the words for whole and Solomon use the same consonants],
    C. He created sun and moon in their fullness,
    D. stars and planets in their fullness.
        E. Bar Qappara said, "Adam and Eve were created at the age of twenty years."

3. A. "King Solomon":
    B. On the king to whom peace belongs.

4. A. Another explanation of the phrase, "Upon King Solomon":
    B. upon the king [meaning, God} who brought peace between his works and his creatures.
    C. How so?
    D. He made peace between fire and our father Abraham.
    E. He made peace between the sword and Isaac,

F.   He made peace between the angel and Jacob.

5.   A.   Another interpretation of the phrase, "Upon King Solomon":
      B.   upon the king [meaning, God} who brought peace among his creatures.

      6.   A.   It was taught on Tannaite authority by R. Simeon b. Yohai: "The firmament is made of snow and the heavenly creatures of fire.
            B.   "The firmament is made of snow: 'and over the heads of the living creatures there was the likeness of a firmament, like terrible ice' (Ez. 1:22).
            C.   "...and the heavenly creatures of fire: 'As for the likeness of the living creatures, their appearance was like coals of fire' (Ez. 1:13); 'And the living creatures ran and returned as the appearance of a flash of lightning' (Ez. 1:14).
            D.   "But this one does not extinguish that, and that does not extinguish this.
            E.   "Michael is the angelic prince of ice, and Gabriel is the angelic prince of fire.
            F.   "But this one does not extinguish that, and that does not extinguish this."
            G.   Said R. Abin, "It is not the end of the matter that he makes peace between one angel and another, but even within a single angel, half of whom is made up of fire and half of ice, the Holy One, blessed be He, brings peace within."

            7.   A.   There are five aspects in which [in Scripture this power of God to make peace is illustrated,] and these are they:
                  B.   "His body also was like the beryl and his face as the appearance of lightning" (Dan. 10:6), yet the one does not do injury to the other, and the other does not do injury to the one.
                  C.   One verse of Scripture says, "Who lays the beams of your upper chambers in the water" (Ps. 104:3), and another says, "For the Lord your God is a devouring fire" (Dt. 4:24), and also, "His throne was fiery flames" (Dan. 7:9), yet the one does not do injury to the other, and the other does not do injury to the one.
                  D.   Said R. Yohanan, "'He makes peace in his high places' (Job 25:2):
                  E.   "The firmament is made of water, the stars of fire, yet the one does not do injury to the other.

F. "The sun has never behold the defect of the moon [Simon, p. 172, n. 1: the hollow of the moon's crescent is never turned to the sun, as this would give offense to her]."

G. Said R. Jacob of Kefar Hanan: "'Dominion and fear are with him' (Job 25:2).

H. "'Dominion' is Michael, 'fear,' Gabriel.'

I. "'...with him': they make peace in him."

J. Said R. Levi, "You have no planet that rises out of turn before the other.

K. "You have no star that sees what is above it, but only what is below it, like a man descending a ladder, who cannot see what is behind him."

L. Even among the plagues that he brought on Pharaoh he made peace:

M. "There was hail, fire flashing up amidst the hail" (Ex. 9:24).

8. A. [Supply: "There was hail, fire flashing up amidst the hail" (Ex. 9:24):]

B. R. Judah, R. Nehemiah, and Rabbis:

C. R. Judah said, "The cup of hail was filled with fire, but this did not extinguish that, nor did that extinguish this."

D. Said R. Hanin, "That statement of R. Judah suggests that it was like a fully-ripened pomegranate, in which every pip can be seen through [the skin]."

E. R. Nehemiah said, "The fire and the hail mingled with one another."

F. Said R. Hanin, "That statement of R. Judah suggests that it was like light in a glass, the water and oil are mixed but the fire goes on burning, but this did not extinguish that, nor did that extinguish this."

G. And rabbis said, "It kept going out and kindling again so as to carry out the will of its creator."

9. A. Said R. Aha, "The matter may be compared to the case of a king who possessed two crack platoons.

B. "They bore a grudge against one another.

C. "But when they saw that the battle of the king was going against him, they made peace with one another so as to make war for the king.

D. "So fire and water bore a grudge against one another, but when they saw the war of the King of kings, the Holy One, blessed be He, which he fought against the Egyptians, they made peace with one another and did battle for the Holy One, blessed be He, against the Egyptians.

E. "Thus: 'so there was hail and fire flashing up amid the hail' (Ex. 9:24) – a miracle."

XLIV:ii

1. A. "...with the crown with which his mother crowned him":

    B. Said R. Yohanan, "R. Simeon b. Yohai asked R. Eleazar b. R. Yosé, saying to him, 'Is it possible that you have heard from your father [Yosé b. R. Halafta] the meaning of the phrase, "with the crown with which his mother crowned him"?'

    C. "He said to him, 'Yes.'

    D. "He said to him, 'And what was it?'

    E. "He said to him, 'The matter may be compared to the case of a king who had an only daughter, whom he loved exceedingly, calling her "My daughter."

    F. "'But he loved her so much that he called her, "My sister," and he loved her so much that he called her, "My mother."

    G. "'So did the Holy One, blessed be He, exceedingly love Israel, calling them, "My daughter." That is shown in this verse: "Listen, O daughter, and consider" (Ps. 45:11).

    H. "'Then he loved them so much that he called them, "My sister," as in this verse, "Open to me, my sister, my love" (Song 5:2).

    I. "'Then he loved them so much that he called them, "My mother," as in this verse, "Listen to me, my people, and give ear to me, my nation" (Isa. 51:4), and the word for "my nation" is written "my mother."'"

    J. R. Simeon b. Yohai stood up and kissed him on his head and said, "If I had come only to hear from your mouth this explanation, it would have sufficed."

    2. A. [Supply: "with the crown with which his mother crowned him":]

        B. Said R. Hanina b. R. Isaac, "We have made the rounds of the entire Scripture and have not found evidence that Bath-Sheba made Solomon her son a crown, and yet you say, 'with the crown with which his mother crowned him'!

        C. "But just as a crown is studded with precious stones and pearls, so the tent of meeting was marked off with blue and purple, crimson and linen."

3. A. R. Joshua of Sikhnin taught in the name of R. Levi: "When the Holy One, blessed be He, said to Moses, 'Make me a tabernacle,' Moses might have brought four poles and spread over them [skins to make] the tabernacle.

   B. "But this is not how the Holy One, blessed be He, did it. Rather, he took him above and showed him on high red fire, green fire, black fire, and white fire. He then said to him, 'Make me a tabernacle like this.'

   C. "Moses said to the Holy One, blessed be He, 'Lord of the ages, where am I going to get red fire, green fire, black fire, or white fire?'

   D. "He said to him, 'After the pattern which is shown to you on the mountain' (Ex. 25:40)."

4. A. Said R. Abun [Pesiqta deRab Kahana I:III.10: R. Berekhiah in the name of R. Levi], "[The matter may be compared to the case of] a king who had a beautiful icon.

   B. "He said to the manager of his household, 'Make me one like this.'

   C. "He said to him, 'My lord, O king, how can I make one like this ?'

   D. "He said to him, 'You in accord with your raw materials and I in accord with my glory.'

   E. "So said the Holy One, blessed be He, to Moses, 'See and make.'

   F. "He said to him, 'Lord of the world, am I god that I can make something like this?'

   G. "He said to him, 'After the pattern which is shown to you on the mountain' (Ex. 25:40)."

5. A. R. Berekhiah in the name of R. Bezalel: "The matter may be compared to the case of a king who appeared to his household manager clothed in a garment covered entirely with precious stones.

   B. "He said to him, 'Make me one like this.'

   C. "He said to him, 'My lord, O king, how can I make one like this [Pesiqta: where am I going to get myself a garment made entirely of precious stones]?'

   D. "So said the Holy One, blessed be He, to Moses, 'Make me a tabernacle.'

E. "He said to him, 'Lord of the world, can I make something like this?'

F. "He said to him, 'See and make.'

G. "He said to him, 'Lord of the world, am I god that I can make something like this?'

H. "He said to him, 'After the pattern which is shown to you on the mountain' (Ex. 25:40)."

6. A. [Supply: "...of acacia trees, standing up" (Ex. 26:15):]

B. What it says is not, "set up acacia trees," but rather, "acacia trees standing up."

C. It is like the ones that are stationed in the council above.

7. A. [Continuing No. 5, supply, "He said to him,] 'Moses, if you make what belongs above down below, I shall leave my council up here and go down and reduce my Presence so as to be among you down there.'

B. "How so?

C. "Just as up there: 'seraphim are standing' (Isa. 6:2), so down below: 'boards of shittim-cedars are standing' (Ex. 26:15).

D. "Just as up there are stars, so down below are the clasps."

E. Said R. Hiyya bar Abba, "This teaches that the golden clasps in the tabernacle looked like the fixed stars of the firmament."

8. A. "...on his wedding day":

B. this refers to the day of Sinai, when they were like bridegrooms.

C. "...on his day of joy":

D. this refers to the words of the Torah: "The precepts of the Lord are right, rejoicing the heart" ()Ps. 19:9).

9. A. Another interpretation of the phrase, "on his wedding day, on his day of joy":

B. "...on his wedding day" refers to the tent of meeting.

C. "...on his day of joy" refers to the building of the eternal house.

D. [Pesiqta deRab Kahana concludes with its base verse: Therefore it is said, "On the day that Moses completed the setting up of the Tabernacle, he anointed and consecrated it" (Num. 7:1).]

Part Four
PARASHAH FOUR

45

Song of Songs Rabbah to
Song of Songs 4:1

4:1   *Behold, you are beautiful, my love, behold you are beautiful! Your eyes*
are doves behind your veil. Your hair is like a flock of goats moving
down the slopes of Gilead.

XLV:i

1. A.   "Behold, you are beautiful, my love, behold you are beautiful:"
   B.   "Behold you are beautiful" in religious deeds,
   C.   "Behold you are beautiful" in acts of grace,
   D.   "Behold you are beautiful" in carrying out religious obligations of commission,
   E.   "Behold you are beautiful" in carrying out religious obligations of omission,
   F.   "Behold you are beautiful" in carrying out the religious duties of the home, in separating priestly ration and tithes,
   G.   "Behold you are beautiful" in carrying out the religious duties of the field, gleanings, forgotten sheaves, the corner of the field, poor person's tithe, and declaring the field ownerless.
   H.   "Behold you are beautiful" in observing the taboo against mixed species.
   I.   "Behold you are beautiful" in providing a linen cloak with woolen show-fringes.
   J.   "Behold you are beautiful" in [keeping the rules governing] planting,
   K.   "Behold you are beautiful" in keeping the taboo on uncircumcised produce,
   L.   "Behold you are beautiful" in keeping the laws on produce in the fourth year after the planting of an orchard,
   M.   "Behold you are beautiful" in circumcision,
   N.   "Behold you are beautiful" in trimming the wound,
   O.   "Behold you are beautiful" in reciting the Prayer,

Song of Songs Rabbah

	P.	"Behold you are beautiful" in reciting the *Shema*,
	Q.	"Behold you are beautiful" in putting a *mezuzah* on the doorpost of your house,
	R.	"Behold you are beautiful" in wearing phylacteries,
	S.	"Behold you are beautiful" in building the tabernacle for the Festival of Tabernacles,
	T.	"Behold you are beautiful" in taking the palm branch and etrog on the Festival of Tabernacles,
	U.	"Behold you are beautiful" in repentance,
	V.	"Behold you are beautiful" in good deeds,
	W.	"Behold you are beautiful" in this world,
	X.	"Behold you are beautiful" in the world to come.
2.	A.	"your eyes are doves:"
	B.	"your eyes" stand for the Sanhedrin, which is the eyesight of the community.
	C.	That is in line with this verse: "If it is hid from the eyes of the community" (Num. 15:24).
	D.	There are two hundred forty-eight limbs in a human being, and all of them function only through eyesight.
	E.	So the Israelites can function only in line with their Sanhedrin.
3.	A.	"doves:"
	B.	Just as a dove is innocent, so the Israelites are [Simon supplies: innocent; just as the dove is beautiful in its movement, so Israel are] beautiful in their movement, when they go up for the pilgrim festivals.
	C.	Just as a dove is distinguished, so the Israelites are distinguished: not shaving, in circumcision, in show-fringes.
	D.	Just as the dove is modest, so the Israelites are modest.
	E.	Just as the dove puts forth its neck for slaughter, so the Israelites: "For your sake are we killed all day long" (Ps. 44:23).
	F.	Just as the dove atones for sin, so the Israelites atone for other nations.
	G.	For all those seventy bullocks that they offer on the Festival of Tabernacles correspond to the nations of the world, so that the world should not become desolate on their account: "In return for my love they are my adversaries, but I am all prayer" (Ps. 109:4).
	H.	Just as the dove, once it recognizes its mate, never again changes him for another, so the Israelites, once they recognized the Holy One, blessed be He, never exchanged him for another.
	I.	Just as the dove, when it enters its nest, recognizes its nest and young, fledglings and apertures, so the three rows of the disciples of the sages, when they take their seats before them, knows each one his place.

J.   Just as the dove, even though you take its fledglings from under it, does not ever abandon its cote, so the Israelites, even though the house of the sanctuary was destroyed, never nullified the three annual pilgrim festivals.

K.   Just as the dove renews its brood month by month, so the Israelites every month renew Torah and good deeds.

L.   Just as the dove goes far afield but returns to her cote, so do the Israelites: "They shall come trembling as a bird out of Egypt" (Hos. 11:11), this speaks of the generation of the wilderness; "and as a dove out of the land of Assyria" (Hos. 11:11), this speaks of the Ten Tribes.

M.   And in both cases: "And I will make them dwell in their houses, says the Lord" (Hos. 11:11).

4.   A.   Rabbi says, "There is a kind of dove, who, when it is being fed, attracts her fellows, who smell her scent and come to her cote.

B.   "So when an elder is in session and expounding, many proselytes convert at that time, for example, Jethro, who heard and came, and Rahab, who heard and came.

C.   "Likewise on account of Hananiah, Mishael, and Azariah, many converted: 'For when he sees his children...sanctify my name...they also that err in spirit shall come to understanding' (Isa. 29:23)."

5.   A.   Rabbi was in session and expounding, but the community's attention wandered, so he wanted to wake them up. He said, "A single woman in Egypt produced six hundred thousand at a single birth."

B.   Now there was present a disciple, named R. Ishmael b. R. Yosé, who said to him, "Who was this?"

C.   He said to him, "This was Jochebed, who produced Moses, and he was numbered as the equal to six hundred thousand Israelites: 'Then sang Moses and the children of Israel' (Ex. 15:1); 'And the children of Israel did according to all that the Lord has commanded Moses' (Num. 1:54); 'And there has not arisen a prophet in Israel like Moses' (Dt. 34:10)."

6.   A.   "your eyes are doves:"

B.   They are like doves.

C.   Your likeness is similar to that of the dove:

D.   Just as a dove brought light to the world, so you bring light to the world: "And nations shall walk at your light" (Isa. 60:3).

      E. When did a dove bring light to the world?

      F. In the time of Noah: "And the dove came in to him in the evening, and lo, in her mouth was an olive leaf, freshly plucked" (Gen. 8:11).

7.   A. [Supply: "And the dove came in to him in the evening, and lo, in her mouth was an olive leaf, freshly plucked" (Gen. 8:11).] What is the meaning of "freshly plucked"?

      B. It was killed: "Joseph is without doubt torn in pieces" (Gen. 37:33).

      C. Said R. Berekhiah, "Had she not killed it, it would have turned into a great tree."

8.   A. **[Genesis Rabbah XXX:VI.3]** Whence did the dove bring the olive branch?

      B. R. Levi [Gen. R.: Abba] said, "She brought it from the young shoots in the Land of Israel."

      C. [Gen. R.: R. Levi said, "She brought it from the Mount of Olives,] for the Land of Israel had not been submerged in the flood. That is in line with what the Holy One, blessed be He, said to Ezekiel, 'Son of man, say to her: "You are a land that is not cleaned nor rained upon in the day of indignation"' (Ez. 22:24)."

      D. R. Yohanan said, "Even millstone cases dissolved in the water of the flood."

      E. R. Tarye [Gen. R.: Birai] said, "The gates of the Garden of Eden opened for the dove, and from there she brought it."

      F. Said to him R. Abbahu, "If she had brought it from the Garden of Eden, should the dove not have brought something of greater value, such as cinnamon or balsam? But in choosing the olive leaf, the dove gave a signal to Noah, saying to him, 'Noah, better is something bitter from this [source, namely,] the Holy One, blessed be He, than something sweet from you.'"

XLV:ii

1.   A. "[Your eyes are doves] behind your veil:"

      B. Said R. Levi, "In the case of a bride whose eyes are ugly, her whole body has to be examined. But in the case of a bride whose eyes are beautiful, her whole body does not have to be examined.

      C. "When a woman ties up her hair in a pony-tail [the words for tie up and veil use the same consonants], that is an ornament for her.

> D. "So too the great Sanhedrin went into session behind the house of the sanctuary, and that was an ornament to the sanctuary."
>> E. Said R. Abbuha, "They appeared to be cramped [which uses the same consonants as veil], but in fact they had ample room, like the great [hall] of Sepphoris."
>> F. And R. Levi said, "[The word for behind] is Arabic.
>> G. "If one wants to say, 'Make room for me,' he uses that word."

2. A. "Your hair is like a flock of goats moving down the slopes of Gilead:"
    B. "The mountain that I tore away [spoil] I made a standing witness to the other nations."
>> C. And what was this?
>> D. The Red Sea [Simon, p. 179, n. 1:] referred to as a mountain perhaps because the waters stood upright."
>> E. And R. Joshua of Sikhnin in the name of R. Levi said, "It is a mountain from which you streamed away. When a woman's hair thickens, she thins it; when pumpkins sprout in profusion, they must be thinned.
>>> F. "What did I tear away from it?
>>> G. ""Your teeth are like a flock of shorn ewes that have come up from the washing, all of which bear twins, and not one among them is bereaved" (Song 4:2)."

46

Song of Songs Rabbah to Song of Songs 4:2

4:2   *Your teeth are like a flock of shorn ewes that have come up from the washing, all of which bear twins, and not one among them is bereaved.*

XLVI:I
1. A. "Your teeth are like a flock of shorn ewes:"
    B. well-defined things,
    C. the spoil of Egypt and the spoil of the sea.
2. A. "that have come up from the washing:"
    B. R. Abba b. R. Kahana said in the name of R. Judah b. R. Ilai, "Before the song [of Deborah] it is written, 'And the children of Israel did

again that which was evil in the sight of the Lord' (Judges 4:1), but afterward, 'And the children of Israel did that which was evil in the sight of the Lord' (Judges 6:1).

C.   "Was it now the first time?

D.   "But the Song had bestowed forgiveness for what had been done in the past.

E.   "Along these same lines: 'Now these are the last words of David' (2 Sam. 23:1).

F.   "What were the first ones?

G.   "But the Song had bestowed forgiveness for what had been done in the past."

3.   A.   "all of which bear twins:"

B.   For all of them were situated between the angel and the Presence of God: "And the angel of God who went before the camp of Israel removed" (Ex. 14:19).

4.   A.   "and not one among them is bereaved:"

B.   not one of them was injured.

47

Song of Songs Rabbah to Song of Songs 4:3

4:3   *Your lips are like a scarlet thread, and your mouth is lovely. Your cheeks are like halves of a pomegranate behind your veil.*

XLVII:i

1.   A.   "Your lips are like a scarlet thread:"

B.   When they said the Song at the Sea: "Then sang Moses" (Ex. 15:1).

2.   A.   "and your mouth is lovely:"

B.   For they pointed in respect with their finger and said, "This is my God and I will glorify him" (Ex. 15:2).

C.   Then Moses began to praise them: "Your cheeks are like halves of a pomegranate behind your veil."

3.   A.   [Supply: "Your cheeks are like halves of a pomegranate behind your veil:"]

B.   The emptiest in your midst is as full of religious deeds as a pomegranate is with seeds,

C.   and it is not necessary to say, those who are "behind your veil."

D. That is to say, the modest and self-restrained in your midst [the words for self-restrained and veil sharing the same consonants].

48

Song of Songs Rabbah to Song of Songs 4:4

[4:1]   *"...behind your veil. Your hair is like a flock of goats moving down the slopes of Gilead. 4:2 Your teeth are like a flock of shorn ewes that have come up from the washing, all of which bear twins, and not one among them is bereaved. 4:3 Your lips are like a scarlet thread, and your mouth is lovely. Your cheeks are like halves of a pomegranate behind your veil.] 4:4 Your neck is like the tower of David, built for an arsenal, whereon hang a thousand bucklers, all of them shields of warriors. [4:5 Your two breasts are like two fawns, twins of a gazelle, that feed among the lilies.]*

XLVIII:i

1. A. "Your neck is like the tower of David:"
   B. This is how David extolled you in his book.
   C. And how did David extol you in his book? "To him who divided the Red Sea in two...and made Israel pass through the midst" (Ps. 136:13-14).
2. A. "built for an arsenal:"
   B. What is the sense of "arsenal?"
   C. It is a book that was said by many mouths [the words for mouths and arsenal use the same consonants].
   3. A. Ten men said the book of Psalms:
      B. the first Man, Abraham, Moses, David, Solomon, thus five.
      C. As to these five none differs.
      D. Who were the other five?
      E. Rab and R. Yohanan:
      F. Rab said, "Asaph, Heman, Jeduthun, the three sons of Korach, and Ezra.
      G. R. Yohanan said, "Asaph, Heman, Jeduthun are one; the three sons of Korach and Ezra."
         H. In the view of Rab Asaph is not covered by the sons of Korach, and in the view of R. Yohanan, the

Asaph here is the same as the Asaph there [the Asaph mentioned in Psalms is the one in 1 Chr. 25:2].

I. But because he was a master of the Torah, he had the merit of reciting a Psalm with his brothers, and he had the merit also to recite a Psalm entirely on his own.

J. In the opinion of Rab, it was another Asaph: "Under the hand of Asaph, who prophesied according to the direction of the king" (1 Chr. 25:2).

4. A. [Supply: Jeduthun:]

    B. Rab and R. Yohanan:

    C. Rab said, "'For Jeduthun' means, for the one who prophesied, and 'upon Jeduthun' means, a psalm concerning the decrees and punishments that happened to him and to Israel."

    D. R. Yohanan said, "'For Jeduthun' means, for the one who prophesied, and 'upon Jeduthun' means, a psalm concerning the decrees and punishments that happened to him and to Israel."

5. A. [Reverting to No. 3:] R. Huna in the name of R. Aha: "Even though ten men wrote the book of Psalms, among them all, the only one of them in whose name the Psalms are said is David, king of Israel.

    B. "The matter may be compared to the case of a group of men who wanted to recite a hymn to the king. Said the king to them, 'All of you sing pleasantly, all of you are pious, all of you are praiseworthy to say a hymn before me. But Mr. So-and-so is the one who will say it in behalf of all of you.

    C. "'Why so? Because his voice is sweet.

    D. "Thus when the ten righteous men proposed to say the book of Psalms, said the Holy One, blessed be He, to them, all of you are praiseworthy to say a hymn before me. But Mr. So-and-so is the one who will say it in behalf of all of you.

    E. "'Why so? Because his voice is sweet.

    F. "So when the ten righteous men proposed to recite the book of Psalms, said the Holy One, blessed be He, to them, 'All of you are praiseworthy to say a hymn before me.

But David is the one who will say it in behalf of all of
you.

G. "'Why so? Because his voice is sweet.'

H. "That is in line with the following verse of Scripture: 'The
sweet one of the songs of Israel' (2 Sam. 23:1)."

  6. A. [Supply: "The sweet one of the songs of Israel" (2
Sam. 23:1)"]

    B. R. Huna in the name of R. Aha said, "It is the one
who sweetens the songs of Israel, namely, David
son of Jesse."

7. A. "whereon hang a thousand bucklers:"

  B. All those thousands and myriads who stood at the Sea and whom I
protected, I protected only on account of the merit of that one who
will come in a thousand generations. [Simon, p. 181, n. 4: Moses,
who came to give the Torah, "commanded to a thousand generations"
(Ps. 105:8).]

8. A. "all of them shields of warriors:"

  B. This encompasses the one who stands and rules over his inclination
to do evil and overcomes his inclination to do evil,

  C. for instance, Moses in his time,

  D. David in his time,

  E. Ezra in his time.

  F. The entire generation depends on him [the words for shield and depend
use the same consonants].

  G. And through whom is the Red Sea opened up for you? It is through
your two breasts, Moses and Aaron.

XLVIII:ii

1. A. [Supply: 4:1 "...behind your veil. Your hair is like a flock of goats
moving down the slopes of Gilead. 4:2 Your teeth are like a flock of
shorn ewes that have come up from the washing, all of which bear
twins, and not one among them is bereaved. 4:3 Your lips are like a
scarlet thread, and your mouth is lovely. Your cheeks are like halves
of a pomegranate behind your veil. 4:4 Your neck is like the tower of
David, built for an arsenal, whereon hang a thousand bucklers, all of
them shields of warriors. 4:5 Your two breasts are like two fawns,
twins of a gazelle, that feed among the lilies.] R. Yohanan interpreted
the passage to speak of Israel at Mount Sinai:

  B. "The 'flock' that stood at Mount Sinai were not standing in a happy
mood.

  C. "'behind your veil:' for they were shrinking together [a word that
uses the same consonants as veil] at every word, and did not stand in
a happy mood but in fear, trembling, and agitation."

2.   A.   R. Abba b. Kahana in the name of R. Yohanan derives proof of the same proposition from the following verse of Scripture: "For that nation and kingdom that will not serve you shall perish; yes, those nations shall be utterly wasted" (Isa. 60:12).

B.   "'they were wasted' from Horeb [the words Horeb and utterly wasted use the same consonants].

C.   "They were then sentenced to death."

3.   A.   [Resuming 1:C:] "'Your hair is like a flock of goats moving down the slopes of Gilead:"

B.   R. Joshua in the name of R. Levi said, "[Gilead is] the mountain from which you streamed away, the mountain from which you tore away I made into a heap and a witness for the nations of the world.

C.   "And what is it? It is Mount Sinai.

D.   "And what did you strip away from it? 'Your teeth are like a flock of shorn ewes.'

E.   "These are things that are counted out in number [the words for flock of shorn ewes and counted out in number use the same consonants],

F.   "namely, two hundred and forty-eight affirmative religious duties, and three hundred and sixty-five negative religious duties.

G.   "'that have come up from the washing:' for all of them were cleansed of sins."

4.   A.   R. Aha and R. Mesharshia in the name of R. Idi says, "In connection with all other additional offerings [of Sabbaths and festivals], a sin-offering is included, for example, 'one he goat for a sin-offering' (Num. 28:22), 'a goat for a sin-offering.'

B.   "But as to Pentecost, there is no sin-offering mentioned.

C.   "This serves to teach you that at that time they were not subject to either transgression or sin."

5.   A.   "all of which bear twins:"

B.   Said R. Yohanan, "On the day on which the Holy One, blessed be He, came down onto Mount Sinai to give the Torah to Israel, with him came down sixty myriads of ministering angels.

C.   "In the hand of each one of them was a crown with which to adorn each Israelite."

D.   R. Abba b. Kahana in the name of R. Yohanan said, "There were a hundred and twenty myriads of ministering angels that came down with the Holy One, blessed be He,

E.   "one to put on a crown on each one, the other to put a girdle on him."

6.   A.   What is the sense of the word translated as girdle?

B. R. Huna the Elder of Sepphoris said, "It is a proper garment, in line with this usage: 'He looses the bond of kings and binds their loins with a girdle' (Job 12:18)."

7. A. "and not one among them is bereaved:"
   B. For not a single one of them was injured.

8. A. "Your lips are like a scarlet thread:"
   B. This is the thunder that came before the act of speech [the Ten Commandments]:
   C. "'for your voice is sweet:' this is the voice after the Ten Commandments: 'And the Lord heard the voice of your words...and said...they have said well all that they have spoken' (Dt. 5:25)."

9. A. [Supply: "And the Lord heard the voice of your words...and said...they have said well all that they have spoken" (Dt. 5:25).]
   B. What is the meaning of "they have said well all that they have spoken"?
   C. R. Hiyya b. R. Ada and Bar Qappara:
   D. One said, "It was like the act of trimming [which uses the same consonants as the word well] in the trimming of the lamps."
   E. The other said, "It was like the act of preparation in the preparation of the incense."

10. A. At that moment Moses began to praise them, saying, "'Your cheeks are like halves of a pomegranate [behind your veil].'
    B. "The most empty-headed among you is as filled with Torah-teachings as a pomegranate,
    C. "and it is not necessary to say, 'behind your veil,'
    D. "the most modest among you, the most self-restrained among you [where we find the consonants used in veil]."

11. A. "Your neck is like the tower of David:"
    B. That is how David extolled you in his book. [The words for tower and extol share the same consonants].
    C. And how did David extol you in his book?
    D. "God, when you went forth before your people" (Ps. 68:8) – and then? "The earth trembled" (Ps. 68:9).
    E. Along these same lines, "The mountains quaked at the presence of the Lord" (Judges 5:5), and then, "Even Sinai at the presence of the Lord the God of Israel" (Judges 5:5). This "Even Sinai..." adds nothing. [Simon, p. 184, n. 1: "Sinai is obviously included in 'the earth' already mentioned. Hence Sinai here must be an allusion to the Israelites who stood there to receive the Torah and it is mentioned to their credit. This then is the eulogy.]

12. A. "built for an arsenal:"
    B. It is the book that was said by many mouths.

13. A. "whereon hang a thousand bucklers:"
    B. All those thousands and myriads who stood at the Sea and whom I protected, I protected only on account of the merit of that one who will come in a thousand generations [Simon, p. 181, n. 4: Moses, who came to give the Torah, "commanded to a thousand generations" (Ps. 105:8).]

14. A. "all of them shields of warriors:"
    B. This encompasses the one who stands and rules over his inclination to do evil and overcomes his inclination to do evil,
    C. for instance, Moses in his time,
    D. David in his time,
    E. Ezra in his time.
    F. The entire generation depends on him [the words for shield and depend use the same consonants].
    G. And through whom is the Red Sea opened up for you? It is through your two breasts, Moses and Aaron.

XLVIII:iii

1. A. [Supply: 4:1 "...behind your veil. Your hair is like a flock of goats moving down the slopes of Gilead. 4:2 Your teeth are like a flock of shorn ewes that have come up from the washing, all of which bear twins, and not one among them is bereaved. 4:3 Your lips are like a scarlet thread, and your mouth is lovely. Your cheeks are like halves of a pomegranate behind your veil. 4:4 Your neck is like the tower of David, built for an arsenal, whereon hang a thousand bucklers, all of them shields of warriors. 4:5 Your two breasts are like two fawns, twins of a gazelle, that feed among the lilies.] R. Isaac interpreted the passage to speak of the war with Midian:
    B. "'Your hair is like a flock of goats:'
    C. "the platoons that went to war against Midian went only on account of the merit of Moses and Phineas: 'And Moses and Eleazar the priest took the gold' (Num. 31:51).
    D. "'moving down the slopes of Gilead:'
    E. "the mountain from which I tore away [spoil] I made a standing witness to the other nations. And what is that? It is the war against Midian.
        F. "And what is the spoil that was torn away?
        G. "'Your teeth are like a flock of shorn ewes:' this refers to matters of a fixed number [the word for fixed and shorn ewes use the same consonants],
        H. "the twelve thousand volunteers, and the twelve thousand draftees: 'So were delivered out of the thousands of Israel a thousand of a tribe, a thousand of a tribe' (Num. 31:5)."

I. Said R. Hananiah b. R. Isaac, "With twelve thousand they went forth to do battle against Midian [and not the twenty-four thousand just now posited]."

2. A. "that have come up from the washing:"
   B. R. Huna said, "The meaning is that not a single one of them put on the phylactery of the head before putting on the phylactery of the hand. For if one of them had put on the phylactery of the head before the phylactery of the arm, Moses would not have praised them, and they would not have gone up from there in peace.
   C. "One must therefore conclude that they were the most righteous men."

3. A. "all of which bear twins:"
   B. [That is to say, they went about in pairs,] for when they would go in pairs to a [Midianite] woman, one of them would blacken her face, the other would remove her jewelry.
   C. But the women would say to them, "Are we not of those that have been created by the Holy One, blessed be He, that you treat us in such a way?"
   D. And the Israelites would say to them, "Is it not enough for you that you have taken what is ours on your account: 'And the Lord said to Moses, Take all the chiefs of the people and hang them up' (Num. 25:4)."

4. A. "and not one among them is bereaved:"
   B. For not one of them was suspect of transgression.

5. A. "Your lips are like a scarlet thread:"
   B. When they said to Moses, "Your servants have taken the sum of the men of war that are under our charge, and not one of us is missing" (Num. 31:49) – on account of transgression or sin.

6. A. "and your mouth is lovely:"
   B. For they said to him, "And we have brought the Lord's offering" (Num. 31:50).
   7. A. Said to them Moses, "What you say is contradictory. You have said, 'not one of us is missing' (Num. 31:49) – on account of transgression or sin,
      B. "and you also have said, 'And we have brought the Lord's offering.'
      C. "If you have not sinned, then how come this offering?"
      D. They said to him, "Our lord, Moses, we went about in pairs to each woman, and one of us would blacken her face, the other would remove her jewelry. Is it possible that the impulse to do evil was in no way stirred? On account of that stirring of the impulse to do evil, we want to bring an offering."

E. At that moment Moses began to praise them: "'Your cheeks are like halves of a pomegranate:'

F. "The emptiest of you are filled with religious duties and good deeds like a pomegranate.

G. "For whoever is saved from a transgression that falls within his power and does not do it has carried out an enormous religious duty.

H. "And it is not necessary to say, 'behind your veil,' meaning that the same is so of the most modest and self-restrained among you.

I. "'Your neck is like the tower of David:' this is how David extolled you in his book.

J. "And how did David extoll you in his book? It was in saying, 'Sihon, king of the Amorites and Og king of Bashan...and gave their land for a heritage' (Ps. 135:11-12).

K. "'Built for an arsenal:' This refers to a book that many mouths spoke.

8. A. "Whereon hang a thousand bucklers:" [God says,] "all the thousands and myriads who went out to do battle against Midian and whom I shielded, I shielded only on account of the merit accruing to him who is to come for a thousand generations.

B. "Nor do you alone depend upon him, but rather, 'all of them shields of warriors:' whoever stands and shields himself and overcomes his impulse to do evil is called a warrior,

C. "for instance, Moses in his time, David in his time, Ezra in his time.

D. "And their entire generation depends upon them.

9. A. "And through whom was the war against Midian carried out?

B. "It was through 'Your two breasts,'

C. "namely, Moses and Phineas."

XLVIII:iv

1. A. [Supply: 4:1 "...behind your veil. Your hair is like a flock of goats moving down the slopes of Gilead. 4:2 Your teeth are like a flock of shorn ewes that have come up from the washing, all of which bear twins, and not one among them is bereaved. 4:3 Your lips are like a scarlet thread, and your mouth is lovely. Your cheeks are like halves of a pomegranate behind your veil. 4:4 Your neck is like the tower of David, built for an arsenal, whereon hang a thousand bucklers, all of them shields of warriors. 4:5 Your two breasts are like two fawns, twins of a gazelle, that feed among the lilies.] R. Huna interpreted the passage to speak of the Jordan:

B. "'Your hair is like a flock of goats moving down the slopes of Gilead:'

C. "The flock that crossed the Jordan crossed only on account of the merit accruing to our father, Jacob: 'Then you shall let your children know, saying, Israel came over this Jordan on dry land' (Josh. 4:22)."

2. A. R. Judah bar Simon in the name of R. Yohanan: "In the Torah, in the Prophets, and in the Writings we find proof that the Israelites were able to cross the Jordan only on account of the merit achieved by Jacob:

B. "In the Torah: '...for with only my staff I crossed this Jordan, and now I have become two companies.'

C. "In the prophets: 'Then you shall let your children know, saying, "Israel came over this Jordan on dry land"' (Josh. 4:22), meaning our father, Israel.

D. "In the Writings: 'What ails you, O you sea, that you flee? You Jordan, that you burn backward? At the presence of the God of Jacob' (Ps. 114:5ff.)."

3. A. [Reverting to 1.C:] "'moving down the slopes of Gilead:'

B. "the mountain from which I tore away [spoil] I made a standing witness to the other nations. And what is that? It is the Jordan.

C. "And what is the spoil that was torn away?

D. "'Your teeth are like a flock of shorn ewes:' this refers to the spoil of Sihon and Og.

4. A. "that have come up from the washing:"

B. Said R. Eleazar, "It was by sixty thousand troops that the land of Canaan was conquered."

C. That is consistent with the view of R. Eliezer, who said, "Any war that involves more than sixty thousand troops is a total snafu."

5. A. R. Judah in the name of R. Hezekiah said, "Any passage in which it is said, 'about ten,' 'about twenty,' 'about thirty,' 'about forty,' may involve more or less than that number.

6. A. "About forty thousand ready armed for war" (Josh. 4:13) as against "Forty four thousand seven hundred and sixty" (1 Chr. 54:18):

B. Said R. Aha, "They were a full thousand and the left fell off on the route-march."

C. Then [reverting to 4.B:] where were the other sixty thousand?

D. He said to them, "They were guarding the baggage, and Scripture did not count them."

7. A. "all of which bear twins:"

B. For they were enclosed [the words for twins and enclosed using the same consonants] between the vanguard [Simon, p. 187, n. 5: the tribes of Gad, Reuben, and half of Manasseh] and the rear guard [Simon: the tribe of Dan]:

C. Thus: "And the armed men went before the priests...and the rearward..." (Josh. 6:9).

8. A. "and not one among them is bereaved:"

B. For not a single one of them was injured.

9. A. "Your lips are like a scarlet thread:"

B. When they said to Joshua, "All that you have commanded us we will do" (Josh. 1:16).

C. "and your mouth is lovely:"

D. When they said, "Whoever he is who will rebel against your commandment" (Josh. 1:18).

10. A. Then Joshua began to extol them: "'Your cheeks are like halves of a pomegranate behind your veil:'

B. "The emptiest among you is full of Torah-teachings like a pomegranate,

C. "And it is not necessary to say, 'behind your veil,' meaning that the same is so of the most modest and self-restrained among you.

D. "'Your neck is like the tower of David:' this is how David extolled you in his book.

E. "And how did David extoll you in his book? It was in saying, 'To him who smote great kings' (Ps. 136:17).

F. "'Built for an arsenal:' This refers to a book that many mouths spoke.

11. A. "Whereon hang a thousand bucklers:" [God says,] "all the thousands and myriads who went out to do battle against Midian and whom I shielded, I shielded only on account of the merit accruing to him who is to come for a thousand generations.

B. "Nor do you alone depend upon him, but rather, 'all of them shields of warriors:' whoever stands and shields himself and overcomes his impulse to do evil is called a warrior,

C. "for instance, Moses in his time, David in his time, Ezra in his time.

D. "And their entire generation depends upon them.

12. A. "And through whom did the Israelites cross the Jordan?

B. "It was through 'Your two breasts,'

C. "namely, Joshua and Eleazar."

XLVIII:v

1. A. Another interpretation of the verse, "...behind your veil. Your hair is like a flock of goats moving down the slopes of Gilead:"

B. the mountain from which I tore away [spoil] I made a standing witness to the other nations.

    C. And what is that?

    D. It is the house of the sanctuary: "Fearful is God from your holy place" (Ps. 68:36).

    E. Now whence does fear go forth? Is it not the house of the sanctuary?

  2. A. That is in line with the following:

    B. "You shall keep my Sabbaths and fear my sanctuary" (Lev. 26:2).

    C. This indicates that it is sanctified when it is in ruins just as much as it is sanctified when it is standing intact.

    D. And that fact yields an argument *a fortiori:*

    E. if the Holy One, blessed be He, did not show favor to his own sanctuary,

    F. then, when he comes to exact punishment from those who destroyed it, how much the more so!

3.   A. And what is that which I tore away [spoil]?

    B. It is "Your teeth are like a flock of shorn ewes."

    C. That is to say, things that are subject to a definite and fixed number, specifically, the garments of the high priesthood.

  4. A. For we have learned in the Mishnah:

    B. **The high priest serves in eight garments, and an ordinary priest in four:**

    C. **tunic, underpants, head-covering, and girdle.**

    D. **The high priest in addition wears the breastplate, apron, upper garment, and frontlet [M. Yoma 7:5A-C].**

    E. The tunic would atone for bloodshed: "And they dipped the coat in the blood" (Gen. 37:31).

    F. Some say, "It atoned for those who wear mixed varieties: 'And he made him a coat of many colors' (Gen. 37:3)."

    G. The underpants atone for fornication: "And you shall make them linen underpants to cover the flesh of their nakedness" (Ex. 27:42).

    H. The head-covering atones for arrogance: "And he set the head-covering on his head" (Lev. 8:9).

    I. For what did the girdle atone?

    J. For the double-dealers.

    K. Others say, "For thieves."

    L. The one who says that it was for thieves maintains that view because the garment was hollow, standing for thieves, who work in hiding.

M. The one who says that it was for the double-dealers is in accord with that which R. Levi said, "It was thirty-two cubits long, and he would twist it on either side."

N. The breastplate would atone for those who pervert justice: "And you shall put in the breastplate of judgment the Urim and the Thummim" (Ex. 28:30).

O. The apron [ephod] would atone for idolatry: "And without ephod or teraphim" (Hos. 3:4).

P. The upper garment [robe] would atone for slander.

5. A. R. Simon in the name of R. Jonathan of Bet Gubrin: "For two matters there was no atonement, but the Torah has provided atonement for them, and these are they:

B. "Gossip and involuntary manslaughter.

C. "For gossip there was no atonement, but the Torah has provided atonement for it, specifically through the bell of the robe: 'And it shall be upon Aaron to minister, and the sound thereof shall be heard' (Ex. 28:35).

D. "Let the sound that this makes come and atone for the sound of slander.

E. "For involuntary manslaughter there was no atonement, but the Torah has provided atonement for it, specifically through the death of the high priest: 'And he shall dwell therein until the death of the high priest' (Num. 35:25)."

6. A. [Resuming 4.P:] The frontlet would atone for impudence.

B. Some say, "It was for blasphemy."

C. The one who says it was for impudence cites the following verse of Scripture: "And it shall be upon Aaron's forehead" (Ex. 28:38), and also, "Yet you had a harlot's forehead" (Jer. 3:3).

D. The one who says it was for blasphemy cites the following verse of Scripture: "And it shall always be upon his forehead" (Ex. 28:38) along side, "And the stone sank into his forehead" (1 Sam. 17:49).

7. A. "And he fell upon his face to the earth" (1 Sam. 17:49):

B. Why did he fall upon his face?

    C.   To begin with you interpret as follows: "His height was six cubits and a span" (1 Sam. 17:4).

    D.   It is so that that righteous man [David] should not have to be troubled to walk the entire length [of the giant],

    E.   therefore it is written, "And he fell upon his face to the earth."

    F.   Said R. Huna, "It was because Dagon, his god, was engraved on his heart.

    G.   "Thus was carried out this verse: 'And I will cast your carcasses on the carcasses of your idols' (Lev. 26:30)."

8.   A.   Another interpretation of the verse, "And he fell upon his face to the earth" (1 Sam. 17:49):

    B.   [Supply: Why did he fall upon his face?]

    C.   Said Rabbi, "It was so that that foul mouth, which had blasphemed and cursed, might be buried in dirt: 'Hide them in the dust together' (Job 40:13)."

9.   A.   Another interpretation of the verse, "And he fell upon his face to the earth" (1 Sam. 17:49):

    B.   [Supply: Why did he fall upon his face?]

    C.   It was so that that righteous man should not be troubled to go back [his full length].

10.   A.   Another interpretation of the verse, "And he fell upon his face to the earth" (1 Sam. 17:49):

    B.   [Supply: Why did he fall upon his face?]

    C.   It was so that that righteous man should come and tread upon his neck,

    D.   so fulfilling this verse: "And you shall tread upon their high places" (Dt. 33:29).

11.   A.   [Returning to No. 3's inquiry:] "that have come up from the washing:"

    B.   For they atone for Israel.

12.   A.   "all of which bear twins:"

    B.   This speaks of the two wreathen chains that issued from the middle of the breastplate and looked like two tassels hanging down from it.

13.   A.   "and not one among them is bereaved:"

B. None of them ever wore out.
14. A. Your lips are like a scarlet thread:"
B. This is the holy crown.
15. A. "and your mouth is lovely:"
B. This refers to the plate.
16. A. [In the Version of Genesis Rabbah XXXII:X.1:] [Supply:"And the waters prevailed so mightily upon the earth that all the high mountains under the whole heaven were covered, the waters prevailed above the mountains, covering them fifteen cubits deep" (Gen. 7:19):]
B. R. Jonathan went up to pray in Jerusalem. When he went by the Palatinus, a Samaritan saw him and asked him, "Where are you going?"
C. He said to him, "To pray in Jerusalem."
D. He said to him, "Wouldn't it be better for you to pray on this holy mountain and not on that dunghill?"
E. He said to him, "Why is it regarded as blessed?"
F. He said to him, "Because it was not submerged by the water of the Flood."
G. For a moment R. Jonathan lost his learning in the law. His ass driver said to him, "Sir, give me permission and I shall answer him."
H. He said to him, "Go ahead."
I. He said to him, "If this place falls into the category of mountains, then it is written, 'And it covered all the high mountains' (Gen. 7:19). And if it does not fall into the category of mountains, then Scripture had no need to make special reference to it [since obviously it was submerged]."
J. At that moment R. Jonathan got off the ass and mounted the ass-driver on it for a span of three *mils*, and he recited in his regard the following verses of Scripture:
K. "'There shall not be barren among you, male or female, or among your cattle' (Deut. 7:14), even among your cattle drivers.
L. "'No weapon that is formed against you shall prosper, and every tongue that shall rise against you in judgment you shall condemn' (Isa. 54:17)."
M. "'Your empty heads are like pomegranates split open' (Song 4:3), meaning that even the emptiest head among you is as full of good replies as a pomegranate is full of seeds.
N. "'behind your veil:' needless to say, the modest and self-controlled among you.

XLVIII:vi

1.   A. Another interpretation of the verse, "...behind your veil. Your hair is like a flock of goats moving down the slopes of Gilead:"

     B. the mountain from which I tore away [spoil] I made a standing witness to the other nations.

     C. And what is that?

     D. It is the priestly watches.

     E. And what did you strip away?

     F. "Your teeth are like a flock of shorn ewes" – things that are counted out,

     G. this refers to the twenty-four priestly watches, the twenty-four Levitical watches, and the twelve divisions [1 Chr. 27].

     H. "that have come up from the washing:" who guard Israel.

     I. "all of which bear twins:"

     J. For we have learned: At three seasons of the year all of the priestly watches were equivalent to one another.

     K. "and not one among them is bereaved:"

             L. **For we have learned in the Mishnah: (1) the first, with the head and a hind-leg, [the head in his right hand, with its muzzle along his arm, and its horns in his fingers, and the place at which it was slaughtered turned upwards, and the fat set on top of it [that place], and the right hind leg in his left hand, and the flayed end outermost; (2) the second, with the two forelegs, that of the right hand in his right hand, and that of the left in his left, with the flayed end outermost; (3) the third, with the rump and the [other] hind leg, the rump in his right hand, and the fat tail hanging down between his fingers, and the lobe of the liver and the two kidneys with it, the left hind leg in his left hand, with the flayed end outermost; (4) the fourth, with the breast and the neck, the breast in his right hand, and the neck in his left, and with its ribs between his fingers; (5) the fifth with the two flanks, that of the right in his right hand, that of the left in his left, with the flayed ends outwards; (6) the sixth, with the innards put in a dish, and the shanks on top of them, above; (7) the seventh, with the fine flour; (8) the eighth, with the baked cakes; (9) the ninth, with the wine] [M. Tamid 4:3].**

M.   "Your lips are like a scarlet thread:"

          N. As we have learned in the Mishnah: **[They gave him wine to pour out. The prefect stands at the corner, with a flag in his hand, and two priests stand at the table of the fat pieces, with two silver trumpets in their hands. They sounded a prolonged sound, a wavering sound, and a prolonged sound. They came and stood near Ben Arza, one on his right, one on his left.]** He stepped down to pour out the wine, and the prefect waved the flag, and Ben Arza dashed the cymbal, and the Levites broke out in song] **[M. Tamid 7:4K-O]**.

O.   "and your mouth is lovely:"

P.   This refers to the song.

          Q. For we have learned in the Mishnah there: **The singing which the Levites did sing in the sanctuary: On the first day they did sing, The earth is the Lord's and the fulness thereof, the world and they who live therein (Ps. 24). On the second day they did sing, Great is the Lord and highly to be praised in the city of our God, even upon his holy hill (Ps. 48). On the third day they did sing, God stands in the congregation of God, he is a judge among the gods (Ps. 82). On the fourth day they did sing, O Lord God to whom vengeance belongs, thou God to whom vengeance belongs, show yourself (Ps. 94). On the fifth day they did sing, Sing we happily to God our strength, make a joyful noise to the God of Jacob (Ps. 81). On the sixth day they did sing, The Lord is king and has put on glorious apparel (Ps. 93). On the Sabbath day they did sing, A Psalm, A song for the Sabbath day (Ps. 92) A psalm, a song for the world that is to come, for the day which is wholly Sabbath rest for eternity. [M. Tamid 7:4]**.

XLVIII:vii

1.   A.   Another interpretation of the verse, "Your hair is like a flock of goats moving down the slopes of Gilead:"

      B.   the mountain from which I tore away [spoil] I made a standing witness to the other nations.

C.   And what is that?
D.   It is the offerings.
E.   And what did you strip away?
F.   "Your teeth are like a flock of shorn ewes" – things that are counted out,
G.   "The one lamb you offer in the morning" (Num. 28:4).
H.   "that have come up from the washing:"
I.   For they perpetually make atonement for Israel.
J.   "all of which bear twins:"
K.   For we have learned: The ram is brought by eleven priests, by fifteen.
L.   "and not one among them is bereaved:"
M. The inwards and the fine flour and wine are brought by three at a time. [Compare M. Tamid 3:1:] **The superintendent said to them, "Come and cast lots [to determine] (1) who executes the act of slaughter, (2) who tosses the blood, (3) who removes the ashes of the inner altar, (4) who removes the ashes of the candlestick, (5) who carries up the limbs to the ramp: (1) the head, (2) the [right] hind leg, (3) the two forelegs, (4) the rump, and (5) the [left] hind leg, (6) the breast, (7) the neck, (8) the two flanks, (9) the innards, (10) the fine flour, (11) the cakes, (12) the wine." They drew lots. Whoever won won.]**

XLVIII:viii

1.   A.   Another interpretation of the verse, "Your hair is like a flock of goats:"
B.   the mountain from which I tore away [spoil] I made a standing witness to the other nations.
C.   And what is that?
D.   It is the Sanhedrin.
E.   And what did you strip away?
F.   "Your teeth are like a flock of shorn ewes" – things that are counted out,
G.   these vote to acquit, those vote to condemn.
H.   "that have come up from the washing:"
I.   For they acquit Israel.
J.   "all of which bear twins:"
K. For we have learned in the Mishnah: **If they found him innocent, they sent him away. If not, they postpone judging him till the next day. They would go off in pairs and would not eat very much or drink wine that**

entire day, and they would discuss the matter all that night. And the next day they would get up and come to court [M. Sanhedrin 5:5A-C].

L.   "and not one among them is bereaved:"

M.   R. Levi said, "For they make connections between one thing and another."

N.   R. Abba said, "For the law is not dim for them."

O.   "Your lips are like a scarlet thread:"

P.   R. Yudan said, "Like the decree of the king is the decree of the court.

Q.   "They give an order at their own authority for death through stoning, burning, decapitation, and strangulation."

R.   R. Hunia said, "The verse, 'Your lips are like a scarlet thread,' refers to blood.

S.   "For we have learned in the Mishnah: **And a red line goes around it at the middle, to effect a separation between the drops of blood which are tossed on the top and the drops of blood which are tossed on the bottom. [And the foundation extended all the length of the north side and all the length of the west side, and projects one cubit to the south and one cubit to the east] [M. Middot 3:1Q-S]."**

T.   R. Azariah in the name of R. Judah: "Just as the red line divides the blood to be tossed above from the blood to be tossed below,

U.   "so the Sanhedrin distinguishes that which is unclean from that which is clean, that which is prohibited from that which is permitted, that which is exempt from liability from that which is liable."

XLVIII:ix

1.   A.   Another interpretation of the verse, "Your lips are like a scarlet thread:"

      B.   this refers to the crimson strip [of wool, tied to the scapegoat on the Day of Atonement].

      C.   "and your mouth is lovely:"

      D.   [Since the word for mouth uses consonants that can yield the word for wilderness, we interpret:] This refers to the goat that is sent forth.

      E.   Said the Israelites before the Holy One, blessed be He, "Lord of the world, we no longer have the crimson strip and the goat that is sent forth."

      F.   He said to them, "'Your lips are like a scarlet thread:' the utterance of your lips is as precious to me as the strip of crimson."

2.   A.   [Supply: "Your lips are like a scarlet thread:"]

B. On this verse R. Abbahu said, "'So shall we render for bullocks the offering of our lips' (Hos. 14:3):

C. "What shall we pay instead of the bullocks and the goat that is sent away?

D. "Our lips."

3. A. "and your mouth is lovely:"

B. [Since the word for mouth uses consonants that can yield the word for wilderness, we interpret:] Your wilderness is lovely.

C. [Since the word for mouth uses consonants that can yield the word for statement, we interpret:] Your statement is lovely.

4. A. [Supply: "and your mouth is lovely:" Since the word for mouth uses consonants that can yield the word for wilderness,] R. Abba b. Kahana said, "Even though [the Temple mount] is a wilderness, people are liable for its boundaries [should they walk through the sacred space in a condition of cultic uncleanness]

B. "even now, when it is a ruin, just as they are liable for its boundaries when it is intact."

C. Said R. Levi, "Said the Holy One, blessed be He, 'During the time that it has lain in ruins, it has raised up for me righteous persons, while during the time that it was standing, it produced for me wicked persons.

D. "'During the time that it has lain in ruins, it has raised up for me righteous persons, for example, Daniel and his allies, Mordecai and his allies, Ezra and his associates.

E. "'while during the time that it was standing, it produced for me wicked persons, for instance, Ahaz and his co-conspirators, Manasseh and his, Amon and his.'"

F. R. Abba b. Kahana in the name of R. Yohanan concerning this statement of R. Levi said, "'For more are the children of the desolate than the children of the married wife' (Isa. 54:1): 'During the time that it has lain in ruins, it has raised up for me more righteous persons than during the time that it was standing.'"

5. A. "Your cheeks are like halves of a pomegranate:"

B. R. Abba b. Kahana and R. Aha:

C. One said, "The emptiest head in the three rows [of disciples, sitting before the Sanhedrin] is as full of Torah as a pomegranate is filled with seeds, and one need not say, those who are 'behind your veil,' that is, those who are seated on the Sanhedrin itself."

D. The other said, "The emptiest of those who are on the Sanhedrin are as full of Torah as a pomegranate is filled with seeds, and one need not say, those who are 'behind your veil,' that is, those who are seated under the olive, vine, and fig tree and are taken up with words of the Torah."

6. A. "Your neck is like the tower of David:"

    B. This is the house of the Sanctuary.

    C. And why is it compared to the neck?

    D. For so long as the house of the sanctuary endured, the neck of Israel was raised proudly among the nations of the world.

    E. But now that the house of the sanctuary lies in ruins, then it is as though the neck of Israel is bowed down: "And I will break the pride of your power" (Lev. 22:19), which is the house of the sanctuary.

7. A. Another explanation of ["Your neck is like the tower of David:" this is the house of the Sanctuary. And] why is it compared to the neck?

    B. Just as the neck is located in his highest part, so the house of the sanctuary was in the highest place in the world.

    C. Just as most of the ornaments are hung around the neck, so the priesthood is attached to the house of sanctuary.

    D. And just as if the neck is removed, a person cannot live, so once the house of the sanctuary was destroyed, [those who hate] Israel have no life.

8. A. "built for an arsenal:"

    B. Four square.

9. A. [Since the word for "arsenal' and the words for beauty and ruin use the same consonants,] Hiyya b. R. Bun said, "It was beautiful but is now a ruin.

    B. "Said the Holy One, blessed be He, 'I am the one who made it a ruin in this world, I am the one who is going to make it beautiful in the world to come.'"

10. A. [Since the word for "arsenal' and the words for ruin and mouth use the same consonants,] there is another explanation of the word translated arsenal:

    B. It is the ruin for which all mouths pray.

    C. In this connection they have said:

    D. Those who stand up to say the Prayer outside of the Land turn toward the Land of Israel: "And pray toward their land which you gave their fathers, the city which you have chosen, and the house which I have built for your name" (2 Chr. 6:38). Those who are in the Land of Israel turn toward Jerusalem: "And they pray to you toward this city which you have chosen and the house which I have built for your name" (2 Chr. 6:34). Those who are in Jerusalem turn toward

the Temple: "When he comes and prays toward this house" (2 Chr. 6:32). Those who are in the Temple turn toward the Chamber of the Holy of Holies and say the prayer: "When they pray toward this place" (1 Kgs. 8:30) It turns out that those standing in the north face south, those in the south face north, those in the east face west, those in the west face east. Thus all Israel turns out to be praying toward one place" (T. Berakhot 3:16A-F, cf. M. Ber. 4:5-6].

E. And how do we know that all Israel is to turn out to pray toward one place?

F. R. Joshua b. Levi said, "'That is, the temple before the sanctuary' (1 Kgs. 6:17), meaning, it is the Temple toward which all faces are to turn."

G. So much for the age in which the Temple was standing. How about the time that it lies in ruins?

H. Said R. Abin, "'built for an arsenal:' [Since the word for "arsenal' and the word for mouth use the same consonants,] the sense is, the Temple for which all mouths pray.

I. "In connection with reciting the *Shema,* one says, '...who builds Jerusalem.'

J. "In connection with the Prayer, one says, '...who builds Jerusalem.'

K. "In connection with the Grace after Meals, one says, '...who builds Jerusalem.'

L. "Thus: 'that for which all mouths say prayers before the Holy One, blessed be He.'

M. "He will rebuild it and bring his Presence to dwell in it."

11. A. One verse of Scripture says, "And my eyes and heart will be there perpetually" (1 Kgs. 9:3), and another says, "I will go and return to my place" (Hos. 5:15):

B. How are the two to be harmonized?

C. His face is above, but his heart is below.

D. For so it has been taught: [And if he cannot turn his face,] he should direct his heart toward the Chamber of the Holy of Holies [M. Ber. 4:5C].

E. R. Hiyya the Elder and R. Simeon b. Halafta:

F. R. Hiyya the Elder said, "Toward the Holy of Holies that is above."

G. R. Simeon b. Halafta said, "Toward the Holy of Holies that is here below."

H. Said R. Phineas, "I shall confirm the opinions of both of you: it must be toward the Holy of Holies that is above, which is directly over the Holy of Holies that is here below,

I.   "in line with this verse: 'The place O Lord that you have made for you to dwell in' (Ex. 15:17), that is, directly above your dwelling place, the sanctuary above."

12. A.   "Mount Moriah" [the consonants of which can be read as bitter or as awe]:

    B.   R. Hiyya the Elder and R. Yannai:

    C.   One said, "For from there flows bitterness to the world."

    D.   And the other said, "For from there flows awe to the world."

13. A.   "Ark" [the consonants of which can be read as light or curse]:

    B.   R. Hiyya the Elder and R. Yannai:

    C.   One said, "For from there flows light to the world."

    D.   The other said, "For from there flows a curse to the nations of the world."

14. A.   "Sanctuary" [a word that uses the same consonants as the word for speech and for commandments]:

    B.   The household of R. Hiyya the Elder and R. Yannai:

    C.   One said, "For from there went forth speech to the nations of the world."

    D.   The other said, "For from there went forth commandments to the world."

15. A.   "whereon hang a thousand bucklers:"

    B.   Said R. Berekhiah, "Said the Holy One, blessed be He, 'A thousand generations I have folded together and brought him who serves as shield to you, whom your heart has yearned for.' [Simon, p. 198, n. 2: The Torah should have been given after a thousand generations but was actually given after twenty-six.]"

16. A.   [Supply "whereon hang a thousand bucklers:"]

    B.   Said R. Berekhiah in the name of R. Isaac, "Said Abraham before the Holy One, blessed be He, 'Lord of the world, For me have you been made a shield, while for my children are you not made a shield?'

    C.   "Said to him the Holy One, blessed be He, 'For you I am only a single shield: "I am your shield" (Gen. 15:1).

D. "'But for your children, I shall be many shields: "whereon hang a thousand bucklers."'"

17. A. "all of them shields of warriors:"

B. This refers to the priesthood and the monarchy.

49

Song of Songs Rabbah to Song of Songs 4:5

4:5 *Your two breasts are like two fawns, twins of a gazelle, that feed among the lilies.*

XLIX:i

1. A. "Your two breasts are like two fawns:"

B. This refers to Moses and Aaron.

C. Just as a woman's breasts are her glory and her ornament,

D. so Moses and Aaron are the glory and the ornament of Israel.

E. Just as a woman's breasts are her charm, so Moses and Aaron are the charm of Israel.

F. Just as a woman's breasts are her honor and her praise, so Moses and Aaron are the honor and praise of Israel.

G. Just as a woman's breasts are full of milk, so Moses and Aaron are full of Torah.

H. Just as whatever a woman eats the infant eats and sucks, so all the Torah that our lord, Moses, learned jhe taught to Aaron: "And Moses told Aaron all the words of the Lord" (Ex. 4:28).

I. And rabbis say, "He actually revealed the Ineffable Name of God to him."

J. Just as one breast is not larger than the other, so Moses and Aaron were the same: "These are Moses and Aaron" (Ex. 6:27), "These are Aaron and Moses" (Ex. 6:26), so that in knowledge of the Torah Moses was not greater than Aaron, and Aaron was not greater than Moses.

2. A. R. Abba said, "The matter may be compared to the case of a king who had two first-rate pearls, which he put in the balance.

B. "This one was not greater than that, and that was not greater than this."

C. "So Moses and Aaron were equal."

3. A. Said R. Hanina b. R. Pappa, "Blessed is the Omnipresent, who has chosen these two brothers.

   B. "For they were created only for the Torah and the glory of Israel."

4. A. R. Joshua of Sikhnin in the name of R. Levi: "There were two species of snakes in Alexandria, one of which induced cold, the other heat.

   B. "There was a case in which physicians sent for some of them and made a compound out of them with which they healed [snake bites]."

5. A. R. Abbah in the name of R. Simeon: "A mortal cannot put on the poultice before seeing the wound.

   B. "But the One who spoke and thereby brought the world into being is not that way. But rather he puts on the poultice and only afterward inflicts the wound.

   C. "'Behold I will bring it healing and cure and I will cure them' (Jer. 33:6); 'When I would heal Israel' (Hos. 7:1).

   D. "Said the Holy One, blessed be He, 'I have come to heal the transgressions of Israel, and 'Then is the iniquity of Ephraim uncovered and the wickedness of Samaria' (Hos. 7:1).

   E. "But as to the nations of the world, he smites them and then heals them: 'And the Lord will smite Egypt, smiting and healing' (Isa. 19:22),

   F. "smiting through Aaron, healing through Moses."

6. A. Happy are these two brothers, who were created only for the glory of Israel.

   B. That is what Samuel said, "It is the Lord that made Moses and Aaron and brought your fathers up" (1 Sam. 12:6).

7. A. Thus "Your two breasts are like two fawns:"
   B. This refers to Moses and Aaron.

XLIX:ii

1. A. "twins of a gazelle:"
   B. R. Joshua of Sikhnin in the name of R. Levi: "Just as in the case of twins, if one of them leaves the breasts, the breasts dry up, so it is written, 'And I cut off the three shepherds in one month [Moses, Aaron, Miriam]' (Zech. 9:8).

C.   "Now is it not the fact that they died only in the same year?

D.   "But the decree concerning them [that they were to die] was made in the same month for all three: 'The princes of the people are gathered in' (Ps. 47:10)."

2.   A.   R. Yosé says, "Three good providers arose for Israel, and these are they: Moses, Aaron, and Miriam.

    B.   "On account of the merit accruing to them were given to them three good gifts: the well, manna, and clouds of glory.

    C.   "The manna on account of the merit of Moses, the well on account of the merit of Miriam, and the clouds of glory on account of the merit of Aaron.

    D.   "When Miriam died, the well went dry, and they said, 'This is no place of seed or of figs' (Num. 20:5), but the well again returned on account of the merit of Moses and Aaron.

    E.   "When Aaron died, the clouds of glory departed: 'And when all the congregation saw that Aaron was dead' (Num. 20:29) may be read not 'saw' but 'feared.'

    F.   "So both [the well and the clouds] were restored on account of the merit of Moses.

    G.   "But when Moses died, all three of them departed, and never returned,

    H.   "the hornet did not cross the Jordan with them,

    I.   "and the Israelites never again from that time on saw tranquillity."

3.   A.   "that feed among the lilies:"

    B.   Said Samuel b. R. Nahmani, "Miriam and Jochebed were the midwives of Israel, and they would shepherd Israel, whose hearts were as soft as lilies.

    C.   "And where was the feeding ground of Israel? In Egypt at the Red Sea."

50

Song of Songs Rabbah to Song of Songs 4:6

4:6   Until the day breathes and the shadows flee,
I will hie me to the mountain of myrrh and the hill of frankincense.

L:i

1. A. "Until the day breathes:"
    B. R. Abbahu and R. Levi:
    C. One said, "[Genesis Rabbah XLVII:VII.1. "Then Abraham took Ishmael his son and all the slaves born in his house [or bought for his money, every male among the men of Abraham's house, and he circumcised the flesh of their foreskins that very day, as God had said to him]" (Gen. 17:23)]
    D. "When Abraham circumcised himself, his sons, and those who were born of his house, he made a mountain of foreskins, and the sun shone on them, and they putrefied. The stench rose to heaven before the Holy One, blessed be He, like the scent of incense and like the scent of the handful of frankincense thrown onto the offerings made by fire.
    E. "Said the Holy One, blessed be He, 'When my children will come into transgressions and bad deeds, I shall remember in their behalf that scent and will be filled with mercy for them and convert the attribute of justice into the attribute of mercy for them.'
    F. "What verse of Scripture indicates it? 'I will hie me to the mountain of myrrh and the hill of frankincense.'"
    G. R. Levi said, "When Joshua circumcised the children of Israel, he made a mountain of foreskins, and the sun shone on them, and they putrefied. The stench rose to heaven before the Holy One, blessed be He, like the scent of incense and like the scent

of the handful of frankincense thrown onto the offerings made by fire.

H. "Said the Holy One, blessed be He, 'When my children will come into transgressions and bad deeds, I shall remember in their behalf that scent and will be filled with mercy for them and convert the attribute of justice into the attribute of mercy for them.'

I. "What verse of Scripture indicates it? 'I will hie me to the mountain of myrrh and the hill of frankincense.'"

2. A. "In that same day Abraham circumcised himself" (Gen. 17:26):

B. Said R. Berekhiah, "Had Abraham circumcised himself by night, his generation would have said, 'If we had witnessed it, we would not have let him do it.

C. "Thus: 'In that same day Abraham circumcised himself.'

D. "If anyone is offended, let him say so."

3. A. R. Abbahu b. R. Kahana and R. Levi:

B. R. Abbahu said, "He felt the pain and was hurt, so that the Holy One, blessed be He, could increase his reward.

C. "'He who is born of your household and he who is bought with your money must be circumcised' (Gen. 17:13).

D. "Said the Holy One, blessed be He, 'Will an unclean person come and take up the tasks of a clean one? That is not possible. But...must be circumcised.'

E. "'I am clean and Abraham is clean; it is right for the person who is clean to take up the task of one who is clean.'"

4. A. R. Abin in the name of R. Simeon said, "The Holy One, blessed be He, joined his right hand with Abraham's and circumcised him:

B. "'you made the circumcision with him' (Neh. 9:8)."

5. A. Another reading of the verse, "I will hie me to the mountain of myrrh:"

B. This speaks of Abraham, who is the head of all the righteous men.

C.   "and the hill of frankincense:"

D.   This speaks of Isaac, who was offered like a "handful of frankincense on the altar."

51

Song of Songs Rabbah to Song of Songs 4:7

4:7   *You are all fair, my love; there is no flaw in you.*

LI:i

1.   A.   "You are all fair, my love:"

      B.   This refers to our father, Jacob.

      C.   [Supply: "there is no flaw in you:"]

      D.   For his bed was whole before him, and there was no unfit [descendant] produced upon it.

2.   A.   What is the meaning of the verse, "You are all fair, my love; [there is no flaw in you]"?

      B.   R. Simeon b. Yohai taught on Tannaite authority, "When the Israelites stood before Mount Sinai and said, 'All that the Lord has spoken we will do and obey' (Ex. 24:7),

      C.   "at that moment there were not found among them persons afflicted with flux, persons afflicted with *saraat,* lame, blind, dumb, deaf, lunatics, imbeciles, fools or hangers-on.

      D.   "And with regard to that moment, Scripture says, 'there is no flaw in you.'

      E.   "But once they had sinned, in only a little while there were found among them persons afflicted with flux, persons afflicted with *saraat,* lame, blind, dumb, deaf, lunatics, imbeciles, fools and hangers-on.

      F.   "At that time it was said, 'Let them put out of the camp every leper and all who has suffered a flux' (Num. 5:2)."

            3.   A.   Said R. Helbo, "'And he who presented his offering the first day was Nahshon son of Amminadab...on the second day Nethanel son of Zuar made the offering' (Num. 7:12, 18).

                  B.   "Why has Judah been treated as subordinate?

    C. "It was so that Judah should not take pride and say, 'Since I made my offering first of all, I am the greatest among you all.'

    D. "Rather, the Holy One, blessed be He, credited it to them as though all of them had made their offerings on the first day and on the final day."

4. A. Said R. Eleazar, "'This was the dedication-offering of the altar, in the day when it was anointed' (Num. 7:84).

    B. "Now had not each one of them made his offering of one basin, one spoon, and the like [on the successive days]? Why does Scripture tote it all up: 'Twelve silver dishes, twelve silver basins, twelve golden pans' (Num. 7:84)?

    C. "It was so that Judah should not take pride and say, 'Since I made my offering first of all, I am the greatest among you all.'

    D. "Rather, the Holy One, blessed be He, credited it to them as though all of them had made their offerings on the first day and on the final day."

5. A. Said R. Berekhiah, "'All these are the twelve tribes of Israel...every one according to his blessing he blessed them' (Gen. 49:28):

    B. "Since it is stated, 'And he blessed them" (Gen. 49:28), why was it necessary to repeat, '...blessing each with the blessing suitable to them'?

    C. "This teaches that Jacob our father went and compared them to wild beasts. Since he had bestowed a blessing on Judah as a lion, 'Judah is a lion's whelp' (Gen. 49:9); Dan as a serpent, 'Dan shall be a serpent in the way' (Gen. 49:17); Naphtali as a hind, 'Naphtali is a hind let loose' (Gen. 49:21); and Benjamin as a wolf, 'Benjamin is a wolf that ravens' (Gen. 49:27).

    D. "Then he drew them together into a single blessing, so stating that all of them are wolves, serpents, fiery serpents, scorpions.

    E. "That is in line with this verse: 'Dan shall be a snake' (Gen. 49:17), while Moses called him a lion: 'Dan is a lion's whelp' (Deut. 33:22).

[Genesis Rabbah XCIX:IV adds:] "In line with this verse [the message is clear]: 'You all are fair, my love, and there is no blemish in you' (Song 4:7)."

6. A. Said R. Idi, "We find in connection with the offerings made by the princes that what this one offered that one offered.

    B. "This one brought a burnt-offering and that one brought a burnt-offering, this one brought a meal-offering and that one brought a meal-offering, this one brought a sin-offering and that one brought a sin-offering, this one brought peace-offerings and that one brought peace-offerings.

    C. "Why was this so?

    D. "For all of them were flawless and all of them equal with one another."

7. A. Why did Scripture give the genealogies, in the book of Exodus, for Reuben, Simeon, and Levi [at Ex. 6:14-19, leaving out the others]?

    B. R. Hanina and R. Levi:

    C. One said, "It was because their father had spoken critically of them."

    D. The other said, "It was because Scripture imputed to them genealogies connected with Moses and Aaron."

    E. Now we do not know who held the one opinion, and who held the other.

    F. But on the basis of that which R. Yudan in the name of R. Judah b. R. Simeon in the name of R. Huna said, "'The ear that listens to the reproof of life abides among the wise' (Prov. 15:31)," it must follow that it is R. Huna who said, "It was because their father had spoken critically of them.

    G. "It was because they accepted the rebuke of their father that they had the merit of being assigned a genealogy connected to Moses and Aaron.

H. "That is why it is said, 'there is no flaw in you.'"

8. A. [Supply: Why did Scripture give the genealogies, in the book of Exodus, for Reuben, Simeon, and Levi at Ex. 6:14-19, leaving out the others?]

B. R. Judah, R. Nehemiah, and rabbis:

C. R. Judah said, "It is because all the other tribes did not guard their genealogies in Egypt, but Reuben, Simeon, and Levi did guard their genealogies in Egypt."

D. R. Nehemiah said, "It was because all the other tribes worshipped idols in Egypt, but Reuben, Simeon, and Levi did not worship idols in Egypt."

E. Rabbis said, "It is because all the other tribes did not exercise authority over the Israelites in Egypt, while these tribes did exercise authority over the Israelites in Egypt.

F. "How was this so? When Reuben died, authority was transferred to Simeon, when Simeon died, authority was transferred to Levi, when Levi died, he proposed to transfer authority to Judah.

G. "But an echo came forth and proclaimed, 'Leave it alone until its time shall come.'

H. "When did its time come [for authority to be transferred to Judah]?

I. "After the death of Joshua: 'And it happened after the death of Joshua...that the Lord said, Judah shall go up' (Judges 1:1)."

9. A. [Supply: "His younger kinsman, Othniel the Kenizzite, captured it" (Judges 1:13):]

B. He had three names: Judah, Othniel, and Jabez [cf. 1 Chr. 4:9].

C. [As to the Judah to whom authority was transmitted,] R. Berekhiah and R. Levi in the name of R. Hama b. R. Hanina: "This is Boaz."

D. R. Simon in the name of R. Joshua b. Levi: "It is Othniel."

10. A. [Supply: "You are all fair, my love; there is no flaw in you:"]

B. "Son of man, the house of Israel has become dross to me, all of them are brass and tin" (Ezek. 22:18).

C. By contrast, said Zechariah, "I have seen it as entirely gold: 'I have seen, and behold a candlestick all of gold, with a bowl on top of it...and two olive trees by it' (Zech. 4:2)."

D. Two Amoras:

E. One said, "The word translated bowl are to be read to spell the word, exile."

F. The other said, "The letters of the word translated bowl should be read redemption."

G. The one who reads the letters to spell "exile" holds that they went into exile to Babylonia and the Presence of God went with them.

H. The one who reads the letters to spell "redemption" holds that the sense is, the one who redeems her is the one who saves her, as in this sense: "Our redeemer, the Lord of hosts is his name" (Isa. 47:4).

I. Said the Holy One, blessed be He, "Since that is the case, then: 'You are all fair, my love; there is no flaw in you.'"

52

Song of Songs Rabbah to Song of Songs 4:8

4:8   *Come with me from Lebanon, my bride; come with me from Lebanon. Depart from the peak of Amana, from the peak of Senir and Hermon, from the dens of lions, from the mountains of leopards.*

LII:i

1. A. "Come with me from Lebanon, my bride, come with me from Lebanon:"

B. Said the Holy One, blessed be He, "'Come with me from Lebanon.'

C.   "There we have learned in the Mishnah: '**They give a virgin twelve months to provide for herself from the time that the husband has demanded her [hand in marriage, that is to accomplish the consummation of the marriage]. [And just as they give a time of preparation to the woman, so they give a time of preparation to a man to provide for himself]' [M. Ketubot 5:2A-B].**

D.   [God continues,] "But that is not how I did it. Rather, while you were still occupied with the mortar and brick [of Egyptian bondage] [the words for brick and Lebanon use the same consonants], I lept and redeemed you" [Simon, p. 205, n. 3: "...straight from the bricks and mortar I took you for my bride by giving you the Torah, though you had had no time yet for spiritual preparation"].

2.   A.   The oleaginous intellect of Ahasuerus allowed "six months of oil of myrrh" (Est. 2:12).

3.   A.   [Supply: "six months of oil of myrrh" (Est. 2:12)]

B.   R. Judah b. R. Ezekiel said, "This refers to oil of boxwood."

C.   R. Yannai said, "This refers to oil of unripe oils, which removes hair and smoothens the skin."

4.   A.   [Reverting to 2.D:] [God continues,] "But that is not how I did it."

5.   A.   R. Berekhiah and R. Jeremiah in the name of R. Hiyya b. R. Abba said, "In Nehardea R. Levi b. Sisi gave the following exposition:

B.   "'"They saw the God of Israel and there was under his feet the like of a brick work of sapphire stone" (Ex. 24:10). This was before they were redeemed.

C.   "'But after they were redeemed, where the brick work was normally kept, there it was put away."

D.   Said R. Berekhiah, "'A brick work of sapphire' is not what is written here, but rather, 'like a brick work of sapphire.' [The meaning is that] both it [the Torah] and all the implements that belong to it were given, it, the basket, and the trowel were given."

6.   A.   Bar Qappara said,, "Before the Israelites were redeemed from Egypt, as it were, [the Torah] was written in the firmament. After they were redeemed, it no longer appeared in the firmament.

B.   "What is the Scripture proof for this view? 'It is like the very heaven in its purity' (Ex. 24:10), when it is clear of clouds."

7.   A.   Said the Holy One, blessed be He, to them, "When you went into exile in Babylonia, I was with you: 'For your sake I have been sent to Babylon' (Isa. 43:14).

B.   "And when you return to the chosen house in the near future, I shall be with you: 'with me from Lebanon, my bride.'"

8.   A.   [Supply: "with me from Lebanon, my bride:"]

B.   Said R. Levi, "It was necessary for Scripture to say only, 'with me *to* Lebanon, my bride.' How come, 'with me *from* Lebanon, my bride'?

C.   "To begin with, he leaps forth out of [and abandons to destruction] the house of the sanctuary, and only then does he exact punishment from the nations of the world [for destroying the place]."

9.   A.   Said R. Berekhiah, "In three hours the Holy One, blessed be He, will exact punishment from the wicked Esau and his troops:

B.   "'Now will I arise, says the Lord' (Isa. 33:10). [The word now appears three times in the cited verse, each standing for an hour, so Simon, p. 207, n. 1]."

10. A.   [Supply: "Now will I arise, says the Lord" (Isa. 33:10):]

B.   R. Simeon b. R. Yannai: "'Now will I arise:' so long as she [Israel] is wallowing in the dirt, as it were, so is he.

C.   "And that is in line with what Isaiah says, 'Shake yourself from the dust, arise, and sit down O Jerusalem' (Isa. 52:2).

D.   "At that moment: 'Be silent, all flesh, before the Lord' (Zech. 2:17).

E.   "Why so? 'Because 'he is aroused out of his holy habitation' (Zech. 2:17)."

F.   Said R. Aha, "Like a chicken that shakes its wings free of ashes."

LII:ii

1.   A.   "Depart from the peak of Amana, [from the peak of Senir and Hermon, from the dens of lions, from the mountains of leopards]:"

B.   Said R. Hunia in the name of R. Justus, "When the exiles [returning to Zion when the Messiah brings them back] reach Taurus Munus, they are going to say a Song.

C.   "And the nations of the world are going to bring them like princes to the Messiah."

D.   "What verse of Scripture indicates it? 'Depart from the peak of Amana.'

E.   "The sense of the word for 'depart' is only 'offering,' as in the following verse: 'There is not a present to bring to the man of God' (1 Sam. 9:7)."

2.   A.   [Supply: "There is not a present to bring to the man of God" (1 Sam. 9:7):]

B.   "It is suitable, but I am not suitable." [Following Simon, p. 207, n. 5: Saul speaks and says that "what he had might have sufficed as a gift for an ordinary person, but not for Samuel."]

3.   A.   [Reverting to 1.E:] "[God speaks,] 'Have I not done as much in the time of Hazael: "So Hazael went to meet him and took a present with him, even of every good thing of Damascus, forty camels' burden" (2 Kgs. 8:9).'

      4.   A.   [Supply: "So Hazael went to meet him and took a present with him, even of every good thing of Damascus, forty camels' burden" (2 Kgs. 8:9):]

          B.   Said R. Judah, "And was the entirety of the good things of Damascus merely forty camels' burden?

          C.   "But this serves to tell you that he had in hand precious stones and jewels that were worth in value all the good things of Damascus, thus, 'took a present with him, even of every good thing of Damascus.'"

5.   A.   [Reverting to 3.A:] "But the [nations of the world] are going to bring [following Simon:] them as gifts to the royal messiah: 'And they shall bring all your brethren out of all the nations for an offering to the Lord, upon horses and in chariots and in litters and on mules and upon swift beasts' (Isa. 66:2).

      6.   A.   [Supply: "And they shall bring all your brethren out of all the nations for an offering to the Lord, upon horses and in chariots and in litters and on mules and upon swift beasts" (Isa. 66:2):]

          B.   What is the meaning of the word translated "swift beasts"?

          C.   R. Berekhiah in the name of R. Judah said, "They are like old men who cannot ride any sort of vehicle but have to be carried on a litter [by hand]."

7.   A.   [Continuing 5.A:] "That [view, that the nations will present Israel as a gift to the Messiah,] is in line with this verse of Scripture: 'Give to the Lord families, you peoples' (Ps. 96:7)."

    B.   Said R. Aha, "What is written is not, 'Peoples, give to the Lord the families,' but 'give...families, you peoples, give to the Lord glory and strength.'

    C.   "[The meaning is,] 'When you bring them, do not bring them in a casual way, but with 'glory and strength.'"

      8.   A.   How did the Israelites merit [being made a gift to the Messiah brought by the nations]?

          B.   It is by reason of the merit that they gained when they said the Song at the Sea.

          C.   R. Nahman said, "It was by reason of the merit that was gained by the faith with which Abraham believed: 'And he believed in the Lord' (Gen. 15:6)."

D. R. Helbo in the name of R. Yohanan said, "'And Israel saw the great work [which the Lord had wielded against the Egyptians, the people feared the Lord; they had faith in the Lord and his servant Moses]' (Ex. 14:31).

E. "Now he was still leading them, and should they not have believed?! Is there someone who can see and yet not believe?

F. "Rather, it must be because of the merit gained by the Israelites when, while still in Egypt, they yet believed: 'And the people believed' (Ex. 4:31)."

LII:iii

1. A. Another reading of "Depart from the peak of Amana, [from the peak of Senir and Hermon, from the dens of lions, from the mountains of leopards]:"

   B. This refers to Abraham: "And he believed in the Lord" (Gen. 15:6).

2. A. "from the peak of Senir:"

   B. This refers to Isaac.

   C. Just as the letters of the word "Senir" yield the sense "hates the furrow," so Isaac was tried only one time alone.

3. A. "and Hermon:"

   B. This refers to Jacob:

   C. Just as all the good of Hermon is located on the lower slopes,

   D. so the priesthood derives from Jacob, the Levites derive from Jacob, the monarchy derives from Jacob.

4. A. "from the dens of lions:"

   B. This refers to Sihon and Og.

   C. Just as a lion is proud, so Sihon and Og were proud and strong.

   D. For the distance from the one to the other was merely a day, and yet this one did not come to help that one, nor did that one come to help this one.

5. A. "from the mountains of leopards:"

   B. This refers to the Canaanites.

   C. Just as the leopard is bold, so these are bold [for they all went out to fight against the Israelites, as is shown in this verse]: "And there was not a man left in Ai" (Josh 8:17).

   6. A. R. Berekhiah in the name of R. Eliezer said, "The Israelites really ought to have recited a song at the fall of Sihon and Og.

      B. "Hezekiah really ought to have recited a song at the fall of Sennacherib: 'But Hezekiah rendered not according to the benefit done for him' (2 Chr. 32:25).

C. "How come? 'For his heart was lifted up' (2 Chr. 32:25).'"
7. A. [Supply: "For his heart was lifted up" (2 Chr. 32:25):"]
B. Now you know full well that Hezekiah was king and righteous, and yet you say, "his heart was lifted up"?
C. Rather, his heart was too proud to say a song.
D. Isaiah came to Hezekiah and his court and said to them, "Sing to the Lord [for he has done gloriously. Let this be made known in all the world" (Isa. 12:5-6)].
E. They said to him, "Why should we?"
F. "For he has done gloriously."
G. They said, "This already has been 'made known in all the world.'"
H. Said R. Abba b. Kahana, "Said Hezekiah, 'The Torah with which I am occupied makes atonement for the song [that I have not sung].'"
I. Said R. Levi, "Said Hezekiah, 'Why are we supposed to recite the miracles and mighty acts of the Holy One, blessed be He? This is already known from one end of the world to the other!
J. "'After all, didn't the orb of the sun stand still in the middle of the firmament, so that the miracles and mighty acts of the Holy One, blessed be He, were already made known from one end of the world to the other!'"
8. A. R. Ishmael b. R. Yosé in the name of R. Abba says, "Pharaoh, king of Egypt, and Tirhaka, king of Ethiopia, were subject to that same miracle, when they came to the aid of Hezekiah.
B. "Sennacherib took note of them, and what did the wicked Sennacherib do to them?
C. "In the evening he chained them.
D. "At midnight the angel went forth and smote the armies of Sennacherib: 'And the angel of the Lord went forth and smote the camp of the Assyrians' (Isa. 37:36).
E. "Now at dawn Hezekiah got up and found them chained. He said, 'It appears that these have come only to assist me, and he freed them.

F.   "So they went and reported the miracles and mighty acts of the Holy One, blessed be He: 'Thus says the Lord, Egypt's wealth and Nubia's gains [and Sabaites, long of limb, shall pass over to you and be yours, pass over and follow you in fetters, bow low to you and reverently address you: "Only among you is God, there is no other god at all! You are indeed a God who concealed himself, O God of Israel, who brings victory!"]' (Isa. 45:14-15)."

9.   A.   [Supply: "Thus says the Lord, Egypt's wealth and Nubia's gains and Sabaites, long of limb, shall pass over to you and be yours, pass over and follow you in fetters, bow low to you and reverently address you: 'Only among you is God, there is no other god at all! You are indeed a God who concealed himself, O God of Israel, who bring victory!'" (Isa. 45:14-15):]

     B.   "Egypt's wealth:"
     C.   This refers to Pharaoh.
     D.   "and Nubia's gains:"
     E.   This refers to Tirhaka, king of Ethiopia.
     F.   "and Sabaites, long of limb:"
     G.   This refers to their troops.
     H.   "shall pass over to you:"
     I.   This refers to Hezekiah and his company.
     J.   "and be yours:"
     K.   They are already handed over to you.
     L.   "pass over and follow you in fetters:"
     M.   In chains.
     N.   "bow low to you:"
     O.   That is, to Jerusalem.
     P.   "and reverently address you:"
     Q.   That is, the house of the sanctuary.
     R.   And what will they say?
     S.   "Only among you is God, there is no other god at all."
     T.   Said Isaiah before the Holy One, blessed be He, "Lord of the world, 'You are indeed a God who concealed himself.'"

U. What is the sense of "indeed"?

W. [Since the words for indeed and where use the same consonants, the sense is:] "Where are you hiding, O God?"

X. [Or, alternatively:] "Indeed, you have power, but you are hiding."

Y. He said to him, "'The God of Israel is the one who will bring victory:' I shall come back and take vengeance."

10. A. [Supply: "Now I know that the Lord will give victory to his anointed, will answer him from his heavenly sanctuary with the mighty victories of his right arm. They call on chariots, they call on horses, but we call on the name of the Lord our God. They collapse and lie fallen, but we rally and gather strength. O Lord grant victory! May the King answer us when we call" (Ps. 20:7-10):]

B. R. Joshua b. Levi said, "If Hezekiah had said a song at the fall of Sennacherib, he would have been designated as the royal Messiah, and Sennacherib would have been marked as Gog and Magog. But that is not what he did.

C. "Rather: 'Now I know that the Lord will give victory to his anointed, will answer him from his heavenly sanctuary with the mighty victories of his right arm. They call on chariots, they call on horses, but we call on the name of the Lord our God. They collapse and lie fallen, but we rally and gather strength. O Lord grant victory! May the King answer us when we call.'" [Simon, p. 211, n. 2: Because he did not become the Messiah through his neglect to hymn God, he found it necessary to pray for the future...otherwise this prayer would have been unnecessary.]

53

Song of Songs Rabbah to
Song of Songs 4:9

4:9   *You have ravished my heart, my sister, my bride, you have ravished my*
             heart with a glance of your eyes, with one jewel of your necklace.

LIII:i

1. A.   "You have ravished my heart, my sister, my bride, you have ravished
         my heart:"
    B.   Said the Holy One, blessed be He, "You had one heart in Egypt, but
         you gave me two hearts."
    C.   "you have ravished my heart with a glance of your eyes:"
    D.   It was through the blood of the Passover-offering and the blood of
         circumcision.
    E.   "with one jewel of your necklace:"
    F.   This is Moses, who was unique, the hero of all your tribes.
2. A.   Another interpretation of the verse, "You have ravished my heart,
         my sister, my bride, you have ravished my heart:"
    B.   Said the Holy One, blessed be He, "You had one heart at the Sea, but
         you gave me two hearts."
    C.   "you have ravished my heart with a glance of your eyes:"
    D.   "For you stood before me at Mount Sinai and said, 'All that the Lord
         has spoken we shall do and we shall obey' (Ex. 24:7)."
    E.   "with one jewel of your necklace:"
    F.   this is Moses, who was unique, the hero of all your tribes.
3. A.   Another interpretation of the verse, "You have ravished my heart,
         my sister, my bride, you have ravished my heart:"
    B.   Said the Holy One, blessed be He, "You had one heart in the
         wilderness, but you gave me two hearts."
    C.   "you have ravished my heart with a glance of your eyes:"
    D.   This is setting up the tabernacle: "And on the day that the tabernacle
         was set up" (Num. 9:15).
    E.   "with one jewel of your necklace:"
    F.   This is Moses, who was unique, the hero of all your tribes.
         G.   There are those to say, "This refers to the women of the
              generation of the wilderness, who were virtuous. When
              that foul deed came around, they went and took counsel

among themselves, and did not give a thing of their jewelry to the making of the calf.

    H.   "Further, when they heard that, in their menstrual periods, they were prohibited to them, they forthwith went and locked their doors."

4.   A.   Another interpretation of the verse, "You have ravished my heart, my sister, my bride, you have ravished my heart:"

    B.   Said the Holy One, blessed be He, "You had one heart in the matter of the spies, but you gave me two hearts."

    C.   [Supply: "you have ravished my heart with a glance of your eyes:"]

    D.   This refers to Joshua and Caleb: "Except for Caleb son of Jephunneh the Kenizzite and Joshua the son of Nun" (Num. 32:12).

    E.   "with one jewel of your necklace:"

    F.   This is Moses, who was unique, the hero of all your tribes.

5.   A.   Another interpretation of the verse, "You have ravished my heart, my sister, my bride, you have ravished my heart:"

    B.   Said the Holy One, blessed be He, "You had one heart at Shittim, but you gave me two hearts."

    C.   "you have ravished my heart with a glance of your eyes:"

    D.   This refers to Phineas: "Then arose Phineas and carried out judgment...and that was counted to him for righteousness" (Ps. 106:30-31).

    E.   "with one jewel of your necklace:"

    F.   This is Moses.

54

Song of Songs Rabbah to Song of Songs 4:10

4:10   *How sweet is your love, my sister, my bride! How much better is your love than wine, and the fragrance of your oils than any spice!*

LIV:i

1.   A.   "How sweet is your love, my sister, my bride! How much better is your love than wine:"

    B.   R. Berekhiah and R. Helbo in the name of R. Samuel b. R. Nahman said, "There are ten passages in which Israel is called bride, six here [in the Song of Songs] and four in the prophets.

C.   "Six here: 'Come with me from Lebanon, my bride; come with me from Lebanon. Depart from the peak of Amana, from the peak of Senir and Hermon, from the dens of lions, from the mountains of leopards' (Song 4:8); 'You have ravished my heart, my sister, my bride, you have ravished my heart with a glance of your eyes, with one jewel of your necklace' (Song 4:9); 'How sweet is your love, my sister, my bride! How much better is your love than wine, and the fragrance of your oils than any spice!' (Song 4:10); 'Your lips distill nectar, my bride; honey and milk are under your tongue; the scent of your garments is like the scent of Lebanon' (Song 4:11); 'A garden locked is my sister, my bride, a garden locked, a fountain sealed' (Song 4:12); 'I come to my garden, my sister, my bride, I gather my myrrh with my spice, I eat my honeycomb with my honey, I drink my wine with my milk. Eat, O friends, and drink; drink deeply, O lovers!' (Song 5:1).

D.   "And four in the prophets: 'The voice of mirth and the voice of gladness, the voice of the bridegroom and the voice of the bride' (Jer. 7:34); 'And as a bride adorns herself with jewels' (Isa. 61:10); 'And gird yourself with them like a bride' (Isa. 59:18); 'And as the bridegroom rejoices over the bride' (Isa. 62:5).

E.   "And, correspondingly, the Holy One, blessed be He, puts on ten [nuptial] robes: 'The Lord reigns, he is clothed in majesty' (Ps. 93:1); 'The Lord is clothed' (Ps. 93:1); 'He has girded himself' (Ps. 93:1); 'And he put on righteousness as a coat of mail' (Isa. 59:17); 'And he put on garments of vengeance' (Isa. 59:17); ' 'For clothing' (Isa. 59:17); 'This one who is glorious in his apparel' (Isa. 63:1); 'Wherefore is your apparel red' (Isa. 63:2); 'You are clothed with glory and majesty' (Ps. 104:1).

F.   "This is so as to exact punishment from the nations of the world, who kept from the Ten Commandments the Israelites, who are [Simon] bound closely around them like the ornaments of a bride."

2. A.   "and the fragrance of your oils than any spice:"
    B.   Said R. Samuel b. R. Nahman, "Just as oil is odorless, but if you scent it, it takes on the fragrance of any number of odors,
    C.   "so a given verse you interpret and find in it any number of good flavors."

55

Song of Songs Rabbah to
Song of Songs 4:11

4:11   *Your lips distill nectar, my bride; honey and milk are under your tongue; the scent of your garments is like the scent of Lebanon.*

LV:i
1. A. "Your lips distill nectar, my bride:"
    B. R. Derosa and R. Jeremiah in the name of R. Samuel b. R. Isaac: "Sixty myriads of prophets arose for Israel in the time of Elijah."
        C. R. Jacob in the name of R. Yohanan said, "One hundred two myriads."
        D. For said R. Yohanan, "From Gibeath to Antipatris were sixty myriads of towns. And you have no more corrupt towns among them all than Beth El and Jericho, the latter because of Joshua's curse, the former because of the fact that Jeroboam's two calves of gold were located there.g
        E. "Now one verse of Scripture states, 'And the sons of the prophets who were at Beth El came to Elisha' (2 Kgs. 2:3), and the smallest number of a plural is two."
    2. A. [Supply: "And the sons of the prophets who were at Beth El came to Elisha'"(2 Kgs. 2:3):]
        B. [If there were so many prophets,] why were their prophesies not published?
        C. It was because the coming generations had no need of them.
        D. One must then conclude that any prophecy which applies for the here and now and which also was needed for coming generations was published,
        E. and every prophecy that applies for the here and now but for which coming generations had no need was not published.
        F. But in the age to come the Holy One, blessed be He, will collect them and publish all of their prophecies: "And the Lord my God shall come and all the holy ones with you" (Zech. 14:5).

3.   A.   [Reverting to 1.B:] R. Berekhiah in the name of R. Helbo said, "Just as the Israelites had sixty myriads of male prophets, so they had sixty myriads of female prophets.

      B.   "Solomon came and publicized them: 'Your lips distill nectar, my bride.'"

4.   A.   [Supply: "Your lips distill nectar, my bride:"] R. Huna and R. Halafta of Caesarea in the name of R. Simeon b. Laqish said, "Just as a bride is adorned with twenty-four adornments, and should she lack one of them, she is null,

      B.   "so a disciple of a sage has to be conversant with the twenty-four books [of the written Torah], and should he lack one of them, he is null."

            C.   R. Huna in the name of R. Simeon b. Laqish: "Just as a bride is modest, so a disciple of a sage has to be modest."

            D.   R. Halafta in the name of R. Simeon b. Laqish: "Just as a bride sits on her throne and says, 'See that I am pure, and this, my bridal accoutrements, gives testimony about me,'

            E.   "so a disciple of a sage likewise must be above all reproach."

                  5.   A.   [As to the word translated nectar,] R. Eleazar b R. Simeon and R. Yosé b. R. Hanina and rabbis:

                        B.   R. Eleazar b. R. Simeon says, "Whoever teaches words of the Torah in public, and they are not so pleasing to those who hear them as fine flour that one has sifted in a sieve [a word that uses the consonants for the word translated nectar] would have been better off not to have said them."

                        C.   R. Yosé [b. R. Hanina] says, "Whoever teaches words of the Torah in public, and they are not so pleasing to those who hear them as honey from the comb, would have been better off not to have said them."

                        D.   Rabbis say, ""Whoever teaches words of the Torah in public, and they are not so pleasing to those who hear them as honey and milk mixed together would have been better off not to have said them."

                  6.   A.   [As to the word translated nectar,] R.Yohanan and R. Simeon b. Laqish:

                        B.   R. Yohanan said, "Whoever teaches words of the Torah in public, and they are not so pleasing to those who hear them as a bride, who gives pleasure to those who see her when she is sitting in her bridal bower, would have been better off not to have said them."

C. R. Simeon b. Laqish said, "Whoever teaches words of the Torah in public, and they are not so pleasing to those who hear them as a bride, who gives pleasure to her groom, would have been better off not to have said them."

LV:ii

1. A. "honey and milk are under your tongue:"
   B. R. Berekhiah said, "There is no drink that is more rotten than the drink that is under the tongue, and yet you say, 'honey and milk are under your tongue'!
   C. "But if there are laws that are obscure under your tongue like honey and milk, laws that are firmly in hand how much the more so!?
   D. Said R. Levi, "Also concerning one who recites Scripture in accord with its proper modulation and intonation, it is said, 'honey and milk are under your tongue.'"

2. A. "the scent of your garments is like the scent of Lebanon:"
   B. "And he came near and kissed him, and he smelled the smell of his clothes" (Gen. 27:27):
   C. Said R. Yohanan, "You have nothing so foul-smelling and gross as washed goatskins, and yet you say, 'And he came near and kissed him, and he smelled the smell of his clothes'!
   D. "But when our father, Jacob, came in, with him came the Garden of Eden: 'See, the smell of my son is like the smell of a field that the Lord has blessed' (Gen. 27:27).
   E. "But when the wicked Esau came in to his father, with him came the [stench of] Gehenna: 'When pride comes, then comes shame' (Prov. 11:2).
   F. "That is why he said to him, 'Who then' (Gen. 27:33), as if to say, '[Since the words for 'then' and 'baked use the same consonants], 'who is baked in this oven?'
   G. "The Holy Spirit replied, 'He who has taken venison' (Gen. 27:33).
   3. A. R. Eleazar b. R. Simeon asked R. Simeon b. R. Yosé b. Laqonia, his father-in-law, "Did weaving looms go forth with the Israelites to the Wilderness?"
      B. He said to him, "No."
      C. He said to him, "Then where did they get clothes all those forty years that the Israelites spent in the wilderness?"
      D. He said to him, "It was from the clothing that the ministering angels provided for them to wear: 'I clothed you also with richly woven work' (Ezek. 16:10)."

4. A. [Supply: "I clothed you also with richly woven work" (Ezek. 16:10):]

B. R. Simai said, "It was purple."

C. Aqilas translated, "It was embroidered."

5. A. [Reverting to 3.D:] He said to him, "But didn't the clothes wear out?"

B. He said to him, "Have you never studied Scripture in your entire life? 'Your clothing did not get old on you' (Dt. 8:4)."

C. He said to him, "But didn't the children grow up?"

D. He said to him, "Go learn the lesson of the snail, for as it grows, its shell grows with it."

E. He said to him, "But didn't the clothes need laundering?"

F. He said to him, "The cloud would rub against them and clean them."

G. He said to him, "But didn't they burn up [in the fire that went along with the cloud]?"

H. He said to him, "Go learn the lesson of the asbestos thread, which is cleaned only in fire."

I. He said to him, "But didn't they breed lice?"

J. He said to him, "If after they died they did not produce lice, did they produce them when alive?"

K. "But didn't they have B.O. from the sweat of their bodies?"

L. He said to him, "They would roll around in the grass by the well: 'He makes me lie down in green pastures' (Ps. 23:2).

M. "So their good smell wafted from one end of the world to the other.

N. "And Solomon came and made the matter explicit: 'the scent of your garments is like the scent of Lebanon.'"

56

Song of Songs Rabbah to
Song of Songs 4:12

4:12   *A garden locked is my sister, my bride, a garden locked, a fountain sealed.*
[4:13   *Your shoots are an orchard of pomegranates with all choicest fruits,*
         henna with nard.]

LVI:i

1.   A.   "A garden locked is my sister, my bride, [a garden locked, a fountain sealed]:"

     B.   R. Judah b. R. Simon in the name of R. Joshua b. Levi: "[The matter may be compared to the case of] a king who had two daughters, an older and a younger, and who did not take time out to marry them off but left them for many years and went overseas.

     C.   "The daughters went and took the law into their own hands, and married themselves off to husbands. And each one of them took her husband's signature and his seal.

     D.   "After a long time the king came back from overseas and heard people maligning his daughters, saying, 'The king's daughters have already played the whore.'

     E.   "What did he do? He issued a proclamation and said, 'Everybody come out to the piazza,' and he came and went into session in the antechamber [holding court there].

     F.   "He said to them, 'My daughters, is this what you have done and have ruined yourselves?'

     G.   "Each one of them immediately produced her husband's signature and his seal.

     H.   "He called his son-in-law and asked, To which of them are you the husband?'

     I.   "He said to him, 'I am the first of your sons-in-law, married to your elder daughter.'

     J.   "He said to him, 'And what is this?'

     K.   "He said to him, 'This is my signature and my seal.'

     L.   "And so with the second.

     M.   "Then the king said, 'My daughters have been guarded from fornication, and you malign and shame them! By your lives, I shall carry out judgment against you.'

N.   "So too with the nations of the world: since they taunt Israel and say, "'And the Egyptians made the people of Israel work with rigor" (Ex. 1:13), if that is what they could make them do in labor, how much the more so with their bodies and with their wives'!'

O.   "Then said the Holy One, blessed be He, 'A garden locked is my sister, my bride.'"

2.   A.   [Supply: "A garden locked:"]

B.   What is the meaning of "A garden locked"?

C.   Said the Holy One, blessed be He, "My garden is locked up, and yet she is maligned!"

3.   A.   [Continuing the account of 1.O:] said R. Phineas, "Then the Holy One, blessed be He, summoned the angel in charge of pregnancy and said, 'Go and form them with all the distinctive features of their fathers.'

B.   "And whom did their fathers resemble? The founders of their families, thus of Reuben, 'The families of the Reubenites' (Num. 26:7)."

C.   Said R. Hoshaiah, "Reuben [produced] the Reubenites, Simeon the Simeonites."

D.   Said R. Merinus b. R. Hoshaia, "But this is as people say, 'Baronites, Sabronites, Sibuyites.' [Simon, p. 218, n. 2: The name does not prove legitimacy.]"

E.   R. Huna in the name of R. Idi: "The word 'the' at the beginning of the name and the addition of 'ites' at the end indicates of them that they really are the sons of their designated fathers."

4.   A.   [Supply: "A garden locked is my sister, my bride, a garden locked, a fountain sealed:"]

B.   Said R. Phineas, "'A garden locked:' this refers to the virgins.

C.   "'a garden locked:' this refers to the married women.

D.   "'a fountain sealed:' this refers to the males."

5.   A.   [Leviticus Rabbah XXXII:V.1: "A garden locked is my sister, my bride, a garden locked, a fountain sealed:"]

B.   It was taught in the name of R. Nathan, "'a garden locked, a fountain sealed:'

C.   "one refers to vaginal, the other to anal intercourse [neither of which has taken place]."

6.   A.   [Leviticus Rabbah XXXII:V.4:] R. Huna in the name of Bar Qappara: "It was on four counts that the Israelites were redeemed from Egypt:

B.   "Because they did not change their names [from Jewish to Egyptian ones], because they did not change their language, because they did not gossip, and because they did not go beyond the bounds of sexual decency.

C. "Because they did not change their names: Reuben and Simeon – whoever went down Reuben and Simeon came up bearing the same names.

D. "They did not call Reuben Rufus, Judah Julian, Joseph Justus, or Benjamin Alexander.

E. "They did not change their language: elsewhere it is written, 'And a refugee came and told Abram the Hebrew' (Gen. 14:13), and here it is written, 'The God of the Hebrews has met with us' (Ex. 3:18); and 'For my mouth it is that speaks with you' (Gen. 45:12) – all in the holy language.

F. "Because they did not gossip: 'Speak into the ears of the people and let them ask jewels or silver from their neighbors' (Ex. 11:2). Now you find that this matter of taking away the wealth of Egypt had been set in trust with them for twelve months prior to the exodus, but not a single one of them turned out to have revealed the secret, and not a single one of them ratted on his buddy.

G. "Because they did not go beyond the bounds of sexual decency: you find that that was the case, for there was only a single Israelite woman who actually did so, and Scripture explicitly identified her: 'And the name of his mother was Shulamit, daughter of Dibri, of the tribe of Dan' (Lev. 24:11). [She was the only Israelite woman who bore a child to an Egyptian man.]"

7. A. [Leviticus Rabbah XXXII:V.3: R. Huna in the name of R. Hiyya b. Abba] R. Abba b. Kahana said, "Sarah went down to Egypt and fenced herself off from sexual licentiousness, and all the other Israelite women were kept fenced off on account of the merit that she had attained.

B. "Joseph went down to Egypt and fenced himself off from sexual licentiousness, and all the other Israelite men kept fenced off on account of the merit that he had attained."

C. Said R. Phineas in the name of R. Hiyya, "It was truly worthy that through the fence that kept people from licentious behavior, Israel should be redeemed."

D. [Song of Songs Rabbah now adds:] "How do we know it? Because Scripture says, 'A garden locked is my sister, my bride, a garden locked, a fountain sealed,' and then, 'Your shoots are an orchard of pomegranates with all choicest fruits, henna with nard.'"

8. A. [Supply from Leviticus Rabbah XXXII:V.2: Another interpretation of "A garden locked" (Song 4:12):] R. Phineas in the name of R. Hiyya bar Abba, "Because the Israelites locked themselves up and avoided licentious sexual behavior with the Egyptians, they were redeemed from Egypt. On that account was 'your being sent forth' [that is, 'your shoots'] 'are an orchard of pomegranates with all choicest fruits.' That interpretation is in line with the following: 'And it came to pass, when Pharaoh sent forth...' (Ex. 13:17). [The shoots of Song 4:13) calls to mind the "sending forth' of Pharaoh, and the Israelites were sent forth by virtue of the fact that they had protected the integrity of their 'shoots,' that is, their offspring.]

B. R. Simeon b. Yohai taught on Tannaite authority, "[The Egyptians were] in the position of someone who inherited a piece of ground that was a dumping ground. The heir was lazy, so he went and sold it for some trifling sum. The buyer went and worked hard and dug up in the dump heap and found a treasure, and with it he built himself a big palace. The buyer would walk about the marketplace, with servants following in a retinue, all on the strength of that treasure that he had bought with the dump heap.

C. "The seller, when he saw this, he began to choke, saying, 'Woe, what I have lost!'

D. "So too, when the Israelites were in Egypt, they were enslaved in mortar and bricks, and they were held in contempt by the Egyptians. But when they saw them with their standards, encamped at the sea, in royal array, the Egyptians began to choke, saying, 'Woe, what have we sent forth from our land!'

E. "That is in line with this verse, 'And it came to pass [a word that contains consonants that can be read, 'woe,'] when Pharaoh had let the people go' (Ex. 13:17)."

9. A. Said R. Jonathan, "They were in the position of someone who had a field the size of a kor who went and sold it for a piddling sum.

B. "The buyer went and dug wells in it and made in it gardens and orchards.

C. "When the seller saw this, he began to choke, saying, 'Woe, what I have lost!'

D. "So too, when the Israelites were in Egypt, they were enslaved in mortar and bricks, and they were held in contempt by the Egyptians. But when they saw them with their standards, encamped at the sea, in royal array, the Egyptians began to choke, saying, 'Woe, what have we sent forth from our land!'

E. "That is in line with this verse, 'And it came to pass [a word that contains consonants that can be read, 'woe,'] when Pharaoh had let the people go' (Ex. 13:17)."

10. A. R. Yosé says, "They were in the position of someone who had a grove of cedars, who went and sold it for a piddling sum.

B. "The buyer went and made of the wood boxes, chests, towers and carriages.

C. "When the seller saw this, he began to choke, saying, 'Woe, what I have lost!'

D. "So too, when the Israelites were in Egypt, they were enslaved in mortar and bricks, and they were held in contempt by the Egyptians. But when they saw them with their standards, encamped at the sea, in royal array, the Egyptians began to choke, saying, 'Woe, what have we sent forth from our land!'

E. "That is in line with this verse, 'And it came to pass [a word that contains consonants that can be read, 'woe,'] when Pharaoh had let the people go' (Ex. 13:17)."

57

Song of Songs Rabbah to Song of Songs 4:13

4:13 *Your shoots are an orchard of pomegranates with all choicest fruits, henna with nard.*

LVII:i

1. A. Another explanation of the verse, "Your shoots are an orchard of pomegranates:"

B. [Reading "your shoots" as "the gifts that you have sent" (Simon),] they are like "an orchard of pomegranates,"

C. as in the speech of ordinary people, for instance, "What did so-and-so send to his betrothed?" "Pomegranates."

2. A. [On the subject of exchanges of gifts between God and Israel, there is this discussion between] R. Hanina and R. Simon:

B. One said, "She [the community of Israel] brought him thirteen things, and he brought her thirteen things.

C. "She [the community of Israel] brought him thirteen things, as made explicit in the book of Exodus: 'And this is the offering...gold and silver and brass, and blue and purple and scarlet and fine linen and goats' hair, and rams' skins dyed red and sealskins and acacia wood...onyx stones and stones to be set' (Ex. 25:3-7).

D. "and he brought her thirteen things as spelled out in Ezekiel: 'I clothed you also with embroidered garments [and gave you sandals of tahash leather to wear and wound fine linen about your head and dressed you in silks. I decked you out in finery and put bracelets on your arms and a chain around your neck. I put a ring in your nose and earrings in your ears and a splendid crown on your head]' (Ezek. 16:10-12)."

3. A. [Supply: "I clothed you also with embroidered garments:"]

B. R. Simi said, "This is purple."

C. Aqilas translated, "embroidered work."

4. A. "and gave you sandals of tahash leather to wear:"

B. the counterpart of the sealskins of the tabernacle.

5. A. "and wound fine linen about your head:"

B. the counterpart of the fine linen and goatskins.

6. A. "and dressed you in silks:"

B. R. Aibu said, "He made them something substantial in the world [the words for substantial and silk share the same consonants]."

C. R. Judah b. R. Simon said, "He wrapped them in clouds of glory: 'The pillar of cloud...did not depart' (Ex. 13:22) [the words for silk and depart share the same consonants]."

7. A. "I decked you out in finery:"

B. This refers to weapons of war.

8. A. It has been taught on Tannaite authority:

B. R. Simeon b. Yohai says, "The weapon that he gave to them at Horeb has the Ineffable Name of God incised in it.

        C.   "But when they sinned, it was taken away from them."

        D.   How was it taken away from them?

        E.   R. Aibu said, "It peeled away on its own."

        F.   Rabbis say, "An angel came down and peeled it off."

9.   A.   "and put bracelets on your arms:"

     B.   This refers to the tablets of the covenant on which the Ten Commandments are incised:

     C.   "And the tables were the work of God" (Ex. 32:16).

10. A.   "and a chain around your neck:"

     B.   This refers to teachings of the Torah:

     C.   "bind them perpetually upon your heart, tie them around your neck" (Prov. 6:21).

11. A.   "I put a ring in your nose:"

     B.   This refers to the holy crown.

12. A.   "and earrings in your ears:"

     B.   This refers to the plate:

        C.   for we have learned on Tannaite authority:

        D.   The plate was like a thin plate of gold, two fingerbreadths in width, and it went around the forehead from ear to ear.

13. A.   "and a splendid crown on your head:"

     B.   This refers to the Presence of God:

     C.   "you shall also be a crown of beauty in the hand of God" (Isa. 62:3); "And their king is passed on before them, and the Lord at the head of them" (Mic. 2:13).

        14. A.   [Reverting to 2.B:] what about the other three?

            B.   "You adorned yourself with gold and silver and your apparel was of fine linen, silk and embroidery. Your food was choice flour, honey and oil. You grew more and more beautiful and became fit for royalty. Your beauty won you fame among the nations, [for it was perfected through the splendor which I set upon you]" (Ez. 16:13-14).

15. A.   "with all choicest fruits, henna with nard:"

     B.   R. Huna said, "She brought him thirteen things, and he brought her twenty-six things, as is the way of the groom to double the wedding gift [Hebrew: marriage settlement] of the bride:

     C.   R. Aha said, "She brought him utensils and spices, and he brought her utensils and spices, utensils through Moses, spices through Solomon:

     D.   "'And she gave the king a hundred and twenty talents of gold and of spices a very great quantity, and precious stones; there came no more such abundance of spices as those that the Queen of Sheba gave to King Solomon' (1 Kgs. 10:10)."

E.   R. Simon said, "She brought him utensils and spices that were counted out, but he brought her utensils and spices that were beyond all counting.

F.   "Solomon came along and made it explicit: 'with all choicest fruits, henna with nard.'"

LVII:ii

1.   A.   Another reading of the verse, "Your shoots are an orchard of pomegranates :"

B.   [Reading "your shoots" as though it spoke of irrigated ground, since the words for "shoots" and "irrigated ground" share the same consonants (Simon, p. 222, n. 6):]

C.   the Holy One, blessed be He, is going to make you like an orchard of pomegranates in the age to come.

D.   And what is the sense here?

E.   It is akin to the well of Miriam.

2.   A.   Where did the Israelites get libation wine for all those forty years that they spent in the desert?

B.   R. Yohanan said, "From the well, and from it came most of the things that gave them pleasure."

C.   For said R. Yohanan, "The well would bring up for them all kinds of herbs, vegetables, and trees.

D.   "You may know that that was so, for when Miriam died, the well stopped, and they said, 'It is no place of seed, figs, or vines' (Num. 20:5)."

E.   R. Levi said, "They got it from the grape cluster, in line with this verse: 'They cut down from there a branch with one cluster of grapes' (Num. 13:23)."

F.   Is such a thing possible?

G.   Said R. Abba b. Kahana, "The fruit was unusually fat at that time."

H.   Rabbis said, "They got the wine from what the gentile traders were selling to the Israelites."

I.   It was taught on Tannaite authority by R. Ishmael, "The gentiles' wine at that time was not forbidden to Israelites."

LVII:iii

1.   A.   Another reading of the verse, "Your shoots are an orchard of pomegranates :"

B.   [Reading "your shoots" as though it spoke of irrigated ground, since the words for "shoots" and "irrigated ground" share the same consonants:]

C.   the Holy One, blessed be He, is going to make you like an orchard of pomegranates in the age to come.

D.   And what is the sense here?

E.   It is akin to the stream: "All kinds of trees for food will grow up on both banks of the stream. Their leaves will not wither nor their fruit fail; they will yield new fruit every month, because the water for them flows from the Temple. Their fruit will serve for food and their leaves for healing" (Ezek. 47:12).

3.   A.   [Supply: "Their fruit will serve for food and their leaves for healing" (Ezek. 47:12): What is the meaning of the word for "healing"?]

B.   Rab and Samuel:

C.   One said, "It was to loosen the upper mouth [relieving a speech impediment (cf. Simon)]."

D.   The other said, "It was to loosen the lower mouth [relieving barrenness]."

E.   R. Hanina and R. Joshua b. Levi:

F.   One said, "It was to loosen the upper mouth [relieving a speech impediment (cf. Simon)]."

G.   The other said, "It was to loosen the lower mouth [relieving barrenness]."

LVII:iv

1.   A.   Another reading of the verse, "Your shoots are an orchard of pomegranates :"

B.   [Reading "your shoots" as though it spoke of irrigated ground, since the words for "shoots" and "irrigated ground" share the same consonants:]

C.   the Holy One, blessed be He, is going to make you like an orchard of pomegranates in the age to come.

D.   And what is the sense here?

E.   It is akin to Elijah, of blessed memory.

F.   For we have learned in the Mishnah:

G.   **The family of the house of Seriphah was in Transjordan, and Ben Zion put it out by force. And there was another family there, which Ben Zion drew near by force. It is families of this sort that Elijah will come to declare unclean and to declare clean, to put out and to draw near.**

H. R. Judah says, "To draw near but not to put out."
I. R. Simeon says, "To smooth out disputes."
J. And sages say, "Not to put out or to draw near, but to make peace in the world,
K. "as it is said, 'Behold I will send you Elijah the prophet...and he will return the heart of the fathers to the children and the heart of the children to the fathers' (Mal. 4:23-24)." [M. Ed. 8:7D-J].

58

Song of Songs Rabbah to Song of Songs 4:14

4:14   *nard and saffron, calamus and cinnamon,*
with all trees of frankincense, myrrh and aloes, with all chief spices –

LVIII:i

1. A. "nard and saffron, calamus and cinnamon, with all trees of frankincense, myrrh and aloes, with all chief spices:"
    B. "nard:"
    C. Nard-oil.
    D. "and saffron:"
    E. As stated.
    F. "calamus:"
    G. This is sweet calamus: "And of sweet calamus" (Ex. 30:23).
    H. "and cinnamon:"
    I. R. Huna in the name of R. Yosé says, "Cinnamon used to grow in the Land of Israel, and goats and deer would munch on it."
    J. "[with all trees of frankincense], myrrh:"
    K. Oil of myrrh.
    L. "and aloes:"
    M. R. Yassa said, "This is foliatum [an ointment or oil prepared from leaves of spikenard (Simon, p. 225, n. 1)]."
        N. Why is it called "aloes" [which is spelled with letters that may be read, "tents"]?
        O. R. Abba b. R. Yudan in the name of R. Judah said, "Because it comes by way of tents [through Bedouin]."

P. And rabbis say, "Because it spreads when in a tent['s contained space]."

2. A. And where did the Israelite women get their ornaments to please their men through the forty years that they spent in the wilderness?

B. R. Yohanan said, "From the well: 'a garden fountain, a well of living water and flowing streams from Lebanon' (Song 4:15)."

C. R. Abbahu said, "From the manna: '[translated by Simon as:] Myrrh and aloes and cassia are all your garments, from what is eaten with the tooth' (Ps. 45:9).

D. "'From what is eaten with the tooth' did the modest and righteous Israelite women adorn themselves and please their men all the forty years that they spent in the wilderness."

3. A. "For behold the Lord commands and the great house will be made into ruins and the small one into clefts" (Amos 6:11):

B. "Ruins" are not the same as "clefts,"

C. for a ruin yields fragments, and a cleft does not.

59

Song of Songs Rabbah to
Song of Songs 4:15

4:15 *a garden fountain, a well of living water and flowing streams from Lebanon.*

LIX:i

1. A. "a garden fountain, a well of living water:"

B. Said R. Yohanan, "Forty-eight times the word 'well' is written in the Torah, corresponding to the forty-eight ways through which the Torah is given, thus: 'a garden fountain, a well of living water.'"

2. A. "and flowing streams from Lebanon:"

B. Said R. Azariah, "This one flows a bit in one matter, and that one flows a bit in one matter, until the law stands forth like [a cedar of] Lebanon."

C.   Said R. Tanhuma, "This one fastens a little and that one fastens a
little, until the law stands forth like well-joined beams."

60

Song of Songs Rabbah to
Song of Songs 4:16

4:16   *Awake, O north wind, and come, O south wind! Blow upon my garden,*
let its fragrance be wafted abroad. Let my beloved come to his garden,
and eat its choicest fruits.

LX:i

1.   A.   "Awake, O north wind, and come, O south wind:" [I give the version
of Genesis Rabbah XXII:V.2, which begins: "And Abel brought of
the firstlings of his flock and of their fat portions" (Gen. 4:4).]

B.   R. Eleazar and R. Yosé bar Hanina:

C.   R. Eleazar [Song: Eliezer] says, "The children of Noah
[when they made offerings] offered their sacrifices in the
status of peace-offerings. [They kept portions of the
sacrificial beast, e.g., the hide, and burned up on the fire
only the fats, that is, minimal sacrificial parts.]"

D.   R. Yosé bar Hanina said, "They prepared them in the status
of whole-offerings [burning up the entire animal and not
keeping any portions for the sacrificer and sacrificer]."

E.   R. Eleazar objected to the view of R. Yosé bar Hanina,
"And is it not written, 'And of their fat portions' (Gen.
4:4)? It was an offering in the status of one the fat portions
of which are burned up on the altar [and not eaten by the
sacrificer]."

F.   How does R. Yosé bar Hanina treat this passage? He
interprets it to refer to the fat animals [and not to the
portions of those that were offered up, but only referring
to "the best of the flock"].

G.   R. Eleazar objected to the view of R. Yosé bar Hanina,
"And lo, it is written: 'And he sent the young men of the
children of Israel, who offered burnt-offerings and
sacrificed peace-offerings of oxen unto the Lord' (Ex.
24:5)? [This was before revelation, and hence would

indicate that the children of Noah, belonging to the
category of the Israelites at that time, prior to the Torah,
in fact offered not only whole-offerings but also peace-
offerings, just as Eleazar maintains.]"

H. How does R. Yosé bar Hanina treat this verse? He
interprets the reference to "peace-offerings" to mean that
they offered up the beasts with their hides, without flaying
them and cutting them into pieces. [So even though the
verse refers to peace-offerings, in fact the animals were
offered up as whole-offerings, hide and all.]

I. R. Eleazar objected to R. Yosé bar Hanina, "And is it not
written, 'And Jethro, Moses' father-in-law, took a burnt-
offering and sacrifices' (Ex. 18:12)? [The reference to a
burnt-offering would suffice, so the inclusion of the further
reference to "sacrifices" indicates that there was an
offering made in a different classification, hence, peace-
offerings.]"

J. How does R. Yosé bar Hanina deal with this verse? He
accords with the view of him who said that Jethro came
to Moses *after* the giving of the Torah, [at which point
Jethro was in the status of an Israelite. Hence the type of
offering Jethro gave would indicate only what Israelites
did when they made their sacrifices and would not testify
to how children of Noah, prior to the giving of the Torah,
in general offered up their animals.]

K. [We shall now deal with the point at which Jethro rejoined
Moses.] Said R. Huna, "R. Yannai and R. Hiyya the Elder
differed on this matter."

L. R. Yannai said, "It was prior to the giving of the Torah
that Jethro came."

M. R. Hiyya the Elder said, "It was after the giving of the
Torah that Jethro came."

N. Said R. Hanina, "They did not in fact differ. The one who
said that it was prior to the giving of the Torah that Jethro
came holds that the children of Noah offered peace-
offerings [in addition to offerings in accord with the rules
governing the classification of whole-offerings]. The one
who maintains that it was after the giving of the Torah
that Jethro came takes the position that the children of
Noah offered up animals only in the status of whole-
offerings."

O. The following verse supports the view of R. Yosé bar Hanina, "Awake, O north wind" (Song 4:16) refers to the whole-offering, which was slaughtered at the north side of the altar. What is the sense of "awake"? It speaks of something that was asleep and now wakes up.

P. "And come, you south" (Song 4:16) speaks of peace-offerings, which were slaughtered [even] at the south side of the altar. And what is the sense of "come"? It speaks of a new and unprecedented practice. [Hence the rules governing peace-offerings constituted an innovation. Freedman, trans. *Genesis Rabbah,* p. 184, n. 1: Thus it was only now, after the giving of the Torah, that the practice of sacrificing peace-offerings was introduced.]

Q. R. Joshua of Sikhnin in the name of R. Levi: "Also the following verse supports the view of R. Yosé bar Hanina: 'This is the Torah governing the preparation of the whole-offering, that is the whole-offering [of which people already are informed]' (Lev. 6:2) meaning, that whole-offering that the children of Noah used to offer up.

R. "When by contrast the passage speaks of peace-offerings, it states, 'And this is the law of the sacrifice of peace-offerings' (Lev. 7:11), but it is not written, '*which they offered up*,' but rather, 'which they *will* offer up' (Lev. 7:11), meaning, only in the future. [Hence peace-offerings' rules, allowing the sacrificer and sacrificer a share in the animal that is offered up, represented an innovation, not formerly applicable, in support of the view of R. Yosé bar Hanina that such offerings' rules constituted an innovation.]"

S. [Reverting to the text of Song:] How does R. Eliezer interpret this same verse, "Awake, O north wind, and come, O south wind"?

T. When the exiles living in the North will wake up and come and encamp in the south, as in this verse, "Behold I will bring them from the north country and gather them from the uttermost parts of the earth" (Jer. 31:8).

    U. When Gog and Magog, who are situated in the north, come and fall upon the south: "And I will turn you around and lead you on and I will cause you to come up" (Ezek. 39:2).

    V. When the Messiah, located in the north, will awake and come and rebuild the Temple, which is located in the south: "I have awakened one from the north and he has come" (Isa. 41:25).

2.   A. "Blow upon my garden, let its fragrance be wafted abroad:"

    B. Said R. Huna in the name of R. Joshua b. R. Benjamin b. R. Levi, "It is because in this age, when the south wind blows, the north wind does not, and when the north wind blows, the south wind does not.

    C. "But in the age to come, the Holy One will bring a strong clearing wind into the world, and he will lead both winds to blow together, and both of them will serve: 'I will say to the north, give up, and to the south, do not hold back' (Isa. 43:6)."

3.   A. "Let my beloved come to his garden:"

    B. Said R. Yohanan, "The Torah here teaches you proper conduct,

    C. "specifically, that the groom should not enter 'the marriage canopy' until the bride gives him permission to do so:

    D. "'Let my beloved come to his garden.'"

South Florida Studies in the History of Judaism

40001	Lectures on Judaism in the Academy and in the Humanities	Neusner
40002	Lectures on Judaism in the History of Religion	Neusner
40003	Self-Fulfilling Prophecy: Exile and Return in the History of Judaism	Neusner
40004	The Canonical History of Ideas: The Place of the So-called Tannaite Midrashim, Mekhilta Attributed to R. Ishmael, Sifra, Sifré to Numbers, and Sifré to Deuteronomy	Neusner
40005	Ancient Judaism: Debates and Disputes, Second Series	Neusner
40006	The Hasmoneans and Their Supporters: From Mattathias to the Death of John Hyrcanus I	Sievers
40007	Approaches to Ancient Judaism: New Series, Volume One	Neusner
40008	Judaism in the Matrix of Christianity	Neusner
40009	Tradition as Selectivity: Scripture, Mishnah, Tosefta, and Midrash in the Talmud of Babylonia	Neusner
40010	The Tosefta: Translated from the Hebrew: Sixth Division Tohorot	Neusner
40011	In the Margins of the Midrash: Sifre Ha'azinu Texts, Commentaries and Reflections	Basser
40012	Language as Taxonomy: The Rules for Using Hebrew and Aramaic in the Babylonia Talmud	Neusner
40013	The Rules of Composition of the Talmud of Babylonia: The Cogency of the Bavli's Composite	Neusner
40014	Understanding the Rabbinic Mind: Essays on the Hermeneutic of Max Kadushin	Ochs
40015	Essays in Jewish Historiography	Rapoport-Albert
40016	The Golden Calf and the Origins of the Jewish Controversy	Bori/Ward
40017	Approaches to Ancient Judaism: New Series, Volume Two	Neusner
40018	The Bavli That Might Have Been: The Tosefta's Theory of Mishnah Commentary Compared With the Bavli's	Neusner
40019	The Formation of Judaism: In Retrospect and Prospect	Neusner
40020	Judaism in Society: The Evidence of the Yerushalmi,Toward the Natural History of a Religion	Neusner
40021	The Enchantments of Judaism: Rites of Transformation from Birth Through Death	Neusner
40022	Åbo Addresses	Neusner
40023	The City of God in Judaism and Other Comparative and Methodological Studies	Neusner
40024	The Bavli's One Voice: Types and Forms of Analytical Discourse and their Fixed Order of Appearance	Neusner
40025	The Dura-Europos Synagogue: A Re-evaluation (1932-1992)	Gutmann
40026	Precedent and Judicial Discretion: The Case of Joseph ibn Lev	Morell
40027	Max Weinreich Geschichte der jiddischen Sprachforschung	Frakes
40028	Israel: Its Life and Culture, Volume I	Pedersen
40029	Israel: Its Life and Culture, Volume II	Pedersen
40030	The Bavli's One Statement: The Metapropositional Program of Babylonian Talmud Tractate Zebahim Chapters One and Five	Neusner

South Florida Academic Commentary Series

South Florida-Rochester-Saint Louis Studies on Religion and the Social Order

South Florida International Studies in Formative Christianity and Judaism